IN PRAISE OF *THREE TESTAMENTS: T*

"*Three Testaments: Torah, Gospel, and Quran* invites readers to study the interdependence of the Scriptures claiming the tradition of Abraham, Sarah, and Hagar as their heritage. I especially appreciate the use of inclusive language and the voice of (wo-)men scholars, introducing the progressive edge of Jewish and Muslim Scriptures. This volume is a very unique and helpful resource for introductory Scripture courses and interreligious dialogue. I highly recommend it." —**Elisabeth Schüssler Fiorenza**, professor, Harvard Divinity School

"Since the medium is indeed a great part of the message, *Three Testaments*—bringing together the Torah, the Christian Scriptures, and the Quran in one volume—is already transformative, simply by challenging all of us to look each other in the face and to see in each face the Face of God. Besides that, Brian Brown's proposal for seeing the Zoroastrian tradition as having set the context for new Revelations in Judaism, Christianity, and Islam may open us up to fuller spiritual and religious explorations." —**Rabbi Arthur Waskow**, director of Shalom Center

"*Three Testaments* is appropriately inclusive in many ways. The use of inclusive Scripture is entirely appropriate for the twenty-first century, both scholarly and evocative. To leave women out of Scripture in our time is to distort the message entirely." —**Sister Joan Chittister**, author of *Called to Question*; columnist in *National Catholic Reporter*

"After prequels demonstrating the many ways in which Jewish, Christian, and Islamic sacred texts manifest influences and parallels, Brown and his associates turn to a deeper investigation of the common as well as the distinctive features of the monotheistic world faiths present in the Torah, the Gospel, and the Quran, including some possible influence in each by Zoroastrianism." —**Max L. Stackhouse**, professor of theology and public life emeritus, Princeton Theological Seminary

"*Three Testaments* suggests new paradigms that could considerably enrich interfaith discussions for each of these three faiths: 'a new paradigm for Jews about the origin of monotheism in world religion, a new paradigm for Christians about the savior of the world, and a new paradigm for Muslims about the people of the book.'" —**Mark Toulouse**, principal and professor of the History of Christianity at Emmanuel College, Victoria University, University of Toronto

"As a member of the Jewish faith, born in a Muslim country and educated at a Catholic convent, I believe this book is destined to be a defining spiritual landmark for the twenty-first century." —**Her Excellency Houda Ezra Nonoo**, US ambassador from the Islamic Kingdom of Bahrain

"We hope and pray that this book will find its way to every home, every library, school and worship center, and to every heart." —**Sayyid M. Syeed**, national director of the Islamic Society of North America

IN PRAISE OF *FOUR TESTAMENTS: TAO TE CHING, ANALECTS, DHAMMAPADA, BHAGAVAD GITA* (2016)

"Brian Brown has done it again with his usual mix of good scholarship and good humor. *Four Testaments* is the companion volume to *Three Testaments* and covers the major Eastern religions. It provides primary texts, as well as material to help nonspecialists understand those texts, and shows us the connections between our religious traditions." —**Amir Hussain**, editor, *Journal of the American Academy of Religion*

"*Four Testaments* is an important work, suited to the times in which we live. It is a necessary work. Of course, the reading is not so simple or arbitrary as to end with just one volume. One needs to keep the *Four Testaments* on one's desk or nightstand alongside the *Three Testaments*, moving back and forth between the two volumes and their several great texts." —**Francis X. Clooney, SJ**, director, Center for Study of World Religions, Harvard University

"There is a phenomenon that permeates this book, characterized by the fact that our engagement with another religious tradition helps us understand our own tradition, as well as the other tradition, better. We see this phenomenon at work at the level of scriptures in these pages." —**Arvind Sharma**, McGill University, Montreal

"This book continues the important work begun in *Three Testaments*. The editor and contributors are to be commended on their valuable contribution to inter-religious studies. If *Three Testaments* is your text for an 'Introduction to Scriptures of Western Monotheism' in the autumn semester, *Four Testaments* should be your text for 'Scriptures of Eastern Monism' in the spring." —**Jonathan Kearney**, religious studies, St. Patrick's College of Dublin City University

"Brown shows both an abundance of circumstantial evidence and more than enough proof that all the major world religions have been informed by Vedic precedents via the Axial Age prophecies of Zoroaster." —**K. E. Eduljee**, creator of the popular Heritage Institute website on Zoroastrian studies at www.zoroastrianheritage.com

"Brown has illustrated how Eastern monism and Western monotheism developed at the same time and perhaps in tension with the same stimulus along the Silk Route, thus connecting the roots of Daoism, Confucianism, Hinduism, and Buddhism with Judaism, Christianity, and Islam." —**Cyril Glasse**, author of the bestselling *New Encyclopedia of Islam* and the just-released *Second Coming of the Judeo-Zoroastrian Jesus of the Dead Sea Scrolls*

"This is an insightful inquiry into the connections between the primary scriptures of the East, in the context of their cultures, and the primary scriptures of the West. This volume expertly affirms the interconnections between various textual traditions. It is a welcome addition to the ever-growing field of intertextual studies." —Sharada and Rasiah Sugirtharajah, University of Birmingham (UK)

"*Four Testaments* is certainly valuable academically in the Global South, though one suspects that it could matter just as much in the community and on the street. Intelligent laity are more open to engagement in these matters than is sometimes realized." —**Reverend Senator Joy Abdul-Mohan**, St. Andrew's Theological College, Trinidad and Tobago

seven testaments of world religion and the zoroastrian older testament

Brian Arthur Brown

Foreword by Karen Hamilton

ROWMAN AND LITTLEFIELD
Lanham • Boulder • New York • London

Executive Editor: Rolf Janke
Editorial Assistant: Courtney Packard
Senior Marketing Manager: Kim Lyons

World Religions and the Theory of the Axial Age, by Jan Assmann in *Dynamics in the History of Religions between Asia and Europe*, is used by permission Koninklijke BRILL NV © 2012.

Quotations from *The Second Coming of the Judeo-Zoroastrian Jesus of the Dead Sea Scrolls*, © 2014 by Cyril Glassé and other materials by Cyril Glassé, are used by his permission.

The appendix F article, "The Sogdians: Prime Movers Between Boundaries," by Jenny Rose, is published with the permission of Duke University Press © 2010.

The appendix G article, "Sogdians in China," an article by Étienne de la Vaissière, is published with permission from the Journal of the Silk Road Foundation © 2004.

The afterword, *Continuing the Magi Journey*, includes an article, "Three Kings and a Star," by Mark Rose, published with the permission of *ARCHAEOLOGY Magazine* © 2004.

Credits for figures and acknowledgments for other material borrowed from other sources, and reproduced with permission, appear on the appropriate page within the text.

Published by Rowman & Littlefield
A wholly owned subsidary of The Rowman & Littlefield Publishing Group, Inc.
4501 Forbes Boulevard, Suite 200, Lanham, Maryland 20706
www.rowman.com

6 Tinworth Street, London SE11 5AL, United Kingdom

ISBN 9781538127865 (paperback)
ISBN 9781538127872 (electronic)

British Library Cataloguing in Publication Information Available

Library of Congress Cataloging-in-Publication Data Available

Library of Congress Control Number: 2019949266

∞™ The paper used in this publication meets the minimum requirements of American National Standard for Information Sciences—Permanence of Paper for Printed Library Materials, ANSI/NISO Z39.48-1992.

In addition to acknowledged contributors, there are other colleagues to whom this work is dedicated:

The Society of Scholars of Zoroastrianism for wordsmithing the material for this book during its annual North American conference in Chicago, October 19–21, 2018, and for careful vetting of the text by members of the society during final editing in 2019 for publication in 2020

The Parliament of the World's Religions for workshopping the material for this book during sessions of the parliament in Toronto, November 1–7, 2018, with all seven scholarly contributors to the book and the author being members of those sessions of the parliament

Faculty and students of Emmanuel College of Victoria University at the University of Toronto, the venue for the first presentations of the *Seven Testaments Trilogy* as curriculum material after exhaustive review procedures, and participation in book launch activities in 2012, 2016, and 2020, as well as the first performance of the play *Three Testaments: Shalom, Peace, Salam*; the use of the study guide, *Three Testaments Companion*; and the first cold readings of the play *Older Testaments: Encounters on the Way*, as the college was moving toward developments in interfaith education described in this book, providing mutual stimulation as these resources evolved

contents

part one: indo-european connections in all seven testaments of world religion

part two: creation and apocalypse in world religions: avestan models in torah, tao te ching, analects, dhammapada, bhagavad gita, gospel, and quran

part three: appendices

ᖴOREᗯOᖇᗪ

Holy Toledo!

Karen Hamilton, Co-Chair: The Parliament of the World's Religions, Toronto 2018

A S AN EXPRESSION OF AMAZEMENT, *HOLY TOLEDO* IS A PHRASE THAT HAS MADE ITS WAY INTO recent Western culture with little memory of its origins. It refers to the city of Toledo in Spain, a city only forty minutes away from Madrid but rarely on the itinerary of those visiting the country. This is a mistake for those engaged in interfaith dialogue, reflection, writing, or action, but there are many other such travel opportunities. The journeys of the Magi are still going on, East and West, and this book is one such expedition.

Toledo is still, in 2019, the most holy city in Spain for the three faiths of Judaism, Christianity, and Islam. It has a long history of being so. The reality and complexity of Al-Andalusia, as manifest in the Spanish cities of Cordoba, Seville, and Granada, is one that merits careful study and reflection in our time and place. For many hundreds of years in and around a period loosely referred to in the West as the Middle Ages, and for a wide variety of reasons (including economic ones), Jews, Christians, and Muslims lived together in peace and mutual respect. This was the reality in Toledo and points to a current universal quest facilitated by *Seven Testaments of World Religion and the Zoroastrian Older Testament*, with an expectation of wide global circulation and conversation.

Toledo was a translation center. As with Al-Andalusia, the faithful adherents, particularly the scholars of the various religions, spoke each other's languages. They read each other's literature and scholarship, and they knew each other's holy texts well. They even reveled in shared architecture and the beauty of gardens and were strategic about beneficial trade. *Seven Testaments* points to such perspectives as found in the text of *Three Testaments: Torah, Gospel, and Quran* and in *Four Testaments: Tao Te Ching, Analects, Dhammapada, Bhagavad Gita.*

In other places around and beyond the Mediterranean, the writings of such scholars as John of Damascus and Patriarch Timothy demonstrate that not only did some faith leaders know the languages the other faiths were writing in, but they also knew the sacred texts of the other faiths intimately and well. This was not and is not a simple signpost, and such knowledge was often used for refuting or converting the other traditions. However, the texts of the various faith traditions were known, read, and taken seriously, even if not read together in the manner of the practice of "Scriptural Reasoning" in the twenty-first century. In *Seven Testaments of World Religion and the Zoroastrian Older Testament*, the trilogy introduced by this volume goes a step beyond simply comparing textual quotes by proffering the unique treasures of each, uncut. The seven primary sacred texts of world religions are permitted to speak for themselves in full through the volumes that follow this one.

Seven Testaments of World Religion builds on the past and projects forward into a universal future that is changed forever by the spread and speed of information, a future in which the relationship between and among faith traditions is as crucial as it was in the Middle Ages, and perhaps even more so. Bringing together, as a whole, the holy texts of the seven world religions is a daring act. It is a unique act, and yet it builds on past possibilities, carefully considers current realities, and offers a path forward in hope and relationship. The trilogy introduced by this volume is built on writing, editing, compiling, and dreaming, woven together with solid historical scholarship, cutting-edge contemporary scholarship, and a deep and broad sense of time and place. *Seven Testaments* itself, the introductory volume, is a particularly accessible book. This book indicates how the holy texts of East and West can stand together in volumes 2 and 3, with crucial articles that give context and can be read separately.

This volume introduces a trilogy for a lifetime of reading by anyone interested in any faith and the relationships among the faiths. It is a set that lives and breathes and has its being in mutual respect—respect for Judaism, Taoism, Confucianism, Buddhism, Hinduism, Christianity, Islam, and also Zoroastrianism's "Older Testament" in its original Vedic setting. The respect is for the past, the present, and the holy future that we can build together—that we must build together in response to the spiritual needs of our world. This project also sets the tone for respectful inclusion of newer and more localized religions in future conversations.

It is appropriate that this book, introducing the previously published *Three Testaments* and *Four Testaments*, was first introduced itself at the 2018 Parliament of the World's Religions in Toronto. This happened while volume 1 was still "under construction," giving nearly ten thousand scholars the opportunity for input prior to the book's publication before a three-day international launch conference at US and Canadian venues on both sides of Niagara Falls. Since 1893, and with particular frequency in recent decades, the Parliament has brought together thousands of people of all faith traditions and from all around the world. They come together to hear profound global faith leaders, to learn from each other and from each other's traditions, and to encounter not only the broad diversity and unity of faith traditions but also their depth and articulation through word, music, ritual, and conviction.

That introduction of *Seven Testaments* by a panel of its contributors prior to the final edit is a perfect example of the Parliament at work. *The Seven Testaments of World Religion* speaks to that diversity, and they speak to threads of commonality and unity, but not in a facile way. There is no attempt to extinguish the differences, some of which are deep, even when there are common historical roots or common contemporary geographies. These endeavors are about listening, observing, reflecting, hearing the common call to action for the sake of a holy vision of peace and justice, and then listening to each other again. There is not just one clearly defined path forward, but there is a journey, and there are beacons of light along the way. This volume, and gatherings like the Parliament and the scholarly launch conference for *Seven Testaments* and the other texts of the trilogy at Niagara Falls, are such beacons of light. They are important but not alone, as such lights are beginning to glimmer increasingly elsewhere.

The fact that *Seven Testaments* has a focus on Zoroastrian traditions and the Vedic influences upon it is fascinating and invites much future study and reflection. This is timely, as there is current interest in traditions of the Zoroastrian Magi and their earlier journey to follow a beacon of light. The town of Ravenna in Italy has claims to fame as the spot where Caesar crossed the Rubicon River, and also as the site of the best collection of fifth-century mosaics in the world. In the basilica of St. Apollinare Nuovo there is a large, very detailed, fifth-century mosaic showing the Magi on their journey to visit the Christ child, to present him with gifts of deep meaning from the East. The Magi are portrayed not in the crowns and royal robes that have become a standard depiction in the West, but rather in the ancient caps and robes typical of the East and reaching back into even more ancient traditions.

A similar mosaic, with comparable images of the Magi, once graced the main entrance to the Church of the Nativity in Bethlehem. This book presents new research and attests to the fact that the Magi embarked on many such journeys, breaking trails for us, East and West. Does everybody know that in 1164 Magi relics were brought from Milan to be reinterred in the new cathedral in Cologne, where they naturally became identified with the "Three Wise Men" of biblical fame? Readers may find themselves stimulated by the crosscurrents of information from modern "Magi" who have come from afar more recently to again present gold, frankincense, and myrrh alongside those of us who are in the scene in the twenty-first century.

Seven Testaments of World Religion and the trilogy it introduces will re-form thinking and perceptions. If we journey through them with awareness and appreciation, allowing ourselves to engage the beacons of light along the way, we will find ourselves in a place like Toledo of old, except that in our time Hindus, Buddhists, Taoists, Confucianists, and others will also be there with the Jews, Christians, and Muslims.

No peace among the nations without peace among the religions.
No peace among the religions without dialogue between the religions.
No dialogue between the religions without investigation
of the foundations of the religions.

—Excerpt from 1993 Parliament of the World's
Religions Declaration towards a Global Ethic

prologue

Twenty Years in the Making

L ATE IN THE DAY ON SEPTEMBER 11, 2001, BRIAN ARTHUR BROWN, CANADIAN AUTHOR AND church minister, convened Muslim and Jewish colleagues to seek a new approach to interfaith relations. Notes from this meeting led to a series of joint sermons, printed, expanded, and published in 2006 as *Noah's Other Son* (the one who drowned in the flood in Quran 17). As a parable for our time, this book offered readers a new kind of interfaith study, culminating in *Seven Testaments of World Religion*, to be launched almost twenty years after 9/11, capping off the *Seven Testaments Trilogy*, a welcome new approach to the study of religion.

Forensic Scriptures (2009) was Brown's more academic version of the material in *Noah's Other Son*. It was released at a three-day launch conference at the Riverside Church in New York City, hosted by four seminaries and attended by two hundred scholars. The author moderated six panels of six specialists each, discussing aspects of a paradigm shift from "comparative religion" to "interfaith studies" (from *comparing* to *sharing*) in the then-new discipline of Scriptural Reasoning.

The final day of that conference saw the author "commissioned" by the participants to do commentary for *Three Testaments: Torah, Gospel, and Quran*. This single volume was planned to include the full texts of Jewish, Christian, and Muslim Scriptures. Scholars present promised expert prefaces and introductions to each text of the three traditions.

By a fortuitous coincidence, senior editors of the Jewish Publication Society and Kazi Islamic Publications were at the conference and pledged cooperation in regard to providing copyright permissions. When the Rowman & Littlefield Publishing Group agreed to publish this scriptural trio, the New Testament of the *Inclusive Bible* from Sheed & Ward (a Catholic house under the R&L umbrella) joined the *Contemporary Torah* and the *Sublime Quran* as three versions produced in the twenty-first century. Upon publication, the award-winning *Three Testaments* volume represented the first time the primary Scriptures of Abraham's family had appeared together in one book as Torah, Gospel (the New Testament), and Quran.

Four hundred students, scholars, clergy, and lay people attended the September 10 launch of *Three Testaments* at Ground Zero events in New York City on the eve of the 9/11 anniversary in 2012. The next day, on the 9/11 anniversary, in response to recent burnings of the Quran in the United States, American and Canadian ambassadors Susan Johnson Cook and Gary Doer introduced the *Three Testaments* book to nineteen other ambassadors and state department officials at a reception hosted by the Canadian Embassy in Washington. Prominent academics and religious leaders were present, addressed by Dr. Brown and several of the contributors. Launch activities in eastern North America were followed by similar 3T events, southern, western and northern: Dallas and Austin in Texas, Los Angeles and San Francisco in California, Chicago and Toronto in the north.

Positive responses to *Three Testaments* led to the 2013 publication of *Three Testaments Companion: Torah, Gospel, Quran & More*, a study guide. It was followed by the stage play *Three Testaments: Shalom, Peace, Salam*, premiering in upstate New York through June 2015. These publications and productions had the amplification of *Three Testaments* and preparation for the publication of *Four Testaments* as their objectives.

Brian Arthur Brown writes collaboratively, and *Four Testaments: Tao Te Ching, Analects, Dhammapada, Bhagavad Gita* continued this "compelling concept" with prefaces and introductions by Taoist, Confucian, Buddhist, and Hindu experts. Published by Rowman & Littlefield in 2016, with input from the Zoroastrian community, *Four Testaments* has been marketed with its predecessor as an engaging "set," containing the primary sacred texts of the seven world religions and winning a number of awards.

Seven Testaments of World Religion is a final iteration of this material, including annotated commentary on the Vedic background and the Zoroastrian role in the sacred texts. It offers important excerpts from the previous published volumes 2 and 3, the play script, study guides for volumes 2 and 3, an appendix on the now confidently identified tomb of Zoroaster, and previously unpublished photos of tombs of Hebrew prophets that were maintained for more than a millennium by Muslim trusts. The latter photos represent a trove bequeathed to this "pre-capitulation" from the estate of Irving Kleigfield, late editor of *Saturday Evening Post*.

The three-day launch conference for this book and the *Seven Testaments Trilogy* in Niagara Falls was modeled on the Riverside conference in New York City that initiated *Three Testaments*: twenty specialist contributors serving on four panels for a hundred scholars, May 29–31, 2020, with all contributing scholars to the trilogy in attendance, preceded by an archaeological expedition with expert conference participants confirming the site of Zoroaster's tomb as presented in *Seven Testaments of World Religion*—an identification regarded by some as "the big reveal" of 2020.

Huston Smith's *The World's Religions* has sold three million copies since 1956, a standard text in *comparative* religion, in which faiths are *compared*. That classic text may find a worthy successor in the *Seven Testaments Trilogy*, in which insights and faiths are *shared*. While aspiring to see the *Seven Testaments Trilogy* as a standard resource in departments of religious studies, seminaries, and congregations, it may be that in some circumstances the first volume, *Seven Testaments of World Religion*, will become the text in classes and book clubs. *Three Testaments* and *Four Testaments* will then serve the needs of students and readers who wish to zero in on or delve further into specific aspects of this study, such as the parallel sayings of Buddha and Christ, the female transmitters of the Quran, or detailed identification of passages from the Dead Zee Scrolls of Zoroaster, buried as verses in the seven testaments themselves.

acknowledgments

THE PARLIAMENT OF THE WORLD'S RELIGIONS, MEETING IN TORONTO IN 2018, WAS AN OPPORtunity for a final meeting of the contributors, providing the forum for publicly announcing this project and workshopping the final editing. The foreword was then produced by our host, the Parliament's gracious Canadian co-chair, Rev. Dr. Karen Hamilton, to whom we offer first thanks.

Elsewhere I have thanked the fourteen eminent writers of prefaces, introductions, and other materials in volumes 2 and 3 of the trilogy, but here I especially thank those whose material is quoted again in this volume, written last but positioned first as volume 1, much as a foreword is written last but placed first in a book. David Bruce and Nevin Reda are reintroduced in thumbnail sketches at the end of this book, where we also meet the new contributors Karen Hamilton, Bhante Saranapala, William Thomas, and Roshan Rivetna. The articles by Jenny Rose ("The Sogdians: Prime Movers between Boundaries"), Étienne de la Vaissière ("Sogdians in China"), and Mark Rose ("The Three Kings and the Star") are published here by permission of their publishers, Duke University Press, the Silk Road Foundation, and *Archaeology* magazine, and we acknowledge the value of their special contributions to our shared and growing understanding.

In *Three Testaments* and *Four Testaments*, I also thank those responsible for bringing the seven sacred texts to life in the English language, worth mentioning again to ensure recognition by those contemplating reading or studying the whole trilogy through. The newer translation of the Torah by David E. S. Stein, the Tao Te Ching text by Victor Mair, the New Testament by the late Joe Dearborne, SJ, and the Quran by Laleh Bakhtiar are published by us under licences from the Jewish Publication Society, Random House, Sheed & Ward Catholic Books, and Kazi Islamic Publications, respectively. All four are cutting-edge translations published in the twenty-first century, exemplary of the most recent trends in relation to archaeological discoveries, inclusive language relating to original intent, and other trends in recent scholarship. The translations of the Analects of Confucius by James Legge, the Dhammapada by Sarvepalli Radhakrishnan, and the Bhagavad Gita by Mohandas Gandhi are now in the public domain, cherished as classics. We are also indebted to Sarvepalli Radhakrishnan and Mohandas Gandhi, neither still living, for their monumental exertions in explaining Eastern religions of

Buddhism and Hinduism to Western readers earlier in the twentieth century, setting a standard for all time, in writings we quote that are now also in the public domain.

John Perkin, interfaith chaplain and lecturer at Mount Allison University, drew to my attention the fact that Zoroaster's Gathas contain the first examples of apocalyptic literature in the world, suggesting that the several others immediately afterward might owe a debt to him. We found this to be so and applied the same approach to creation stories in part two of this book. Thank you, John. James "Manu" Sinton and Olivier Lapierre researched the fixation of teenagers with the unrelenting apocalypticisms in electronic gaming as an expression of latent spiritual concerns.

I owe a particular debt of gratitude to Mark Toulouse, who, during his years as principal of Emmanuel College in Toronto, helped me bridge the gaps in language styles between three readerships—university departments, seminaries, and lay individuals—and who skillfully moderated the New Axial Age event at the 2018 Parliament of the World's Religions, from which several papers are reproduced in this volume. Bhante Saranapala of the University of Toronto lately joined the team to amend a perceived deficiency reference to modern Buddhism in the previously published *Four Testaments* text.

Contributors who presented a penultimate draft of the manuscript at the 2018 Parliament of the World's Religions appeared nervous upon hearing a rumor that "the chief legal counsel for the US Library of Congress" was present in one of their workshops. Who knows when one might misspeak, but I met Kersi Shroff later and discovered that this distinguished gentleman was not there as a critic. As an aficionado of *Three Testaments* and *Four Testaments*, he was keen to become one of the final readers to prevent egregious errors in *Seven Testaments*. As it turned out, he is a Zoroastrian interfaith activist and was invaluable in suggesting new material for the part three appendix section, including important updates on new information about the substantial presence of Zoroastrians in ancient China and related matters.

Under Shroff's influence, the last four appendices became the forum for an exciting new dimension of this study, only hinted at in the other volumes of this trilogy, and he provided the context for appendix H in historical narrative style, identified as fodder for a movie script. Because he did not write these appendix materials, I cannot claim Kersi Shroff as a contributor, but I thank him here with the hope that, having recently retired from the Library of Congress, he might honor us with a blurb for the back cover upon publication of the book.

My interfaith tutors of earlier years, to be always gratefully acknowledged, include Wilfred Cantwell Smith and Willard Oxtoby at McGill University in 1963 and 1964, respectively, and Mary Boyce in a series of lengthy conversations through the winters of 2004, 2005, and 2006, the latter abbreviated by her untimely death. These were occasions when she pointed me in the direction of unsolved issues and gave hints of possible new resolutions of certain Zoroastrian mysteries.

Anne Bauman and Stanley Algoo are proofreading, language, and grammatical experts who shared wordsmithing and fact-checking with readers Kobad Zarolia, Dave Davies, Joe Heasley, and Donna Flood. The skillful conversion of forty color pictures to striking grayscale images was accomplished by Mike Koster of PrePrint Design of Niagara Falls, Ontario. Rolf Janke, my editor at Rowman & Littlefield; his assistant Courtney Packard; and technical wizard Patricia Stevenson all deserve much credit for the final annotated product as enhanced in the publishing process.

My wife, Jenny Sutacriti, is a seasoned veteran in research tasks related to all my books, and it was she who coined the phrase *the Z factor* to categorize Zoroastrian passages in various scriptures. She also conceived the expression *Dead Zee Scrolls* to identify the missing parts of the Avesta Scriptures in a manner evocative of the Dead Sea Scrolls, which had disappeared in such similar circumstances, and it was she who identified the one possible repository of those documents.

The Embrace at St. John's Stevensville United Church in Fort Erie, Ontario, has provided facilitation for sponsors and corporations in promotional and publicity endeavors undertaken by Rev. Cheryl Wood-Thomas, my Canadian agent, and in the United States by James Flood, administrator of First Baptist Church in Niagara Falls, New York. Cheryl's husband, Rev. William Thomas, is the playwright from whom we gratefully received the script of *Older Testaments: Encounters on the Way*, based in large part on the *Four Testaments* book, by permission. Wider promotional pursuits have been undertaken by the Winberg Foundation of Toronto in book launch events throughout the long process, beginning with our tour of North America's largest cities during the 2012 launch of *Three Testaments*. Jenny and I were accompanied even then by ubiquitous senior scholar David Bruce, who will be representing us at *Seven Testaments* introductory events at various places in the future.

I nearly always write collaboratively, but even such a lengthy list of acknowledgments cannot do justice to the many scholars in Australia, Trinidad, Turkey, Ireland, the United Kingdom, Israel, Hong Kong, India, the United States, and Canada who responded electronically to *Three Testaments* and *Four Testaments* with helpful suggestions and modifications of concepts that appear now in this introductory volume of the trilogy. As this material appears in final form as *Seven Testaments of World Religion and the Zoroastrian Older Testament*, more than nine hundred scholars, students, and interested readers of this series have been linked by my blog, offering questions and participating in research. With all of the above, they are labeled by early reviewer Joseph Montville as comparable to the glorious "Symphony of a Thousand," the popular description of Mahler's Eighth Symphony. I am so honored to have had the privilege of conducting this orchestra.

illustrations

THE MAP INSERTED AT THE BEGINNING OF THIS BOOK WAS PRODUCED WITH THE ASSISTANCE of cartographer Len Guelke, brought into our circle by "mapmaker" and our consultant Ward Kaiser. The chart of sources of the Jewish Torah on the back of that insert was executed by technical specialist Karen Arbour under the direction of the author/contributing editor. The Great Intersection map introducing chapter 5 was executed by phenomenologist Indira Brown Sinton under the direction of the author/contributing editor. Both insert images and the Great Intersection are specifically copyrighted in the name of Brian Arthur Brown.

Except for a few designated otherwise, illustrations in appendix C ("Where the Bodies Are Buried") are from the Counsel Collection, bequeathed to readers of this trilogy by Paul and Roy Kligfield, sons and heirs of the late publisher of the *Saturday Evening Post* magazine, art collector, and philanthropist Irving Kligfield, and published first in the *Three Testaments Companion*.

Illustrations presenting images of archival pages of sacred Scriptures, placed strategically throughout part two (Avesta, Torah, Tao Te Ching, Analects, Dhammapada, Bhagavad Gita, New Testament, and Quran), are all from the British Library and are used under license. A *Jewish Text from Dunhuang* is also from the British Library, and *The Court of King Akbar* is from Bridgeman Images, also under license.

In chapter 16, the calligraphy *Ardently Anxious over You* is from Mohamed Zakariya, obtained through the auspices of his friend and ours, Amir Hussain, and used with the artist's kind permission.

preface

What's New in This Book?

THE FIRST FRESH CONCEPT IN THE TRILOGY AS INTRODUCED IN THIS BOOK IS ITS RECOGNITION of an "Older Testament," preceding "revelations" in primary sacred texts of all seven world religions. A second surprise for many may be the extent of Asian "Eastern" influence in the "Western" Bible. A third special feature is the extent to which each of the primary Scriptures speaks for itself in entirety here, compared to other interfaith texts limited to quotes for study or snippets cited for comparative purposes. These three fresh concepts are introduced here and developed more completely in the two related compendia that present Western monotheism and Eastern monism (Western Oneness of divinity in a God who is separate from the created universe/Eastern Oneness of absolutely everything within a Divine Universe). It may be helpful in passing to acknowledge that monism and pantheism are almost the same, though monism suggests that everything is divine, while pantheism holds that there is divinity in everything.

Vedic-Zoroastrian influence on Jews in Babylon has long been recognized. A Zoroastrian perpetual flame in Leviticus and the recent identification of a certain "Krishna" in the Book of Esther are examples that set the scene for a deeper appreciation of Asian realities in the Bible. The concepts of creation and apocalypse, angels and demons, salvation and damnation, resurrection and final judgment, heaven and hell, found first in the complete Hebrew Scripture and shared among the seven world religions, are all Vedic in origin, brought forward in Zoroastrian refinement, with a "Redeemer" who is identified first as the Saoshyant, the savior of the world.

After twentieth-century debates about Greek, Egyptian, and Jewish influence in their Scriptures, Christians may also be astonished at the evidence of a similar Asian underpinning of the New Testament. The appearance of Magi at the nativity of Jesus, and his reference to the Persian "paradise" as the gospel concludes, support a new cognizance that light and dark at creation in St. John's opening chapter, as well as baptism, angels, Satan, hell, final judgment, and salvation, are all concepts originating further East, derived from Zoroastrianism without mediation.

Muslims are aware of Zoroastrian echoes in the Quran. Hindus and Buddhists take their Vedic backdrop as given. Confucianists disregarded sixth-century BCE Magi influence in China, but, under the influence of a contributor to this work, even Chinese Taoists now accept that fact.

The shared Vedic heritage had been reformed and refined by Zoroaster, whose influence was a stimulant throughout the Silk Route in the Axial Age.[1] None of these religions became Vedic or "Zoroastrian," but the Zoroastrian-Jewish interface in the Middle East impacted Christian and Muslim monotheistic traditions in the West. As we now realize, this "Z factor" also encouraged interaction between monistic Taoist, Hindu, and Buddhist traditions in the East. This shared Vedic heritage points to a fourth unique element in this introductory volume: examination of a symbiotic relationship between monotheism and monism, and the beginning of a conversation, even a sharing, between their proponents.

Seven Testaments of World Religion opens with a map indicating the overlaps of ancient religious ideas among migrating peoples, illustrated by the Vedic-Zoroastrian contextual setting of the Jewish Torah, where this reality is first reflected among several religions originating in Asia at the same time at various points on the Silk Route. The "Older Testament" is also foundational in primary texts of Taoism, Confucianism, Buddhism, Hinduism of the Bhagavad Gita, and Christianity, developed concurrently or revealed subsequently. This series of classic and ancient revelations concludes with a "final testament" from Islam, affirming the Divine warrant for validity of all religious traditions. All these elements unfold in this volume 1 of the trilogy and are developed in detail in volumes 2 and 3.

Important newer religions (Sikh, Mormon, Baha'i, "New Age," and others) represent 2.5 percent of the world's religious population, and another 2.5 percent (Shinto, Wicca, Jain, and indigenous religions) are older and also significant. But 95 percent of the world's religionists (about 85 percent of the world's population) relate to the seven world religions that share an "Older Testament" with all the descriptors we have listed and mention again: creation and apocalypse, angels and demons, salvation and damnation, resurrection and final judgment, heaven and hell.

In the twentieth century, many religions moved from essentially negative "exclusivist" attitudes toward each other to "comparative" religion. *Comparing* might be seen as an advance over judging, but it was not the paradigm shift to the *sharing* found now in twenty-first-century interfaith studies. Religion is rising everywhere except on the northeast coast of North America and in Western Europe. The twenty-first century may become an almost worldwide "century of religion," much as the twentieth century was a "century of science," with exciting developments even in the West.

Academic tomes have traditionally been expected to be objective and detached. I and my interfaith colleagues are unapologetically personal and connected to our contributions, as befits a new era of sharing rather than simply comparing. The latest edition of the *Chicago Manual of Style* permits such intimations, and we are nothing if not *au courant*.

There may be a waning in seminary programs these days, but there is now a new and popular religious studies discipline featuring an interfaith smorgasbord at most universities. Faith relations have become as important as race relations in the twenty-first century, in which religion affects community life, politics, and international affairs. On the negative side, genocides and terrorism appear to be delineated by religious identities. On the positive side, religion may now be able to make genuine and significant contributions to the quest for peaceful coexistence.

It is hoped that this book and the others in this trilogy may contribute to that goal.

note

1. Lao Tzu (floruit 575 BCE) and Socrates (floruit 400 BCE) are regarded by us and others as effective Axial Age boundaries.

introduction

Setting the Scene

David Bruce

ITH MOST CANADIANS AND AMERICANS, I REMEMBER QUITE CLEARLY WHERE I WAS when I first heard of the terrorist attack on the World Trade Center in New York on September 11, 2001. I remember asking myself whether the reports were false or exaggerated; I remember wondering whether the world would ever be the same again. I also remember stepping into the pulpit days later to address a congregation reeling from that unthinkable tragedy, pleading with God: *Don't be silent, Lord! Speak to us! And help us to listen.*

While "nine-eleven" may have made its mark on me, other events have taken their toll elsewhere: tribal genocide in Africa; forced migrations in Southeast Asia; displacement of indigenous peoples in colonial territories; and border skirmishes everywhere. Humanity's need to live according to the "better angels of our nature" has never been greater. The problem is: *How do you listen to angels?*

Perhaps . . . we begin with simply listening to one another. In *Noah's Other Son*, Brian Arthur Brown introduced me to Quranic supplements to stories found in Christian Scriptures, similar to the supplements to Jewish Scriptures found in Christian Scriptures. I was intrigued enough to be drawn into conversation with Brian, and quite quickly after that I joined the editing team for *Forensic Scriptures*. And even though I've never known him to be a shrinking violet, I think it's fair to say that Brown hit a whole new level of audacity with the publication of *Three Testaments*, the first copublication of the Torah, the New Testament, and the Quran in one volume. He soon followed up that landmark with the *Three Testaments Companion* and the much-appreciated off-Broadway production of *Three Testaments*: *Shalom, Peace, Salam*.

Paper presented by David Bruce to Parliament of the World's Religions, Toronto, November 5, 2018.

I thought, *Phew; that was quite a ride.* But with the encouragement of his publisher, Brown took yet another hyperleap and compiled *Four Testaments*, featuring the first copublication of Tao Te Ching, the Analects, the Dhammapada, and the Bhagavad Gita. And, not yet quite done, the upcoming publication of *Seven Testaments of World Religion* will bring the entire project to yet another level.

In all of these works, Brown's fundamental message is deceptively simple: he asks us to *listen.* Our greatest intellectual and spiritual questions will only find their answers through listening deeply, both to the texts and to the peoples of other traditions, sometimes mediated through and sometimes impacted by traditions we once viewed as contrary to our own. The listening that Brown is asking us to do isn't just another hermeneutic of suspicion, but rather a hermeneutic of friendship, one that supposes that people in ancient times—as much as or more than today—sometimes shared their intuitions and insights regarding the purpose and value of human existence.

In the Analects we read,

> Tsze-lu asked, saying, "What qualities must a man possess to entitle him to be called a scholar?" The Master said, "He must be thus earnest, urgent, and bland: among his friends, earnest and urgent; among his brethren, bland." (Analects 13:28)

By this measure, Brown is writing for his friends, rather than fellow scholars, because he is anything but bland. Rather than dryly defending a scholarly position three millimeters to the left of some other scholarly position, Brown writes with unbridled enthusiasm as he shares his discoveries with others whom he presumes to be his friends. One of Brown's central theses—perhaps *the* central thesis—woven throughout the entire *Seven Testaments Trilogy* is that understanding the Vedic roots of Zoroastrianism is critical to mutual understanding among the major religious traditions of the world. If he sometimes seems to overstate his case, it's because he is sketching the outline of a huge area of study that will require a whole generation of scholars to fill in—such is the fate of a pioneer in any field.

To be clear, Brown is not claiming to have identified the original "fountainhead" of the seven major religious traditions, as if to provide some simple charting of religious evolution. Nor is he claiming to have identified the mechanism by which religious traditions give rise to one another, as if historical causation is ever as simple as "A causes B." Brown knows that religion is carried in the arms of art, music, dance, literature, and language and involves politics, economics, the presence or absence of heroes, and other accidents of history. Nor is Brown resurrecting the tired old image of some primordially pure religious tradition tragically displaced by local corruptions. Instead, he appreciates the majesty of the world's major religious traditions and celebrates that majesty by insisting that major texts from each tradition be published together *in their entirety*, rather than a curated collection of selected passages. He would rather let the major religious traditions speak for themselves than arrogantly claim he can see what none of them are willing or able to see about themselves.

Brian Brown is more interested in listening and, yes, wondering and speculating than he is in pronouncing his findings as once-and-for-all. And the collection of works in the *Seven Testaments Trilogy* invites us to listen along with him.

First, Brown invites us to listen for those archetypes that transcend cultural specificity. Light and darkness, the heavens and the earth, purity and defilement, reality and illusion are all perennial themes finding expression in the major religious traditions of the world. Brown further invites us to listen to how these perennial themes are foundational in the Zoroastrian iteration of traditional Vedic lore, indicating how Zoroastrianism remains the most likely vehicle of transmission of thematic elements found in ancient traditions from East to West and West to East. He is aware that there would not have been such extensive cross-fertilization of the world's religious traditions unless these themes resonated with something we might call "the human condition." Please understand that nothing in Brown's works *reduces* religious expression to psychological phenomena, but also understand that appreciation of parallel language and imagery among the world's great traditions can't really help but undercut religious exclusivism.

Second, Brown invites us to listen for the universal tension between transcendence and immanence found in all seven of these great faiths. In Western traditions, the Heavenly Reality is typically regarded as being self-identified as personal. God's redeeming action is personal, and human personhood is ultimately enduring. The personal redeemer reconnects people (individually and collectively) to a personal God. By contrast, in Eastern traditions the Heavenly Reality is more typically regarded as impersonal. Heaven's redeeming action calls the quester to transcend the needs of personhood, and thus the means of redemption is transpersonal: the faithful teacher exemplifies transcendence of egoism for the greater good. Even though I'm sure I'm clumsy in my oversimplification, it's clear that these expressions aren't opposed to one another but reflect the unanimity that the Heavenly Reality is, in relation to us, a redemptive force, whether actively intervening in human affairs or patiently exuding a spiritually gravitational pull.

Third, Brown invites us to consider the relationship of history to religious truth. While Eastern traditions appreciate and recognize the influence of historical persons—Lao Tzu, Confucius, Gautama—their larger interpretive frameworks view these persons as enlightened expositors of what is perennially true. By contrast, Western traditions see historical persons—from Moses the Lawgiver through to Muhammad the final Prophet—as effecting permanent change in the spiritual economy.

Many Western scholars and commentators seek to sideline the competing historical claims of Western traditions by identifying religions with ethical principles, effectively "Easternizing" Western traditions, but I think it's pretty plain that this strategy disregards the central importance of history to Judaism, Christianity, and Islam. The Eastern perspective has not, as we in the West sometimes naively assume, rescued Eastern religions from the temptations of exclusivism and geopolitical conquest; unfortunate inquisitions and crusades are universal—and, Brown would suggest, universally unnecessary. Brown invites us to reimagine history not as the source of conflict but as the medium in which all religious traditions have shared and can share their insights in friendship, rather than attempting to conquer one another in misguided enmity. It has happened before; it can happen again.

And, finally, Brown invites us to engage the stranger in a familial relationship. I cannot glibly reconcile all the distinctive claims of the world's great religious traditions. Am I to live again in the flesh *and* seek escape from the flesh in Nirvana? Do I acknowledge Jesus as the only begotten Son of God *and* allow for Krishna as an avatar of the divine? Can I agree that propriety is the highest ideal *and* attempt to live the provocative life of the prophet? And yet, for all their differences, I can just as easily be strangely warmed by the important resonances between the Dhammapada of the Buddha and the "Sermon on the Mount" of Jesus. Perhaps in the world of religions, there is ultimately no "us" and "them," but rather a larger "us" than we have but rarely imagined, each opening ourselves, in the ways that our traditions have taught us, to the Ultimate Reality, through our particular understandings of what the followers of Zoroaster called the Saoshyant.

Eight or nine years ago, I was volunteering as the on-call clergy for a hospital here in Toronto. Late one night I was called to the hospital to minister to a Hindu family who had just found out that the child they had long hoped for had died in the womb. The doctors had suggested that they induce a stillbirth of the unborn child, and while the family was pretty much agreed, they didn't want to go ahead without consulting with a chaplain—even if that chaplain was me! I did my best to empathize with the family and encouraged them to draw strength from the teachings of their own spiritual traditions. As the mother was wheeled into the operating theater, the father and his mother accompanied me to the chapel to pray. There I was, saying the rosary in honor of Jesus's mother, while grandmother entered into a meditative state she had been taught as a child, or so I supposed. While we were praying, a Muslim orderly entered the chapel, looked at the family members, and then looked at me with a quizzical expression as if to ask whether he should leave. I smiled warmly and nodded as if to welcome him. He crossed the chapel and quietly found a mat on which to say his prayers. And there we were, under the umbrella of three faiths, praying, but also listening, listening deeply, for the presence of the divine in the midst of our daily struggles.

Our presence here today confirms that a new Axial Age is at hand, to which the work of Brian Arthur Brown and others call our attention. Are we ready—am I ready—to engage it? I have spoken, but am I ready to listen? Thank you for listening, not to me, but with me. Thank you.

ðisclaimers

What If? and Other Questions

I AM GRATEFUL FOR THE CONFIDENCE PLACED IN ME BY LEARNÈD COLLEAGUES. HOWEVER, SOME disclaimers may be in order to protect their reputations and my own. At first glance, it might appear that this book and the trilogy of which it is a part are based on three assumptions that may be correct but the refutation of which could cause this shrine of texts to collapse like a house of cards unless there is an alternative explanation.

First, we accept traditional dates of "Zoroastrian scholars" for Zoroaster's life as 628–551 BCE, the dates maintained by Persian, Arabic, and early Christian sources. But what if the eleventh-century BCE dates preferred by many European and some American unaffiliated "scholars of Zoroastrianism" are correct?

In fact, we acknowledge that if Zoroaster was born earlier and his religious reforms had hibernated for five hundred years, our thesis then simply depends on an outburst of Zoroastrian enthusiasm by Vedic Magi, who converted en masse under the Zoroastrian monarch, Cyrus the Great, "in deference to his most gracious majesty."[1] If this was the case, it would have been these Magi who spread the word throughout the Silk Route in the sixth century BCE rather than Zoroaster himself and his first followers, but with the same effect. However, that having been said, during the course of presenting our material we hope to resolve the dating question once and for all by proving when Zoroaster died and by showing where and when he was buried—the "big reveal" of our presentation, in the opinion of some.

Second, and in a similar way, while we also place his birth in one of the more traditionally accepted locations west of the Caspian Sea, we recognize modern scholarship that speculates about his birth having been possibly farther west, even to the recent and almost convincing article by Himanshu Bhatt at the University of Alberta, described in *Hindupedia*, suggesting that he was born in India. Again, that affects neither the dates nor the central arguments of this text with respect to his ministry beginning in Balkh and headquartered there for nearly forty years.

Third, we are hopeful that missing pages of the Avesta will be found in caches of material discovered in the present flurry of high-tech archaeological activity, verifying our thesis. We even go so far as to speculate that the most likely location of such a find (or finds) would be near Balkh, in Samarkand, or east from there on the Silk Route into China proper. But again, we concede that nothing depends entirely on finding the physical Dead Zee Scrolls in a cave somewhere, since they can now be unearthed largely from where they are buried within the scriptural testaments of the seven world religions under investigation.

Fourth, what if there never were any scrolls, and the text of the Avesta was not written down until books appeared early in the Common Era, perhaps under Sasanian rule sometime after 224 CE, as first proposed by Mary Boyce?[2] We would then have to ignore the vast array of ancient testimonies to the existence of written copies, which we present, but even that still leaves us with the power in an oral tradition of these poem-prayer-songs that was as precise in older times as print is to modern people. We could accept that the oral tradition functioned in much the same way that we assume written material would have functioned. Accordingly, critical rejection of any or all of our key assumptions detracts little from the groundbreaking theses of this book.

In a similar vein, we know that wider aspects of scholarship fluctuate. In the twentieth century, there was doubt that Lao Tzu, the father of Taoism, ever existed, though that has been revised again in the twenty-first century. We simply take his reported meeting with Confucius at face value, believing that when we see something like the results of such a meeting, something similar to that legend must have transpired in the transmission of ideas across the ancient world and in countries that we now know to have been more fluid and porous than previously imagined. There are other such examples of fluidity even if tradition got some of the names wrong, though we are increasingly discovering that tradition is usually at least as trustworthy as artifacts in pointing to the facts.

Another disclaimer here, while we have the opportunity, relates to a chart in chapter 9 of the *Three Testaments* book in this trilogy, already published, purporting to identify strands of the Quran in the same manner as the chart of sources of the Jewish Torah in this volume. The theory is valid, but its execution requires much more work on the part of expert Islamic scholars, as has been promised. We have had good advice in the meantime, but students should ignore the details of that chart in future reading.

We do not claim that 100 percent of the material in this "introductory" volume is original. Almost 10 percent of part one is replicated from volume 2 and volume 3 of this trilogy. This includes "specialist" language in a piece by Karl Friedrich Geldner and several pages about Baruch Spinoza, not usual for an introduction to a subject like this one. They appear again in *Three Testaments* (Geldner) and *Four Testaments* (Spinoza) but are introduced here as related to Zoroastrian material expanded and annotated in this volume—heavy going, which may require a second reading at a later time to be fully appreciated. All of part two is fresh and original. One appendix in part three is a play already being used by interfaith classes as cold readings, available in script format from Stageplays.com and as a book from Amazon, but scheduled to go out of print there upon publication of this volume. "Where the Bodies Are Buried" appeared earlier in the *Three Testaments Companion* (2014). That *Companion* is also now intended to go out of print but remain available electronically from Amazon. All the above are briefly still available from their publishers, from Amazon, and at Barnes & Noble and other sources at the time of publication of *Seven Testaments of World Religion*. Two important appendices and an afterword conclude with "contributions" provided not by the respected authors but by their publishers in a cooperative spirit and under license.

One final disclaimer acknowledges that some will find this introductory text to be not strictly academic on every page. A few paragraphs here and there are simply practical in suggesting to students and other readers how the findings of this book might be applied in the world of the New Axial Age. For example, chapter 8, "Monism and Monotheism in Actual Practice," is not intended to be definitive, but rather to serve as the beginning of a conversation between two groups of cousins in what we now find to be an extended family. Academic purists may decry departures from objective analysis and ventures into application of the principles, but we regard the changing scene of religious practice as sufficiently academic to warrant attention, whether it is in Muslims loving Jesus (as did Muhammad) without leaving the mosque, or the government of Germany funding multifaith "cathedrals" in which Muslims may worship on Friday, Jews on Saturday, Christians on Sunday, and "Eastern" religions on Monday, Tuesday, Wednesday, and Thursday. The latter is a switch from government funding only for Christians (the usual German practice), similar to the government in Muslim-majority Kazakhstan building a spiritual Palace of Peace and Accord with seven chapels for the same seven religions featured in this book in its new capital at Astana. None of the many such examples we give represent syncretism or homogenization of religion, but they fit with the ethos of an emerging New Axial Age sufficiently to merit some attention.

Many of the issues raised here are dealt with in notes and appendices, but not everyone reads these, so we especially recommend appendices E and H to students, lay readers, and Zoroastrians for what we regard as sheer pleasure.

Volumes 2 and 3 of this trilogy—namely, *Three Testaments: Torah, Gospel, and Quran* and *Four Testaments: Tao Te Ching, Analects, Dhammapada, Bhagavad Gita*—are more strictly academic in content, but for an introductory volume 1, it may be appropriate to occasionally digress into religious experience in *Seven Testaments of World Religion and the Zoroastrian Older Testament*. We hope to at least begin an overdue conversation between monotheists and monists in the newer discipline of Scriptural Reasoning, which had its beginnings among Western monotheists alone.

notes

1. The phrase used by Samuel de Champlain to justify his switch from Protestantism to Catholicism to please the king in his application to gain a trading rights monopoly in early French Canada.

2. Mary Boyce, *Zoroastrians: Their Religious Beliefs and Practices* (London: Routledge & Kegan Paul, 1979), 17.

part one

INDO-EUROPEAN CONNECTIONS IN ALL SEVEN TESTAMENTS OF WORLD RELIGION

1
breakthroughs in the study of world religions

THE SOURCE CHART OF THE JEWISH TORAH NEAR THE BEGINNING OF THIS STUDY HAS A HIS-tory in development. The pious fiction that Moses wrote the five books of the Torah (long before there was a Hebrew alphabet) was first challenged in the eleventh century CE by Spanish physician Isaac ibn Yashush, who realized that the list of the Edomite kings in Genesis chapter 36 all lived centuries after Moses. For this observation, he got the nickname "Isaac the Blunderer" from his literalist rabbi, Abraham Ibn Ezra, but the cat was out of the bag.

Martin Luther's friend Andreas Karlstadt observed that Deuteronomy describes the grave of Moses, the location of which, as the Bible says, "No one knows even to this day"[1]—not likely a comment by Moses himself. In 1651, English philosopher Thomas Hobbes noted that whoever wrote the Torah referred to Moses in the third person. At about the same time, Baruch Spinoza humorously drew attention to a verse that claims "Moses was the most humble man who ever lived,"[2] which could not be true if Moses made the comment himself. Roman Catholic writer Richard Simon next pointed out that when the writer spoke of place names like "Dan," it was often about places that had other names in the time of Moses. This would be as if the early history of America was purported to be written by one of the Dutch pioneers who kept referring to New York instead of New Amsterdam.

Finally, French and German scholars Jean Astruc and Karl Graf realized that various names for God and other hallmarks of style indicated that there were likely several authors. This enabled the father of textual analysis, Julius Wellhausen, to describe four strands of material in his famous 1886 "documentary hypothesis," as identified on our chart as J, E, D, and P. In the twentieth century, numerous subsets of material were identified in tentative "fragmentary" and "supplementary" hypotheses, to which we now add the twenty-first-century recognition of the Z factor in the Torah. Z also appears in other parts of the Hebrew Scriptures and in the other six sacred texts featured in *Seven Testaments Trilogy*.

In 1959, I entered Dalhousie University in Halifax, Nova Scotia. My pretheology degree in arts and science included some sciences as broad programs to understand how the world works and liberal arts in Greek, Latin, and English literature, plus philosophy, history, and psychology. This four-year honors degree was intended to prepare one for the rigors of theological studies, still then referred to as "the queen of the sciences." Theology and religious studies were offered only in seminaries, separate colleges, and a few faculties of theology or "divinity" (like McGill, Harvard, and Oxford), which were separate from the rest of the academic community in such places.

There was then no department of religious studies at Dalhousie, or at any other university that I knew of, though they are ubiquitous in the twenty-first century, which is now tackling the subject of religion more rigorously in public. Back then, at Dalhousie, there was but one lone religious half-course in the English Department, called "Introduction to the English Bible," so I signed up.

On the first day, Professor John Corston introduced the notion that we do not know who wrote the opening books of the Bible. But I drew his attention to my copy of the King James Version, which opened with the words "The First Book of Moses, called Genesis." He wanted the class to use the then newer Revised Standard Version, but he was suddenly distressed to realize that the RSV also began with the title "The First Book of Moses, Commonly Called Genesis." He insisted that the phrase *commonly called* was significant and predicted that future editions would simply be called *Genesis*. He was correct, of course, with the New Revised Standard Version of 1989 and most others since then having dropped the reference to Moses, which is not in any of the ancient manuscripts.

Corston seemed rattled by my impertinent interjections, but he persevered in explaining the likelihood of multiple communal authorship of this part of the Bible, introducing us to the documentary hypothesis of Julius Wellhausen. The Torah, or "Pentateuch," as Christians then called it, was presented as among the most precious documents in the world. We now see it as also pointing toward a Vedic subtext of world religions, an aspect then well beyond the horizon. We recognize Z verses as appearing in two books of the Torah, elsewhere in Hebrew Scriptures, undoubtedly in Christian and Islamic texts, and in three of the four Eastern iterations of world religions, even including Confucian writings much later—the latter being a very recent realization.

The good professor fared ever so much better when we reached the New Testament, with the aid of a four-color chart, about a square meter in size. It depicted the four main sources of material in what we call the Synoptic Gospels, the "look-alike" Gospels that may be viewed together: Matthew, Mark, and Luke. We students could see clearly how one might have copied from another, which gospel was likely written first, and how Luke probably spoke for the others in acknowledging that his own material was obtained from various sources and eyewitness accounts, which he then edited together in a manner very similar to the books of the Torah.

I was beginning to learn, and by this time John Corston and I had become quite friendly. So, I said to him, "Don't you wish you had that kind of chart to illustrate the opening books of the Old Testament?" His reply was a direct challenge: "Since you are going into theology when you leave here, you should construct such a chart and eventually submit it as your thesis project." I thought I might just do that, so while the idea was fresh, and to prepare for the coming exam, I produced my first draft of the chart over the Christmas break at my grandparents' home in late 1959. I used a pen and ruler, an Underwood typewriter, and some children's crayons . . . just sixty years before submitting this manuscript to my publisher in 2019.

The original chart was an almost amusing but helpful aid to my classmates at the Faculty of Divinity at McGill University when I arrived in Montreal a few years later. There my depiction of the original Wellhausen documentary hypothesis was massaged in favor of decisions about J, E, D, and P by McGill's dean of graduate studies, our Old Testament professor, Stanley Brice Frost, in his book, *The Beginning of the Promise*.[3] Its appendix remains the basis of identifying strands in the chart presented in this book, though it has been slightly amended by a range of experts since then. The most recent insights to influence the final draft of this chart are the work of Richard Elliott Friedman in the appendix of what may be his final word on the matter in *Who Wrote the Bible?*[4] and comments by Marc Zvi Brettler in *How to Read the Bible*.[5] However, among the welter of "supplementary" and "fragmentary" hypotheses in the intervening years, none had yet ventured a nomenclature for the Z factor, despite growing recognition of the interface between Jews and Zoroastrians in Babylon. That is my final touch-up to the chart, but it is just the tip of the iceberg for the uses of Z in the future.

This trilogy offers the central premise and discerning thesis that Vedic religious stimulus was introduced by Magi in China at the very time the Jews were in Babylon, at either end of the Silk Route, which we now identify as the "axis of the Axial Age." The Zoroastrian iteration of Vedic heritage stimulated the development of Buddhism and the reform of Hinduism in India, appearing there as almost "between the lines" of primary Scriptures such as the Dhammapada and the Bhagavad Gita, but increasingly possible to identify in the current postcolonial era. Having intersected with Judaism during the Babylonian Captivity, this "Z factor" also influenced Christianity and Islam in dramatic ways only now recognized in the New Axial Age of the twenty-first century. Its appearance in the Eastern texts is even easier to identify.

Zoroastrianism, which itself may have been exposed to earlier Hebrew influence some seventy years prior to their interface in Babylon, was neither foundational nor dominant in any of those religions, but it was at least simulative in all areas connected by the Silk Route in the sixth century BCE. Serving as the state religion of the Persian Empire through a thousand years of association with the world's first superpower, Zoroastrianism thus influenced, or at least helped refine, the seven world religions. We can now point to echoes of Vedic-Zoroastrian stimulus in many places, and, as an interesting sidebar, we present the current search for the lost portions of Zoroastrian Scriptures (the Dead Zee Scrolls) as almost a holy grail of archaeology in the view of some of our contributors.

Were there Magi in ancient China, connected with Persia, introducing religious concepts from the Middle East and the Middle West to the Chinese culture that was believed, until recently, to have developed in total isolation? Was Spinoza, the framer of philosophy that shaped modern Europe, actually informed and influenced by Vedanta Hinduism through his family connections with the Dutch East India Company? The proof of the first is now conclusive, the evidence for the second is mounting, and these are but two of the links between the major religious traditions in human history to be explored in this book. These breakthroughs are seminal in influence in the twenty-first-century field of "religious studies."

The sacred texts themselves take preeminent place in the discussion of *Our Religions*, to use the term employed by a publication of that title that came out of the 1993 Parliament of the World's Religions to describe the seven truly "world" religions. In this trilogy, our own 2016 study of four Eastern, mainly "monistic," texts in *Four Testaments: Tao Te Ching, Analects, Dhammapada, Bhagavad Gita* is presented in tandem with our 2012 publication of *Three Testaments: Torah, Gospel, and Quran* of Western monotheism, both from the Rowman & Littlefield Publishing Group.

This deliberate juxtaposition raises a quintessential question: If monism and monotheism can be shown to have some common roots, are they as totally incompatible as is usually presumed, or might there be ways in which these traditions can enrich each other? This is a key consideration in what follows here.

There was a dramatic spiritual stirring along the Silk Route early in the sixth century BCE, triggered by the prophetic ministry of the aforementioned Persian prophet named Zoroaster, reaching from Europe to China through connections between Magi who were already in "The Land of the Heavenly Dragon" and still connected with their Iranian counterparts. The name *China* comes from the Sanskrit Cina (derived from the name of the Chinese Qin Dynasty, pronounced "Chin"), which was translated as "Cin" by the Persians and seems to have become popularized by Iranian-speaking Sogdian traders along the Silk Route from China to the rest of the world. The reverberations of this spiritual stirring among the Magi apparently inspired a custodian of the Imperial Archives in China's imperial palace to venture into the new dimension of religion we call Taoism. That development may have led to an "equal and opposite" initial reaction in Confucianism, based on China's own best traditions.

The response to this stimulus in India was different, beginning with Buddhism as a positive development, which prompted not resistance but reform of religion across the board in India. This resulted in the development of Z-related Jainism, but more significantly a renewal of Hinduism, making Buddhism almost redundant in India but ready for export throughout neighboring lands. At this very time, the most easily recognized reaction or response to this Vedic-Zoroastrian spiritual revolution is the further development and advancement of Hebrew religion during the Babylonian Exile of Jews, documented in Hebrew Scripture, which had its own reverberations in subsequent religious developments of Christianity and Islam.

When I entered the Master of Divinity program at McGill University in the mid-twentieth century, Western Christians were just beginning to recover the Jewish heritage of the church. In the previous fifty years, its theology had been largely shaped by Greek and Roman, as well as Egyptian and Gnostic, influences developed in the West. This new balance in both theology and biblical studies prevailed until early in the twenty-first century, when a "postcolonial" agenda began to emerge around the world. A change in perspective appeared inevitable in reference to "Asia in the Bible," another central thesis in this work.

To illustrate the change as it may be seen in a wider, parallel phenomenon, most dictionaries of the twentieth century gave the Greek and Latin roots of words, but as the twenty-first century dawned, dictionaries began to show the "Indo-European" roots of most words. The same is now happening in the search for the Vedic roots of Christian theological concepts. We are not saying that there were no other influences, nor that they did not influence each other. The power, insight, and majesty of each of the seven Scriptures under consideration in this book validate the claim of divine inspiration of them all, as affirmed in the Quran,[6] the final testament in the series. But what we are indeed saying is that the Zoroastrian iteration of Vedic lore is as profoundly significant in the Christian Scriptures as it was in the Hebrew and is also in the Tao Te Ching, the Dhammapada, the Bhagavad Gita, and the Quran, and eventually in Confucian writings (if not in the initial analects of Confucius).

Of course, Jewish and Islamic studies have been developing corresponding links in the same direction as Christian theology, and the influence of Eastern theology on all three Western Scriptures is beginning to be recognized at last in this postcolonial era. In 2013, R. S. Sugirtharajah of the UK University of Birmingham could write in a watershed judgment, "In modern times there has been a grudging acknowledgement that some of the key theological concepts in Christianity might have their origins in Zoroastrianism,"[7] a Vedic imprint from the East impressed upon the West, but almost invisible until recently.

In addition to providing a link between the three Western testaments and their many offshoots (Mormon, Baha'i, and others), in the East the Vedic umbrella shelters the identifiable commonalities of Taoism, Buddhism, and Hinduism, as well as reactions from Confucianism and connections to Jainism, distinctively Tibetan Buddhism, and perhaps earlier Shinto and certainly later Sikh traditions, reflecting an essence of a religious quest that is more than the coincidence of humans responding to similar phenomena. Vedic lore, as discerned in *Seven Testaments of World Religion and the Zoroastrian Older Testament*, may be described perhaps better as the deep, subterranean aquifer from which the world draws its waters of Christian baptism, Islamic ablution, Hindu sacred bathing, the flow of the Tao, water bowls in Buddhist funerals, and *tevilah* and *netilat vadayim* in Orthodox Judaism. The symbolism of water in these religions may be, again, more than just coincidental to all religions. It is not found in Confucianism, nor in many others. From the beginning, Zoroastrians have believed that pollution is evil and that pure water symbolizes the sacred. They seek to avoid pollution of any kind (physical or spiritual) and perform ritual ablutions before saying their prayers five times a day facing a source of light and before any religious ceremonies, such as weddings. This may seem especially familiar to practitioners of some others of our world religions. It may not be the only time that we appear to be stretching almost too far in making connections, but the volume of other examples eventually becomes overwhelming.

CHAPTER 1

As the Vedic bridge between Eastern and Western religious traditions, Zoroastrianism is of peculiar interest because its influence in the West is identical, but like the mirror opposite of its reforming impact on Eastern Religion and its formative influence on Eastern philosophy during the Axial Age in the fifth and sixth centuries BCE. The humorous observation that "Zoroastrianism is the next big thing, and always will be" may be about to give Zoroastrians the last laugh.

In his seminal analysis of the situation among Jews and Christians, Sugirtharajah summarizes the point by referencing the late Professor Norman Cohn of Sussex University to the effect that "the Judeo-Christian faith tradition owes an intellectual debt to Zoroastrianism for such theological ideas as a universal god, notions of angels, Satan, heaven, hell, resurrection of the body, life after death, and the final apocalyptic ending of this world."[8] Narrowing further to Christianity alone, he quotes J. C. Hindley, New Testament instructor at West Bengal's Serampore College, the current interfaith trailblazer in India, that "it is no longer possible to relegate Zoroastrianism to the fringe of Christian interest."[9]

This trilogy will broaden the Jewish and Christian Western analyses to include their relationships with Islam. More particularly, it will show how that process not only engages Eastern religions and philosophy through a common ancestor but also connects them contextually with Western religions and philosophy today in a manner previously unimaginable. Far from any homogenization of these traditions, it is their different developments that may contribute now to the unique contribution of each at an even deeper level and serve as an enrichment to them all, a point first raised by David Bruce in our introduction.

If our frequent attributions to Zoroastrianism seem like a stretch to some traditional scholars, let me just suggest that we may be at the beginning of an epochal new awareness, something like the cross-fertilization of ideas between East and West along the "Silk Route" long before that conduit functioned as primarily a trade route for goods. It may turn out that there were links other than the Zoroastrian-tinged Vedic connection we are proposing, like perhaps Manichaeism a little later, but at this point it would appear that Zoroastrianism in the mid-sixth century BCE needs to be taken more seriously as the stimulus we are attempting to identify for what is now frequently referred to as the Axial Age.

Every time this text refers to whatever Silk Route influence reached over into China, down into India, and back to Israel-in-Babylon as "Zoroastrianism," the reader may be thinking, "or whatever." But the premise here is that the sixth-century BCE eruption of "something," under the aegis of the Persian superpower, was a resophisticated Vedic influence, moving through the conduit we now call the Silk Route and acting as a stimulant in all seven of these world religions, embraced in the case of six and possibly later in the seventh. If it waddles like Zoroastrianism and quacks like Zoroastrianism, we feel justified in identifying it as Zoroastrianism.

There were hints of monism in various places in the ancient world, and we know that monotheism had been incubating in Israel since the time of Moses. But we can observe how "Westernism" (i.e., in religion and in philosophy) rather suddenly veered from polytheism toward monotheism at almost precisely the same moment that "Easternism" moved just as suddenly from polytheism to monism, both emphasizing the Oneness of God. The parallel timing, as well as Zoroastrian geographical connections both east and west along the Silk Route, suggests that something was going on that may not fully explain these phenomena but that implies a link or a shared stimulation. If so, modern occidental and oriental philosophers may have more grist for their mills, and Western and Eastern religions have a clear agenda for their "interfaith" discussions in the twenty-first century.

Are human beings creatures who have the privilege of knowing, worshipping, and serving one God (monotheism), or are they consciously able to realize their participation in One divine whole (monism)? Is the role of religion to provide "atonement" in the sense of reconciliation between creatures and their Creator, or is it truly "at-*One*-ment*," meaning an emptying of individual "selves" into the glorious fullness of God? If the latter, what is the role of the individual in striving toward realization of the divine? And what is the status of individual elements in relation to the Godhead after integration? Is it possible to conceive of monotheism as a way station in the direction of monism, or does monism simply fail to recognize and accept God's creativity in the divine authentication of separate elements in creation? Where is the line between monotheism and monism, or is there a dynamic continuum between them?

In the simplest of human terms, these may be among the questions facing analysts of religion and theologians of the twenty-first century. Lately one keeps meeting people who say they are both Jewish and Buddhist. Hindus are often regarded as being the most able to embrace other religious traditions, while Muslims are often regarded as most closely guarding their religious distinctiveness, despite Quranic affirmation of revelations of Allah to all human communities.

This trilogy represents the first time the four main popular Scriptures of Eastern monism are linked to each other (in mutual support or in reaction), to the Western traditions, and to the earlier Zoroastrian iteration of Vedic lore. We hope to help launch a field of studies with the potential to engage academic research in areas from ancient Greek and Roman classics through Mesopotamian history, back to investigations of the Vedic origins of spiritual development from one end of the Silk Route to the other, and forward to a whole new Western understanding and appreciation of religion and philosophy in India and China. The expectation is, as Amir Hussain suggests in his foreword to *Three Testaments*, that if he is becoming a better Muslim through appreciation of Christianity and Judaism, in this self-same process of interfaith studies Hindus may become better Hindus, Christians better Christians, and so on, with even atheist readers and agnostics becoming wiser and better as persons.

We might acknowledge that a certain level of dedication will be required to plod through the "Exordium" by Karl Friedrich Geldner, at the conclusion of the next chapter, which presents Zoroastrianism as the Vedic godparent of all major religions, east and west. In a lengthy précis here, this document, over a hundred years old, will be referenced again in *Three Testaments* and *Four Testaments* because it has considerable value, not merely in the information it presents but also in presenting a religious ethos integral to Western culture just a century ago that is foreign to many people now. This ethos is still part of life in the East and is closer to the spirit of the ancient world than we are in the West. It may both inform and enthrall those who can endure the old-world archaisms in this presentation, which lays a foundation for much that follows later.

We hope to illustrate how Western and Eastern traditions of theology and philosophy may be understood as illuminating each other through their shared Zoroastrian connections. To begin with, the Vedic and Semitic traditions may connect with each other more than previously realized through intersections right on the Silk Route. These traditions do not run parallel and may in fact encounter each other directly only once, twice, or perhaps three times that we know of, though such momentous intersections perhaps affected the whole world.

The first such interaction may have happened between Abraham's relatives and early Aryan migrants in places like Mitanni in Assyria. The second intersection now appears to have happened when the Vedic tradition, migrating southward toward India through Iran, crossed the path of Israelite exiles moving northward toward Europe—significant not only for the numbers involved but also for the particular personas putatively engaged. The third direct connection took place as monotheistic Vedic-Zoroastrian Persian conquerors encountered their monotheistic Jewish civil service in newly captured Babylon. Neither group used the modern term *monotheism*, preferring to speak of the Oneness of God. These last two meetings were perhaps less than seventy-five years apart, and we contend that their ramifications are still reverberating in the field of religious studies.

Our focus on Taoism, Confucianism, Buddhism, and Hinduism as the Eastern complement to Judaism, Christianity, and Islam in the West was inspired and confirmed by the publication of the aforementioned survey of seven religions, which might be properly designated as truly "world religions." *Our Religions: The Seven World Religions Introduced by Preeminent Scholars from Each Tradition* was authored and edited by Arvind Sharma of McGill University, one of our own commentators in this trilogy. It was a response to the 1993 acknowledgment of those seven by the Parliament of the World's Religions, a book currently regarded by many as a preeminent text in the field of interfaith studies.

We intend to indicate how these seven religions have some common scriptural roots and have influenced each other more significantly than was previously thought. We have no interest in homogenizing these religions, and we recognize that the differences between them are more enlightening at what may be points of common stimulation. We urge the study of *Our Religions* by Arvind Sharma, and other resources, to follow through on how these religions evolved or grew to the character and the status they enjoy in the twenty-first century, an area of study far beyond the mandate of this trilogy. Here we provide only the raw religious data and initial commentary.

Many seminarians, university undergraduates in "comparative religion," and members of congregations venturing into the interfaith arena are overwhelmed by the number of sects and variant versions of oriental religions. In this trilogy, our approach is more selective, beginning with the first or primary "testament"-sized Scripture of each religion. Without giving breathing exercises or guidelines for meditation, our material sometimes verges on the experiential with respect to the seven sacred texts on exhibition in this trilogy. For context, however, and to illustrate wider trends in passing, my colleagues and I also present glimpses of past religious knowledge, related socio-political realities that affect the current world, and future developments in religious archaeology that may bring forth stunning new information in our lifetimes. One development representing these three elements is unfolding just as this book is going to press, as presented in appendix E.

Judaism is small in numbers today but widely disseminated. The majority of Christians are now found outside the Western Hemisphere, and Islam has spread far beyond its Arabic origins. Because of where they were written in western Asia, we continue to refer to the Scriptures of these three religions as Western. The Western Scriptures are all presented here in twenty-first-century translation, chosen to illustrate current trends in textual criticism, such as inclusive language to the extent reflected in the meaning of the originals, the roles of women in both writing and dissemination, and accuracies verified by very recent archaeological discoveries. The Hebrew Scriptures are in the *Contemporary Tanakh* version of the Torah. The New Testament is from the *Inclusive Bible*, a Jesuit translation initially spurned (but not forbidden) by the Vatican under Pope Benedict XVI but increasingly now emulated by other translations favored by Pope Francis. Our Islamic Scripture is *The Sublime Quran*, noted for its scholarly resolution of thorny gender questions. These three sacred texts are used under license and with gracious permissions from the Jewish Publication Society, Sheed & Ward Catholic Books, and Kazi Islamic Publications, publishers that are preeminent in those traditions.

The four Eastern Asian testaments, together with extant remnants of the "Eastern" Zoroastrian Avesta, represent the quintessence of Eastern sacred texts, like four fingers and a thumb, presented in the context of their Vedic glove. We present a several sections of the Avesta in original paraphrase, but archaeologists are still looking for the bulk of the original, a search introduced in detail in appendix F of *Four Testaments* by Professor Richard Freund of Hartford University. We present the other four sacred Eastern testaments in a manner we hope renders the originals as faithfully as possible in translation, portraying the understanding of these Scriptures down through the ages, and appropriately representing their position in today's world. Our *Tao Te Ching* is the twenty-first-century version by one of our contributors, Victor Mair, used by his permission and under license from Random House. Our English classic versions of the Analects by James Legge, the Dhammapada by Sarvepalli Radhakrishnan, and the Bhagavad Gita by Mohandas Gandhi are all currently in the public domain.

The "evidence" for a close and direct relationship between Zoroastrian and Jewish priests and scholars in Babylon can be divided into three categories: circumstantial, collateral, and absolute proof. The absolute proof of Vedic and Zoroastrian influence in Hebrew Scriptures seems to consist in small but concrete things, like the sudden emergence of *Redeemer* (Saoshyant), appearing twenty-two times as an actual name for God during the parts of Isaiah written in Babylon.[10] Or we might highlight the hitherto strangely unnoticed appearance of the name *Krishna*[11] in the Book of Esther and the sudden appearance of fire sacrifice and even perpetual fire[12] in Leviticus, one of the priestly scrolls almost certainly begun in Babylon. Additionally, the circumstantial and collateral evidences we present are so abundant that a pattern emerges that is impossible to ignore. Within Christianity this pattern of Zoroastrian influence gets unexpectedly stronger, as we shall see, and is perhaps even more so in Islam, in which previous revelations are confirmed, corrected, or amplified. In both of these latter cases, this appearance of the Z factor is an interesting new development, with even less previous basis in scholarship of the twentieth-century than in the case of Judaism, where at least substantial hints existed prior to this study.

notes

1. Deuteronomy 34:6.
2. Numbers 12:3.
3. S.P.C.K., London, 1960.
4. San Francisco: HarperCollins, 1997.
5. Philadelphia: Jewish Publication Society, 2005.
6. Quran 5:48.
7. *The Bible and Asia*, 44.
8. *Cosmos, Chaos and the World to Come: The Ancient Roots of Apocalyptic Faith* (New Haven, CT: Yale University Press, 2001).
9. "A Prophet Outside Israel? Thoughts on the Study of Zoroastrianism," *Indian Journal of Theology* II, no. 3 (1962), 107.
10. Isaiah 40–66.
11. Esther 1:14.
12. Leviticus 6:12–13.

2

from the z factor to zoroaster (including a historic exordium by friedrich geldner)

HERE ARE CHRISTIAN BIBLES THAT HIGHLIGHT THE WORDS OF JESUS IN RED INK, AND JEWISH Bibles that highlight the creation story and Scriptures of environmental interest in green ink. We contemplated exhibiting the Zoroastrian-related Z verses in bold type in all the sacred texts presented in this trilogy. This might be doable in the Torah, but we demurred from doing so because this critical analysis is still embryonic in the New Testament, the Islamic contribution needed more work than our team was prepared to undertake, and some parts of the oriental texts contain so much Z-related material that the rest might seem inconsequential. The Z verses in the Hebrew Scriptures are quite easily identified, but we limited ourselves in this exercise to the bold portions of the "Sources of the Jewish Torah" chart, in which small parts of Genesis and Leviticus contain Z in the Torah as an illustration.

Were such a purely scriptural publication of at least the three Western texts to be printed, the publisher might refer to the Zoroastrian passages in bold as "the Z factor," a nomenclature we have used and hope to see adopted now in all such studies in much the same way that J, E, P, D, and other initials are regarded in studies of the Hebrew Torah. In New Testament studies, we use Q for traces of a document hidden between the lines of the three Synoptic (look-alike) Gospels, and S for the original "Signs Gospel," thought by many scholars to lie behind the Gospel According to St. John. The designation M is becoming established in Quranic studies to identify the Meccan surahs, as over and against the longer Medina surahs, known as Md. While no scriptural trilogy with such verses in bold is possible at this juncture, it is entirely appropriate to adopt the "Z" nomenclature for academic study purposes in all three Western Scriptures at least.

There is a thin line between identification of Z passages attributable to Zoroastrian material and simple similarities found in all or most religions, but we hope to be able to make the distinction correctly. For example, while the Quran condemns lying as a general principle, there are no particular verses that appear to represent the previous revelation to Zoroaster about the destructive power of "the Lie," strident enough to be printed in bold. However, the Jewish sect that compiled the Dead Sea Scrolls deprecated their enemies with titles like "The Man of the Lie" and "The Spouter of Lies," which, while not scriptural, could give such passages Z standing in academic circles. Indeed, Jesus denounced Satan as a "Liar" and "The Father of Lies,"[1] identical to phrases in the Zoroastrian Avesta, and exactly the kind of Z factor references that would certainly qualify for bold print. There are many more such Z passages scattered between the appearance of Magi[2] at the nativity of Jesus to his use of "Paradise"[3] rather than "heaven" when speaking to the thief dying beside him on the cross.

Cyril Glassé, author of *The Second Coming of the Judeo-Zoroastrian Jesus of the Dead Sea Scrolls*, provides one of the more succinct summaries of these points:

> Jesus rises from the dead in three days, an interval taken directly from Zoroastrianism. In that religion, the dead linger near the grave for three days before continuing their afterlife journey. Half or more of Christianity is composed of elements from Zoroastrianism compounded with elements from Semitic religion. . . . Then there is Jesus himself, born of a virgin, as Zoroaster said would happen, the *Saoshyant*, the world savior. Isaiah (duly repeating Zoroastrian doctrine) says: "Therefore the Lord himself shall give you a sign: Behold, a virgin shall conceive. And bear a son, and call his name Immanuel." (God is with us.)[4] Isaiah is quoting Zoroastrian dogma on the subject, and ignoring this or pretending otherwise is either longstanding ignorance or deliberate obfuscation. The Zoroastrian prophecy is attested by the visit of the Magi, who were Zoroastrian priests, following the "Star out of Jacob"[5] to bring gifts to the baby Jesus to certify that everything was in accordance with the most ancient of religions. This marks him as the Zoroastrian "Saoshyant," or world savior.[6] The Koran calls these Zoroastrians *Majus*. Muslim authorities, going back to the Caliph Umar, accept Zoroastrians as a People of Scripture, with a revealed religion, and thus qualified for the protection of the Islamic State.[7]

In its Zoroastrian iteration, the ancient Vedic heritage may be seen as the foundation of Eastern religions. Hinduism, Jainism, Buddhism, and even Taoism are monistic, with Confucianism perhaps initially a reaction to the introduction of this stimulus in China. The only comparable overarching influence in world religions is the Semitic heritage as the cradle for Western monotheistic religions—Jewish, Christian, and Islamic. The Jewish expression of Middle Eastern religious experience was as generic to expanding Semitic traditions as Zoroastrianism was to new iterations of Vedic tradition. Judaism also influenced subsequent Eastern religious developments through its impact on Zoroastrianism in an early interface, just as Zoroastrianism influenced subsequent Western religious developments through its impact on Judaism, and also on its own as experienced personally by Jesus and Muhammad—all easily identified.

In the Vedic tradition, any situation "is what it is," and devotees are enjoined to "go with the flow" and act correctly within it (the flow being the dynamic and complete One monistic universe, the ultimate Divinity). By way of contrast, in Semitic tradition no situation is what it should be (at least not since the "fall" of humanity), and believers are challenged to change things and act accordingly. Aryan Vedic notions of "super race" (lamentably promoted in Germany in the middle of the last century, but not limited to that) and Semitic concepts of "chosen people" (held by Jews, Christian, and Muslims in equal but different ways) are both mitigated by universal Zoroastrian principles, as we shall see, but it is little wonder that communities have sometimes clashed under Vedic and Semitic influences. We are entering an era in which it is increasingly necessary that they contribute to each other in our one world in ways that enhance the faith of those engaged in practically all major world religions.

Extensive missing portions of the Zoroastrian "Avesta" Scriptures may be the Rosetta Stone of common ground among the "world religions" and could contribute generously to mutual respect among believers when found. These "Dead Zee Scrolls" would certainly contain material related to the *Three Testaments* of western monotheistic religion (Torah, Gospel, and Quran) and to at least three of the *Four Testaments* of Eastern monistic religion (Tao Te Ching, Analects, Dhammapada, and Bhagavad Gita), all of which developed in the churning wake of Zoroaster or in its aftermath on the Silk Route.

The Avesta, as the Zoroastrian scriptural corpus is called, was once the most broadly circulated and widely translated written material in the world, disseminated east and west along and beyond the Silk Route. The Zoroastrian tradition of respect for others and tolerance of their religion was established by Cyrus the Great in the Persian Empire. This generosity was eventually rejected by the Greeks in their promotion of a European vision of "civilization" and by Muslims who encountered a later Zoroastrianism that had lost its focus on the Oneness of God, a matter they found offensive.

The main corpus of Zoroastrian Scriptures was deliberately destroyed twice, first by the Europeans under Alexander the Great and again by Muslims after Muhammad. But copies had undoubtedly been stored by accident or hidden in various places, much like the Dead Sea Scrolls and the Nag Hammadi Library, so valued now by Jews and Christians. Until now the existence of what we call the Dead Zee Scrolls has had only mythical status, much like the existence of Troy in the writings of Homer until the site was discovered by Heinrich Schliemann in 1870. The search for this Zoroastrian treasure has only now begun in earnest. The discovery of the tomb of Zoroaster might have been regarded as even less likely until recently identified under the Blue Mosque in Mazar-i-Sharif, Afghanistan, as detailed in our appendix C.

In their prayers today, Zoroastrians employ only some 15–20 percent of the ancient Avesta material, rescued or remembered from those destructive calamities. This book details the ancient references to that vast earlier collection and points to the near certainty that complete versions of three distinct editions existed, following Zoroaster, reconstituted after Alexander, and reconstituted again after Muhammad, though the latter may be little more than the remnant Avesta treasured as their Scriptures by Zoroastrians today. The first two versions will eventually be found, perhaps sooner rather than later, and conceivably rivaling the Dead Sea Scrolls in both size and significance. In this trilogy, we exhibit material found to date and examine the prospects for an unearthing of the entire mother lode, even while looking for clues between the lines of the seven other Scriptures that emerged in the wake of the appearance of the first Zoroastrian Avesta Scripture along the Silk Route.

Archaeologists in Uzbekistan and western China are now turning up interesting Zoroastrian artifacts from the fifth century CE, but these are just remnants of a religious tradition that actually flourished more significantly a thousand years earlier. A pristine bronze statue of Apollo was found off Gaza in 2014, a cuneiform disk from Mesopotamia showing blueprints of the ark modeled by Noah was displayed in 2013, and a Roman eagle turned up under the streets of London in 2012, all from that prime earlier Zoroastrian era. So why should we not assume that the most widely published book in the world of that era will eventually turn up under the streets of Samarkand, among tens of thousands of as yet uncataloged manuscripts stored in the library of the Southwest University of Nationalities in China, or even as artifacts buried with Zoroaster in the stone crypt under the tomb of Ali in the Blue Mosque currently under investigation in Afghanistan?

Current archaeological expeditions employ space-age technology and infrared camera techniques capable of finding troves of artifacts and caches of documents, some of which might have been hidden in circumstances remarkably similar to the concealment of the Dead Sea Scrolls and the burial of the Nag Hammadi Library. Whether by design or by accident, the finding of the "Dead Zee Scrolls" mother lode is now only a matter of time, and with it, new clues to the origins of Eastern and Western Scriptures and the use of theological phraseology East and West.

The search for clues to what may have been in the scrolls of the complete Avesta will unfold in this trilogy, chapter by chapter. Excitement has been mounting about the possibilities of locating copies of the ancient originals, and even during the writing of *Four Testaments* our interest was piqued by a press conference announcement from the Institute of Archaeology of the Academy of Sciences of Uzbekistan.[8] A fifth-century BCE temple at Khorazm (a province of the ancient Persian Empire just north of Bactria, Zoroaster's headquarters, near the borders of today's Turkmenistan and Afghanistan) had just been identified as a Zoroastrian fire temple from the precise era of our interest. Being unearthed in good condition except for four towers at the corners, the 625-square-meter temple was then yielding intact pitchers, jugs, vessels, bowls, jars, terracotta figurines, bronze medallions, pins, and arrowheads in bright and expressive condition. The excavation is now almost complete but has yielded no documents, as the search continues in this area. Among ancient artifacts, documents are always the last to be discovered.

One important site to which we will refer was unearthed early in the twentieth century, as the field of Zoroastrian studies began to get organized, but the pace is picking up in the twenty-first century. Even as we go to press again, archaeologists in northwest China's Xinjiang Uygur Autonomous Region have discovered major Zo-roastrian tombs, dated to more than 2,500 years ago on the sparsely populated Pamir Plateau. This find purportedly exceeds all previously known Zoroastrian cultural artifact troves, though yet again yielding no complete Avesta.

We follow the leading universities of Russia, China, India, Europe, and North America in the hunt for this important written artifact in the quest to discover that we are one world and to prove that important religious developments have been interrelated. We already know that Zoroastrianism provides a model precedent for mutual respect in the diversity we must cherish in mixed societies in the twenty-first century. Not even the excavation of Troy in Turkey near the end of the nineteenth century, or the puta-tive discovery of Atlantis in southern Spain in photos taken from space at the end of the twentieth century, could match the communal or cultural significance for our era of finding the complete Avesta Scriptures. This will be a treasure for religious people, provide grist for the academic mill through the twenty-first century, and appear as front-cover material for tabloids at supermarkets in the future as superficial headlines melodramatically proclaim, "SOURCE OF ALL SCRIPTURES FOUND."

Meanwhile, we will experience a new appreciation of the Zoroastrian Avesta from "testaments" of the religions whose monism exploded upon a vast region of the East within the same era that monotheism burst beyond its Semitic base in the West. Both developments may have happened in response to stimuli in the Axial Age, triggered by that certain Persian prophet and his vision of the Oneness of God, understood variously by those who pray to either the God above all or the Godhead within a divine universe.

In Zoroaster's teaching, from that perspective, the possibility of evil in the world is presupposed from the beginning as at least a powerful illusion, in opposition to good-ness, or Divinity. Both Ahura Mazda (the Divinity) and Angra Mainyu (the Deceiver) possess power, which manifests itself as light in the divine One and as darkness in the deceptive illusion. But the dark does not actually exist, and nothing makes things dark except for the absence of light. Light can lighten, but there is no dark that somehow "darkens" or makes darkness. Light is the reality; dark is an illusion, or a dependent reality at best. Likewise, there is no such thing as cold, though there is such a thing as heat. Cold itself does not exist, though in the absence of heat the illusion of cold seems very real to humans. Both "dark" and "cold" are dependent realities. And so it is with evil, which does not exist on its own, while good is real. The absence of good creates a void in which the illusion of evil can be very painful.[9]

While the devil (Angra Mainyu / Ahriman / Satan / Lucifer / Iblis) does not "exist," he does "appear" in human thoughts and seeks to rule in human hearts. In Zoroastrian monistic understanding, Divinity (Ahurah Mazda / Ormazd / Godhead / God / Allah) does exist, infused in the universe and offering Divine energy to everything and ev-eryone. In human experience, darkness, cold, and evil appear to be very real, and to experience life according to Divine purpose, it is up to each individual to choose light, warmth, and goodness rather than false illusions or dependent realities like darkness, cold, and evil. The Avesta Scriptures make it clear that humans have complete freedom of choice in this matter: "O Mazda, from the beginning you created soul and body. You granted people the mental power and knowledge. You placed life in the physical body and gave humanity the power to act, speak and think. You willed that everyone should choose their own faith and path freely."[10]

Ultimately, in Zoroastrianism, Ahura Mazda is God and Angra Mainyu is a false god, an illusion. Treating the latter as also real brings about a dualism that has frequently "bedeviled" Zoroastrianism, always to eventually fail and fade. Meanwhile, however, humans must deal with the illusion of cold—either that or freeze to death. Humans need the light of the sun, or they will perish in what they experience as darkness. Likewise, the essence of spiritual life is found in facing up to the powerful appearance of evil in the war between God and the illusionary False God. Knowing with Zoroaster how it will ultimately end does not lessen the danger or reduce the necessity of choosing which side to serve: the warm embrace of life or a cold shoulder to the world, the light of understanding or the power of dark foreboding, the positive reality or the negative illusion. Many are called to the warmth and light of the good, but the cold dark delusion has its attraction to many among its legion of warriors.

The context for human experience in this seeming competition is set in the ancient Zoroastrian creation story, maintained at least orally since the time of Cyrus the Great, committed to writing in appendix verses of the Avesta,[11] and almost certainly to be found in the texts of the Dead Zee Scrolls, highlighted in part two of this book, along with the apocalypse tradition that builds on the Final Judgment motif, addressed to all who faced the choice and made the decision of who to serve.

The following exordium might have been included as an appendix in part three of this volume, except that it is so important to the argument that we felt we had no choice but to publish its additional basic knowledge about Zoroaster here.

exordium

by karl friedrich geldner

ZOROASTER, one of the great teachers of the East, the founder of what was the national religion of the Perso-Iranian people from the time of the Achaemenidae to the close of the Sasanian period. The name is the corrupt Greek[12] form of the old Iranian Zarathustra.[13] Its signification is obscure, but it certainly contains the word *ushtra*, or "camel." Zoroaster was famous in classical antiquity as the presumed founder of the widely renowned wisdom of the Magi.

The ancients also recount a few points regarding the childhood of Zoroaster and his hermit-life. Thus, according to Pliny,[14] he laughed on the very day of his birth and lived in the wilderness upon cheese.[15] Plutarch speaks of his intercourse with the deity.[16] Dio Chrysostom, Plutarch's contemporary, declares that neither Homer nor Hesiod sang of the chariot and horses of Zeus so worthily as Zoroaster, of whom the Persians tell that, out of love for wisdom and righteousness, he withdrew himself from men and lived in solitude upon a mountain. The mountain was consumed by fire, but Zoroaster escaped uninjured and spoke to the multitude.[17] Plutarch speaks of Zoroaster's religion in his *Isis and Osiris*.[18]

As to the period in which he lived, most of the Greeks had by then lost a true perspective. Hermodorus and Hermippus of Smyrna place him 5,000 years before the Trojan war, Xanthus 6,000 years before Xerxes, Eudoxus and Aristotle 6,000 years before the death of Plato. Agathias remarks,[19] with perfect truth, that it is no longer possible to determine with any certainty when he lived and legislated. "The Persians," he adds, "say that Zoroaster lived under Hystaspes, but do not make it clear whether by this name they mean the father of Darius or another Hystaspes. But, whatever may have been his date, he was their teacher and instructor in the Magian religion, modified their former religious customs, and introduced a variegated and composite belief."

He is nowhere mentioned in the cuneiform inscriptions of the Achaemenidae, although Cyrus, Darius, and their successors were without doubt devoted adherents of Zoroastrianism. The Avesta is, indeed, our principle source for the doctrine of Zoroaster; on the subject of his person and his life it is comparatively reticent; with regard to his date it is, naturally enough, absolutely silent. The whole thirteenth section, or *Spend Nask*, which was mainly consecrated to the description of his life, is among the many sections which have perished, while the biographies founded upon it in the seventh book of the *Dinkard* (ninth century CE), the *Shāh-Nāma*, and the *Zardusht-Nāma* (thirteenth century), are merely legendary—full of wonders, fabulous histories, and miraculous deliverances.

The Gatha poem prayers alone within the Avesta make the claim to be the *ipissima verba*, the very words of the prophet; in the rest of that work they are described as being from Zoroaster's own mouth[20] and are expressly called "the Gathas of the holy Zoroaster."[21] The litanies of the Yasna and the Yashts refer to him as a personage belonging to the past. The Vendidad section also merely gives accounts of the dialogues between Ormazd (a late spelling of Ahura Mazda) and Zoroaster. The Gathas alone claim to be authentic utterances of Zoroaster, his actual expressions in the presence of the assembled congregation. They are the last genuine surviving remnants of the doctrinal discourses with which—as the promulgator of a new religion—he appeared at the court of King Vishtaspa in Bactria.

According to the epic legend, Vishtaspa (Greek: Hystaspes) was king of Bactria. According to the *Arda Vīrāf*,[22] Zororoaster began his teaching before this regal convert, in round numbers, some three hundred years before the invasion of Alexander. Probably he emanated from the old school of Median Magi and appeared earlier in Media as the prophet of a new faith but met with sacerdotal opposition and turned his steps eastward. It was to the east of Iran that the novel creed first acquired a solid footing and only subsequently reacted with success upon the West.

His doctrine was rooted in the old Iranian—Aryan—folk religion, of which we can only form an approximate representation by comparison with Vedic religion. The Aryan folk religion was polytheistic. Worship was paid to popular divinities, such as the war god and dragon slayer Indra, and to natural forces and elements such as fire (Igni), but the Aryans also believed in the ruling of moral powers and of an eternal law in nature.[23] Numerous similarities with Vedic religion survive in Zoroastrianism, side by side with marked reforms. The *daēvas*, unmasked and attacked by Zoroaster as the enemies of mankind, are still in the Gathas, without doubt the gods of old popular belief—the idols of the people. For Zoroaster, they sink to the rank of spurious deities, even while maintaining spiritual vigor.

Some few of these have names, and among those names of the old Aryan divinities emerge here and there (for example, Indra and Nāonhaitya). With some, of course—such as Igni, the god of fire—the connection with the good deity was a priori indissoluble. Other powers of light, such as Mithra,[24] the god of day, survived unforgotten in popular belief until the later system incorporated them into the angelic body. Beyond the Lord and his Fire, the Gathas only recognize the archangels and certain ministers of Ormazd, who are, without exception, personifications of abstract ideas. An Essence of Ormazd is Truth and Law;[25] an Essence of the wicked spirit is falsehood; and falsehood, as the embodiment of the evil principle, is much more frequently mentioned in the Gathas than Ahriman or Satan himself.

Zoroaster says of himself that he had received from God a commission to purify religion.[26] He purified it from the grossly sensual elements of *daēva* worship and uplifted the idea of religion to a higher, purer sphere. The body of Vedic Aryan folk belief, when subjected to the unifying thought of a speculative brain, was transformed to a self-contained theory of the universe and a logical dualistic principle. But this dualism is a temporally limited dualism—no more than an episode in the world-whole—and is destined to terminate in monotheism, or perhaps in the Oneness of God. Later sects sought to rise from it to a higher unity in other ways. Thus the Zurvanites represented Ormazd and Ahriman as twin sons proceeding from the fundamental principle of all—*Zrvana Akarana*, or limitless time.

At the beginning there appeared the existence or the possibility of two spirits who represented good and evil.[27] Ormazd is light and life; this God is known as Ahura Mazda, who creates all that is pure and good—in the ethical world of law, order, and truth. His antithesis, Ahriman, also known as Angra Mainyu, is darkness, filth, and death and produces all that is evil in the world. The ultimate triumph of the good spirit in ethical consciousness of the religious community is the quintessence of Zoroaster's religion.[28]

In the Avesta version, as soon as the Wise Lord and the Evil Spirit encountered one another in the human heart following creation,[29] the conflict began. The history of this conflict is the history of the world: all creation divides itself into that which belongs to Ahura Mazda and that which Ahriman claims. Not that the two potentialities carry on the struggle in person; they leave it to be fought out by their respective creations and creatures that they send into the field. The field of battle is the present world.

In the center of battle is humanity: its soul is the object of the war. Humanity is the creation of Ormazd / Ahura Mazda, who therefore has the right to call them to account. But Ormazd created them free in their determinations and in their actions, so they are accessible to the influences of the evil illusions. This freedom of the will is clearly expressed in the Avesta: "Since thou, O Mazda, didst at the first create our being and our consciences in accordance with thy mind, and didst create our understanding and our life together with the body, and works and words in which humans according to their own will can frame their beliefs, the liar and the truth-speaker alike lay hold of the word, the knowing and the ignorant each after their own hearts and understandings."[30]

If all this seems esoteric, it is little wonder that Zoroastrianism has been the forum for much confusion through the ages, to both believers and scholars. Whether Zoro-astrianism is dualistic, monotheistic, or even monistic is the kind of question to which students will return again and again, but it must be acknowledged that these reforms of Vedic lore are of foundational importance in the revelations and evolutions of the seven world religions and others that followed.

In Zoroastrianism, humanity takes part in this eternal conflict by life in the world and activity in the infinite universe. The life of humanity falls into two parts—its earthly portion and that which is lived after death is past. The lot assigned to humans after death is the result and consequence of their life upon earth. No ancient religion had so clearly grasped the ideas of individual guilt and of merit. On the works of humans here below a strict reckoning will be held in heaven. All the thoughts, words, and deeds of each are entered in the book of life as separate items—all the evil works as debts. Wicked actions cannot be undone, but in the heavenly sphere their account can be counterbalanced by a surplus of good works. It is only in this sense that an evil deed can be atoned for by a good deed.

After death the soul arrives at the *cinvatō peretu,* or accountant's bridge, over which lies the way to heaven. Here the statement of his life account is made out. If he has a balance of good works in his favor, he passes forthwith into paradise[31] and the blessed life. If his evil works outweigh his good, he falls finally under the power of Satan, and the pains of hell are his portion forever.

Zoroaster experienced within himself the inward call to seek the amelioration of mankind and their deliverance from ruin and regarded this inner impulse, intensified as it was by long, contemplative solitude and by visions, as the call addressed to him by God Himself. Like Muhammad after him, he often speaks of his conversations with God and the archangels. He calls himself most frequently *manthran* ("prophet"), *ratu* ("spiritual authority"), and *saoshyant* ("the coming helper"—that is to say, when men come to be judged according to their deeds).

Like John the Baptist and the Apostles of Jesus, Zoroaster believed that the fullness of time was near, that the kingdom of heaven was at hand. Through the whole of the Gathas runs the pious hope that the end of the present world is not far distant. He himself hopes, with his followers, to live to see the decisive turn of things, the dawn of the new and better eon. Ormazd will summon together all his powers for a final decisive struggle and break the power of evil forever; with his help, the faithful will achieve the victory over their detested enemies, the *daēva* worshippers, and render them impotent. Thereupon Ormazd will hold a *judicium universale,* in the form of a general ordeal, a great test of all mankind by fire and molten metal, and will judge strictly according to justice, punish the wicked, and assign to the good the hoped-for reward.

Satan will be cast, along with all those who have been delivered over to him to suffer the pains of hell, into the abyss, where he will henceforward lie powerless.

Zoroaster, with the heavenly sphere, facing Ptolemy and the earthly sphere, in *The School of Athens*, painted by Raphael at the papal residence of the Vatican in 1510.

Forthwith begins the one undivided kingdom of God in heaven and on earth. This is called sometimes the good kingdom, sometimes simply the kingdom. Here the sun will forever shine, and all the pious and faithful will live a happy life, which no evil power can disturb, in the eternal fellowship of Ormazd and his angels.

The last things and the end of the world are relegated to the close of a long period of time, when a new Saoshyant is to be born of the seed of the prophet, the dead are to come to life, and a new incorruptible world to begin.

notes

1. John 8:44.
2. Matthew 2:1.
3. Luke 23:43.
4. Isaiah 7:14.
5. Numbers 24:17.
6. The Second Coming of the Judeo-Zoroastrian Jesus of the Dead Sea Scrolls, 164–65.
7. Quoted at greater length in *Four Testaments*, 18.
8. *Uzbekistan Today* newspaper, November 20, 2013.

9. The substance of a discussion at the Conference of the Society of Scholars of Zoroastrianism (SSZ) in Chicago, October 19–21, 2018, an event supported by the Federation of Zoroastrian Associations of North America (FEZANA) and the World Zoroastrian Organization.

10. Yasna 31:11 as referenced in Geldner's exordium; this is from *The Divine Songs of Zarathustra* by IJS Taraporewalla, available in English from Whitefish, MT: Kissinger Publishing, 2010.

11. Bundahishn 1:3.

12. Ζωροάστρρης.

13. New Persian, *Zardushi*.

14. *Nat. Hist.*, vii. 15.

15. xi. 97.

16. *Numa*, 4.

17. vol. ii., 60.

18. cc. 46–47.

19. ii. 24.

20. *Yasna*, 9, 1.

21. *Yasna*, 57, 8.

22. *Arda Vīrāf, I, 2.*

23. *v.* Ed. Meyer in the article PERSIA: *History,* § *Ancient.*

24. Iranian *Mithra.*

25. *asha* = Vedic *rla.*

26. *Yasna*, 44, 9.

27. *Yasna*, 30, 3.

28. Reference has been made to Zoroaster's natural monotheism or emphasis on the Oneness of God in the divinity of all that is real and true. It is not difficult to understand how the religion sometimes veered off course to dualism, supposing the evil spirit to be a god. That spirit is the spirit of falsehood and is itself false, whereas Ahura Mazda represents the complete oneness of God in all that is true.

29. Bundahish I, 4.

30. *Yasna*, 31, 11.

31. *Garō demāna.*

3

fROm the foundations of the earth

Vedic and Semitic Prehistories East and West

HE FOLLOWING DEPICTION OF TWO ANCIENT AND SURVIVING RELIGIO-CULTURAL TRADITIONS related to our theme is not meant to settle any outstanding disagreements among either Vedic or Semitic scholars, and it is therefore painted in broad strokes to give an introductory summary that is relatively beyond dispute. This is for the benefit of readers new to the material in preparation for understanding how these traditions intersected in possibly one of the most dramatic interchanges of religious ideas in world history, with repercussions East and West as reflected in the Scriptures under investigation in this trilogy.

Proto-Vedic religion is the hypothesized religion of Proto-Indo-European peoples (often abbreviated as PIE) around 3600 BCE, based on the existence of similarities among sacred linguistic terms, deities, religious practices, and mythologies among those later referred to as "Indo-European" peoples in the Russian steppes prior to large, energetic migrations southeast through Iran and into India and the smaller Aryan migration across northwest Europe.

In 1147 CE, the new city of Moscow was named after the ancient Moscva River, on which the city is situated. This name is cognate with *moksha*, the Sanskrit Vedic word meaning "salvation," often associated with river rites, no doubt practiced in the Moscva and remaining significant among Hindu descendants of Vedic-related traditions to this day. This linguistic marker is but one of the more obvious among a great number that locate the proto-Vedic religion of Aryan migrants as originating in Russia, right down to the current Russian word *vedat*, which means "knowledge," clearly derived from the Indo-European roots *veda* and *Vedic*. Other evidence for this origin of Vedic religion relates to Aryan archaeology and religious traditions. We will limit ourselves to the latter in this study, secure in the knowledge that evidence for the overall thesis is easily accessed elsewhere. The Aryan migration into India and Persia (Iran) took place for the most part between 2500 and 1500 BCE, with trailblazers before and stragglers after.

In the religious connection, the most obvious link is the names of gods from the area we now call the Russian steppes, as they appear in the Vedic Scriptures known as the Rig Veda and other Vedic sacred materials that followed in India and Persia. Indra, Mitra, and Varuna were among these Vedic gods: Varuna the sky, Mitra the sun, and Indra representing the power of nature. In the various iterations of these Aryan gods found in Scandinavia and Central Europe, Persia, and India, these three also represent a tripartite theology found in all Indo-European religions except Greek polytheism. The three functions are sacerdotal, martial, and fecundity (worship, war, and sex). We cannot ignore other important gods found throughout this swath of humanity, like Agni, the god of fire (ignite and ignition) and acceptor of sacrifices, whose name is actually the first word in the first verse of the ancient Rig Veda Scripture.

The Rig Veda, a collection of more than one thousand hymns and mythic poems, is the oldest continuously used scriptural material in the world. Written down around 1200 BCE, the Rig Veda was "composed" as a song earlier than Zoroaster's Gathas and maintained orally in the final form we have it by the Aryans in India around 1500 BCE. While also showing influence from the ancient Harappan high culture they overran in northern India, the Rig Veda was being developed hundreds of years earlier, before the Aryans left Russia, as shown by place names, linguistic markers, names of gods, and other evidence. When it was written down, it was first written in Vedic, an early form of Sanskrit, closely related to the earlier Avestan language employed by Zoroaster. If its composition began in Russia and was completed in India and written down later there, we can only guess what oral stage it was at, or what status it enjoyed, en route from the Russian steppes to the Indus River. However, as it passed through Persia much of it appeared, not dissimilar to the classic mode in which we have it, judging by the use Zoroaster makes of this material as quoted in his poetic "Gatha" prayers in the Avesta, the Scriptures of his "new" reformed Vedic religion . . . portions all remaining as having been memorized and rewritten after destructions of the larger texts.

Indeed, by the early seventh century BCE Zoroaster may have even been familiar with the final accepted version of the Rig Veda, produced in India, or at least the transitional material that led to its production. It seems likely that he adopted its then archaic Avestan dialect of the twelfth century BCE to authenticate his reforms in much the same way that twentieth-century evangelical Christians used the dialect of the King James Version of the Bible to endow many of their new hymns with authenticity and a familiar sense of holiness, despite a similar time lapse. Official pronouncements from the Roman Catholic Church are still issued in Latin to this day in order to produce that same effect.

While the Rig Veda is the oldest of the Vedas, there are three other Vedic Scriptures, the Sama Veda chants, the Yajur Veda rites, and the Athara Veda teachings, all entirely composed and written down in India. These later compositions had little or no influence on Zoroaster in the Persian Empire. Among the Vedic influences, it is his material, reformed from the Rig Veda alone, which impacted the Jews in Babylon under the aegis of Zoroastrian rulers and their Magi priests. It was the creation story from the Rig Veda that he adapted for the beginning of time, or of the age, or of the cycle. The apocalyptic corollary, so prominent in his writings, appears to have been his own, perhaps inspired by the Rig Veda notion of the beginning, both to be copied subsequently in the sacred texts of all seven world religions, as illustrated in part two of this book.

Proto-Semitic culture is the hypothetical progenitor of historical Semitic languages in the Middle East. Locations that have been proposed for its origination include northern Mesopotamia, the Arabian Peninsula, and the Levant (Greater Syria), with recent estimates that this antecedent of Semitism may have originated around 3,700 BCE, approximately the same era as the very first stirrings of Aryan identity in Russia.

The word *Semitic* is an adjective derived later from Shem, one of the sons of Noah in the biblical book of Genesis, from the Greek version of that name—namely, Σημ (Sēm). The concept of "Semitic peoples" is derived from biblical accounts of the origins of the cultures known to the ancient Hebrews. In an effort to categorize the peoples known to them, those closest to them in culture and language were generally deemed to be descended from their forefather, Shem. Those in other parts of the world were considered as having descended from the two other surviving sons of Noah, as they moved out following the biblical account of the flood—his fourth son, Canaan (the disobedient), having drowned in the deluge after refusing to get on board the ark (as recounted in the Quran).[1]

In Genesis 10:21–31, Shem is described as the father of Aram, Ashur, and Arpachshad, who are presented in the Bible as the ancestors of the Arabs, Assyrians, and Aramaeans, as well as Babylonians, Chaldeans, Sabaeans, and Hebrews, all of whose languages are closely related. This whole language family was accordingly named "Semitic" by linguists, with the term *anti-Semitic* only coming into existence since 1879, strangely in reference to the Jews alone, when William Marr founded the "League for Anti-Semitism" in Germany.

Mesopotamia is generally held to be "The Cradle of Civilization," where writing, the wheel, and the first organized nations or city-states arose during the middle of the fourth millennium BCE. Rivaled in certain developments by only the pre-Aryan Harappan civilization in northern India (and perhaps as yet undocumented developments in early China), the Sumero-Akkadian states that arose in Mesopotamia from 3500 to 2400 BCE were the most advanced in the world at the time in terms of engineering, architecture, agriculture, science, medicine, mathematics, astronomy, and military technology. They had highly sophisticated socioeconomic structures and the world's earliest examples of written law, together with structurally advanced and complex trading, business, and taxation systems, a well-structured civil administration, currency, and detailed record keeping. Schools and educational systems existed in many states. By the time of the Middle Assyrian Empire in the mid-second millennium BCE, early examples of zoology, botany, and landscaping had emerged, and during the Neo-Assyrian Empire in the early to mid-first millennium BCE, King Ashurbanipal built the world's first public library in the ancient Mesopotamian city of Nineveh. Mesopotamian religions were highly organized, and astrology was widely practiced. The oldest records are astrological omens preserved from the reign of King Ammi-saduqa (1683-1647 BCE), a thousand years before Zoroaster, but it is only of late that the obvious has been noted. Mesopotamian "gods" are all identified with astrological bodies in a manner similar to the earlier Vedic religious traditions. This is a dramatic challenge to the notion that much religious material the Hebrews received from the Mesopotamians was original to them. The plot thins until the two traditions connect shortly before, during, and following the Babylonian Captivity.

In the nineteenth century BCE, a wave of polytheistic Semitic "relatives" entered Egypt, possibly at the same time Abraham and his family also made their pilgrimage there. By the early seventeenth century BCE, these Hyksos, as they were known by other Egyptians, had conquered the country, with possibly "Sons of Israel" as their slaves, forming the 15th Dynasty, to be succeeded by the 16th and 17th Dynasties. The New Kingdom, next in sequence from possibly 1550 until about 1050 BCE, was the Egyptian era the world knows best, with its famous pharaohs, the biblical account of Moses leading the Israelites out of slavery, and an interlude of monotheism under Akhenaten. Akhenaten was swayed in this direction by his wife, the legendary Queen Nefertiti, who was a Mitanni princess and a distant relative of Abraham's clan. Nefertiti apparently brought monotheism to Egypt from the Assyrian desert, though her Semitic community there also worshipped the Aryan Vedic gods, Mitra, Varuna, Indra, and the Nasatya twins (Sunrise and Sunset)—an early preview of the coming encounter between the two main religious traditions of the ancient world.

All early Semites across the entire Middle East appear to have been originally polytheist, except for the tentative emergence of what we might call the proto-monotheism of some desert people: Abraham, possibly Nefertiti, and so on. Mesopotamian religions are the earliest recorded in writing in their own time, and for three millennia they were rivaled in influence only by Vedic traditions, exerting strong influence in what is today Syria, Lebanon, Jordan, Israel, Palestine, and the Sinai Peninsula. Their religious ideas, rejected, "corrected," or improved upon, may be seen in the later Semitic monotheistic religions of Judaism, Christianity, and Islam as well as dualistic Gnosticism, Manichaeism, and Mandaeism.

Some of the most significant of the Mesopotamian deities were Anu, Ea, Enlil, Enki, Ishtar (Astarte), Ashur, Shamash, Shulmanu, Tammuz, Adad (Hadad), Sin (Nanna), Dagan (Dagon), Ninurta, Nisroch, Nergal, Tiamat, Bel, Ninlil, and Marduk. They may have been inspired by Vedic predecessors in connections lost back in the mists of time but were developed as an entirely independent subset of theological ideas. If the Vedic Aryans got the wheel from Mesopotamia but used it for a whole new purpose, it appears that the opposite happened with religion, with Mesopotamians borrowing a basis in religious astrology but developing it in a whole new direction. It was out of this welter of Mesopotamian divinities that the Semitic monotheistic religions of Judaism, Christianity, and Islam came forth, beginning with the Israelites, regardless of mistaken populist and new age notions about Zoroaster being the world's first monotheist. Zoroaster follows Abraham by at least a millennium and Moses by several centuries, as we shall see.

Israel, as the very first among surviving examples of monotheism, gradually evolved with the founding of Judaism and the belief in one single god, Yahweh—often unpronounced in reverential respect and frequently written using only the Hebrew consonants, יהוה or YHWH. The Hebrew language, closely related to the earlier attested Canaanite language of Phoenicians, would become the vehicle of the religious literature of the Torah (referred to by Muslims as *Taurat*) and the more complete Tanakh (referred to by many Christians as the *Old Testament*), thus eventually having global ramifications. We will see hints of its influence in the East as well, and for all these reasons it numbers it among the seven world religions, despite its smaller size today.

Scholars may observe that monotheism and its ramifications appear to have "evolved" in this culture, but religious records and the experience of many believers attest to an understanding that such developments were usually triggered by specific experiential incidents in which God's very self was "revealed" to leaders like Moses and the prophets who were chosen by God. These revelations were then shared with others by people who were similarly called to prophetic utterance, as we shall attempt to illustrate.

The point that there is no "Aryan gene" and no "Aryan super race" would not be worth making, were it not for the immature delusions of a miniscule but dangerous remnant of fanatics who can be found today in the strangest of places, growing in Europe and sometimes vociferous in the United States. The Aryans were a hybrid tribal polyglot that became concentrated in valleys west of the Ural Mountains and east of the Danube River system until they burst upon the world with great energy. They then moved in several directions, but especially into India and "Iran" (the "Aryan" nation), from whence their Magi emissaries made their way from one end of the Silk Route to the other.

I have elsewhere compared the claim of Aryan racial superiority to a naïveté of a child hearing from a parent that their new dog is a mongrel and going forth to proclaim to playmates with pride that "our dog is a pure-bred mongrel." Sometimes mongrels or hybrids do very well. Something similar obtains with respect to the Semitic peoples, who are also not a "race" but a language group with dynamic histories and impacts upon the world, derived from the vibrancy of an early mix of people at the great hinge of the world where three continents connect. Again, we are more interested in the ideas, including religious ideas, that emanated from this group than their particular genetic composition, except for purposes of tracking their migrations.

We shall return to the peripatetic Aryans and their Vedic religion shortly, but meanwhile some comment about changing perspectives on movements of Semitic peoples might be in order. The Jews in particular are of interest with their gift of monotheism to the world. They did this on their own and through Zoroaster and other influences, including later Christians and Muslims (the Muslims in possibly a derivative sense, without disputing their account of a direct relationship between Muhammad and God, correcting or amplifying previous revelations, a subject for discussion further along). The Jews migrated in several directions in search of economic and other opportunities, sometimes triggered by expulsions or persecutions. Their presence in business and other activities along the Silk Route throughout history has been documented and is increasingly attested by DNA evidence among populations from Israel to India and China, both amid people who have always claimed a Jewish identity for themselves and among others who have lost all memory of such a connection.[2]

People now usually identified as "Jews" also went up into Europe through Asia Minor and Scythia beginning with the Assyrian expulsion of the ten northern "Israelite" tribes in 722 BCE. They were followed by some others who went to Europe en route through Egypt more than a hundred years later, when separate groups from Jerusalem and Judah also went into exile in Babylon in 598 and 587 BCE. Another migration took place after the destruction of Jerusalem by the Romans in 70 CE (with a further dispersal in 136 CE), with the difference being that there were significant Jewish populations already present to greet them in the cities of Egypt, Turkey, Greece, Italy, the Balkan countries, and, to a lesser extent, Spain, France, and Germany, to use the current place names. Were subsequent robust concentrations of Jewish inhabitants mainly recent migrants, or were they populations related to earlier exiles in 722 BCE, 598 BCE, 587 BCE, or 70 CE? The jury is out on the question of whether these scattered and vibrant Jewish communities were based on a combination of all these Mediterranean and European accumulations of monotheistic Semites over many centuries, but that appears to be the case.

DNA research now attests to a long-standing Jewish presence in Central Asia, along the Silk Route, and into both China and India. Such pockets of genetically specific Semitic Jews are often now identified as the "lost tribes of Israel" of the seventh century BCE by gravesites in places like Merv and by documents and historical artifacts in many places. Similar research proves beyond doubt that Spain continued to harbor a large Semitic presence, both Jewish and Arabic, despite the determination of Ferdinand and Isabella to expel all such populations in 1492. Similar studies are ongoing to identify Jewish presence in both Africa (from Ethiopia to Zimbabwe among tribes who have traditionally claimed a Jewish identity) and parts of Europe where such collective memories have been suppressed or even ridiculed, as in the case of "British Israel."

The point of this digression is to illustrate that the extent of movement by Semitic peoples may be almost as extensive as that of the Indo-European Aryan migrations and that the intersection of the two cultures and their religious interchange was formative in world culture. Periodic tragic experiences of interface between them, as in Germany in the twentieth century, are as much a support to this thesis as detraction from it. Obviously more was going on than meets the eye, and folk traditions are increasingly regarded as having the potential for historical veracity if corroborated by other evidence such as DNA and archaeological investigations.

The point in reference to this study is that just as genes mix and migrate, so do ideas and beliefs. All people make their contributions to warlike and peaceful mentalities, sporting competition and culture, musical composition and performance, scientific discovery and technology, and, of course, religion, in various measures and at various times. We return then to the thesis behind this trilogy—that Vedic religion forms a backdrop behind much of what endures to our time in both Western and Eastern religions. This may be especially true of a particular Vedic tradition that crossed paths with a certain Semitic tradition in a dynamic interface which has had ramifications through the ages.

Research a hundred years ago demonstrated that well before their migrations in the 2500 to 1500 BCE millennium, the Aryans worshipped *Dyaus Pitr*, the "Divine Father," who created the universe.[3] Known as *Gitchi Manitou* on the Great Central Plains of North America, and called *Shang Di* in the "Border Sacrifice" of ancient China, *Altjira* in the Australian Outback, *Nyambe* in the west tropics of Africa, and *Brahman* in earliest India, this religious instinct was shared by aboriginal peoples around the world. Before 1500 BCE, the remoteness of God resulted in a growing Vedic adulation of life forces called *devas* (from which we get both "divinities" and "devils") that were nearer at hand to these spirited Aryans.

Agni (reference *ignite*), the fire spirit (or divine energy), existed in concurrence with other forces of nature that needed to be harnessed through communal worship. *Varuna*, representing the night, the waters, the underworld, and the unconscious, maintained order. *Indra*, the power of nature and divine warrior, defended the people from their foes. *Mithra*, the deva of sun and rain, would nourish and replenish the earth. *Mazda*, whose name means "wisdom," would engender the cult of Wisdom and all the Wisdom traditions that form subtexts of many religions down through the ages. It was the Lord of Wisdom, Ahura Mazda, who rose in Zoroastrianism to represent (and ultimately replace) the *Dyaus Pitr*, as being both transcendent and closer at hand and available to those seeking guidance in the midst of chaos. God was at last seen to be both transcendent and immanent (echoing discussions among believers in many religions today).

Mithra would develop from a peaceful fertility deva to become the favorite mascot-god of the Roman Legion as some of the legions of that army became Aryanized. More dramatically, and even earlier, the Aryans had adopted bronze weapons from the Armenians and learned to hitch their wild horses to wagons acquired from Kazakh neighbors, leading to their invention of the war chariot. In their sweep into India, Indra was transformed from a defensive patron to a spirit of the scourge: "Heroes with noble horses ready for war, and chosen warriors, call upon me! I am Indra, Lord of plunder. I excite the conflict. I stir up the dust. I am the Lord of unsurpassed vigor."[4] Chaos had come with a new stirring of the spirit of adventure and even conflict in the era of migration.

The movement of these peoples into Persia appears less violent than the move into India, where they met greater resistance. The migration to Persia appears to have attracted gentler elements of the Aryan culture, including many who sought to simply maintain the old pastoral ways. However, some in their midst were stirred with the spirit of plunder and adventure, even to preying on their fellow Aryans in the name of strife that brought victory and reward to the strong, certainly in India but also in Persia. "Dog eat dog" and "every man for himself" are slogans that might have been appropriate for the times, and the price was high for women and children, farmers settling into production, the elderly, and anyone with cattle that could be rustled. What kind of gods were these devas now? This question would have been uppermost in the mind of the young Zoroaster as reflected in his prayers, even with archaic cultural content and vocabulary.

The account of the revelation Zoroaster received at the river may appear to be identical to the biblical story of Daniel at the River Ulai,[5] which is also located in Persia, but the young prophet Zoroaster, in the first instance, was a hundred years earlier. No one need doubt the meaning or the significance of the reported appearance of the archangel Gabriel to Daniel just because that epiphany is identical in format to the earlier appearance to Zoroaster, as recorded in the ancient but still extant Avesta Scriptures of Zoroastrianism. Apocryphal or otherwise, Daniel's epiphany is placed at the beginning of the reign of Cyrus the Great, Persia's first Zoroastrian monarch, but similar appearances by Gabriel also heralded the births of John the Baptist[6] and Jesus Christ[7] in the Gospel According to Luke.

The unexpected appearance of Gabriel to Muhammad in the Cave of Hera[8] also bears a striking resemblance to the angelic appearances to Zoroaster and to Daniel, Zechariah, and Mary. It was this same archangel who appeared time and again to Muhammad over the next twenty-three years, always unannounced and unexpected, to present the Recitations that stand now as the final chapters of Scripture in the Abrahamic family trilogy of Torah, Gospel, and Quran. This is not the forum in which to address skeptics who are unable to rationally fathom the reality or the meaning of angelic appearances. Suffice it to say that the powerful phenomenological occurrences reported in Zoroastrianism bear an uncanny resemblance to critical embryonic junctures in the three Western religions in particular, the Scriptures of which were the substance of the *Three Testaments* volume prior to this trilogy. In chaotic times a spectral appearance addressed a spiritually questing individual, and a commitment to share the ways of God in peace and service ensued. The appearance to Zoroaster and his response is merely the first of these analogous events.

The moment when Zoroaster was confronted and instructed by the archangel was not the first or the last occasion when religion changed from ritual, from philosophy, and from theology into experience, and from communal rites into personal encounter with the divine. God's call for Abraham to leave home,[9] the story of Jacob's ladder[10] (and Jacob's wrestling all night that changed him into Israel),[11] and Moses at the burning bush[12] (and again on Mount Sinai)[13] are all examples of this phenomenon. St. Paul, knocked off his horse on the road to Damascus,[14] and Muhammad, so tightly embraced by the angel Gabriel in the Hera cave that he could hardly breathe, were long into the future but further testimony to religious convictions born of experiential rather than philosophical phenomena.

Ritual, philosophy, and theology have also survived, in formal religious guise and otherwise, but what Karl Jaspers has helped us recognize as the Axial Age[15] of reform may be attributed in significant measure to that moment of revelation experienced by Zoroaster at the river. Within a hundred years after Zoroaster, to the east the Buddha was transforming Hinduism and founding his religion of Enlightenment, and further east Lao Tzu elucidated the Tao and Confucius promoted noble traditions as a way of life in reaction to it. To the west the classical age of prophecy emerged with dramatic impact in Israel, while even further west the philosophers of Greece swept away an old mythology with deeper passions of the mind, based on questions of individual responses to transcendent realities or even Reality.

If Semitic Jewish genes could spread throughout the earth in ancient, middle, and modern times, how much more easily could seminal ideas spread? Much current research about Zoroastrianism comes from the Sasanian epoch as late as the fifth, sixth, seventh, and eighth centuries CE, accessible to us but possibly not entirely typical of earlier Zoroastrian influence and dynamic supremacy. In fact, the fifth-century CE era, currently under international investigation along the Silk Route, while yielding exciting information and insights, might almost be characterized as a "dark age" period for Zoroastrianism, immediately before its near disappearance. Of infinitely greater significance would be the Zoroastrian situation and its influence a full thousand years earlier. At this point we can only examine that phenomenon through observation of its churning wake along the Silk Route and just beyond, east and west. That may be about to change; now there is more even in that wake than first meets the eye, whether stirred by Zoroaster himself, as we contend, or by the Magi, converted to his banner.

The significance of the dates 628–551 BCE for Zoroaster has been recognized partly as a result of growing acceptance of the Axial Age theory, popularized now by writers like Karen Armstrong in *The Great Transformation*. Sometimes called *The Pivotal Age* in English,[16] Jaspers originally used his "axistime" to describe a slightly broader era of a few centuries, though he was then still unable to identify a specific "pivot," or what we might call "the axis of the Axial Age." He locates Zoroaster just prior to Cyrus in Persia, as we do, but the connection of the Axial Age directly to Zoroaster depends on dates and other issues not resolved before Jaspers died in 1969.

It would now appear that Zoroaster died about a dozen years before Cyrus the Great occupied Babylon and began Persian rule over some 127 former kingdoms of various sizes. This empire of the world's first superpower comprised nearly one-fifth of the then-known world's land mass, similar to the Roman Empire at its height, the British Empire at its zenith, or the Soviet Union before its collapse. The state religion was a tolerant and inclusive Zoroastrianism, and the era under Cyrus represents the Axial Age in full bloom. The influence and the power of the Zoroastrian movement over the next thousand years is difficult to picture or imagine for many now because, even at its zenith as the state religion of the world's first superpower, it was the religion of an oriental culture outside the mainstream of Western historical reportage.

The Persian Empire may be compared in this regard to the Mongol Empire of the thirteenth and fourteenth centuries CE in failing to register significantly in Western consciousness, but even more obscure, given its greater antiquity.

In *Three Testaments: Torah, Gospel, and Quran*, it was suggested that we might now think of Zoroaster as the "axis of the Axial Age." On reflection and in subsequent discussions, it is realized that a better use of terms would be to speak of the Silk Route as the axis along which Zoroaster and Zoroastrianism provided inspiration, drawn from Vedic religion (possibly cross-fertilized with Semitic religion), which stimulated the major religious reforms of the era. These developments permeated the Silk Route from one end to the other over the hundred-year period following the life of Zoroaster.

Zoroastrianism reached great heights, though it was eventually decimated both militarily and politically by Alexander the Great and then revived for hundreds of years in a degraded form. Finally, it was practically eliminated by Islam, except for monistic elements in China and purely monotheistic elements that lived on in Iran and India. The latter survive and even flourish in small numbers there today and in pockets of the United Kingdom, Canada, Australia, and the United States, where they are usually identified as Parsees.

However, the once pervasive sway of this movement, which may have contributed key elements to the spiritual foundation of the whole world, can be glimpsed in the West in the politics and theological development of ancient Israel after the Return from the Babylonian Exile, and also in historical accounts of its near domination of Europe in the failed Persian invasions of Greece. A more objective appraisal of these events than found in Hollywood films may be found even in the biased reports in Greek history. The adulation of Cyrus in Hebrew literature presents the beginning of a brief overview of the reigns of Zoroastrian monarchs whom we know at least peripherally, like Cyrus, Xerxes, and Darius. Both the Bible and ancient writers provide additional information from their own records and from inscriptions about a line of such monarchs as who ruled the Persian Empire at the apex of the Zoroastrian era in a world just beyond the horizon of the West.

Vishtaspa, the first Zoroastrian monarch, is mainly known to us because of his relationship to Zoroaster. Not a lot is known about his rule beyond that connection, though this available information serves to introduce life in the court of a typical monarchy of minor but growing status in an era and a part of the world unfamiliar to many. Cyrus the Great (Cyrus II, or simply Cyrus), however, is well known both to historians and to readers of the Hebrew Scriptures. In 559 BCE, almost a decade before Zoroaster died, Cyrus succeeded to the throne of Anshan, a vassal kingdom of Media (in what is now northern Iran) then ruled by his grandfather, Cyrus I, another early Zoroastrian monarch, and an ally of Vishtaspa. Within two decades Cyrus had subdued Media itself, conquered Asia Minor, and marched into northern India. After consolidation, in 539 BCE his forces fought their way into the city of Babylon, then the vast urban center of the ancient world.

The supreme potentate of Babylonia, King Belshazzar, was killed, and Cyrus assumed rule of the entire Babylonian Empire. This was just as prophesied by Daniel, as the apocryphal account appears in the Hebrew Scriptures, when Belshazzar and his court were feasting out of the sacred vessels stolen from the temple in Jerusalem. This travesty resulted in their guilty vision of *Mene, Mene, Tekel, Parsin*, the "writing on the wall," interpreted for them by Daniel in terms of God's judgment. Babylon's time was up: it was "found wanting, divided, and ready to be conquered."[17] In assuming and extending his control, Cyrus ruled the largest and most powerful empire the world would see until that of Alexander the Great and the later Roman Empire.

The success of Cyrus was built on combining military strategy with enlightened diplomacy based on Zoroastrian spirituality. For example, the Kingdom of Lydia had been difficult to conquer on the way to hegemony, but upon finally defeating the wealthy King Croesus, instead of killing him, Cyrus made him prime minister. He even referred to him as one of his "Companions,"[18] an inner circle of advisors to the Zoroastrian monarch, perhaps emulated by Jesus with his disciples, and almost certainly a model for Muhammad and his "Companions." That title may have been suggested by Salman the Persian, a Zoroastrian, and briefly a Christian before his attachment to Muhammad as confidant and trusted advisor.

In all the places he conquered, in addition to displaying graciousness toward the vanquished, Cyrus allied himself with those who had been oppressed by their former rulers. A famous but not entirely unique example reflects his relationship with the elite Jewish exiles, many of whom had earned high places in the civil service of Babylon. His sponsorship of their return to Jerusalem, and his funding of the rebuilding of their temple and culture, won him the loyalty of a new province on his Egyptian flank. This buffer faced the Egyptian power that would not be integrated into the Persian Empire until the rule of Cambyses II (in power 530–522 BCE), his son and successor, named for Cambyses I, his own father.

The empire's new religion under Cyrus appears as Zoroastrianism in its pristine, complete, and uncorrupted manifestation, based on the Oneness of God. It was articulated in this context at the core of the brilliantly successful policies of Cyrus toward enemies and subjects alike. This Zoroastrianism was monotheistic, at least on the surface and as understood by the Jews on location. This Zoroastrianism was undiluted by later dualism, again suggesting chronological closeness to the originator of the faith who was dedicated to the Oneness of God, but it was also less all-encompassing than the monism of the Western Zurvanite Zoroastrians and Eastern monists who drew inspiration from Magi who increasingly shared the monistic view in secret.

In a time after Cyrus, an altered form of the religion did shift the balance toward dualism in the struggle between good and evil, light and darkness. While he recognized the necessity of the struggle with evil forces, which are real in human experience, Zoroaster himself believed fervently in the ultimate exclusivity of the prerogatives and final reign of the Lord of Wisdom, and in the goodness of the religion he was commissioned to promote. Cyrus appears to have embraced the pristine Zoroastrian religion much as it was first promulgated by its founding prophet. The Jewish exiles recognized the affinity of this religion with their own, possibly even before Cyrus formally ascended the throne of Babylon.

We will return to the reign of Cyrus time and again, especially in his relationship with the Jews, as the main illustration of the Zoroastrian phenomenon that appears to have triggered a "reformation" among all religious and philosophical traditions connected by the Silk Route. We will not be suggesting that adherents of the new Taoist religion appearing in China, or the old traditions of Confucianism, were actually Zoroastrian. Nor were the new Buddhism or the reformed Hinduism of India Zoroastrian per se—in the same way that the Jews did not become Zoroastrian in spite of profound influence from that quarter. We merely point to simultaneous religious upheavals or stimuli in all these cases at the same time, within a hundred years of Zoroaster and his influence across the length of the "Silk Route," as it came to be called much later. Developments under the successors of Cyrus are documented by memorial inscriptions. Many other contemporaneous developments were independent of Persian control, farther east and farther west, as testimonials to the power of sweeping ideas.

After Cyrus, the reign of Cambyses was a brief eight years, but it brought Egypt into the Persian Empire. Darius then tried to do the same with Greece and Europe but was turned back by the Greeks at the battle of Marathon. Despite the Persian employment of forces numbering in excess of a million men, including soldiers, sailors, and support personnel, Xerxes was the next to fail at the same project. Just a decade after the Persian defeat led by Athens at Marathon, Xerxes prevailed briefly against Greek land forces, including the Spartan 300 at Thermopylae. This incident caused the superior Athenian navy to withdraw from the Straits of Artemisium until a combined Greek naval force won a decisive sea battle at Salamis, followed by a decisive Greek land victory at Plataea. These battles have been depicted by Hollywood in movies that got almost every detail wrong except for the realization that much of world history was thus determined. The list of monarchs passes on to Artaxerxes, who extended the sponsorship of the Jewish Return to Jerusalem by refunding Nehemiah and Ezra, before he was succeeded by Xerxes II, Darius II, and Artaxerxes II (Ahasuerus in the story of Esther).

Finally, Artaxerxes III and Darius III extended the drift toward dualistic theology, and when Xerxes III was about to mount the peacock throne, Alexander the Great crossed the Hellespont in 334 BCE. This European avenger subdued the whole Persian Empire in just two years, finally sacking Persepolis in 330 BCE with a fiery holocaust of Scriptures and other writings at that city's great library. During this attempt at "civilizing" Asia, the Greeks apparently imagined that nobody would think to hide a personal copy of the precious Avesta Scriptures. We hope they did, on purpose or by accident, and if so, they will be found, probably soon now, given dramatic advances in archaeological search techniques in the twenty-first century.

The Achaemenid Empire founded by Cyrus was succeeded by Alexander in 334 BCE until his death in 323 BCE, when his empire was divided among his four successors. In Persia proper, this meant the Seleucid kings, a Macedonian dynasty that ruled until 83 BCE, a period in which Zoroastrianism survived but languished. Classical Zoroastrianism did better under Parthian rule, roughly 83 BCE until 224 CE, but in that year a Persian officer led a coup against the Parthians and established the Sasanian dynasty, a restoration of Persian control over most of its ancient empire. The state religion was fully reinstated, but while monotheism appears to have survived in Zoroaster's old Bactrian stronghold, in the villages of Fars province and among traders on the Silk Route, the creeping dualism of later Achaemenid monarchs had become entrenched during the Seleucid years. It now fostered a rivalry of near equals between Ahura Mazda and the Adversary (*Ahriman*, later Satan) in a neo-Zoroastrianism, and in the cognate Manichean and Mithra religions that developed in part out of Zoroastrianism and grew under its influence.

Even though the original Avesta poems by Zoroaster were cherished, this dualistic perversion of the pristine faith in the Oneness of God flourished under the Sasanian dynasty, which came next until its collapse in 651 in the face of the Islamic advance. During the Sasanian era, new Scriptures were added to the remnants of the earlier Avesta corpus. The Islamic invaders eventually disenfranchised this version of Zoroastrianism, again burned all the Scriptures that could be found, and enforced a strict monotheism, all the while recognizing Zoroastrians as potentially "People of the Book," were it not for this perversion. Were some copies of the second compilation of the Avesta Scriptures, including more nasks, also buried somewhere once more? Again, time will tell, and it is becoming increasingly difficult to imagine that such a time is not imminent.

Let us return briefly to Cyrus, and back before him, in general summary prior to more detailed investigation of salient elements of the story. The pristine Zoroastrianism appearing in edicts, inscriptions, and documents from the reign of Cyrus, and their similarity to prophetic pronouncements of Zoroaster in his Gathas, is one more aid in dating Zoroaster's life and ministry. That convergence of justice elements and the Oneness of God are among the most persuasive arguments for a new understanding of the Zoroastrian contribution to world culture that is emerging again in our time. A reasonably complete picture may become achievable as we add the Quranic confirmations of true Zoroastrian revelations, new perspectives that Jewish sources can teach us, and unique Christian Gospel material from Zoroastrianism in the time of Jesus, all referenced in *Three Testaments*, plus material from sources in the related religious traditions much further East, featured in the *Four Testaments* text.

The Zoroastrian revelation that stimulated religions throughout the ancient Silk Route may have been triggered by an encounter with a more western Semitic religion, but it originated in the more easterly Vedic vortex. Religious developments in the Semitic "holy land" are sometimes attributed to its position at the hinge of three continents, but Vedic religious fervor erupted in a similar crucible in the Russian steppes, east of Ukraine in modern Kazakhstan. There a confluence of developments shaped a society, migrating from northwestern Russia to a previously barren plain, which blossomed when they adopted innovations from European societies to their west in a hybrid culture. This burgeoning population became mobile due to invention of the wheel, brought from the Mesopotamian south and adapted to the wagon from the Kazakh east, eventually producing the war chariot that extended their power.

None of these advances were invented on the steppes, but the cross-fertilization was dynamic. The same thing happened to their Proto-Indo-European (PIE) language in tension with Hittite and other influences, a process that was paralleled in Rig Veda religious terms as the hybrid society began to desert this marginal land and migrate in several directions. As the invention of the automobile shaped modern society in a manner similar to the influence of the wheel of old, the advent of computers and the internet might resemble the impact of PIE linguistic development throughout much of the ancient world. Religious turmoil was the next stage for the ancients, followed by "worldwide" spiritual creativity along the Silk Route, emanating from this dynamic

Painted clay and alabaster head of a Zoroastrian priest wearing a distinctive Bactrian-style headdress found in the Greco-Bactrian kingdom of Tajikistan in third to second century BCE.
SEBASTIAN TER BURG, CREATIVE COMMONS CC0.

culture that could not be supported by the marginal land in which it developed. Under their influence, the Silk Route became the internet of the original Axial Age, "and the rest is history," coming to light again.

notes

1. According to the Quran and Muslim tradition as described in *Noah's Other Son* by Brian Arthur Brown.

2. Irwin M. Berg, "Among the Jewish Descendants of Kaifeng," *Judaism: A Quarterly Journal of Jewish Life and Thought* (Winter 2000). Hosted at Kenyon College.

3. William Schmidt, *The Origin of the Idea of God* (New York: University Press of America, 1912).

4. As quoted by Karen Armstrong, *The Great Transformation*, 8.

5. Daniel 8:16.

6. Luke 1:19.

7. Luke 1:26.

8. Quran 96:1–3.

9. Genesis 12:1.

10. Genesis 28:12.

11. Genesis 32:24–28.

12. Exodus 3:2.

13. Exodus 19.

14. Acts 9.

15. *Achsenseit* or "axistime" in Karl Jaspers, *Vom Ursprung und Ziel der Geschichte* (The Origin and Goal of History).

16. Jaspers's use of the German word *Achse* is translated equally as *axis* or *pivot*.

17. Daniel 5.

18. William Barclay, *The Revelation of John, Vol. 1*, 122.

4
commissioned at the river

A Priest Becomes a Prophet

To AMPLIFY WHAT WE ONCE KNEW ABOUT ZOROASTER, THE TIMES WERE TOUGH AND THE PEOPLE of his religious community were oppressed. According to the Avesta, the young priest went down to the river to prepare a water sacrifice and to meditate on his need, and that of his people, and to hear a word from God. As he waded out of the river, quite unexpectedly an angel appeared in the shining form of a man who both confronted him and instructed him.[1]

The pensive young priest had waded into the river almost distracted from his improvisational incantations by the social disintegration all around him. As he emerged, a vision came to him in which he was personally addressed by a specter he could only identify as one of the Immortals, beings then identified with or symbolized by the seven major celestial bodies visible to the naked eye in the universe. This story is important enough that it is repeated three times in extant remnants of the Avesta Scriptures.[2]

After establishing rapport, the shining figure led him in the spirit into an audience with the Lord of Wisdom, *Ahura Mazda*, who was also the deva of justice, and who was attended by six other Immortals. Ahura Mazda was both immanent and entirely lucid in authorizing Zoroaster to energize his people to oppose mayhem and to confront the cold, dark evil they were experiencing. Zoroaster had gone into the water as a priest and come out to become a prophet.

Zoroaster learned in this revelation that even divinities had to choose between order and disorder in support of either harmony or chaos. The human race was being enlisted to join the forces of nature in a new era that would lead to eventual victory of light over darkness, warmth over frigidity, and goodness over evil.

Zoroaster had experienced the immanence of the Lord of Wisdom; the glory of the moment triggered his immediate realization that this Ahura Mazda was also transcendent and should be identified as the Creator of the Universe. The Divinity was uncreated, and all the forces of nature must become subservient to God alone. Ahura Mazda is not alone in the universe, but he alone is God. It was also revealed or became clear that the Lord had an evil counterpart whose status as a spirit appeared great, though his purpose was less lofty and destined to fail as humans joined the struggle on the side of goodness. Zoroaster was instructed to put the invitation clearly to his people. Some suggest this was not technically monotheism at first, since the Immortals participated in divinity, but they were soon correctly understood as angels in the service of the only One worthy of worship. Ahriman, Angra Mainyu, or Satan, as he became known, was a deceiver and an illusion, eventually referred to as a "fallen angel," though a troublesome sidetrack to humanity on frequent occasion and in definable eras of Zoroastrianism dualism.

Spiritually precocious, even as a child, Zoroaster had trained to be a priest from the age of seven and was recognized early for his ability to improvise incantations during sacrificial ceremonies.[3] Hebrew monotheism had been in the air throughout neighboring nations since the time of Moses, and the prophetic ministry of Jeremiah may have included visits to the Israelites who had been exiled by Assyria a hundred years earlier, between 730 and 710 BCE. The Bible has many Israelites then living in places like Hala,[4] Harbor,[5] and Hara,[6] cities eventually absorbed into the Median Empire, all mentioned in Zoroaster's own story in the Avesta and also mentioned in the Bible as communities to which Israelites were exiled by the Assyrians.

The coincidence of place names in the Avesta and the Bible may not have been noticed heretofore, but we present it as part of the welter of circumstantial evidence of a relationship between Zoroaster and the Israelites. Even before the matter of Zoroaster's dates was adequately addressed, twentieth-century historian Arnold J. Toynbee put this matter thus: "The date of Zarathustra is a matter of dispute and we cannot say for certain whether his religious discovery was independent . . . or whether his voice was a mere echo of the cry of forgotten Israelite prophets who had been marooned in the cities of the Medes."[7]

The scriptural indications of a possible direct connection with Jeremiah are slender, but Israel's lamenting prophet did have something of a fixation with the exiles, wherever they were, visiting many such communities, as attested by several references in the Bible. Jeremiah even prophesied that if the northern and southern kingdoms of Israel and Judah reunited, they would be rejoined by the exiles from "the north,"[8] almost certainly a reference to deportees in places like Scythia. He also demonstrated direct knowledge of the Scythians themselves when he described the "rising waters of the north," their ability and their possible interest in flooding the enemies of Israel with galloping steeds and rumbling chariots.[9]

By Jeremiah's time, many Israelite exiles may have intermarried with the Scythians in northern Syria, Media, and elsewhere, so Zoroaster may have even had Semitic Hebrew relatives. Given the meshing of their dates, as we now understand the overlap, it is entirely possible that as a teenager, Zoroaster could have heard Jeremiah, his elder contemporary, preaching to the Israelites, "Hear, O Israel, the Lord our God is One," and issuing a plea for the exiles to keep the faith. The appeal of the Oneness of God might have had significance to a young Zoroaster at a time when religious and political turmoil was affecting his community. Would a youthful student of Vedic religion have heard this as a message that "there is One God," or was it a message that "God is One"? This fine distinction might be something with which his followers and others he influenced would struggle, whether or not he was yet aware of the difference.

The possibility of a direct connection between Zoroaster and Jeremiah is not contended here with any degree of certainty, but it is offered as an example of ancient transcultural interchanges. Given a number of hints in the Talmud and early Arab Christian references, the Jeremiah connection to Scythians and the exile communities in Zoroaster's homeland may be a promising area of future study in support of this thesis. However, if Zoroaster's initiation into awareness of the Oneness of God was not through a connection with Jeremiah, it could well have been through one of the other prophets, commercial or other visitors to the Israelite community in exile, or simply the Israelite exiles themselves, some of whom no doubt remained devout, as many did elsewhere.

We do not yet have physical proof of an intersection between Semitic and Vedic traditions at this juncture, but it is clear that the Jews got an expanded theology of "creation and apocalypse, angels and demons, salvation and damnation, resurrection and final judgment, heaven and hell" from Zoroastrians just a few years later in Babylon. Before that the Zoroastrians themselves had been introduced to monotheism or the Oneness of God, almost certainly by the Israelites, and this happened somewhere other than either Babylon or Israel. Our conjecture is merely a plausible example of the exchange of ideas that certainly happened among ancient peoples, and the conjunction of dates and geography facilitating such intercourse in this case is too great to discount out of hand.

We have already recognized that Judaism was influenced, some might say "transformed," by God under Zoroastrian stimulus in Babylon, and that Zoroastrianism had this indirect and possibly other direct influence in Christianity and Islam. What is less well recognized, even in academia, is the seeming likelihood that Zoroastrianism was profoundly influenced during its Vedic incubation by the Semitic Israelites in exile, with whom Zoroaster himself may have crossed paths. From the Israelites this particular Vedic tradition would have received the vision of the Oneness of God (monotheistic or monistic), the understanding of personal responsibility to God (the commandments or dharma), and the hope for a Redeemer (an avatar, messiah, or saoshyant), all of which appeared in other Eastern religions also within a generation after Zoroaster. That last exchange could have gone either way. The messianic prophecies of the first Isaiah preceded our putative dates for Zoroaster, though the Redeemer thrust in the writings of Deutero-Isaiah (the second to use the Isaiah name, all in the same scroll) is patently Zoroastrian, and it is entirely possible that the second Isaiatic writer edited the first to insert the messianic prophecies into the writing of his respected predecessor.

Either way, the Jews got messianic theology from the Zoroastrians, or Zoroaster got it from the Israelite exiles or some such Hebrew source. The Islamic vision of the masih is closer to the Jewish version, compared to the messiah passed on to Christians in a more Zoroastrian mode (Savior of the world rather than a restorer of the monarchy in Israel). Mary Boyce noted the dichotomy: "It was out of a Judaism enriched by five centuries of contact with Zoroastrianism that Christianity arose in the Parthian period, a new religion with roots in two ancient faiths, one Semitic, the other Persian."[10]

We do know that following the "revelation at the river" Zoroaster commenced his mission at the age of thirty, launched by two events emulated exactly by Jesus, long into the future. In both cases, the river rite or "baptism" at the age of thirty was followed by the challenge of a satanic adversary, "tempting" them to renounce their faith. However, through the first several years of his ministry, Zoroaster gained only one reliable disciple: his cousin, Miadhyoimah. He also earned the enmity of the religious establishments and was forced to migrate from the western end of the Silk Route, where he was born, to the eastern end, where he flourished. His opportunity came at Balkh, in the minor kingdom of Bactria, just west of China, north of India, and at the far eastern tip of what would become the Persian Empire, in an event regarded as a godsend by his later followers. After a lengthy and successful prophetic ministry centered there, he would be buried nearby in a site to be called *The Tomb of the Exalted*, currently designated as that of a Muslim saint buried there later, as will become apparent.[11]

Zoroaster was given a chance to discuss his mission with the priests of the royal court at Balkh, the capital of the Kingdom of Bactria, an area covering today's northern Afghanistan and parts of contiguous Islamic republics. After three days they dismissed him and had him jailed for challenging Vedic orthodoxy. But he had caught the eye of young King Vishtaspa, nearly twenty years his junior, who must have seen the divine spark in the prophet-priest, now forty years old. When Vishtaspa's favorite horse became paralyzed and unable to rise, the established priests could do nothing, so the king took the opportunity to send for Zoroaster, who prayed over the beast and somehow raised it to renewed vigor, to the delight of the king, the queen, and the whole royal household. They converted to the cause of peace and justice for possibly both spiritual and political reasons, as the young king cleaned house and asserted his rule. Zoroaster flourished, his influence growing rapidly throughout the region coincident with the expansion of Vishtaspa's realm, which the king's descendants would expand even further and parlay into the Persian Empire, adopting the prophet's "mazdianism" as the state religion.

Zoroaster's utterances were poetic and couched in the evocative dialect of his proto-Vedic forebears, a language regarded as sacred due to its connection to the Rig Veda. That was an almost primordial and rudimentary articulation of the evolving Vedic tradition that had taken root in India and would eventually be reformed there under Buddhist influence and reflected in the Bhagavad Gita, all in the wake of Zoroaster's stimulus. Within a few years the corpus of Zoroaster's poetic utterances was so precious in his expanding circle that King Vishtaspa put his literate prime minister in charge of the texts. Jamaspa undertook this responsibility with such devotion that, according to the tradition, he produced two archetypical scrolls with gold lettering on ox-hide sheets.

This new devotion to sacred texts per se was emulated by Jews not long after, by elaborate Christian monogrammed texts in due course, and by Islamic adulation of sacred words in the final iteration of "The Book." Testimony to the plethora of copies and translations of these Avesta Scriptures in the ancient world has been referenced earlier and will be elaborated upon again later, but it needs to be kept in mind here too. Even among ancient Jews and in the early church there was never such prodigious production of copies of a treasured text. Are we to believe that not even a single complete copy has survived somewhere?

Zoroaster trained three orders of disciple-missionaries who fanned out across the ancient world and organized the community of faith in Ahura Mazda, the Lord of Wisdom. The horse itself became an enduring symbol of the Zoroastrian religion, and, as trends sometimes do, Zoroaster's spiritual influence galloped all over the world of the first superpower and beyond. Zoroaster had relocated from near the gates of Greece at the western end of the Silk Route to his new headquarters near the gates of China and India at the eastern end of the Silk Route. His followers became ensconced at its center but moved throughout the twenty-eight provinces of the empire, and east and west, especially after the Magi converted en masse under Cyrus and presented Zoroastrianism to the world in both Eastern monistic garb and Western monotheistic attire.

It is not a stretch to realize how Zoroaster, or his message, could extend its reach from one end to the other of the route through a portion of the globe little different in size and shape from the single nation of Chile (in east-west "landscape" rather than north-south "portrait" orientation). Even the landscape of the terrain is similar, passable by indigenous peoples in earliest times and in every age since, with varying levels of activity depending on historical circumstances. Are we to continue to believe that ideas could not traverse such a space, even though often erroneously described as impossibly remote and inaccessible? Such a concept is now understood to relate more to limitations of the dark ages of Western history than to the situation in the time and location of Zoroaster. Recent and indisputable evidence of the presence of Iranian Magi in China before and during Zoroaster's lifetime is elaborated in detail in volume 2 of this trilogy as the pièce de resistance of this new realization.

Zoroaster married, possibly more than once, and established his personal home and religious headquarters in the town of Balkh, the capital of Bactria, some fifteen kilometers to the northwest of the city of Mazar-i-Sharif in today's Afghanistan. That is a city that grew up around a mausoleum called *The Tomb of the Exalted* (a translation of the words *Mazar-i-Sharif*) sometime in the mid-sixth century BCE, following the entombment of the most important figure of the age and time. Zoroaster's three sons took the lead in reorganizing society into three classes: priest-authorities, warrior-police, and landed gentry (later four to include worker-servants), according somewhat with the principal castes organized in India by related Aryan migrants some generations earlier. That reformed social system was now to be employed in bringing order to the spiritual struggle between good and evil.

The challenges were enormous. The mighty prince of darkness, introduced as Ahriman, then Angra Mainyu (later known as Satan in various traditions and eventually Lucifer in some), had a retinue of six additional Anti-Immortals, now including Indra and other forces who served the cause of evil in the world. Following the revelation to Zoroaster at the river, the cosmic battle was to be joined by those prepared to struggle on earth. Zoroaster understood that in the battle between the devas representing good and evil, the Lord of Wisdom was destined for the final victory and that mortals who joined His cause should acknowledge Him as the only One true God. This rapid blossoming of monotheism, and perhaps a nascent expression of monism or the Oneness of God, is reflected in the extant Avestas. It is preserved by the modern Zoroastrian communities of Parsees and others, though the seeds of an eventual flowering of dualism in much of the Iranian community were also there from the very beginning, a dangerous enshrining of evil.

All of this and the subsequent Avestan Scriptures are presented in dramatic apocalyptic language, the first appearance of this form of expression in the world. We meet this style again in Daniel and a few other places in the Hebrew Scriptures. The apocalyptic style appears in the Gospels and dominates the Book of Revelation, concluding the Christian Scriptures. Its use is predominant again through almost the whole of the Quran—more circumstantial evidence of the foundational role of Zoroastrianism in these three religions. The place of both creationism and apocalypticism is perhaps less dominant in the Eastern traditions but prominent there too, as will be discovered in part two, a significant link between East and West documented here for the first time.

Zoroaster lived long and saw the impact of his mission spread throughout all areas of Persian influence and well beyond, the harbinger of what many scholars now call the "Axial Age" of religion and philosophy. Peasants and royal families alike flocked to his banner. Until recently, it was believed that he died a mysterious and violent death at the hands of assassins in the fire-temple at Balkh at seventy-seven years of age. Judging by the later dialect used, suspicions have arisen that this story was a fabrication placed in the record by detractors some centuries later. He probably died at a great age, having seen his revelations reshape Vedic religion. His religious reforms soon redefined society in the Persian Empire and influenced all religions throughout the ancient world.

The original name "Zarathustra" was Persian, but the Greeks called him *Zorastres*, the Romans called him *Zoroastres*, and the anglicized *Zoroaster* has now become almost universal for a prophet who is himself almost mythical in popular culture and remains largely unknown in academic circles. An exception is the German title from Friedrich Nietzsche's book, *Also Sprach Zarathustra*, and the music by Richard Strauss that used that title. Indeed, the *Also Sprach Zarathustra* music was popularized by Stanley Kubrick's movie *2001: A Space Odyssey*, and it was used as the opening number for almost all concerts by Elvis Presley, but the character for which it was named remained off the radar screen for most people, with rare exceptions.

Even in an era before scholarship had revealed as much as we now know, Zoroaster appears as "Sarastro" in Mozart's opera *The Magic Flute*, noted for its Masonic elements, where he represents moral order in opposition to the "Queen of the Night." He is also the subject of the 1749 opera *Zoroastre* by Jean-Philippe Rameau, set in the

Mercury Dime. Through the last millennium, Zoroastrianism barely survived, behind the scenes and just beneath the surface of world culture. The barsom, a bundle of twigs as pictured above right, represents the tree of life. Zoroastrians still use it as it appeared first in ancient ceremonies, including state functions of the Persian Empire. It is pictured here as the Roman ceremonial fasces (bundle) in its (Zoroastrian) Mithraic derivation on the US dime of the 1940s. On the obverse, we see Mercury, the Roman messenger and god of financial gain, wearing a Phrygian (or Mithraic) cap, popularized by the Roman Legion that adopted Mithra as their mascot and brought his cap from Zoroastrian regions of Anatolia (Turkey) to Europe.
UNITED STATES, MERCURY DIME, 1944, US MINT, PHILADELPHIA.

ancient kingdom of Bactria, where the forces of good, led by Zoroastre, the "founder of the Magi," struggle against the forces of evil. During the Enlightenment, Voltaire and other encyclopaedists promoted research into Zoroastrianism, considering it a rational Deism more acceptable than Christianity. In essence, Zoroaster was a reformer of the older Vedic religion that provided the raw materials for all emerging religions at the Middle Eastern hinge of continents, the area where both monism and monotheism took root.

Despite the beginnings of academic interest, even through the twentieth century, Zoroastrianism remained just beyond the horizon of mainstream Western history and consciousness, largely because his movement was so successfully quashed by Alexander, by the followers of Muhammad, and finally further east in the collapse of the Zoroastrian Yan Dynasty in China—a part of world history hardly known in the West but covered well in our appendices F, G, and H.

Zoroaster's birthplace appears to have been the city of Urmiah, now known as Rizaijeh, in the Shiz district of present-day Azerbaijan. Arabic and Persian scholars mark his birth date as 628 BCE[12] by noting that the sacking of the Persian capital of Persepolis by Alexander the Great in 330 BCE took place 258 years after the "appearance" or epiphany of Zoroaster. This is possibly a reference to his birth, but it is traditionally regarded as referring to the establishment of the Zoroastrian religion in Bactria under King Vishtaspa. Avesta records show that Zoroaster was some forty years old at that time.[13]

As referenced in our earlier Exordium, an alternate ancient tradition reported by Xanthus of Lydia about 450 BCE, and adopted by Greek and Roman historians, places the birth of Zoroaster some six thousand years before Xerxes. This pushes Zoroaster's dates back to about 6500 BCE, a popular mythology that survived until very recently, though it makes Zoroaster appear approximately twelve times as ancient as in the Persian record.[14] This is the basis of the mythical image of Zoroaster adopted in New Age circles, rather than the historical reality. While readers often abjure books with too many dates, a more accurate dating of Zoroaster's impact on the world is key to the argument in this story, so some heavy plodding is now necessary in this regard.

Whenever we see what appear to be fantastic or impossible dates and ages in the ancient world, the first question we must ask is whether these numbers are divisible by 12. Most primitive societies measured time by cycles of the moon, rather than the solar calculations employed in the Common Era. This was the practice of early Hebrew, contiguous, and related societies, and "how many moons" is what counted into the modern era among aboriginal societies in some parts of the world. In the Bible, Methuselah[15] may have lived to a very old age for his time, but it is obvious that his age represents 969 cycles of the moon, or, if divided by 12, some eighty cycles of the sun. We would call these eighty "years" in the solar method of time measurement, which was adopted shortly before the Common Era. By this computation, Noah lived 950 moons,[16] or seventy-nine years. He was "six hundred" when the flood came, or fifty years old by our calculations. After the adoption of solar time measurement, we are given to understand that Jesus lived approximately thirty years and Muhammad some sixty-three years, both ages described in the system employed in the current era, and most frequently used now for Lao Tzu, Confucius, the Buddha, and the dating of the Bhagavad Gita, all germane to this study.

The confusion concerning Zoroaster's birth date might be illustrated by the current switch in measurement of temperature. The United States continues to use the Fahrenheit scale, while the rest of the world has switched from various systems to Celsius. A thousand years from now, perhaps the whole world, including America, will have been using Celsius for centuries. At that point a study of our times would reveal that while temperatures peaked at 30 or 40 degrees everywhere else in the twenty-first century, a hot day in America was represented by 100 degrees or more, misunderstood as surely the hottest place on earth with almost unbelievable heat.[17]

So when Xanthus reports that Zoroaster was born six thousand "cycles" before Persian king Xerxes invaded Asia Minor and Greece in 480 BCE, we should presume that he meant six thousand cycles of the moon. But the Roman historian Diogenes Laertius, among others, took this to be six thousand cycles of the sun, since they lived in the solar era, placing the birth of Zoroaster at a seemingly impossibly remote date in relation to the Aryan activities that preceded him and the religious developments in Persia and elsewhere that succeeded him. When Xanthus recorded that period as six thousand cycles, he really meant five hundred of our solar years before 480 BCE, or the year 980 BCE according to our calculations, a recurrence of the biblical examples as given.

This is not precisely the same as the Persian record accepted in this book and throughout the trilogy, but it is a difference measured in a couple of centuries, not many thousands of years. The choices for birth dates of Zoroaster are three. First, we should accept 6500 BCE if we believe that Xanthus and documents like the Bible really measured time in solar years rather than moons. Second, we would accept a date of somewhere roughly around 1000 BCE if we adjust this rounded-up Greek and Roman account from moons to solar years. Third, the date of Zoroaster's birth would be 628 BCE if we accept the Arabic and Persian records, commonly held throughout the centuries in regions of the East, similar to certain European and American estimates in the twentieth century and some experts in the twenty-first century.

In this study, and with the support of recent European conclusions, we employ the later Arabic and Persian date of 628 BCE, partly because it fits with our thesis regarding Persian Zoroastrianism as the direct immediate predecessor of scriptural Judaism. The slightly earlier revised Greek and Roman date of 930 or about 1000 BCE would not be a major problem, since it too follows Moses by some centuries. It is preferred by some scholars of Zoroastrianism, who base their calculations on linguistic analysis of the Gathas, but it does not fit quite as well when we begin to compute backward from the Jewish experience in Babylon, a technique to be elaborated upon later.

Impressive corroboration of our position is also bolstered by information now known about the birth of Darius I, in 551 BCE, the factor that tipped the balance for several scholars in the recent debate in Europe and America. This son of the first royal convert, the now elderly King Vishtaspa, grew up to succeed to the Persian throne in 522, the third king, eight years after the death of Cyrus. Darius would have known Zoroaster as the revered priest and prophet in his father's court. Cyrus too would have known Zoroaster as a child, slightly earlier. Debate, controversy, and final resolution of this important matter will be presented in a subsequent part of this trilogy.

Certain scholars may continue to give weight to other factors, but leading writers on the topic, from experts like Amir Hussain[18] and Susan Whitfield[19] through Sol Nigosian[20] to Karen Armstrong,[21] have increasingly tended toward more recent dates as evidence mounts. The substantiation of a birth date of around 628 BCE is convincing and important in our thesis that Zoroaster's revelation at the river occurred around 600 BCE in a region populated in part by Israelite exiles who were at least nominally monotheistic. If that is conceded, permitted, or imagined, a great many other things fall into place with respect to both Eastern and Western religious developments.

Zoroaster's prophetic ministry exploded some ten years later and dramatically impacted the whole of the ancient Middle East and beyond for the next fifty years. A generation later, Cyrus, the rising Zoroastrian conqueror, marched into Babylon in 539 to establish the Zoroastrian faith at the heart of the first realm in history to be appropriately described as a superpower. The significance of Cyrus establishing Zoroastrianism as the *de facto* "state religion" in the Persian Empire just twenty years after the death of Zoroaster (or a century after his birth) has yet to be entirely digested in either academic circles or popular imagination. Along with Zoroaster's impact both further west and further east, the interchange between Vedic-Zoroastrian and

Semitic-Jewish influences in Babylon is important as an example of what may well have happened elsewhere, though this is not yet as well documented.

As indicated, the late dates for Zoroaster's birth (either 930 or 628 BCE) place the revelation that was given to him well after the establishment of monotheism in Israel. Even prior to large-scale trade in goods, religious and other ideas traveled in a fluid dynamic all through the ancient East, with the Silk Route as the conduit. For example, Vashti, the great-granddaughter of Nebuchadnezzar and the first wife of Artaxerxes II, was of Indian lineage, through Nebuchadnezzar's son, Amel-Marduk,[22] who distinguished himself in the campaigns of northern India and brought home a wife. The Vashti connection is a given among Indians, where this ancient name remains common, and the scholarly linkage is now typical of research in which northern India is accepted as being in the further reaches of the empire of Artaxerxes II in the time of the Buddha.

Only recently have Westerners noted the presence of a certain Krishna in the book of Esther among those the king consulted before banishing Vashti, the Hebrew letters of his name being "KRiShNA" or Kṛṣṇa.[23] This is patently obvious in transliteration, though the name has been traditionally but inexplicably rendered as "Carshena" (or Karshena) in translation into European languages. Indians who incline to take this reference as the king's invocation of a Hindu god should be content to simply recognize it as Indian influence in the court, including the fluid transmission of ideas we have been describing as typical of Zoroaster's time and the age that followed. This observation by Rasiah Sugirtharaja to a Jewish audience at England's Birmingham University in 2013 sent such shock waves of chagrin through the academic community that it may be safe to say that every Bible translation after 2013 will almost certainly include Krishna (a "postcolonial" concession).

Meanwhile, under Zoroastrian influence, the many deities of the Vedic tradition moved toward the Oneness of All, a monism inclusive of creator and creation, an Eastern development seemingly opposite to related monotheistic developments in the West, a point requiring further discussion. While Zoroastrianism may have facilitated the spread of monotheism as an increasingly dominant belief throughout the Persian Empire and toward the West, the fact that this seminal belief had flourished for hundreds of years in the Israelite community almost next door to Zoroaster's birthplace can hardly be mere coincidence.

We may regard the revelation to Zoroaster as an adult priest at the river as genuine, but monotheism, or something approaching monism, was not exactly new to him at that moment. His worldview was Vedic, but given the seventh-century BCE dating, Zoroaster's inspiration with respect to the Oneness of God was almost certainly Israelite in origin. The exceptional Zoroastrian influence on Judaism during the Persian years of Israel's exile in Babylon may now be understood as but the closing of the circle. A belief in the Oneness of God came to Zoroaster as a teenager and to the world from the Israelites, and the final draft of the Hebrew Torah was facilitated and financed by Zoroastrian monarchs in Babylon. Through the Return to Jerusalem, a belief of the Oneness of God was passed on to the world.

The acceptance of the better, more reasonable date of his birth is only one of the ways the Zoroastrian record helps resolve many conundrums of later Western Scriptures and correlates with the examination of Eastern Scriptures that together form the core material of this trilogy. Extant Avesta information testifies to Zoroaster's birth to his mother, Dughdhova, when she was fifteen years of age and reports it as a "virgin birth."[24] The custom of attributing the birth of an outstanding figure to divine initiative became relatively common in what we now call the Middle East, though Zoroaster's was the first birth so described. This image serves those today who simply relate the truth of the doctrine to a recognition that God initiates salvation rather than humans lifting themselves by their own bootstraps.

Zoroaster's lineage is then traced back through his father, Pourushaspa, forty-five generations to the first human, Gayomard,[25] again in a manner identical in ethos to the way in which the genealogy of another famous son of a virgin is traced by St. Luke back to Adam through his "father," Joseph.[26] Pointing out the similarities to later Scriptures is not meant to challenge the veracity of other accounts, but rather to point to the origins of the imagery and establish the linguistic power of images that may be historical or adopted by faith, in either case proffering profound truths that lie beneath eternal mysteries.

In the twentieth century, attempts were made to establish an academic understanding of Zoroastrianism, a religion long obliterated by the vicissitudes of history and the rivalries that both refined and decimated its heritage. Those initial attempts failed largely because of scholarly disputes on how to read the surviving material and the external references, thanks to uncertainty about Zoroaster's own dates. However, by the end of that century a consensus on many such issues emerged around the findings of Mary Boyce at the University of London's School of Oriental and African Studies, published in 1977 after a year of life "on the ground" in the Zoroastrian villages of Iran. Professor Boyce remained ambivalent about Zoroaster's precise dates, but she at least succeeded in establishing to the satisfaction of all that his "mythical" European dates of 6500 or 6000 BCE were to be replaced by dates somewhere between 1200 and 1000 BCE at a minimum.

These later dates work plausibly with the theses of this trilogy, though not as well as the traditional Persian dates placing his birth late in the seventh century BCE and his death mid-sixth century BCE, about a generation before Cyrus came to power in Babylon. This matter is of some significance, as we get to know Zoroaster by moving backward from the Jews in Babylon to a pristine Zoroastrianism matching the Gathas and necessarily only a generation or two earlier. This is also the key to making sense of the Axial Age—that it has a shared stimulus, rather than occurring through religious flare-ups that somehow happened simultaneously but independently.

A twentieth-century attempt to date Zoroaster by the Persian records got its impetus from earlier European scholarship in 1947, when Ernst Emil Herzfeld, a German (Jewish) archaeologist and Iranologist at Princeton University (having taken refuge from the Nazis), produced new evidence just a year before he died.[27] As the culmination of a lifelong investigation, Herzfeld published facts supporting the Persian view that

King Vishtaspa (German, Wistaspa / Greek, Hystaspes), who is named by Darius I as his father, was the very same king named by Zoroaster in the Gatha sections of the Avesta as his royal patron. This would coincide precisely with the time period in the traditional Persian record concerning the dates of Zoroaster himself.

Herzfeld's views found immediate support from additional convincing arguments by the German scholar W. B. Henning,[28] published in 1951. Henning specifically upheld the authenticity of the Persian view of Zoroastrian tradition as presented by Hassan Taqizadeh, an Iranian politician who was an authority on Middle Eastern calendars. The growing consensus picked up enough momentum that it produced a popular view among literary sophisticates, expressed in *Creation*, a novel by Gore Vidal. This story was narrated by the fictional grandson of Zoroaster in 445 BCE, describing encounters with agéd figures of the Axial Age during his travels, a chronology in accord with our view of these figures.[29]

In the strictly academic sphere, opponents of the traditional Persian dates continued to support the dominant European position, situating Zoroaster at around 1000 BCE. This still works in our view about an understanding of the Oneness of God coming from Israel to Zoroaster, since we find a monotheistic Moses next door at a still earlier time, but it does not fit as well regarding pristine Persian Zoroastrian influence on the Jews in Babylonian Exile. In opposition to the traditional Persian position, the supporters of the dominant European view were led by Gherardo Gnoli, professor of Iranian Philology at University of Naples "L'Orientale" from 1965 to 1993, an authority in the non-English-speaking world perhaps on a par with Mary Boyce.

Opposing scholars who were lining up to side with the old Persian position now included William W. Malandra and R. C. Zaehner, outspoken American and British scholars, respectively, but in 1977 they were all overshadowed by Mary Boyce, who published the fruits of her year spent in the Zoroastrian village of Sharifibad in Iran. Henning was the respected mentor of Mary Boyce, but she never agreed with his traditional Persian dating.

It appeared that Herzfeld, Hemming, Taqizadeh, Vidal, Malandra, Zaehner, and others had failed to carry the day in one of the more engaging scholarly debates of the twentieth century. Then, shortly before his 1996 election as president of the Italian Institute for Africa and the East, Gnoli dramatically changed his opinion on the Darius/Vishtaspa matter, accepting that Zoroaster may indeed have been an early contemporary of Cyrus, living in the sixth century BCE rather than around 1000 BCE. Malandra immediately wrote a new review of Boyce's "Textual Sources for the Study of Zoroastrianism" in the *Journal of the American Oriental Society*,[30] in which he challenged her position on the 1000 BCE era dates. Her supporter, Shapur Shabazi, replied in the *Bulletin of the School of Oriental and African Studies*, with grace, as follows:

> On the basis of a King List and several allusions in medieval sources, many scholars have insisted that an authentic Zoroastrian "tradition" placed Zoroaster in the sixth century B.C. This theory was demolished in 1977, but recently Professor Gherardo Gnoli has restated it in great detail and with seemingly sound arguments.[31]

According to Boyce, Shabazi himself was not personally convinced,[32] but the conversion of Gnoli to the Persian traditional view was the beginning of movement toward that position, and at least openness by Mary Boyce herself and other leading Iranists that has continued and is in line with our thinking. In spite of this consensus, however, there are still respected scholars of Zoroastrianism who cling to the dates between 1000 and 1300 BCE, mainly for philological reasons, since it is clear that the Gathas composed by Zoroaster himself employ a language from that earlier era. The answer to that problem is found in twentieth-century Christian hymns and prayers written in Shakespearean English, the "noble" form of the language employed nearly four hundred years earlier in the beloved King James Version of the Bible. In similar fashion, as he reinterpreted proto-Vedic scriptural traditions for his time, Zoroaster would be inspired to authenticate his words by the use of the still-revered Vedic language and cadence from that earlier era.

Mary Boyce never did commit to a change of her own published position, though she often acknowledged that her mentor, Walter Henning, favored the sixth-century dates, and she was forthcoming in suggesting to the present writer how the Persian position could be supported and maintained. It was she who suggested, perhaps as an original thought, that the philological issue of antiquated language could be resolved by reference to the above "trick" (as she called it) of Christians and others of authenticating their new works by the use of Shakespearean English as the most noble form of English, as employed by the King James translators. This time lapse would be almost exactly the length of the validating throwback employed by Zoroaster.

The argument for a relatively late date for Zoroaster's prophetic ministry is based on several factors, such as refutation of the "orientalism" that dismisses the validity of Eastern opinions, recognition of the frequent adoption of revered ancient styles as a claim of authenticity, and close affinity between the original character of Zorostrianism and the way it was known to Jews and others as practiced by Cyrus the Great. A final argument for the late dating of "Zoroaster" and "Zoroastrianism" is their genesis of apocalyptic literature, which then dramatically appeared in five of the world religions, even eventually including Confucianism by the time of its adoption by Christianity and Islam. It is possible that Zoroaster originally employed the apocalyptic style in his Gatha verses four hundred years before the others somehow all simultaneously discovered a style identical to his. Or it may be that they all received divine revelations in that level of bravura without inspiration from his example at all. But both the four-hundred-year gap and the simultaneous inspirations seem less likely than the probability that Zoroaster preceded the others by little more than a generation and their apocalyptic expressions followed in the wake of his utterances.

But like an elephant in the room, the question remains: "What happens to this entire house of cards if the dates of Zoroaster are not 628–550 BCE?" We cannot totally ignore the strength of expert arguments regarding birth dates proposed between 1000 and perhaps 1270 BCE. Such earlier dates are not as neat for our theory, which is based on the ancient Persian and Arabic sources rather than earlier European estimates. However, while the historic figure recognized as Zoroaster may indeed predate the flare-up of what we identify as Zoroastrianism, there is a cogent theory that can explain the spiritual eruption along the Silk Route that leaves the ramifications of our theory completely intact.

We cannot be certain whether Cyrus the Great was a Zoroastrian emerging from a long-simmering tradition dating back several centuries or simply a dedicated and highly visible devotee of the new religious development, as described in our narrative. What we do know is that Cyrus was indeed a Zoroastrian and that out of respect for, fear of, or love for this absolute monarch, the Magi priesthood of Vedic traditions throughout his empire and beyond converted en masse to his reformed expression of Vedic religion. Through their influence, Zoroastrianism came into the consciousness of Greeks and other Europeans, who actually bought the myth that Zoroaster was the founder or "Father of Magism." The Zoroastrian influence of the Magi touched Southern Europe, reached into Egypt and North Africa, saturated the Middle East, and extended to India and China in ways fully documented in our *Four Testaments* text.

So it could be that Zoroaster's religion simmered for some four centuries and Zoroastrianism, as we know it, emerged under Cyrus and Magian influence, becoming the "state religion" of the Persian Empire for a thousand years and a stimulative influence far and wide. It is either this or else the Persian and Arabic dates are correct, with Zoroaster's apocalyptic Gathas setting the religious world on fire, with results as described. How else do we explain the sudden and nearly universal proliferation of seven days of creation, Saoshyant messianic theologies, last judgments, salvation (*moksha*), condemnations to hell, the cherishing of written texts, Satan, angels, and other phenomena of Vedic lore in both monotheistic and monistic developments that simultaneously replaced the polytheistic religious traditions of most of the world?

Zoroastrianism is therefore the conduit for ancient Vedic lore as reformed and expressed by Zoroaster, whether spread in his time by sons and disciples or four hundred years later by devotees in a great religious "revival" led by the Magi. Zoroaster articulated his reforms to Vedic religious lore as revealed to him at the beginning of a worldwide religions phenomenon in much the same way that biblical stories known by Muhammad and all his Arab contemporaries were revealed afresh to the Prophet of Islam in reformed or annotated form at the conclusion of this classic religious era. This could be described as a web of revelatory inspiration that blankets the world to this day, each portion of the patchwork quilt offering its own symbolic message of eternal truth.

The challenge for believers, as well as scholars, and even scholarly believers, is to cease fighting about which patch of the quilt is "right," to appreciate each other's traditions, and to both cherish and share their own with sincere humility. This is the ethos of the original Axial Age, and there is no reason why it should not prevail in the New Axial Age. Even for skeptics of our position, the place for this all to begin could be an acceptance of the Magi option, making the precise dates of Zoroaster's life and ministry less crucial to the thesis of Zoroastrianism as the source and origin for a spectrum of doctrines found in whole or in part in the seven testaments and claimed by various of the seven world religions as their own. But for good reasons, the team producing this trilogy continues to favor the 628–551 dates for Zoroaster. Readers are welcome to decide for themselves, secure that either choice is compatible with our understandings of the Axial Age, then and now.

The Vedic or proto-Vedic religion of migrants on their way from the Russian steppes to India swept through Asia Minor (Turkey) and into Babylon (Iraq)/Persia (Iran) on their way to India. The Israelite religion of Semitic monotheism stalled briefly in Asia Minor as many of these "lost tribes of Israel" made their way northeast to Europe, while some went west along the Silk Route. In this investigation, it is conjectured that the two religions may have intersected in momentous coincident exchanges in places like ancient Scythia (present-day Armenia/Azerbaijan) and also in Babylon, where exiled Jews were running the civil service seventy years later, when the Zoroastrian Cyrus swept into power, both recognizing each other as something akin to coreligionists.

The profound significance of this intersection for the twenty-first century is only now becoming recognized as the trigger for the Axial Age, in which philosophical ideas and religious ideals stirred in concert from Greece to China, connected by what we now call the Silk Route. To illustrate how such interplay could well have taken place, we present a critical portion of the script of the play *Three Testaments: Shalom, Peace, Salam*, which premiered in Upstate New York in June 2015 at Niagara Falls, produced by James Flood under the direction of Arthur Ari Strimling. The entire ninety-minute production is available on YouTube's NOW channel from videographer John Bedell, on DVD from Amazon, and in downloadable script format from Cyberpress, the original publisher, by contacting administrator@stageplays.com. The play is apparently most valuable in use as cold readings by university and seminary students, perhaps one of each of the ten scenes given per day at the opening of class, preceding lectures or seminar discussions, as described in our study guide in appendix A. The script of Act One in three scenes is reproduced here in our appendix B and contributes to the above understandings among those whose learning style includes creative imagination.

notes

1. Zadspram 20–21.
2. Yasna 31.8, 33.6–7, 43.5.
3. Yasna 33.6, 13.94.
4. II Kings 17:6.
5. II Kings 18:11, a river running through the cities of the Medes.
6. I Chronicles 5:26.
7. Arnold J. Toynbee, *A Study of History* (Abridgement by D. C. Somervell), 387.
8. Jeremiah, chapter 3.
9. Jeremiah, chapter 47.
10. *Zoroastrians: Their Religious Beliefs and Practices* (London: Routledge, 1979), 99.
11. The name *Tomb of the Exalted* translates as Mazar-i-Sharif in today's Afghanistan.
12. Cf. Bundahishn 34:1–9; Arda Wiraz 1:1–5; Denkard 7.7:6; Zadspram 33:11–12, quoted in Dhalla, *History of Zoroastrianism*, xxxi.

13. Al-Biruni, *The Chronology of Ancient Nations*, 1000 CE (Sachau translation), 17.

14. Benvenisti, *The Persian Religion According to the Chief Greek Texts*, 15.

15. Genesis 5:27.

16. Genesis 9:29.

17. This vivid illustration was helpfully introduced by Jenny Brown to my students in a seminary class who were having difficulty recognizing the potential for confusion in the ancient world's change from lunar to solar dating.

18. Amir Hussain et al., eds., *World Religions: Eastern Traditions* (Toronto: Oxford, 2014), 12.

19. Susan Whitfield, *Life Along the Silk Road* (Los Angeles: University of California Press, 1999).

20. Sol Nigosian, *The Zoroastrian Faith* (Montreal: McGill-Queens, 1993).

21. Karen Armstrong, *The Great Transformation* (New York: Random House, 2007).

22. "Evil-merodach" in the books of Nehemiah and Ezra.

23. Esther 1:14.

24. Yasna 46.13, 51.12, and 53.1.

25. Ibid.

26. Luke 3:23.

27. E. E. Herzfeld, *Zoroaster and His World* (Princeton, NJ: Princeton University Press, 1947).

28. W. B. Henning, *Zoroaster, Politician or Witch-Doctor* (1951).

29. Gore Vidal, *Creation* (New York: Random House, 1981).

30. *JAOS* 114 (1994): 498–99.

31. "The 'Traditional Date of Zoroaster' Explained," *BSOAS* 40 (1997): 25–35.

32. Conversation with the author in 2005.

5

the silk route

The Axis of the Axial Age

T**HE PHRASES** *AXIAL AGE* **OR** *AXIAL PERIOD* **ARE ENGLISH TRANSLATIONS OF THE GERMAN** *ACH-senzeit*, "axistime," a term coined in the mid-twentieth century by philosopher Karl Jaspers. The heart of the age is from the sixth to the fifth century BCE, or slightly more than the years 550–400 BCE. Jaspers originally used the term to describe the wider period from 700 to 300 BC, during which comparable transformative religious thinking appeared in Persia, India, China, Israel, and Greece. Described as "the great transformation" by Karen Armstrong, the Axial Age concept now has near universal acceptance, though we and others regard those core years 550–400 BCE as the essence of the age. The German Egyptologist Jan Assmann expresses this essence succinctly in a major new study of *Dynamics in the History of Religions between Asia and Europe.* He writes:

The theory of the Axial Age as put forward by Karl Jaspers in 1949 and elaborated since then, especially by Shmuel Eisenstadt and his circle,[1] is centred on the following principal assumptions: there is but One Truth and One Mankind. At a given point in its moral, spiritual and intellectual evolution, mankind "broke through" to a much clearer apprehension of this Truth. This happened independently in several places at approximately the same time around 500 BCE. The main characteristics of this breakthrough may be summarized as universalisation and distanciation. *Universalisation* is concerned with the recognition of absolute truths, valid for all times and all peoples; this implies features such as reflexivity, abstraction, second order thinking, theory, systematisation, etc. *Distanciation* is concerned with introducing ontological and epistemological distinctions, such as the eternal and the temporal world, being and appearance, spirit and matter, critique of the "given" in view of the true, etc.: in short, the invention of transcendence and the construction of two-world theories.[2]

Fine words profoundly expressed, except for a glaring improbability: that such a major and fundamental shift in human understanding would have happened "inde-

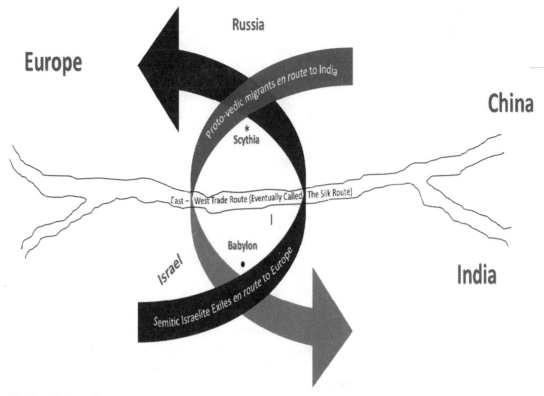

The Great Intersection.
© 2016 BRIAN ARTHUR BROWN. DIAGRAM EXECUTED BY INDIRA BROWN SINTON.

pendently at several places at approximately the same time" with no connection or mutual influence. It is possible that such a phenomenon could have occurred in two places or even three at the same time, but to happen independently everywhere that is connected by the Silk Route, and at a time when there was already a common denominator in the Zoroastrian phenomenon as propagated by the Magi, seems highly improbable. In his book *Vom Ursprung und Ziel der Geschichte* (*The Origin and Goal of History*), Jaspers himself identified a number of key Axial Age thinkers as having had a profound influence on future philosophies and religions, and he identified characteristics common to each area from which those thinkers emerged. Jaspers saw striking parallels in religion and philosophy but failed to identify any obvious direct connection or transmission of ideas between regions. His time span was also slightly longer than more recent analysis suggests, stretching some four hundred years as compared with our acceptance of the core of the Axial Age as being closer to 150 years in length, a period of sustained spiritual dynamism.

Jaspers argued that during the Axial Age, "the spiritual foundations of humanity were laid simultaneously and independently in China, India, Persia, Judea, and Greece. And these are the foundations upon which humanity still subsists today."[3] Jaspers is being seen increasingly as correct, except for the failure to identify the common denominator, a factor he missed by casting his net over an unnecessarily broad span of time. Jewish, Christian, and Islamic scholars, Richard Freund, David Bruce, and

Amir Hussain, tend toward joining other contributors to this trilogy in speaking of the Axial Age as a period lasting from Lao Tzu as an elderly seer in 550 BCE and Socrates as a philosopher who died about 400 BCE, a period spanning 150 years following the death of Zoroaster. We might think of that epoch as including the reign of Cyrus (538–529) as the main political marker, the rise of Jewish prophets and the Buddha as dominant religious factors, with Socrates bookending the era philosophically in the West and Confucius in the East.

Jaspers's failure on this point was natural enough since there were important Greek philosophers like Thales and Pythagoras, even before Parmenides, who was a monist, and Socrates, a monotheist, in the period as we now define it. Likewise, after our preferred span, Plato and Aristotle should be seen as simply worthy students of the trend, building brilliantly on the new accepted framework. Sandwiched between the more famous Parmenides and Socrates, in an aside to his works on physics, we find the Greek scientist Empedocles: "God is a circle whose center is everywhere, and its circumference nowhere."[4] This statement simply bears witness to the Zoroastrian-inspired churning controversy amid Hellenistic intelligentsia at this precise moment. Greek philosophy might have been interesting but not seminal without Parmenides and Socrates, key figures in our core definition of the Axial Age in Greece.

The same could be said of Israel's prophets, with Joel, Elijah, Elisha, and First Isaiah making earlier contributions that would have been valued, except that Jeremiah, Second Isaiah, Daniel, and Ezekiel raised the bar so incredibly high in the Axial Age in response to Zoroaster that they defined the movement and left prophets who also followed them to be described as "the minor prophets." Similar predecessors and successors to the true Axial giants might be seen in China, India, and Persia, though not as well known in Western literature on the subject. Suffice it to say that during the era of the greatest Hebrew prophets, Lao Tzu and Confucius held sway in China. Leading India toward the Bhagavad Gita, it was mostly Buddha in that precise era, except for Mahavira, another great reformer of Indian religion, whose Jain teachings also fit into the Zoroastrian aftermath and whose dates are too exactly in the middle of this epoch to ignore. In Persia, Cyrus himself set everything in motion with his support for monotheistic religion and his application of Zoroastrian moral principles to diplomacy and governance. The dates of these, the greatest among the historic figures, all fit the tighter timeline.

Considering the historical sequencing of these key religious figures, we naturally ask what, if anything, they might have in common. The only outlier on this list is Jeremiah, whose younger years may be "grandfathered" into the record for the sake of a slightly earlier connection as described in our play, found in appendix D. With all these dates being BCE of course, Jeremiah lived his three-score years and ten, 655–586, Lao Tzu 604–524, Ezekiel 622–569, Isaiah 582–512, Cyrus 580–529, Buddha 563–483, Confucius perhaps 551–479 or slightly later, Mahavira 540–468, Parmenides 515–444(?), and Socrates 469–399. They all confronted their worlds with distinctive new thinking about morality and its spiritual basis within 150 years of the life of Zoroaster. Cyrus may be the only one to have met Zoroaster personally, which would have happened when he was a child in the court of Vishtaspa, but the others can all be seen as part of a spiritual upheaval triggered by Zoroaster, whose influence appears in the teachings of every one of them. It is absent from their predecessors and only found in their successors identified as minor prophets and students.

Jaspers himself held Socrates, Confucius, and the Buddha in especially high regard, describing them as exemplary human beings and "paradigmatic personalities." His linking of them as exemplary might have been his clue, clustered as they are within our tighter time frame right after the life of Zoroaster. We concede a similar place of preeminence to the aforementioned contemporary prophets of Israel, and the impact of Cyrus was such that Israel almost took him to be the Messiah, a figure who appears in Zoroastrianism as the *Saoshyant* or Redeemer—which Cyrus almost was to Israel, in a certain sense.

Socrates was officially executed for "atheism," by which his judges meant that he no longer believed in the "gods" (plural), though, as quoted by Plato, he clearly believed in God, a radical new departure eventually to be adopted throughout Greece. In the Axial Age, the gods of Olympus were dethroned in the West, and the Vedic gods continued to exist in the East only as angelic spirits under the canopy of monism, the meaning of which, and its relationship to monotheism, will be discussed in the last chapters of part one. Israel's monotheism was reinforced in Babylon by Zoroastrianism at its height, and the issues in both religion and philosophy were how individuals should live in reference to good and bad, right and wrong, justice and injustice. All this was related to what was now perceived as God's claim upon them and God's invitation to them as set out dramatically in Zoroaster's preaching and writing.

The Gathas are the earliest chapters of the Avesta Scriptures, written by Zoroaster and still extant, but Zoroastrians are not mentioned by name in any of them, just as Jews are not mentioned anywhere in the Torah, and Christians are not mentioned by that name in any of the Gospels. As with Jews and Christians, we rely on later generations to self-identify as Zoroastrians, so it is not surprising that Cyrus (a very young contemporary of Zoroaster) and others of his generation do not refer to themselves as Zoroastrians. The first independent description of Zoroastrian religion (the religion of the government under which the commentator grew up) comes from Herodotus, the Greek "Father of History," who was born in Halicarnassus, a Greek city in the Persian province of Caria (Turkey) in the time of Xerxes I. Even he does not yet use the Zoroastrian name but refers to its practitioners as Magians, the then common designation of Zoroastrian priests in the empire's heartland provinces where the Magi converted or adjusted en masse from the earlier religion of that name. This "shorthand" branding was a conflation of Magianism and Zoroastrianism or a confusion of the two, which lasted many centuries. Indeed, this transition was so smooth that outside observers continued to imagine that Zoroaster founded the Magian religion for some time.

Without much distinction between monotheism (one God) and monism (one Being or "mono-be-ism"), Herodotus testifies to the link between Vedic Aryans and Semitic Jews. According to him, the Zoroastrian Magians of his region both preserved many of the names of the divinities ("singing the Theogony") and held to a belief in a future immortality, going after their death to "Zalmoxis" (the "God of Moses"). They even called their homeland "Moesia," for it was there that many exiled people of Moses also lived. Moesia is best known in history as a province of the Roman Empire in the southeastern Balkans in what was the only part of Scythia controlled by the Romans. In Scythia/Caria/Moesia, we can see at a glance the connection between the Persian religion as Herodotus knew it and that of the Israelite exiles, whose religion was acceptable to the Zoroastrianism as practiced in the general population. This is the kind of thing that was common, though not universal, from Greece to China in the 150 years after Zoroaster, especially in the superpower Persian Empire.

Personal responsibility to God for good thoughts and good actions was not new or unique to Zoroaster any more than being "born again" was new or unique to Billy Graham in the twentieth century. Using the scriptural born-again motif, Graham triggered a worldwide phenomenon in a similar way, much of which was identified with his own Baptist tradition, but which also affected reforms among charismatic Catholics, energized the new Pentecostal movement, and bolstered other young churches, as well as elements within the sometimes-moribund mainline Protestant denominations. The relationship of Oneness-of-God teachings in Zoroastrianism to Judaism, Hinduism, Buddhism, Taoism, and others may be seen in a similar light—stimulating but applied in various ways, but all based on Zoroaster's emphasis on Good Thoughts, Good Words, Good Deeds—*Humata, Hukhta, Huvareshta* in the Avestan language, which connected them all to some extent. Zoroaster linked these laudable concepts to the Oneness of God and personal responsibility of individuals in community. These were both conceivably learned from Israelite neighbors or relatives, and one or more Jewish prophets, but finally integrated with his own revelatory encounter with God (depicted dramatically in our appendix B play), inviting and commanding his response and that of his people.

The first direct classical Greek reference to Zoroaster and the Magi is located in a dialogue by Plato (429–347 BCE). After noting this observation in *Three Testaments* without reference, Dr. Laleh Bakhtiar, the great translator of our *Sublime Quran*, wrote, "The 4 cardinal virtues of Wisdom, Temperance, Courage and Justice have been attributed to Plato in the West. Yet in a dialog between Socrates and a young Greek general named Alcibiades, Socrates clearly mentions the 4 cardinal virtues as having come from the Persian–Magi–Zoroastrian tradition":

> When a young prince is seven years old he is put upon a horse and taken to the riding-masters, and begins to go out hunting. And at fourteen years of age he is handed over to the royal schoolmasters, as they are termed: these are four chosen men, reputed to be the best among the Persians of a certain age; and one of them is the *wisest*, another the *most just*, a third the *most temperate*, and a fourth the *most courageous*.
>
> The *wisest* instructs him of Zoroaster and teaches him also the duties of his royal office; the second, who is the *most just*, teaches him always to speak the truth; the third, or *most temperate*, forbids him to allow any pleasure to be lord over him, that he may be accustomed to being a freeman and king indeed—lord of himself first, and not a slave; the *most courageous* trains him to be bold and fearless, telling him that if he fears he is to deem himself a slave.[5]

In this dialogue, Zoroaster (Zoroastren in Greek) is called "the son of Oromazes" (a Greek form of *Ormazd*, the common corruption of *Ahura Mazda*). In the same play, Zoroaster's religion is called "the magianism of Zoroaster . . . which is the worship of the Gods." A blatant inaccuracy notwithstanding, the inference is that Zoroaster was the founder of the doctrine of the Magi, simply an error in historical chronology. Other passing Platonic or neo-Platonic references to Zoroaster are found in *Alcibiades II*, *Protos*, *The Republic*, and *Anonymmi Vita Platonis*.

It is almost certain that the Vedic and Semitic tradition intersected in Zoroaster's time, resulting in a transformative burst of energy that provided a powerful reinforcement for monotheism as it was emerging in the West and the development of monism in the East, both major departures from earlier polytheism. Between them we have the creative tension of dynamics that form the spiritual agenda of the mid-sixth century BCE and well into the fifth, and that might have a similar reverberation in a New Axial Age of our own twenty-first century.

We do not suggest that the aforenoted Axial Age prophets and philosophers were disciples of Zoroaster or that they lacked their own genius. But genius rarely appears in a vacuum; it is frequently a reaction or a response to some stimulus—in this case, Zoroaster's impact in the matters of morality and personal religion. Our theses may well prove valid, even without the Dead Zee Scrolls for which we are searching. Though we anticipate this momentous discovery before long, we are becoming adept at identifying quotes or inferences from these scrolls buried between the lines of the scriptural testaments of the world religions. There are also two other impact factors in Zoroastrianism that may be of as much value in our quest today as they were 2,500 years ago.

The first of these additional impact factors was the specific content of Zoroastrian Scriptures, doctrine, and practices as reflected in Buddhist enlightenment, in the messianic theology of Jews and Christians, and in the eschatology of Islam. In Zoroastrian spirit, we do not suggest that recognizing the details of Zoroastrian heritage in the major religions of the world should lead to overturning these religions, but rather to mutual respect and understanding. This needs elucidation and illustration yet to come in this study, only part of which is dependent on new documentation, and much of which is found in the religions and philosophies of the East.

The second of these additional factors was Zoroastrianism's ecumenical tolerance and even encouragement of other religions, even while insinuating a certain influence upon them. We have the clearest evidence of this with respect to the Jewish religion, but it was also evident among Buddhists along the Silk Route in early times in a co-existence with Central Asia's Sogdian Zoroastrians[6] in particular, and others, as we shall see. An essence of the Zoroastrian phenomenon was individual religious fervor and personal esoteric communion with God, both populist and elitist, from West to East and back again. With even tentative acceptance of that premise, the rest will fall into place in both monotheistic and monistic traditions West and East.

Since subtexts of volumes 2 and 3 of this trilogy focus on the additional information we may find in the Dead Zee Scrolls, yet to be located, we might conclude this summary by at least whetting our appetites for it in an examination of what Zoroastrian material we do have now. We can begin by turning to another article in the eleventh edition of the *Encyclopedia Britannica* by the same Karl Friedrich Geldner. He gives us the starting point for modern knowledge at the beginning of the twentieth century and manages to preserve a genuine feel for the antiquity of our sources, "warts and all."

Zend-Avesta *Origin and History*—While all that Herodotus (i. 132) has to say is that the Magi sang "the theogany" at their sacrifices, Pausanias is able to add (v. 27. 3) that they read from a book. Hermippus, in the 3rd century B.C., affirmed that Zoroaster, the founder of the doctrine of the magi, was the author of twenty books, each containing 100,000 verses. According to the Arab historian, Tabari, these were written on 12,000 cowhides, a statement confirmed by Masudi, who writes: "Zartusht gave to the Persians the book called Avesta. It consists of twenty-one parts, each containing 200 leaves. This book, in the writing which Zartusht invented and which the magi called the writing of religion, was written on 12,000 cowhides, bound together by golden bands. Its language was Old Persian, which now no one understands."

These assertions sufficiently establish the existence and great bulk of the sacred writings. Parsee tradition adds a number of interesting statements as to their history. According to the *Arda-Viraf-Nama*, the religion revealed through Zoroaster had subsisted in its purity for 300 years, when Iskander Rumi (Alexander the Great) invaded and devastated Iran, and burned the Avesta which, written on cowhides with golden ink, was preserved in the archives at Persepolis. According to the *Dinkard*, there were two original copies, of which one was burned, while the second came into the hands of the Greeks. One of the Rivayato texts relates further: "After the villainy of Alexander, an assemblage of several high-priests brought together the Avesta from various places, and made a collection which included the sacred Yasna, Vispered, Vendidad and other scraps of the Avesta," which, as far as possible, should be a faithful reproduction of the original. King Shapur I (241–272 AD) enlarged this re-edited Avesta by collecting and incorporating with it the non-religious tractates on medicine, astronomy, geography and philosophy. Under Shapur II (309–380 AD) these nasks were brought into complete order, and the new redaction of the Avesta reached its definitive conclusion.

notes

1. Karl Jaspers, *Vom Ursprung und Zeil Geschichte, Munich*: Piper 1949. The debate on the "Axial Age" continued in the 1970s under the beautiful title "The Age of Transcendence." Since then, there have been a series of conferences published in Shmuel N. Eisenstadt (ed.), *The Origins and Diversity of Axial-Age Civilizations* (Albany: SUNY Press, 1987).
2. Koninklijke BRILL NV, 2012, 255.
3. Karl Jaspers, *The Way to Wisdom: An Introduction to Philosophy* (New Haven, CT: Yale University Press, 2003), 98.
4. Frag. B35 (Simplicius, *Physics*, 31–34; *On the Heavens*, 528–530).
5. Plato, *Alcibiades I*.
6. An ancient nation in modern Uzbekistan and Tajikistan, of special interest in the quest to locate the Dead Zee Scrolls.

6
the extant avesta
Pieces of a Jigsaw Puzzle

T HE EARLIEST PARTS OF THE AVESTA SCRIPTURES WERE EVIDENTLY COMMITTED TO WRITING at the insistence of King Vishtaspa, who converted to the faith under Zoroaster's personal influence and became Zoroaster's powerful patron. As a former scribe, this king's own prime minister, Jamaspa, took responsibility for publication of the text. Especially after the death of the monarch, Jamaspa took special care of the portions written to date, as recorded in later verses of the extant Avesta.[1] Another earlier contributor, Tabari, followed by a certain Bundari, affirmed that Vishtaspa had instructed that two copies of the holy texts be inscribed in letters of gold upon ox-hide scrolls, a tradition illustrating Zoroastrianism's devotion to the sacred character of the texts. The Roman commentator Pliny, quoting Hermippus,[2] made reference to the legend that Zoroaster composed no less than two million verses,[3] an exaggeration probably achieved by multiplying two hundred verses of all possible Gathas in the Avesta by an estimate of ten thousand copies of the work, or perhaps twelve thousand, as we shall see.

The two archetypal copies of Zoroaster's original and seminal work were to serve initially as the standard priestly codices throughout Vishtāspa's realm, a pattern of canonization and verification later emulated by all or most Scripture traditions in this extended family of sacred texts. As mentioned, the earliest original reference to written Avestan texts comes from the *Ardā-Vīrāf Nameh*,[4] and these artifacts are also mentioned later in the *Dinkard* and the *Shatrōihā-i-Airān*. Those three works are all portions of the Avesta composed at a later date, witnessing to the Gathas, which introduced the whole Avesta much as the Torah introduces the Hebrew Scriptures and the Gospels introduce the New Testament. The *Ardā-Vīrāf Nameh* contends that twelve thousand copies were produced and disseminated from the royal library at Stakhar Papakan (also known as Ishtakhar), which is near Persepolis.

The faith was to be promulgated throughout the world in accordance with the teaching of these scrolls. We mentioned a tradition to the effect that one of the original copies in gold ink on cowhides came into the hands of the Greeks and was translated into copies in their language. It too has disappeared, but support for this tradition may be found in the Arabic lexicon of Bar-Bahlūl, according to which the Avesta of Zoroaster was available in seven languages—Greek, Syriac, Persian, Aramean, Segestanian, Mervian, and Hebrew. A still earlier Syriac manuscript commentary on the New Testament by 'Ishō'dād, bishop of Ḥadatha, near Mosul, similarly speaks of the Avesta as having been eventually written in twelve different languages. Even if there is hyperbole here, it is clear that there was fervor and devotion surrounding written versions of the original Avesta Scripture. Yet until relatively recent discoveries, like the Dead Sea Scrolls, the Nag Hammadi Library, and other surprising finds, it had been widely assumed that every single copy had perished. Now we are not so sure . . . indeed, we are becoming hopeful that such a treasure may be found.

This material appears to have been more voluminous than all the classical Hebrew writings in our possession—Scriptural, apocryphal texts, and noncanonical materials combined. Like the Bible, the Avesta was, and what still remains of it is, a compendium of documents written in various related languages. The oldest portions contain original materials as well as prayers that were revised by Zoroaster under inspiration from Vedic oral sources, some of which were from a time contemporary to Abraham. The later portions of the Avesta continue down to final texts composed just after the closing of the canon of the Christian Scriptures. The Avesta as a whole may therefore be regarded as beginning slightly before the Torah as we have it and as an influential envelope around the whole of the Bible, as well as the four Eastern texts of world religions. Of the seven, the Quran alone was written entirely outside the Avesta era and would claim to re-present material first seen in the Avesta as either correction or amplification.

The deliberate destruction of the Avesta, beginning in a drunken conflagration under the direction of Alexander the Great in 330 BCE, was part of a program to "Hellenize" his empire, the first of many European attempts to "civilize" the rest of the world. Sometime after the breakup of Alexander's empire, as detailed above, a "Parthian" regime governed Persia from 83 BCE until 224 CE and revived the vigor of the Zoroastrian religion. This was especially evident under King Vologeses, who commissioned the first attempt to recover Avesta materials from scattered fragments, to write down the oral traditions and liturgies, and to gather Zoroastrian quotations from Greek manuscripts. A brief disruption of the project by political and military upheavals was followed by a revival of Zoroastrianism in the Persian Empire during the Sasanian era, 250–650 CE, in which Zoroastrianism resumed its place as the state religion. Its high priests succeeded in collecting the surviving Avesta documents into twelve volumes called *nasks*. This "Sasanian archetype" (as it is called in the Catholic Encyclopedia) was the first official Zoroastrian canon, established not long after the formation of the Hebrew canon and shortly before the closing of the Christian canon.

Sadly, from both monistic and monotheistic perspectives, new materials produced in these popular revivals were increasingly dualistic in nature, so that by the time of Muhammad Zoroastrian monotheism was largely a memory. The surviving portions of the Avesta itself were ambivalent in this regard, so most of what remained was obliterated by the fervently monotheistic Muslims when they took over Persia in the seventh century CE. Both amplification of the early monotheistic truths of the Avesta and condemnation of its latter dualism are almost certainly to be found "between the lines" in the Quran. This is analogous to the presence of material reflecting the Torah and the Gospels in the Quran, except that with the Avesta there is little of the original currently available for comparison.

All that remains today of the original documents are portions from several religious *nasks* (or booklets), both monotheistic and mixed, and one law book of social regulations. These have been put together from documents and fragments hidden in the few remaining Zoroastrian communities in Persia/Iran or spirited out of the country by refugees fleeing to India at that time and later. They were supplemented by familiar and beloved hymns, dating back to Zoroaster himself, which could be reproduced from memory by believers at any time. There is just enough remaining that we can outline the development of the Avesta as a whole, prior to tracing its influence on the Torah, and also considering its influence in the world of the Torah, in which the rest of the Hebrew Scriptures were produced in the form we know and reflected in the New Testament and the Quran. But even prior to that, we may now see traces of certain monistic reactions to Zoroastrian stimulus farther east in our investigations of sacred texts of the Orient.

Westerners were largely unaware of the Avesta until after the seventeenth century, when, in the growth of trade with India, manuscript copies began to reach Europe. The French scholar A. H. Anquetil du Perron (1731–1805) went to India, learned to read the Avestan language from a Parsee priest in Surat, acquired manuscripts, and produced a translation. European study of the Avesta subsequently paralleled and drew support from the study of the earliest Sanskrit literature, which was linguistically related. More recent translations are somewhat more reliable, using tools produced by Mary Boyce, who had a Sanskrit scholastic background and became fluent in the Persian Avestan cognate languages as preserved in the rural Zoroastrian communities of Iran, where she chose to live among Zoroastrian villagers for a considerable period of time some fifty years ago, demonstrating a Margaret Mead–like determination to get inside the culture. A Zoroastrian revival in the East and a blossoming new appreciation of Zoroastrianism in the West are currently moving from infancy phenomena to adolescent vivacity, but the world has barely scratched the surface of a mature understanding of Zoroastrianism for the twenty-first century.

The core of the surviving or extant Avesta is a small collection of Gathas, universally recognized as prophetic utterances by Zoroaster himself. We refer to their language as Gathic Avestan, an ancient Indo-European language that has affinities with Sanskrit and Hindi to the southeast and Greek and Latin to the northwest.

At each stage of the Avesta's development, it also displays a linguistic affinity with Aramaic, its contemporary as spoken in Persia, and a link with Hebrew. The Gathas have an oracular quality that is rhetorical and poetically melodic—an apocalyptic literature, the first of that genre in the world. Like other ancient linguistic traditions, these factors make them difficult to translate, so verses of the Avesta are cherished by Zoroastrians today in the original as memorized. There are only about six thousand words in the Gathas by Zoroaster himself, recorded in five distinct poems, each with its own meter. They present the great Persian prophet's sublime expression of belief in one uncreated Lord of Wisdom, and they outline what this God expects of people in both the universal and the personal struggle between good and evil, between truth and falsehood. God's will is presented as both invitation and command, detailed equally in worship and in good deeds as opposed to false gods and bad deeds.

The second surviving "text" of the Avesta was possibly written by a school of Zoroaster's disciples, probably during his lifetime or soon after, although Mary Boyce, as the world's leading academic authority on the Gathic Avestan dialect, believed it too may have been composed entirely by Zoroaster later in his life. Titled "Worship in Seven Chapters" in translation, it is known in the Zoroastrian community as the *Yasna Haptanhaiti*. The prayers in these seven chapters are more like hymns than poems, invoking the Lord of Wisdom as well as the sacred devas or "guardian angels" who protect the earth, sky, and sea. In direct correspondence to the prophet's teaching, they profess devotion to the truth and seek the happiness and fulfillment of the believers in serving God in worship and in action. These virtues are several times listed as good thoughts, good words, and good deeds, whether communal or personal.

The third book, simply known as *Yasna*, or "Worship," begins at chapter 28, implying that the seven chapters of the Yasna Haptanhaiti, just before it, were once preceded by twenty other chapters or *sutras*, including Zoroaster's five Gathas. This leaves fifteen missing very ancient sutras as the mother lode of what we hope to find in someday unearthing the complete original Avesta, material by either Zoroaster himself or his earliest disciples. Yasna itself is primarily liturgical, consisting of rubrics and instructions for worship. The Yasna has seventy-two chapters at present and appears complete. Written somewhat later in a dialect known as "Younger Avestan," in it we catch a glimpse of cosmological inferences from its introduction of the old devas of the Vedic pantheon. They are called *yazatas*, and they are regarded as spirits whose only purpose now is to serve and glorify the Lord of Wisdom.

A fourth collection, titled the *Visparad*, is much smaller at this point, also written in a Younger Avestan dialect. Its purpose is to simply comment on much of what we find in the first three collections. There may be much of the Visparad yet to be found, but its value will be less than the extended Gathas referred to above, which, as indicated, may hold the key to the Oneness of God in a tension between what eventually became monotheism and monism.

The fifth series of documents is called the *Yashts*, or "Services" of worship. There are twenty-one complete Yashts, and other bits and pieces, all based on ancient Vedic hymns used by Buddhists and Hindus still today. The comparison is instructive, and these may be listed among the Z passages, to use our new nomenclature, possibly printed in bold someday in Buddhist and Hindu hymn books. Most of these Yashts have been reworked in the Avesta to laud the yazatas as models for humans to emulate in service to the Lord of Wisdom. Ahura Mazda is extolled, using the Younger Avestan translation of his name, *Ormazd*, which came into use even before the Common Era, although modern Zoroastrians have maintained or returned to the use of *Ahuramazda*.

In spite of their beauty, in the Yashts the Zoroastrian religion appears in the transition toward dualism, a form of Zoroastrianism that did not ultimately survive. There are yasht hymns to specific yazatas, or reinvigorated Vedic devas, like Mah (the Moonlight), Tir (the Starshine), and Aban (the Waterfall). The latter features a recycled Vedic hymn to the river goddess Ardvi Sura Anahita, a Z hymn still in use "as is" among Hindus in the twenty-first century. These days, a similar concept of angelic presences, long associated with Catholic and Orthodox Christian tradition in the West, appears to be undergoing a revival among Jews, Protestants, and Muslims in popular cultures of the West.

Such hymn-poems are among the most sublime passages in the Avesta, and they may remind us of the romantic devotion to nature found in New Age discourses and in recordings used for meditation today. We may yet find some of them represented in the Quran in a more theologically complete form as revealed to Prophet Muhammad, according to Islamic understanding of such transmissions in corrected or fresh revelations, the Z passages of the Quran.

The mistake in the latter books or nasks of the Avesta, as seen by monotheistic Zoroastrians today, was in compromising the rigorous abstraction of Zoroaster's original monotheistic (or even the monistic) vision of the Oneness of God. That danger is illustrated in Yashts extolling the beauty of green pastures and still waters, but without any shepherd leading as "head" or "Godhead." Others extol the endurance of the *Fravashis*, the souls of good people, but make no reference to the overarching goodness of God. The fire may give a certain charm to the hearth, but without the warmth of God's spirit that it represents, these most beautiful moments may be but fleeting illusions, subscribed to in the twenty-first century by those claiming to be "spiritual but not religious." This false Zoroastrianism may be critiqued as a "greeting card" religion, with beautiful sentiment but few demands, subject only, if we are correct, to such sentiments being revealed to Muhammad in an appropriate form acceptable to God—much like their re-presentation also in Hebrew and Christian revelations. Its more complicated relationship to monistic Eastern religions will be examined in volume 3 of this trilogy, dedicated to them.

The balance needed for the use of such imagery to experience and to reflect God's glory was about to be lost in Zoroastrianism. Once the power of these aesthetic devas was no longer used to serve and glorify God, and as they themselves became the object of meditation or worship, the direct encounter producing either atonement or at-One-ment between humans and God was gone. With it went the impetus for personal morality and the imperative for social justice, both lost in the loveliness and beauty of an antiseptic religion that never dirties its hands—perhaps a precursor to what a Canadian writer has referred to in *The Comfortable Pew*, an analysis of mid-twentieth-century Christianity. Many Western synagogues, churches, and masjids today are responding with prophetic warnings about the failure to distinguish between the requirements of the Creator and the desires of the created. This is a subject also prominent in the Eastern texts we will examine in detail, as discussed in sermons in temples, stupas, and shrines there.

The sixth and concluding section in the extant Avesta material is the *Vendidad*, intended to exorcise demons, but in confirming their power, the Vendidad reinforces many of the negative stereotypes of dualistic Zoroastrianism that have existed in many quarters. Published sometime after 300 CE, halfway between the lifetimes of Jesus and Muhammad, it continues the momentum of Vedic revival in the service of a dualistic worldview that Zoroaster himself would possibly have found abhorrent. Without a solid underpinning based upon the Oneness of God, Zoroastrianism by this time bore little resemblance to the pristine faith encountered by the Jews in Babylon.

The Vendidad appears to be a recapitulation of earlier texts, now lost, but the clumsy use of the Avestan language gives it a strained tone. Its prescriptions for the purification of women in menstruation, priests *in flagrante*, and animals and corpses are said to be still observed in remote rural Zoroastrian villages in Iran, but less so in India and abroad. The Vendidad is either ignored or scorned by many urbane Zoroastrians today in Tehran, Mumbai, London, Toronto, New York, Houston, Chicago, and Sydney, where sins like adultery, child abuse, apostasy, sorcery, and profanity no longer require hanging, flaying, infestation, beheading, or dismemberment—penalties like those also abjured by Christians, Jews, and others in comparatively recent times, despite the appearance of such extreme measures in their own scriptures.

In addition to these large and significant Zoroastrian Avesta texts, there is the *Khordah Avesta*, the "Little Avesta" still in use as a prayer book by Zoroastrians today. Composed and collected at an undetermined time during one of the attempts to recover texts and summarize the teachings in a worshipful context, the Khordah Avesta contains quotes from all the other extant collections, as well as fragments not found anywhere else. A number of verses in which God proclaims his name to be "I AM" will occasion our return to the Little Avesta when we consider Zoroaster's debt to Moses at the burning bush, similar I AM passages uttered by Jesus in the Christian Gospel, and frequent I AMs by Krishna in the Bhagavad Gita, a late addition to the Mahabharata now dated as coming from the Axial Age as we define it.

Translations of sacred texts across all seven traditions in this trilogy exhibit two distinct practices. Those employing "formal equivalence" strive for literal translation, even at the expense of common sense. For example, when in an American idiom "his speech *hit* the program *out of the park*" is translated into languages spoken by people with no knowledge of baseball, the idiomatic expression makes no sense. Translators using "dynamic equivalence" seek to accurately convey the meaning but use other words, like "his speech presented the program in ways appreciated by all," with no reference to "hitting it out of the park." Current translations of the Avesta are largely limited to rather clumsy formal equivalence and are understood by only those who have perhaps lived for a year or more in an Iranian Zoroastrian village.

The extant Zoroastrian Scriptures currently represent about 20 percent of the original, which would have been somewhat larger than the entire Bible of both testaments. What remains now makes up a volume about the size of the Quran, or half the size of the

Christian New Testament. It opens with the Gathas by Zoroaster himself, the poetic psalmlike prayers that establish the style for much of the rest of the collection. The first comprehensive modern translation was completed in 1864 by Professor Friedrich von Spiegel (1820–1905), a German translation of "the original manuscripts" brought out serially from 1852 to 1863 and now at Harvard University. Under the simple title *Avesta*, its English translation was completed in 1864 by von Spiegal's British colleague, Arthur Henry Bleeck. Frequently reprinted and still available, it uses a strict, formal equivalence that has been continued in more recent original translations, though with improved linguistic research.

From within the Parsee community, Piloo Nanavutty offered a charming dynamic equivalent translation of *The Gathas of Zarathustra* in 1999, limited mainly by a surfeit of untranslated phrases unfamiliar to and unmanageable by most English readers, although appreciated in the increasingly English-speaking Parsee community. This has led to our present attempt to offer a paraphrased dynamic equivalent sample, relying on everything we know about Zoroaster's life, passion, impact, and theology, but presented in a style believably representing the clarity and dynamism that must have been characteristic of this prophet whose message so changed the world and stimulated the seven sacred texts under our consideration.

The paraphrase offered in this study is aided by the *Textual Sources for the Study of Zoroastrianism* by Mary Boyce, and it is permeated with the brilliant synthesis of recent linguistic scholarship presented in *The Hymns of Zoroaster* (2010) by M. L. West, emeritus fellow of All Souls College, Oxford, and fellow of the British Academy. While his translation is also somewhat hamstrung by formal equivalence to a language and a sometimes-opaque text with which we are all still struggling, West's accompanying commentary is the new gold standard in Zoroastrian scholarship in our own era of greater certainty about the dates of Zoroaster himself.

Our paraphrases are an attempt to appreciate the power and majesty of the Avesta text and the intimacy between its first author and God. They are dependent upon the four sources mentioned above, based primarily on Spiegel and Bleeck for vocabulary, though enriched by the other three who supply insights to the meaning. Our brief selections from the Gatha section of the Avesta illustrates Zoroaster's belief in the Oneness of God. This concept was clouded later by the appearance of Avestan "divinities" who are first recognized in Zoroastrianism as something akin to angels but who eventually grew in importance to become again gods like their Vedic antecedents, almost equal to their creator. This trend later expanded the motivation of Muslims in their drive to recover a pure monotheism.

In these samples, we include Gatha verses that present Zoroaster's questions about the creation of the earth and the origins of the universe, questions that some of us now believe may have been answered directly by Isaiah in Babylon, as illustrated in some detail in *Three Testaments*. Another of our examples is from the crisis moment early in his ministry when Zoroaster felt compelled to move from his Eastern birthplace in Scythia/Armenia/Azerbaijan to the region of Bactria, where he flourished for the next forty years.

Also included are references to Zoroaster's expectation of Saoshyant redeemers or "saviors," in the plural. They are described elsewhere as three in number who might come early to facilitate creation, to redeem people at a turning point in history, and at the end of time to save the elect. This idea is mirrored exactly in a Christian theology of the Messiah in the Gospel of John, laden as it is with discernable Z passages identified in our volume 3. While using the flowing syntax of dynamic equivalence in these examples, there has been every effort to stick to the formal equivalent language to illustrate what is apparent in all these translations—that the Avesta is indeed echoed in the Torah and Gospel, that its truths are confirmed in the Quran, and that it was a primary stimulus for the Eastern Scriptures considered in this study.

In what follows, we witness a turning point in religious development of the world that swept throughout the region of the emerging Persian Empire and beyond, as humanity quite suddenly shifted from a creaturely dependence to active partnership with the Divine.

Worship[5]

With hands outstretched in worship, I pray to you and seek your help,
O Lord of Wisdom, placing your bountiful will above everything.
I offer right actions combined with good thoughts,
To connect Wisdom with even souls in nature, like that of the cow.

I approach you, O Lord of Wisdom, as a mortal with good thoughts,
So you can bless me personally, both materially and spiritually.
Such blessings are your appropriate responses to the needs of believers.

I will praise you with right actions and good thoughts.
O Lord of Wisdom, your dominion is unimpaired.
My piety is worthy of an answer, so come to my aid.

I have summoned the spiritual resources to lift my thoughts on high,
Knowing that you, O Lord of Wisdom, reward right actions.
As long as I possess ability and strength I will pursue justice.

O Right One, may I see a vision of you as my thoughts rise to you.
Let our compliance become a path to you, O Lord of Wisdom.
In submission may we impress even predators with our hymns.

Join your good thoughts with ours, and make righteousness your gift.
In honest words, O Lord, give support to this camel herder, and to all.
Lord, give us what we need to overcome the acts of hostility by the foe.

O Right One, reward our good thoughts with your blessing.
Out of your holiness, empower King Vishtaspa and me.
O Lord of Wisdom, provide your authority,
Showing the requirements in which we may receive your care.

Revelation[6]

In accord with the laws of primordial existence,
the Day of Judgment shall come.
The wicked and the righteous together
Shall see their falsehoods and their honesty weighed up.

The person who is honest to others, whether kith or kin, O Lord,
Or even the ones who serve the needs of cattle in the field,
Shall themselves find pasture and peace.

So, God, I worship you and seek to avoid disobedience,
Whether in the challenges of family, or in the life of the clan,
In community service, or with ignorance like beasts in the field.

Reveal to me your purpose and your requirements,
So that I may attain your dominion,
The path of life that is in accord with your will.

As your priest, I call for truth and seek to fulfill my calling.
Assist me to undertake my ministry to the people,
By taking counsel with you, O Lord of Wisdom.

Come to me now, in your manifest essence, O God.
May my faith in you be vindicated among the believers.
Let all your promises to me be seen as true.

All that was, everything that is, and all that shall be comes from You.
You reward us all according to our faithfulness, and we pray
That we may grow in righteousness in response to your dominion.

O Lord, you are the Mighty One of Wisdom.
Devotion and truth which nurture human life belong to you.
Hear my prayer and have mercy upon me in any reckoning to be made.

Arise within me, O Lord, and fulfill my desire
To serve you perfectly with unfailing devotion.
Accept my self-offering and confer your power for good.

From afar, draw near and reveal yourself to me.
Let me share in your sovereign reign, O Lord,
And instruct your people in devotion and in truth.

As an offering, this camel herder gives body and breath,
So that you may be served in good thoughts and good deeds,
Described in words that correspond to your dominion.
Everything that is good in life comes from you, O Lord of Wisdom.

Glory to God[7]

I realized that your very nature is bountiful, O God,
When I recognized you as the originator of life.
You offer both words of revelation and deeds which bear fruit.
Sun, moon and stars of creation reflect your glory, as may we.

As this turning point of realization, Lord, you come and bless.
Your sovereignty and your wisdom lead us on to truth.
Our devotion will allow you to guide us in wisdom.

When your wisdom encircled me and inquired of me,
"Who are you? To what people do you belong?
What will it take for your Lord to engage you?"

Then I answered you, first and foremost, I am a simple camel herder.
But I am an enemy of falsehood and lying, as best I know.
My goal in life is to respond to the glory I see in you, Lord,
To worship and praise you with songs of rejoicing.

Salvation[8]

I know I am ineffective here, My Wise Lord.
To which land shall I flee?
Where shall I seek refuge?
I am excluded from family and clan.

The community I would serve has rejected me
And the tyrants of the territory are no better.
How can I please you, Lord, where there is no response?

My cattle are few and my followers are scattered.
I lament my situation to you as my only true friend.
Give me a vision of your strength in Wisdom.

O Lord of Wisdom, when will you send your Redeemers,
To bring in the sparkling light of salvation,
The Redeemers who offer inspiration and guidance?
As for me, here and now, I rely on your Spirit alone.

This I Ask[9]

This I ask of you, so tell me truly Lord,
How are you to be worshipped?
O Lord of Wisdom, will you speak to me as a friend?
And may other worshippers gain wisdom from our encounter?

This I ask of you, so tell me truly Lord,
Can life be renewed by salvation during this existence?
And can human beings be blessed through understanding,
With your truth acting as the healer, and you as our friend?

This I ask of you, so tell me truly Lord,
At the beginning of creation, who was the father of order?
Who set the sun and the stars in their orbits and caused the moon to wax and wane?
These things and many more I long to understand, Lord God of Wisdom.

This I ask of you, so tell me truly Lord,
Who holds up the earth and who keeps the sky from falling?
Who brought water into being to nourish the plants?
Who but you, Wise Lord, is the breath of the wind and the spirit of the cloud?

This I ask of you, so tell me truly Lord,
Which worker of wonders called forth the speed of light
Across the expanse of darkness, in rhythms of sleep and waking?
From whom came times of dawn, mid-day and nightfall to regulate our work?

This I ask of you, so tell me truly Lord,
How am I to grow in understanding of
Your revelations enshrined in sublime teachings?
I learned of them first through your wisdom, my greatest joy.

This I ask of you, so tell me truly Lord,
How am I to remain faithful to you in daily living?
Will you teach me, Lord, how to be loyal to your sovereignty?
Or is it only you that can dwell in truth and wisdom?

This I ask of you, so tell me truly Lord,
Is the revelation I received for everyone,
And will it be enough to sustain my livelihood?
Or am I to live a life of devotion apart from the world?

This I ask of you, so tell me truly Lord,
How shall others who see the vision express their devotion?
I was chosen to spread abroad your truth,
But I look upon others with apprehension.

This I ask of you, so tell me truly Lord,
Who is really a disciple of the truth and who lives by lies?
Am I to proclaim your truth to those who are hostile,
Or is salvation intended for those who receive it gladly?

Day of Judgment[10]

Protect me as long as this perishable world is dominant, O Lord,
Until wickedness and lies are obliterated in the Day of Judgment.
Mortals and immortals alike, both good and evil, abound,
But your promise of salvation gives your devotees the courage to go on.

Tell me, O Lord of Wisdom, since you know all things,
Will the just overcome the unjust in this life,
Or do we await the Day of Judgment
For the glorious renewal of life that is to come?

Right teaching is available to the one who is able to understand
The truth from you, O Lord of Wisdom, giver of all good.
In your benevolence, you provide the most profound insights,
Those that are integral to your wise understanding.

So in your great wisdom, O Lord,
Welcome those mortals who respond to your invitation.
Those whose thoughts and actions are in accord
With your desires and purposes.

Let good rulers govern us rather than corrupt,
So that surrounded by good governance,
We may live in piety and in harmony with nature,
As symbolized by the contentment of the cow.

For it is our cattle that provide for us,
Even as we provide for them.
And the vegetation so prevalent in creation
Remains as the context for the life we share.

In such a life, why should cruelty and violence prevail?
Let all who would triumph do so with understanding
Of the truth which underlies our existence,
And which draws us together for worship in your house, O God.

Truly I acknowledge your dominion, O Wise Lord,
What will you provide for me in response to my devotion?
Where will I find the resources for the followers you desire
To promote your cause of justice and of truth?

When will I be able to perceive the manifestation of sovereignty
Which will pit your truth against the hostile malice all around us?
Let me see the specific expression of your truth
In the coming Savior, who brings his reward with him.

O Lord of Wisdom, when will mortals see salvation?
When do we eliminate our intoxication with power,
Which deludes both the rulers and their people,
And through which these lands are corrupted?

When, O Wise Lord, can we expect to see devotion and justice combine
To give safety and good pasture beneath your sovereign control?
Who will establish peace and security in the midst of bloody conflict?
From whom will the penetrating insights come to set us free in truth?

Such will be the Saviors and Redeemers of the lands,
Working through wisdom in harmony with truth.
Your Saoshyants will fulfill your purposes in the universe.
They are destined to prevail against all the forces of doom.

This selection of clustered verses is paraphrased after the formal equivalence used even by Mary Boyce and others, serving to illustrate the intimacy between Zoroaster and God. It is limited to excerpts from Gathas, universally accepted as being by Zoroaster himself, expressed with a spiritual sophistication that is a breakthrough as compared with both the older theological constructs of his Vedic predecessors and the awkward caricatures of his religion represented by Western translations. It is not suggested that the above paraphrases represent an advance in linguistic scholarship. If there is any improvement in the presentation, it is derived from a more flowing English syntax and the application of our growing knowledge about Zoroaster, his influence, and his prophetic passion, expressed in dynamic equivalence.

In the cadences presented here, we may at last glimpse the turning point in which belief develops into the spiritual power that transformed the people of the ancient world, as stated, "from a creaturely dependence to active partnership with the Divine" through either redemption atonement or at-One-ment. Indeed, we also see something of that understanding in biblical personas who predate Zoroaster: Abraham, Moses, the pre-Zoroastrian Hebrew prophets, and perhaps elsewhere. But it is Zoroaster who sees and presents this partnership or union as a universal vision that is open to all humanity.

The impact of that realization, as articulated and implemented by his followers at the apex of Persian rule as the world's first superpower, with reverberations from Europe and the Middle East to the perhaps more exquisite articulations in China and India, triggered the spiritual tsunami in what we now call the Axial Age. Israel itself was, of course, among those most dramatically impacted due to its close association with Zoroastrians in Persia during the Babylonian Exile. But the birth of Buddhism immediately thereafter, the subsequent reforms of Hinduism, and other related developments, both philosophical and religious, have been well documented elsewhere and will be illustrated in volume 3 of this trilogy. The connections to Christianity and Islam are also presented in volume 2 in summarizing the universal vision.

We also see the reflection of Hebrew and Christian Scriptures in the Quran, but the issue of the place of Zoroastrian Scriptures there falls into the category of what, in conversation, is sometimes called "the elephant in the room"—that is, something clearly obvious but not discussed or acknowledged by anyone. Since the Roman Empire and the rule of Alexander the Great are mentioned in the Quran, and since regional religions like Judaism and Christianity are discussed, how could it be possible that the Quran makes no mention of Persia and Zoroastrianism, Arabia's most powerful neighbor and most significant external religious influence, respectively? The fact is that these influences are indeed addressed in the Quran, but in such a manner that they are so pervasive as to be almost invisible, forming the context of much of the Islamic Scripture. Just as water is invisible to fish and air is invisible to humans, it may be only in an interfaith study like this one that the "water" (Persia) and the "air" (Zoroastrianism) of the Quran can be seen and identified in the "corrected and true" revelations to Muhammad in the understanding of Muslims. We shall also attempt to articulate this phenomenon more completely in volume 2.

Prior to turning to Judaism and the Eastern texts in detail, and before including Christianity and Islam in the wider vision, we need to consider how Zoroastrianism could have inspired both monistic and monotheistic manifestations, and even consider how the former may be considered by some to be the fulfilment or conclusion of the world's spiritual pilgrimage from polytheism through monotheism to monism. This much is required before we are also able to give the Tao Te Ching, the Analects, the Dhammapada, and the Bhagavad Gita their due.

notes

1. Dk. iv. 21; v. 34; vii. 5, 11.
2. Philosopher of Smyrna, ca. 250 BCE.
3. N. H. xxx. 2.
4. By Arda Viraf in the Middle Persian Pahlavi language of the third century CE.
5. Yasna 8:1–27.
6. Yasna 33:1–7 and 10–14.
7. Yasna 43:5–8.
8. Yasna 46:1–3.
9. Yasna 44:1–5 and 8–12.
10. Yasna 48:1–12.

7
the fraternal twins of world religions

R EADERS MAY HAVE BARELY TAKEN NOTE OF THE COMMENT BY KARL FRIEDRICH GELDNER IN the exordium to the effect that "the Zurvanites represented Ormazd and Ahriman as twin sons proceeding from the fundamental principle of all— *Zrvana Akarana*, or limitless time." Who has even heard of the Zurvanites, and yet this Zoroastrian cult in the Near West[1] may be the easiest way to illustrate the Zoroastrian influence also found in mainstream Eastern and oriental thought, particularly Hindu and Buddhist beliefs. Monism and monotheism do not look alike—hence "fraternal" in the title of this chapter—but twins they may be, with spiritual DNA indicating that each has a strand of common parentage in different Zoroastrian manifestations, East and West.

Zurvan, as a name for the *Ultimate*, or God (from the Sanskrit word *Sarva*, via the Avestan *zurvan*), came to mean "infinity," referred to as *The Ancient of Days* in Zoroastrian hymns and prayers, and later in the Bible,[2] an obvious Z reference. The name is also freighted with semantic inferences describing monistic deity, as found in India and throughout the East. In the Middle West (western Persia and west from there to the Mediterranean, from an Eastern perspective), *Zurvanism*, as it existed for centuries, refers to Zurvan as the God of infinity in time and space, known simply as the One. The name *Zurvan* was revived from earlier Vedic traditions about a hundred years after Zoroaster, whose teachings the cult claimed to correctly interpret, rightly or wrongly, regarding monotheism as merely a step to monism. The latent dualism in Zoroastrianism was a problem thus solved by regarding good and bad, justice and evil, right and wrong, and other opposites as manifestations of the two spirits, *Spenta Mainyu* (Benevolent Spirit) and *Angra Mainyu* (Malevolent Spirit), twin brother offspring from Zurvan and his creation. They were known to people as Ahura Mazda (Lord of Wisdom) and Ahriman (The Adversary). By correct and creative dealing with both devas, the devotees aspired to ultimate Oneness with the eternal and infinite Zurvan.

None of this might matter very much, except that Zurvanism is an illustration of Zoroastrian monism accessible to Western scholars, enabling us to understand the impact of Zoroastrianism (regarded by its adherents today as monotheistic) in the development of monism in the East. The Zurvan cult simmered through western areas of the Persian Empire in the last half of the Achaemenid period, during the rule of the descendants of Cyrus. Zurvanism actually held sway in most of the later Sasanid period, finally disappearing soon after 651 CE under the Muslims, while monotheistic Zoroastrianism has survived in reduced circumstances until the modern era. The importance of Zurvanism to us is as an illustration of how Zoroaster's message acted as a stimulus, triggering a variety of responses in the Axial Age, including monism, prevalent in the East but also visible in the West early in the Common Era, through Spinoza to "New Age" religion and other trends in our time.

Monistic Zurvanism had its beginning in the West at about the same time that the Zurvanistic Magi were exerting a similar influence in China and northern India. Their stimulus was resisted by Confucius, massaged by Lao Tzu, taken to rapturous heights by the Buddha, and expressed in universally applicable terms by Hindus by the time of the Bhagavad Gita.

This linkage between Zoroastrianism and monism is thus easily documented in the West, but it is more dominant in the East, where it is pervasive in most religious traditions. The particular dichotomy between monism and monotheism, inherited by the world from the followers of Zoroaster, may form the basis of one of the main religious discussions in the twenty-first-century practice of Scriptural Reasoning. This connection should lay to rest the objections of some critics of the thesis in *Three Testaments* and *Four Testaments* regarding plausible relationships among the seven world religions. We will return to what this means shortly, but before affirming the Zoroastrian heritage of Eastern monism, let us at least establish the bona fides of Zurvanism and monism in the Middle West, since the whole concept may be new to many readers.

The oldest reference to the Zurvan sect is attributed to Eudemus of Rhodes (370–300 BCE) in his *History of Theology*, cited by Damascius in *Difficulties and Solutions of First Principles* in the sixth century CE. In it Eudemus describes a cult among the Persians that considered Eternal Infinity the primordial parent of Light and Darkness,[3] as seeming references to Ahura Mazda and Ahriman. There are also contemporary inscriptions invoking the name of Zurvan, but most written sources on this subject during the Sasanian period are from Christian critics, both Armenian and Syrian.

For that matter, if all we had to go on were those early Christian commentaries on the lengthy Sasanian era, we would assume that Zoroastrianism was thoroughly monistic, as it may have been (by names other than Zurvanite) when it was presented by Magi in the Far East. As it was, Mazdean monotheism was actually the norm in the West through most of the classical Achaemenid era, again after the Sasanians, and then down through the ages to modern times. But we highlight the Zurvanites to show how the monistic phenomenon was an option, even in the West, where its devotees were always the minority party. Even under Sasanian rule, their modus operandi might be compared to modern "Charismatic Catholics" who are enthusiastic in private or in small groups, but who also attend regular mass as loyal members of the Roman Catholic Church. Even when the ancient Persian royal family embraced Zurvanism for a time, the state religion maintained the rituals of what was considered orthodox monotheistic Mazdianism.

After Zoroaster's time, in extant Avesta texts published before the Sasanian era, Zurvan appears in the evolving scriptural trilogy twice. Zurvan is praised as represented by *Vata* and *Vayu* (Space and Air),[4] and plants only thrive as they develop according to the pattern established over "time" as embodied in Zurvan.[5] Zurvan also appears twice in passing in the more recent extant Vendidad section of the Avesta, but without significance, and makes no appearance in the Gathas of Zoroaster himself, nor in the Yazatas, and certainly not in the *Khordah Avesta* (Little Avesta) of enduring popularity.

However, something had apparently given these Zurvanites the idea that Zoroastrianism (even if they did not yet all use that name) should be interpreted in a monistic fashion. In the Avesta, as we have it, the Yasna section on worship begins as "Chapter 28" of the whole. Obviously somewhere between the five opening Gatha poems by Zoroaster and the seven chapters of *Yasna Haptanhaiti*, there were once twenty-three chapters, poems, or sutras of other material that might have been highly influential at some stage of the religion's development. Three scraps of verses, usually prepended to the Gathas, may be from that corpus, where the Gathas habitually address Ahura Mazda (Lord of Wisdom), but the Yasnas after the gap are mainly about the "Mindful Lord." As perhaps from the twenty-three prayer poems now missing in between, the scraps of these "detached mantras," as they are sometimes called, also address a "Mindful One" (a term we will see again and again when we consider monistic aspects of Buddhism and Hinduism).

This is not much to go on since, with five Gathas containing six thousand words, we may assume the missing twenty-three early sutras could contain thirty thousand more. But the opening words of the first one, for example, could have come straight out of the Dhammapada or the Bhagavad Gita:

> Just as he is the Master one would choose,
> So the guidance of right and good thoughts,
> Of actions is assigned to the Mindful One,
> With power to the Lord as guru to the destitute.[6]

In later reconstructions of verses remembered by the majority, were most of these monistic-leaning verses neglected or forgotten because they were the treasure of only the heterodox Zurvanites? Is this the basis of Zoroastrian stimulation that was taken further East by Magi in China and Zurvan travelers and interlocutors in India? We will know if and when we find the Dead Zee Scrolls.

In the seventh century CE, Zoroastrianism was supplanted by Islam throughout the Persian Empire. The transition happened gradually in areas of Mazdean orthodox monotheism, like the northwestern provinces of Zoroaster's heartland and in the villages, but rapidly among the ruling Sasanian elite with their Zurvanistic tendencies. Early Islam would have had little patience with a monism in which people strive to unite with God rather than worship and serve God, especially since that monism presented itself with twin spirits of Ahura Mazda and Ahriman and other dualistic manifestations. Yet Zoroastrians appear in the Quran, where they are most often referred to as Sabaeans or Magians, for better and for worse.

"Truly, those who have believed, those who became Jews and Sabaeans and Christians—whoever believed in God and the Last Day and did as one in accord with morality, then, there will be neither fear in them nor will they feel remorse."[7]

"Truly, those who have believed, those who became Jews and Sabaeans and the Christians and the Zoroastrians, and those who ascribed partners—truly God will distinguish between them on the day of Resurrection. Truly God over everything is a witness."[8]

Islamic respect for Zoroastrian monotheism continued down through the ages in a Persian Islamic culture that still today respectfully reserves a seat in the parliament of Iran for a Zoroastrian representative.

Meanwhile, in Greece, at the beginning of the core Axial Age years, Parmenides of Elia propounded a monistic view of reality in his poem *On Nature*. In one section of the poem,[9] Parmenides says that "what is (i.e., reality) must be understood as being One," that "change is an illusion," and that "existence is timeless." In another section called "The Way of Opinion," he argues that the world of appearances is a false realm from which we must become detached in order to enter into the reality of the One. The monism of Parmenides is virtually identical to Vedantic Hinduism, though it is hard to imagine any link except Zurvanic Zoroastrianism. Parmenides never quotes Zoroaster by name, but he greatly influenced Plato, who does. Indeed, Plato presents Parmenides as being in conflict with Socrates in the play *Parmenides*, where the monism of Parmenides stands in contrast to the monotheism of Socrates, both conceivably responding to the Zoroastrian stimulus that was in the air. Monotheism won out in the West, but we may observe that the collapse of faith in the gods of Olympus happened at the very same time that in the East the old Vedic gods became subsumed under the umbrella of monism, both developments taking place within two generations of Zoroaster's life and prophetic ministry.

There is enough similarity between Zurvan and the Lord of Creation (Prajapati) in Vedic literature,[10] as well as in literature ascribed to the mythical poet Orpheus concerning the origins of the gods, for us to at least recognize the Z factor in them both. The fluidity of these ideas in the fifth century BCE is palpable, despite academic submissions quoted earlier suggesting that these momentous developments took place independently in many places at the same time. To go a step further, these inferences begin to look like mounting evidence that monotheism and monism have roots that are similar, if not intertwined. Practitioners of Scriptural Reasoning may soon be considering the common themes of "creation and apocalypse, angels and demons, salvation and damnation, resurrection and final judgment, heaven and hell," and other elements of the shared heritage of the seven religions, but the overarching discussion will surely be the relationship or the contrast between monotheism and monism.

In the West, an ultimate "One," drawing "all" to itself by operating through the facade of twin deva divinities, good and evil, finally led to a pessimistic fatalism that characterized a classical Zurvanism, not too different from the fatalism sometimes identified with Indian religions. This might stand in contrast to a more positive Mazdeanism in which devotees are encouraged to serve Ahura Mazda in the attainment of the victory of good over evil in the eternal kingdom. Of course, if we acknowledge the fatalism experienced in serene monism, we must also concede the damage of activist monotheism, from warfare to climate change, brought about by human activity, mainly among monotheists.

For Zurvanism to have simmered for several centuries, to have survived foreign domination, and to have flourished in the new Sasanian era, there must have been an agency, if not a separate organization, of these monistic Zoroastrians. Such a zealous tradition can be identified as the Magi, whose earlier religion, before virtually all of them identified with the Zoroastrian state religion, may well have been dualistic. The indications of this would take up too much space to document here, but the opportunity to highlight the potential dualism in Zoroaster's message might have helped the Magi feel at home under the Zoroastrian umbrella. It blended well with the developing Zurvan tendency to present the conflict between Ahura Mazda and Ahriman as a creative tension leading to resolution in the Oneness of God rather than the victory of good over evil. Is this the face of Zoroastrianism the Magi also presented in India and China?

This is speculation, but the Magi did disappear from the stage of world history during the quashing of Zurvanism by Islam, while more orthodox Mazdean Zoroastrians survived. Another conjecture of interest might be regarding the effect, if any, that the conflict between Zurvanism and Islam might have had on the development of militant Shiism in Iran as a distinct branch of Islam. More to the point in reference to evidence that will be presented in this trilogy is the irrefutable fact demonstrated in *Four Testaments* that the Magi became established in China even before Zoroaster's time. They would surely have maintained their Iranian connections and were almost certainly the conduit of Zoroastrian monistic ideas to the East.[11]

Monotheism dominated the scene in the Middle East and all over in the West throughout the Middle Ages by way of Judaism, Christianity, and Islam, while the exact opposite was the case in Southeast Asia and the Orient, where monism prevailed in Taoism, Buddhism, Hinduism, and Jainism (the latter as part of the pattern, though not usually considered a "world religion"). Such equilibrium was challenged in the East by Confucianism, and later by the arrival of European missionaries following the Renaissance and Reformation eras, and in the West by the philosophical writings of Baruch Spinoza (1632–1677).

Regarded by many as the thinker who laid the groundwork for the eighteenth-century Enlightenment, as well as for aspects of modern biblical criticism and current conceptions of the self and, arguably, the universe, Spinoza has come to be considered one of Western philosophy's most important thinkers. Indeed, philosopher Georg Wilhelm Friedrich Hegel said of all contemporary philosophers, "You are either a Spinozist or you are not a philosopher at all."[12]

It is traditionally assumed that Spinoza worked his way into a profound monism in isolation from any monistic precedents elsewhere in the world. A careful analysis, however, not of his writings, but of his family and personal connections, might stimulate some interesting second thoughts in that regard with reference to this study. A resemblance between Spinoza's philosophy and Eastern monistic traditions has been the subject of previous inconclusive investigations based on textual evidence; we will build on them by taking a different approach.

Theodore Goldstucker of Germany, a noted scholar of Sanskrit literature, was one among several in the nineteenth century who noticed a particular textual connection that seemed too obvious to ignore. He described the similarities between Spinoza's religious ideas and the Vedanta beliefs of India in some detail. Spinoza's conception of God is "so exact a representation of the ideas of the Vedanta that we might have suspected its founder to have borrowed the fundamental principles of his system from the Hindus, except that his biography convinces us that he was wholly unacquainted with their doctrines."[13] Others have been equally spellbound by the comparison of ideas: "Spinoza was a man whose very life is a picture of that moral purity and intellectual indifference to the transitory charms of this world, which is the constant longing of the true Vedanta philosopher. Comparing the fundamental ideas of both we should have no difficulty in proving that if Spinoza had been a Hindu, his system would in all probability mark a final phase of the Vedanta philosophy."[14]

In these and other instances, even allowing for translation into another language, we appear to be looking at the same words in Spinoza's writing and the Vedanta written two thousand years earlier. How could this be? Max Muller, in his lectures on the subject, noted the striking connection between Vedanta and the philosophical system of Spinoza, saying that "the Brahman, as conceived in the Upanishads and defined by Sankara, is clearly the same as Spinoza's 'Substantia.'"[15] Helena Blavatsky, a founder of the Theosophical Society, spells out the core detail of Spinoza's religious thought as compared to Vedanta when she says, "As to Spinoza's Deity—*natura naturans*—it is the Vedantic Deity pure and simple."[16]

Is there anything that could be discovered by standing back further than these commentators that would allow us to make an actual connection? As it turns out, Spinoza would have had good reasons to disguise any pagan source for his ideas about God. By the age of seventeen, he had left formal educational pursuits to take over the family business of importing goods from India and elsewhere in the East and to begin his writing career. By the age of twenty-three, he was expelled from the synagogue and spurned in the Jewish community for radical views never completely described in any available source. Books by his pantheist friend and philosophical mentor, Francis Van den Ende (1602–1674), were placed on the *Index of Forbidden Books* by the Catholic Church, and it was not long before Spinoza was given the same honor for theology considered heretical. A few years later Van den Ende would be executed, along with Johan de Witt (1625–1672), Spinoza's political mentor. For Spinoza to publish views that were merely radical would be one thing, but seeking acceptance for ideas originating in pagan India could have put his life in danger in that environment.

So even supposing we could illustrate any probable linkage with Eastern thought, Spinoza would have good reason to shield any connection with the Hindu Vedanta.

As it is, he wore a signet ring that he used to mark his letters and that was engraved with the word *caute* (Latin for "cautiously")[17] under a rose, suggesting his familiarity with the Vedanta legend of two divinities in conversation: "Brahma, the creator and Vishnu, the protector, were discussing which flower was the most beautiful. Brahma favoured the lotus and Vishnu the rose. After seeing the arbour laden with fragrant roses in Vishnu's celestial garden, Brahma acknowledged the supremacy of the rose over all the flowers, including the lotus."[18] This supposedly explains how the rose became the flower associated with the Vedanta. This symbol was adopted by Spinoza, "cautiously," as expressed on his seal.

Spinoza's Jewish family had moved from Portugal to Amsterdam in 1593, having previously established themselves in mercantile endeavors in which connections with Goa, Daman, and Diu in Portuguese India and elsewhere in the East were essential. Seven years after his family's 1595 establishment of a company in Holland, the Dutch East India Company was formed through a union with several other such companies. In Spinoza's personal library, on display in his cottage museum today, we find his copies of books by Pieter and Jean de la Court, including *Political Maxims of the State of Holland*, which critiques the trade in nutmegs, mace, cloves, cinnamon, and, notably, Indian quilts and carpets.[19] In the 1600s, the British East India Company imported perfumes and cosmetics from India after Queen Elizabeth I adopted and popularized the use of imported red lipstick. French fashion in the seventeenth century was dominated by silks from India, despite a late entry into trade there by the French. On their buildings, the Dutch themselves adopted the frilly gables of Indian architecture. We can only speculate about what other fashions from India may have been under critique in Europe, and with Spinoza importing spices and textiles, it is hard to imagine that this brilliant scholar never took note of books or papers—even the used paper employed in packing spices and delicate wares.

But the connections do not end with his business associations. While establishment Protestants were as unimpressed as Jews and Catholics with Spinoza and his ideas (though he was finally buried in a Reformed Church cemetery), from his diaries we know that he had an intimate circle of Mennonite friends. These Mennonites had been prominent in the Dutch East India Company in its early years and had traveled to India. They were "free thinkers" and eventually became an annoyance to the more profiteering shareholders. "The Mennonites withdrew from the trade when the company became involved in conquest and violence."[20] Again we ask the question: How much did Spinoza and his circle know about India and what was going on there? Were their concerns strictly limited to business matters, or did they have access to information and materials of wider, and even spiritual, interest?

Spinoza was considered by some to be an atheist because he used the word *God* (Deus) to signify a concept that was different from that of traditional Judeo-Christian monotheism: "Spinoza expressly denies personality and consciousness to God; he has neither intelligence, feeling, nor will; he does not act according to purpose, but everything follows necessarily from his nature, according to law."[21] Accordingly, we might even say that Spinoza's detached God[22] is antithetical to a Jewish God who chooses and empowers people to serve him, to a Christian God who loves them, to a Muslim God of justice who will call people to account in a Final Judgment, and to all anthropomorphic conceptions of the Divinity. The monistic concept of a God who not only "goes with the flow" but also *is* the Flow will be discussed in volume 3, beginning with the monistic images of Taoism.

Spinoza recommends *amor intellectualist dei* (the intellectual love of God) as the supreme good for man,[23] but Spinoza's God does not have free will,[24] he does not have purposes or intentions,[25] and Spinoza insists that "neither intellect nor emotion will pertain to the nature of God."[26] Moreover, while we may love God, we need to remember that God is really not the kind of "being" who could ever love us back. "He who loves God cannot strive that God should love him in return," says Spinoza.[27] The purpose of prayerful meditation in monism is not to get God to change the natural order of things, which may appear as good or evil, or to plead that events may be tilted in our favor. It is rather that each believer should seek and attain grace to accept and deal with life by attuning one's self with God and God's detached nature, a contrast with monotheists pleading with God to attune himself to humanity's needs and desires. This "becoming One with God" may result in a state of gentle bliss, as we shall consider when we get to the Eastern examples. Or is this akin to fatalism, which may not be pleasing to a monotheistic God who has a program and invites human creaturely participation and who enables humans to engage in a partnership?

This brief summary of Spinoza's life and works has been altogether inadequate as a summary of the great philosopher's religion. Indeed, it presents religion in a cold, detached form, though American critic Harold Bloom has written, "As a teacher of reality, Spinoza practiced his own wisdom, and was surely one of the most exemplary human beings ever to have lived."[28] We hope to remedy that "cold, detached" image of monistic religion in our volume 3 (*Four Testaments*), which presents the same monism in a more appealing light. Since Spinoza, there have been several fringe groups and a few notable individuals in the West who have exemplified a monistic faith, but there has been no significant mass *movement* as such, akin to Zurvanism. Yet the late twentieth-century vogue of interest in Hinduism and Buddhism in the West may have been a harbinger of profound discussions to come in the Scriptural Reasoning of the interfaith environment of the twenty-first century, in which religion is both deterministic and dynamic as well as personal and warm.

Indeed, the religious situation is suddenly once again deterministic and dynamic throughout the whole world, and the relationship between monism and monotheism has become a critical issue. Monotheism and monism might be regarded as the DNA of the spiritual life of humanity. By coincidence or otherwise, both strands of this double helix appeared West and East in the philosophies and religious expressions of the Axial Age, immediately following the burst of spiritual energy emitted by that Persian prophet Zoroaster, whose spectacular prophetic utterances flared into prominence around 588 BCE.

In the new Axial Age of the twenty-first century, Western monotheism continues to attract interest in the East with the spectacular growth of Christianity in China, Korea, the Philippines, southern India, and elsewhere. At the same time, Eastern religious influence grows daily in the West through the influx and increasing pervasiveness of millions of monistic immigrants, establishing temples of many kinds among the churches, synagogues, and mosques in cities large and small. There has perhaps never been such an exciting time in the history of religion, and in spite of uncertainty in Western Europe and North America, the twenty-first century may someday be regarded as the century of religion, much as the twentieth century has become known as the century of science and technology.

Monotheism appeared among the Israelites much earlier and got a tremendous boost among the Jews in Babylonian Exile with the advent of rule there by Zoroastrians whose founder may have accepted the Oneness of God from Israelite exiles in the first place—just seventy-five years earlier. With phenomenal consequences at the beginning of the Axial Age, monism came on the world scene later than monotheism's first appearance with Moses, but it blossomed in the East in the writings and teachings of Lao Tzu in China and the Buddha in India in precisely the same post-Zoroaster historical epoch as monotheism began to spread and flourish in the West. Lao Tzu and the Buddha were followed by the ethical reforms of Confucius in China and a reformation of Hinduism in India, culminating in the Bhagavad Gita, the crown of Vedanta. Confucianism may be seen as a reaction to foreign religious influence on behalf of Chinese traditional values, while developments in Hinduism built on such influences, much as Christianity and Islam eventually followed Judaism to the fore as champions of monotheism.

Lao Tzu and Buddha may have both been stimulated by a degree of spiritual animation surrounding the spread of Zoroastrian influence, but it is not contended that either they or their followers became Zoroastrians. Rather, in response to that vision of personal intimacy with the transcendence of Divinity, and the impact of the Zoroastrian program of "right deeds" to accompany "right words" and "right thoughts," they would have presented their own genius in concert with spiritual advances that, while perhaps not "worldwide," seem to have extended throughout the length of the Silk Route and into its peripheral offshoots at either end.

notes

1. Our term for the Middle East and Greece when matters are considered from an Eastern perspective.

2. *The Ancient of Days* as a name for God also appears in the Bible as a Z phrase, located in Daniel, as might be expected by students and other readers now familiar with the Babylonian connection.

3. Dhalla (1932), 331–32.

4. Yasna 72:10.

5. Yasht 13:56.

6. The author's own rendering of Yasna 27:13, in which "guru" is often rendered "teacher" by Western translators.

7. Quran 5:69 (Sublime Quran).

8. Quran 22:17 (Sublime Quran).

9. *The Way of Truth.*

10. *Rig Veda* 10:129.

11. Victor Mair in *Dynamica in the History of Religions between Asia and Europe*, 97.

12. *Hegel's History of Philosophy*, 146.

13. *Literary Remains of the Late Professor Theodore Goldstucker*, W. H. Allen (1879), 32.

14. *The Westminster Review, Volumes 78–79* (London: Baldwin, Cradock, and Joy, 1862), 478.

15. *Three Lectures on the Vedanta Philosophy*, F. Max Muller (Kessinger Publishing, 2003), 123.

16. *H. P. Blavatsky's Collected Writings*, Volume 13 (Quest Books), 308–10.

17. Matthew Stewart, *The Courtier and the Heretic* (W. W. Norton, 2006), 106.

18. Girija Viraraghavan, *The History of Roses in India*, IndianRoseFederation.org, Pune, India, August 20, 2013.

19. The *Spinoza*-huis or Spinoza Museum in Rijnsburg.

20. Samuel Cramer, "Mennoniten," in *Realencyclopedie für Protestantische Theologie and Kirche*, 24 vols., 3rd ed., edited by J. J. Herzog and Albert Hauck (Leipzig: J. H. Hinrichs, 1896–1913), 611.

21. Frank Thilly, *A History of Philosophy*, § 47 (New York: Holt & Co., 1914).

22. "I believe in Spinoza's God who reveals himself in the orderly harmony of what exists, not in a God who concerns himself with fates and actions of human beings." These words were spoken by Albert Einstein, upon being asked whether he believed in God by Rabbi Herbert Goldstein of the Institutional Synagogue, New York, April 24, 1921, published in the *New York Times*, April 25, 1929; from *Einstein: The Life and Times*, ed. Ronald W. Clark (New York: World Publishing Co., 1971), 413. It is also cited in a telegram to a Jewish newspaper, 1929, Einstein Archive 33-272, from Alice Calaprice, ed., *The Expanded Quotable Einstein* (Princeton, NJ: Princeton University).

23. *Stanford Encyclopedia of Philosophy*, vol. 5, 33.

24. Ibid., vol. 1, 32c1.

25. Ibid., appendix I.

26. Ibid., vol. 1, 17s1.

27. Ibid., vol. 5, 19, http://plato.stanford.edu/entries/pantheism/#Per.

28. Harold Bloom (book reviewer) (June 16, 2006), "'Deciphering Spinoza, the Great Original,' book review of *Betraying Spinoza. The Renegade Jew Who Gave Us Modernity* by Rebecca Goldstein," *New York Times*.

monism and monotheism
in actual practice

WITH APOLOGIES TO THOSE WHO WOULD HAVE US STICK TO A MORE STRICTLY ACADEMIC discourse, we should now fulfill the promise made in our earlier "Disclaimers" to consider these matters as they appear in actual practice. From an academic perspective, this may contribute to an opening up of the Western monotheistic discipline of Scriptural Reasoning to Eastern monists. It may also show how it was possible for some of Zoroaster's followers into the Oneness of God to become monists (mainly in the East) and others to become monotheists (mainly in the West). It is not our intention to endorse or to recommend one over the other, but rather to promote understanding and some sharing of treasures.

The depth of Spinoza's monotheistic theology does not bear a lot of resemblance to the everyday spiritual practice of many who profess to be monists, including most Hindus, many Buddhists, and some Taoists. Spinoza is these days admired and quoted by monistic leaders everywhere, but at the risk of obfuscating the issues, let us attempt to address the differences and the relationships between monotheism and monism in practice. Many in the West have adopted the misconception that oriental religions require those who seek unity with the One to give up their individuality, to perhaps retire to a mountain retreat, and to forswear family, business, and other responsibilities. Some elements of later Buddhism may make the case that such withdrawal is permitted or even required, but that is not our understanding of the earlier Dhammapada or the Tao Te Ching, where we become One with God in the very thick of communal activity and "go with the Flow" in the midst of family life and other responsibilities.

The Western view of "atonement" for sins implies not oneness but reconciliation of particularities that remain very separate as creator and creature, in contrast to the *at-One-ment* with God that monistic faith offers. But in a fulsome understanding of monism, can some sense of individual identity endure in both this life and the life to come? In a marriage, Jews and Christians sometimes employ the biblical image of two becoming one, even described in Scripture as "one flesh,"[1] but their oneness allows for individual particularity within the union. The Oneness of the Divine

Universe does not connote participation in a homogenous blob but rather describes the interconnectedness of All, including many parts.

In discussing the monism of Hindus, interfaith author Adam Hamilton[2] addresses the matter thus, with an overture to the understanding of Christians and other monotheists:

> What happens when we finally have attained knowledge and have exorcised all the bad karma from our lives? We receive salvation—moksha—which is a release from suffering and the cycle of death and rebirth. We are then united with God in a state which is called "nirvana." Some Hindus believe this union is complete; in other words, nothing is left of the individual. We become like a drop of water in a vast ocean, our individuality and distinctness forever lost. Others in Hinduism believe there is a sense in which we remain somewhat distinct, perhaps like a fish that dwells in the ocean.[3]

Both *monotheism* and *monism* are relatively new terms, originating in the seventeenth and eighteenth centuries and completely unknown to the ancients, East or West. Rather than being seen as contradictory, in this early period of the twenty-first century we might begin to consider the two concepts as poles or end points on a continuum. Some believers are at one end and some at the other (and perhaps many in between), but in our time it may be possible to maintain one's own faith position with integrity while benefiting from an enriching vision from the other end of the spectrum.

The three most familiar forms of monotheism in the West are explored in *Three Testaments: Torah, Gospel, and Quran*, volume 2 of this trilogy. Monism also may take a variety of forms, the three most widely recognized being Taoism, Buddhism, and Hinduism, as presented in volume 3 under the title *Four Testaments: Tao Te Ching, Analects, Dhammapada, Bhagavad Gita*. The Oneness we seek is described as the *Flow of Life* in Taoism, in which a person swims against the current, spits into the wind, or rows against the tide at their own peril. A person experiences fulfillment as an individual by finding their destiny within the flow as a part of the whole and playing their role in a positive manner within it. Buddhism finds unity in the liberation that comes from an emptying out of individual particularities into a fullness that is an essence of enlightenment.

Confucianism, if not a reaction to these concepts and trends, is at least distinguished by some distance from monism, though it can hardly be described as merely monotheistic either, given its respect for polytheistic aspects of ancestor worship. Its transformation from a quasi-philosophical status to a religion through the integration of several million Zoroastrians following the disastrous An Lushan Rebellion will be touched on in chapter 12 and explicated more fully in appendix H. Hinduism, as exemplified in the Bhagavad Gita, is described in this study as a bridge between monotheism and monism, with monotheism as a way station en route to the Ultimate, despite the necessity of a respectful nod to earlier polytheism previous to the Axial Age and the Bhagavad Gita.

At the risk of oversimplification, in the interest of stretching the understanding of Protestant Christians for whom this is all religious "new think," let us attempt to explore the relationship of monotheism to monism from a practical perspective. Catholic Christians may have a little less difficulty in this regard, and Eastern Orthodox Christians may almost instinctively relate to the concept. Christianity is chosen first for this exercise not only as the religion of some contributors to this study, and possibly the majority of our readers, but also as being, by about a billion adherents, the largest religion in the world, providing an example most likely to be easily understood by many others, monistic and monotheistic alike.

Some Christian theologians are avowed monists, such as Paul Tillich (1886–1965), the German American existentialist philosopher who is widely regarded as one of the most influential theologians of the twentieth century. Tillich quotes St. Paul that since God is the one "in whom we live and move and have our being,"[4] it follows that everything that has being partakes in God. Tillich's understanding relates to an area of religious life in which twenty-first-century Christians in particular may find their greatest potential "new" spiritual depth, though centuries ago there were mystical traditions of Christian meditation that can now be profitably revisited in this regard.[5]

To begin with, it is perhaps often presumed by casual observers that monotheists pray and monists meditate. Prayer is addressed "to God," as a Being who is separate from us, and meditation is thinking "about God" (or even centering oneself in mindfulness "about" life) as a means of experiencing Oneness with God, or Union with the Divine universe. But it is easily observed that, on the one hand, monotheists frequently recite little poems about God and, on the other hand, monists often address God directly. The prayers of Christian children, like "Now I lay me down to sleep, I pray the Lord my soul to keep" and the mealtime grace "God is great and God is good, Let us thank God for our food," are not actually prayers at all, because they are *about* our intentions, and *about* God, rather than words directly addressed to God. For children to pray to God, they would say, "Now I lay me down to sleep, I pray You Lord my soul to keep," and "You are great, and You are good; we thank you God for this our food." So these pieces of children's devotions in their most popular form are meditations *about* God.

However, in the popular Hindu "meditation on peace" from the opening of the Atharva Veda, we do not really have a meditation as such, but actually a proper prayer, addressed *to* God: "Supreme Lord, let there be peace in the sky and in the atmosphere. Let there be peace in the plant world and in the forests. Let the cosmic powers be peaceful. Let the Brahman, the true essence and source of life, be peaceful. Let there be undiluted and fulfilling peace everywhere."

This distinction is important, as it goes to the heart of spiritual practice. The object of either prayer or meditation is "God" for traditional Christians and "The Godhead" for Hindus, Buddhists, and other monists, all of whom do both meditate and actually pray in public temple rites, as may be easily observed. However, while Christians see Christ as the manifest presence of God, they also think of him as the head of a body that contains all, as in the Scripture, "God has put all things under the feet of Christ and has made him the head over all things,"[6] and, as noted, Hindus and other monists may be equally counterintuitive in directly addressing the Godhead as a separate being, as when one speaks *to* the divinity as "Supreme Lord."

St. Paul links all believers into the one body thus: "The body does not consist of one member but of many. If the foot would say, 'Because I am not a hand, I do not belong to the body,' that would not make it any less part of the body. And if the ear would say, 'Because I am not an eye, I do not belong to the body,' that would not make it any less a part of the body. If the whole body were an eye, where would the hearing be? If the whole body were hearing, where would the sense of smell be? But as it is, God arranged the members in the body, each of them, as he chose."[7]

For Christians, the believer is not the Head, but the believer is in one body with the Head, perhaps as a toenail, offering praise, laments, thanksgivings, and supplications to God in prayer and listening to the Godhead in meditation. No words are adequate to describe these divine realities, but one might think of oneself as a toenail on a body with millions of feet, with a Godhead that appreciates one's role and purpose, even when clipped from time to time or experiencing fungus. All "matter" in the universe is part of this body in which all parts are infused with Divine energy that is personal and has purpose and spirit that humans can experience. Prayer and meditation are appropriate ways for individuals to get in sync or in harmony with the Divine energy or spirit of the universe in our souls. The Godhead gives of God to the body of the universe, perhaps much like the way the brain gives its impulses to the human body. Humans (mind, flesh, and spirit) are part of the body, as is the Divine energy (spirit?) stored in every solid rock and every swaying tree, as well as in all the swirling gasses and debris of space.

Why do Hindus and other monists speak of "Godhead" instead of simply God? It is because all is God and the object of prayers is the God*head* who listens and speaks. The Godhead is the center of creative energy and the compassionate facilitator of our self-realization. The Godhead is the transformative power who changes into energy infused matter and, being responsive to our needs, can and will regenerate those who are faithful to Divinity. My morning meditation on a Hebrew scripture (from the KJV translation of my youth and the only one used on *Jeopardy*—as known well by Christians and those of other religions) may serve as an example. The repeating of "Thou wilt keep him in perfect peace whose mind is stayed on Thee, for he trusteth in Thee" is sometimes interrupted by a voice in an echo of another cherished Hebrew Scripture: "Thus says the Lord God, the Holy One of Israel, 'In returning to me and in waiting upon me, you shall be safe; in peace and quiet you shall find strength and courage.'"[8] I repeat that a few times, but for those building on the same heritage, now centered on the Godhead in the context of the Divinity of the Universe and the individual's place in it, such a mantra might sound like this: "Thus speaks Godhead, the holy crux of All, 'In consciously connecting with me and in awareness of the Divinity of the Universe, you are secure, my Brian'" (if the reader will excuse the maudlin personal reference). Continuing in a monistic vein, "In serenity and tranquility, you shall find strength and courage to do your duty and fulfill your destiny"—the very things that Arjuna heard from Krishna. Jewish and Christian readers may smile as they recite a familiar mantra of meditation to conclude this monistic newspeak: "Those who maintain awareness of their connection to Divinity shall find their strength renewed. They shall mount up with wings like eagles; they shall run and not be weary; they shall walk and not faint."[9] I am then ready for the day.

To reach this state of awareness or redemption, the Buddhist may sit under a tree using certain techniques of meditation until he is awakened. The Hindu may enter the transcendental state through yogic practice in which she becomes empty of the old self and part of the whole Self. Jews may dedicate themselves to what Existence (Yahweh) has done to restore them as a community and as persons. Christians find themselves redeemed through acceptance of how the Godhead with the face of Jesus invited them to Oneness by taking their sin and pain upon the Divinity. Taoists may get there via a more philosophical approach, Muslims through obedience to the Quran. Confucianists of late have been experimenting with "all of the above." Except for Confucianists (as will be illustrated), each of these leans toward certainty that theirs is the only way. The Way of the future may be more generous acknowledgment that we get there by the valid "prophetic" assistance of the other ways that may lead us toward the bliss of Nirvana or heaven in the current New Axial Age of interfaith enlightenment. This is an exciting perspective for some. A Christian leader of the experimental Emergent Church (which he calls "a new form of Christianity") speaks of sharing, but not with the intention of conversion: "I don't believe making disciples of Jesus must equal making adherents to the Christian Church. It may be advisable in many circumstances to help people become followers of Jesus and remain within their Buddhist, Hindu, or Jewish contexts."[10]

The question, then, is no longer whether one "believes in God" but whether one has experienced ("awakened to") an energy that has meaning and purpose for existence, whether in the life of each human or the "life" and purpose infused in each goose and in every space rock. In turning itself into matter, this Divine creative energy of the universe can be experienced without a lot of intellectual understanding, but there is some delight in the realization that the great oneness of the Divine universe is not known or experienced as an eternal and infinite but nebulous blob. Rather, it is a rich and full panoply, designed by the Godhead (not by us in our desires) and with a destiny in which humans may share.

"Awakening" (as Buddhists call it) is the finding or the real-ization of one's God-given place in the All, not according to our desires, our program, or our perceived needs, but in an enlightenment of an ultimate reality that is related to awakening or redemption by the Godhead and our connections to all the other parts of the body. The light comes on in different ways individually and in relation to various traditions. For Jews, it may be in synagogue community, while Confucianists may find it in noble traditions. For Taoists, it is found in going wisely with the Flow, and for Buddhists, it is in mindfulness. Hindus may find enlightenment during yoga or in transcendental meditation, while Christians are "born again" in Christ, and Muslims find that which is beyond words in the hearing or in the recitation of the Quran.

This is not syncretizing of religion, and rather than dismissing it as an oversimplification, the appropriate response is to be loyal to one's own tradition, to be prepared to share one's treasures with others, and to receive from them what they have found to be precious. Converting to another religion is a possibility, though regarded as breaking connections in an abhorrent apostasy in some communities. In this New Axial Age, it may be appropriate for many to simply cherish one's own experience, exchange gifts, and enrich each other, worshipping at the shrine in one's tradition, visiting another temple with one's friends, or meditating alone.

This casts a whole new light on the prayer of Jesus for his disciples and the church: "I ask not only on behalf of these, but also on behalf of those who will believe in me through their word, that they may all be *one* (italics added). As you, Father, are in me and as I am in you, may they also be in us, so that the world may believe that you have sent me. The glory that you have given me, I have given them, so that they may be *one*, as we are *one*."[11]

This oneness with the Divinity is to come by sharing, not by arguing that everyone else is "wrong." And it often comes by receiving the gifts of others, which Christians have long done with Jews (in spite of horrible examples to the contrary), whose prophets, psalms, proverbs, and communal worship have inspired the church in all its branches.

Hindus and Buddhists shared in a similar way in earlier days of India, before Buddhism moved on to build on Taoism in China, which itself began by building on the noble traditions cherished by Confucius and by adding insights inspired by the Magi, all illustrated in the *Older Testaments* play in appendix D. As the world increasingly becomes one, the role of religion changes, not to homogenize the faith traditions but to contribute that which each finds precious to others, who may be thereby enriched, and to receive from others that which enriches the individuals and communities to which we all belong. Examples recommended in this study include Paul Knitter, a Catholic professor of theology at a historically Protestant seminary in New York; Michelle Voss Roberts, the principal of Emmanuel College in Toronto, who introduces those training for Christian ministry to Hindu emotional sensitivities; and Amir Hussain, a Canadian hockey-playing Muslim who teaches in a Catholic University in Los Angeles.

The title of Knitter's book, *Without Buddha I Could Not Be a Christian*, speaks volumes. *Tastes of the Divine: Hindu and Christian Theologies of Emotion* by Voss Roberts deflects from textual studies to emotional aesthetics in religious experience, available even to those who cannot read. Hussain, famous of late for doing the TV documentary *The Story of God* with Morgan Freeman on the National Geographic Network, is found in his foreword to our *Three Testaments* book, articulating a credal summary of United Church of Canada beliefs as describing the manner in which Muslims may find ways to become better Muslims.

Our somewhat awkward presentation of monism is but an attempt to phrase these thoughts often expressed by Hindu gurus in phraseology (like the Godhead and millions of toenails)[12] that may be appreciated by a wider Western audience. The nontraditional emphasis on *oneness* between believers and God and between believers and one another may be uncomfortable for Christians who see such headship and oneness language as merely symbolic when applied to Jesus. But for many, perhaps even including those who believe the words of the Bible literally, these words point to the possibility of a more monistic understanding of Christianity.

This realization may also lead to an understanding of heaven with perhaps less anthropomorphic individualism, though there too the *oneness* may enfold many parts. In Christian prayer, the Godhead may have the face of Jesus and be addressed as Jesus-Godhead-Christ, a helpful concept for those who love Jesus and focus on him, even while now attracted to monism and enriched by new and different concepts like "Godhead." Charles Wesley, the Methodist lyricist, and Felix Mendelsohn, the Jewish-Christian composer, of "Hark! The Herald Angels Sing," may have perceived where this is leading when they lifted up the line "Veiled in flesh the Godhead see" in their famous Christmas carol, bridging other controversies in their lives.

For Jews and Muslims, the face of the Godhead is veiled; for Hindus, it may appear as the face of Vishnu, Krishna, or perhaps Kali, the latter being the feminine face of Divine empowerment. While Taoists will have no such image of the face of the Godhead, in meditation they may picture the great Flow of life, a wide river beyond horizons in which each drop retains a role and has both character and purpose. That may be inadequate for some, or they may enrich their outlook by adding this gift to perspectives of their own, which they in turn might also share.

To appreciate monism, Christians and others should have no need to leave traditional doctrines of their own or expressions they find efficacious, as their monotheistic dichotomy between Creator and creature gently expands in the direction of a monistic enrichment in wholeness. Christians are addressed here as among those who may find some of this especially difficult, but to offer a biblical example, "To tell the truth in love, we must all grow up into Him who is the head, into Christ, from whom the whole body, joined and knit together by every ligament with which it is equipped, as each part is working properly, promotes the body's growth in building itself up in love."[13] The body in this sense is the whole universe, but monotheists who have a new appreciation of monism may still use monotheistic terminology in prayers and songs as a way of getting their minds around the creative tension between talking to and of God and/or the Godhead.

Reviewers and critics have suggested that in articulating classical Buddhism, our *Four Testaments* volume has been somewhat deficient in presenting how these phenomena are experienced in popular culture in the twenty-first century. For readers for whom meditation is new, in the first year this publication appears the Headspace app is available free. Several three-minute guided sessions might be a delightful experience. Other opportunities will be forthcoming in the future. It is in emptying oneself of everything that a person becomes One with the universe and with All. However, the meditative state is not like the vegetative state. Stuff happens in sensitivity to a new reality. The self is not lost but is truly connected, perhaps for the first time. This may be described as an experience of the Divine. Buddhist meditation is not the same as meditation practiced by other traditions, and we wish to avoid syncretism in our suggestion that religious believers and practitioners can both bless and assist each other.

However, in chapter 13, found in part two of this book, we will be treated to a more fulsome presentation of the practicalities of "mindfulness" in the Buddhist tradition by Bhante Saranapala. Toronto's popular "urban monk," as people call him, unites the current vogue techniques of centering one's self in place (here) and focusing in time (now) with more traditional techniques of emptying oneself of desires and personal ambitions into the Divine nothingness in which one finds everything. Even so, we will keep in mind that while the Buddha may have been awakened to his connection to All in the Divine Universe, he remained a person who walked and talked and related to the world we know.

As illustrated above, Hindus have a similar experience of stretching the images, and have been doing so very well for a much longer period of time. The scriptural texts in volume 3 of this trilogy conclude with Bhagavad Gita, the Hindu Z turning point under Buddhist influence, bridging these seeming differences more completely from an Eastern perspective. Readers are blessed there with the guidance of Mahatma Gandhi through the Gita text in commentary said to be perhaps his best work, uniting modern experience with traditional expression as well as Eastern and Western perspectives. He follows on the similarly masterful explication of the Dhammapada text of earliest Buddhism by Sarvepalli Radhakrishnan, two giants of the East who themselves possessed an impressive appreciation of monotheistic religion in its Western context.

Individual Western Jews, Christians, and Muslims, who regard God or the Godhead as Creator, Redeemer, and Sustainer, respectively, may realize how close to monism they come by considering this Methodist New Year's Eve "Covenanting Prayer" in which any of them might empty themselves into the Divine oneness of the universe: "I am no longer my own, but yours. Put me to what you will, place me with whom you will. Put me to doing, put me to suffering. Let me be put to work for you or set aside for you, praised for you or criticized for you. Let me be full; let me be empty. Let me have all things; let me have nothing. I freely and fully surrender all things to your glory and service. And now, O wonderful and holy God, Creator, Redeemer, and Sustainer, you are mine and I am yours. So be it. And the covenant which I have made on earth, let it also be made in heaven." Is this perhaps halfway to monism?

As for language used to express feeling as well as meaning, people continue to speak of "sunset" even though we all know that the earth turns and the sun does not actually set. It is in this sense that Christians and other Westerners, who may now appreciate the monist perspective on the Divinity of All and are praying to and meditating on the Godhead, may continue to employ cherished monotheistic phrases and concepts. Examples of Kabbalist Jews and Sufi Muslims doing so are also provided below, but meanwhile Christian monists may continue to speak of the Godhead, or God being "up there" in the same way that at the funeral for a loved one many of them sing of life "Beyond the Sunset," knowing full well that this is an image rather than a scientific reality. Such devotional activities are as appropriate for Christian monists as they are for Hindus.

Monotheist language and the use of monotheist imagery can be helpfully appropriate for prayers and meditation by monist "toenails" addressing and meditating upon the Godhead. In *Four Testaments*, Mohandas Gandhi illustrates some of the ways this can happen from a Hindu perspective in his discussion of the various forms of yoga. From our own simple perspective, the difference between prayer and meditation might be described as the difference between words and music, or between a shower and a bath. It is entirely possible to pray to the Godhead, as do monistic Hindus, and/or meditate by focusing on aspects of the Whole in the way Orthodox Christians look *through* sacred icons rather than *at* them to see the All.

It is all Divine (or we could say it is all God), not just a homogenized blob or all mashed together, since we have identity in the God "in whom we live and move and have our being,"[14] and at the center of it All, there is Godhead. Our Hindu colleagues might explain it thus, but that does not suggest that Taoist philosophy or Confucian traditions are "wrong," that Buddhist mindfulness or Jewish teachings are less important, or that the resonance of the Quran is less Divine than the redemptive emanations Christians believe they receive from the Saoshyant (Redeemer) whose face they see in the Godhead. People may share these treasures with each other, respectfully, in this new Axial Age. Even purely academic readers might allow this digression into how it All works.

So Existence itself is a new definition of God. Divine Existence is a Universe of both macro (multiverse) and micro (nanoverse) proportions. Existence itself is the ultimate meaning of that which was revealed to Moses in the burning bush moment as the I AM. Existence is awesome. There is a Divine (spiritual) energy in the Universe that, when encountered or realized, causes one to fall down in worship and then to stand up in service to purpose and meaning not of one's own choosing or desire. Reading this may be one of the experiential moments we projected at the beginning. Such phenomena may also be the subject of academic inquiry, even if sometimes a person simply needs to just enjoy the sunset, spiritually speaking.

There are currently Christians who have difficulty believing in the tradition of a God-out-there who is separate from and above the universe. Some of them describe themselves as "non-theistic" Christians, but this does not mean that they necessarily deny Divinity in the universe to which they belong. But in order to share unity or oneness with the community, the traditional language of monotheism may be the only practical way for them to participate in worship. These individual parts of the whole may find themselves comfortable praying to God and singing in the choir while privately communing with the Godhead through meditation. They may join with or even lead and direct the congregation of other equally distinct "parts" in lifting up praise to the Godhead and being uplifted themselves as the Godhead cleanses, trims, and renews (or "redeems") them. The Godhead may well have regenerative purposes for the rest of the universal body in which they participate in old-speak.

A phrase from a recent "Statement of Faith"[15] in the United Church of Canada might help define the line between monotheism and monism. It begins, "God is Holy Mystery, beyond complete knowledge, above perfect description," and continues in monotheistic voice: "Nothing exists that does not find its *source* in God." Changing one word could make this into a monistic statement reading, "Nothing exists that does not find its *being* in God." St. Paul may be ahead of the rest of the church when he quotes the Greek poets, "(God) is not far from any one of us, for in him we live and move and have our being."[16]

Is it possible that while the concepts of God are different, the requirements of religious life may be similar in practice? Might monistic and monotheistic experiences of God result in similar behavior? Is this possibly an area of interfaith conversation that can move forward in Scriptural Reasoning? Is going with the Taoist Flow, as a molecule of water conjoined with the ocean stream, the monist's equivalent of the monotheist seeking to know the will of God and to serve the Creator? To further conceptualize monism from a monotheistic perspective, it might be said that while Jews, Christians, and Muslims may have no difficulty *praying* to the Godhead, they would be more likely to see themselves as *meditating* on the divinity as the Flow—that is, the ongoing will and purpose of God. To put monism simply, while it may be true that God is not separate from the universe, the Godhead is not the same as, or identical with, the other parts of the one universal body.

We have not here touched on an important distinction between monism and monotheism in popular cultures, East and West—namely, the relationship or connection with the natural world. It is commonly supposed that monists are more inclined to live in harmony with nature since they see themselves as being one with it, while monotheists may feel freer to exploit nature for their own benefit. However, the extreme pollution in countries where much of the population espouses monism raises a question about that idea, as it also does for monotheists, whose Hebrew Scripture teaches that humanity is "to have responsibility for the earth and to replenish it"[17]—a passage in Genesis, thought now to have come down to the Bible as possibly a Z verse in a section from Vedic tradition.

Before leaving this exercise of attempting to explore the border between monotheism and monism, and finding it perhaps more porous than traditionally imagined, it may be of interest to note that while monotheistic Judaism flirted with polytheism (as witnessed in Scripture), or at least henotheism (worshipping a God who is merely the best among gods), it has rarely manifested monistic tendencies. To illustrate the uniqueness of Judaism, where the name of God may not even be pronounced, the Hindu and Buddhist (also Jain and Sikh) *japa nama* practice of immersing oneself in God by focused meditation in reciting the names of God is the opposite of the practice among many Jews. Forms of *japa* are actually practiced in certain Christian circles and in Sufi Islam, but in Judaism the very opposite usually prevails in traditions where the name of God may not even be pronounced.

However, some Jewish Kabbalist theologians like Moses ben Jacob Cordovero (1522–1570) and Schneur Zalman (1745–1812) come close to monism. Cordovero taught that all things are linked to God through emanations, making all of existence part of God. Zalman said that God is all that exists and that all particulars are completely undifferentiated. But Kabbalah as a whole is vague on this point, and there are but rare other exceptions, like Spinoza and Rabbi Jacqueline Mates-Muchin, a contributor to our epilogue and to volume 3 of this trilogy. This is passing strange, given that the bedrock verse of the Torah is where God says to Moses, "I am who I am."[18] Thousands of books have been written on the exact meaning of this verse in Hebrew, but the most obvious possibility is rarely mentioned. Exodus 3:14b has the description of God as *ehyeh asec ehyeh*, presented in Exodus 3:15 as the name of God using consonants only, frequently rendered as YHWH or Yahweh, derived from the verb *hayah*, conveying the meaning of "to exist" or the verb "to be." In a footnote in the 1985 JPS Tanakh Version of the Hebrew Bible, the uncertainty over the meaning of *ehyeh/YHWH* is noted, and two possible literal translations identified "I am" and "I will be." Neither of these is as entirely satisfactory in Hebrew, which speaks of something more essentially monistic, like "I am all that is" or "I am Existence."

Is meditation as well as prayer found in Islam? The popular website Islamic Insights says so:

> Meditation is one of the most important aspects of a successful Islamic lifestyle. When we consciously adopt Islam for ourselves, we do so through recognition and cognizance of the Oneness of God. We contemplate and recognize that Allah is worthy of worship and that nothing else is. We recognize Truth in His words and in the guides He sent to us for our benefit. None of this is possible without contemplation, reflection, concentration, observation, and presence of mind. The Prophet (peace be upon him and his progeny) was well-known for his meditation practice. People often related that he would go to the cave in Mount Hira for meditation, contemplation, and prayer. It was during this practice that he first received Qur'anic revelation. Thus, meditation opened the door of revelation.

Indeed, the everyday "prayers" of Muslims are structured around Quranic verses called "duas," and even cursory observation reveals them to be at least as meditative as prayerful.

For that matter, in summarizing the Western expressions of monism widely regarded as Eastern in essence, it may come as a shock for many to realize that the Oneness of God in Islam has one particularly strong monistic Muslim tradition of theology and practice. Its origins are described by Indo-American commentator Keki R. Bhote. He begins with a summary remarkably similar to our own and proceeds from there to present Islamic Sufism in a light that goes some distance in explaining the antipathy of Muslim extremists toward this particular faction.

> In the millennia-old tradition of nature worship and ancestor worship dominated by priests, sacrifices and magic, Zarathustra was the first to break their spell in the 6th Century BC. Within fifty years of each other, Judaism in Palestine, Buddhism and Jainism in India, and Confucianism and Taoism in China, as well as the great philosophers of Greece saw a wave of theological advances that are carried over into this day. Some 1,200 years later, that 6th Century BC phenomenon witnessed another revolt against an entrenched priesthood.[19]

To whit:

> Sufism was created in the crucible of extreme distress felt by devout Zoroastrians when forced by the Arabs to give up their beloved religion and accept Islam in the seventh century AD. So Zoroastrians in Iran flew under the radar of the Muslim clergy to secretly form a new branch of the Muslim faith with decidedly Zoroastrian antecedents. While there is no single founder of Sufism, it was started by Ibrahim Adham, the son of a Zoroastrian prince in Balkh, the center of old Zarathustra's ministry, in 750 AD.[20]

Among the famous Sufi mystics who advocate monism, one of the most notable is the beloved thirteenth-century Persian poet Rumi (1207–1273). In his didactic poem *Masnavi*, Rumi says, "In the shop for Unity (Arabic: *wahdat*), anything that you see there except the One is an idol." Sufism uniquely bridges the divide between Sunni and Shia Muslims with meditation focused on reciting verses of the Quran and repeating the names of God, whether during the "whirling dervish" practice (borrowed from early Zoroastrianism) or otherwise. With Sufism largely found to be practiced in Turkey and other parts of what was the Persian Empire when Zoroastrianism was the state religion, it is difficult to escape the inference that this may well be a remnant of Zurvanistic influence. In any case, the current rapid growth of the Sufi movement in Iran can also be attributed to a desire for a more inclusive Islam among those resisting the ayatollahs.

The Quranic ideal of *Tawhid* is seen by most Muslims as strict "monotheism," the usual translation of the word. There is only one God, Allah, and the universe is his creation. "Allah is the Light of the heavens and the earth,"[21] and the purpose of creation (including humanity) is to obey and serve him. In Sufism, the hybrid concept is that Tawhid should be understood as Absolute Reality. Anything that is real is of God, and illusions are to be eschewed. This Sufistic Tawhid may be distinguished from pantheism ("everything is God"). Rather, the reality is that there is nothing except God ("God is everything"). While both Sunnis and Shias recite *la ilaha illallah* (there is no God but Allah), Sufis take this proclamation a step further in reciting *la mawjuda illallah* (there is nothing but Allah).

Another of the most influential Islamic monists was the Sufi philosopher Ibn Arabi (1165–1240), who developed the concept of "unity of being" (*whadat al-wujud*). In his book, *Fasusu'l-Hikam*, he writes, "Although apparently Creation is distinct from the Creator, in reality the Creator is but the Creation and Creation is but the Creator. All these are from one reality. Nay, it is but He who is the Only Reality, and it is He who manifests Himself in all these realities." God is thus considered the Ultimate Reality, which is transcendent but also immanent in Creation. Worshipping and serving God therefore results in responsibility toward society.

At the same time, Sufism manifests an ascetic tendency by rejecting worldly life on the part of the believer. Cyril Glassé, another contributor to this trilogy, quotes two Sufi authorities in this regard in *The Concise Encyclopedia of Islam*. Ibn 'Ata Allah says, "The source of every disobedience, indifference, and passion is self-satisfaction. The source of every obedience, vigilance and virtue is dissatisfaction with one's self."[22] Lord Krishna himself could not have put it better, as we will see in the Bhagavad Gita.

Glassé then compares Sufi monism to the Hindu Vedanta, to mystical traditions of Eastern Christianity, and to Taoism[23] before quoting the great Islamic theologian and jurist, Al Ghazali, who says in *al-Munqidh mina'l-Dalal*,

> I turned my attention to the way of the Sufis. I knew that it could not be traversed to the end without both doctrine and practice, and that the gist of the doctrine lies in overcoming the appetites of the flesh and getting rid of its evil dispositions and vile qualities, so that the heart may be cleared of all but God. When I considered the intention of my own

teaching, I perceived that instead of doing it for God's sake alone, I had no motive but the desire for glory and reputation. I realized that I stood on the edge of a precipice and would fall into Hellfire unless I set about to mend my ways. Conscious of my helplessness and having surrendered my will entirely, I took refuge with God as a man in sore trouble who has no resources left. God answered my prayer and made it easy for me to turn my back on reputation and wealth and wife and children and friends.[24]

We can here imagine Al Ghazali ascending a mountain in the Himalayas to find complete Nirvana.

notes

1. Genesis 2:23–24.
2. Senior minister of the United Methodist Church of the Resurrection, Kansas City, Missouri.
3. Adam Hamilton, *Christianity and World Religions* (Nashville: Abingdon Press, 2005), 42.
4. The Book of Acts 17:28.
5. Including but not limited to the Desert Fathers and Desert Mothers, Gregory of Nyssa, Hildegard of Bingen, Bernard of Clarivaux, Meister Eckhart, John of the Cross, Brother Lawrence, Blaise Pascal, and the Eastern traditions of mystical prayers dating back to the origins of Orthodox monasticism.
6. Ephesians 1:22, New Revised Standard version of the Bible.
7. I Corinthians 12:14–18, ibid.
8. Isaiah 30:15.
9. Isaiah 40:31.
10. Brian D. McLaren, *A Generous Orthodoxy: Why I Am a Missional, Evangelical, Post/Protestant, Liberal/Conservative, Mystical/Poetic, Biblical, Charismatic/Contemplative, Fundamentalist/Calvinist, Anabaptist/Anglican, Methodist, Catholic, Green, Incarnational, Depressed-Yet-Hopeful, Emergent, Unfinished Christian* (Nashville: Zondervan, 2004), 293.
11. John 17:20–22.
12. The Godhead and toenails illustration is from Swami Chinmayananda addressing Westernized Hindus at the Vidyalaya School in Couva, Trinidad, April 9, 2009.
13. Ephesians 4:15.
14. Acts 17:27b–28.
15. Song of Faith is easily found on the website of that particular church.
16. Acts 17:27b–28.
17. Genesis 1:28.
18. Exodus 3:14.
19. *Zoroastrianism: Mother of all World Religions*, 217.
20. Ibid., 212.
21. Quran 24:35.
22. Cyril Glassé translation, *The New Encyclopedia of Islam*, 4th edition (Lanham, MD: Rowman & Littlefield, 2013), 507.
23. Ibid., 508.
24. Ibid., 508–9.

part two

CREATION AND APOCALYPSE IN WORLD RELIGIONS: AVESTAN MODELS IN TORAH, TAO TE CHING, ANALECTS, DHAMMAPADA, BHAGAVAD GITA, GOSPEL, AND QURAN

9

the dead zee scrolls

Zoroastrian Concepts Buried in the Scriptures of World Religions

AT THE OCTOBER 19–21, 2018, ANNUAL CONFERENCE OF THE SOCIETY OF SCHOLARS OF ZORO-astrianism in Chicago, keynote speaker Brian Arthur Brown was introduced by Rohinton Rivetna as the author of two popular interfaith texts. *Three Testaments: Torah, Gospel, and Quran* presents the Scriptures of Western monotheism from Abraham's family (Jews, Christians, and Muslims) together in one volume for the first time, with commentary. *Four Testaments: Tao Te Ching, Analects, Dhammapada, Bhagavad Gita* contains those Eastern primary texts with commentary on Taoism, Confucianism, Buddhism, and Hinduism of the Bhagavad Gita as reformed in the Axial Age of religious development along the Silk Route from Turkey to China. Brown illustrates how all seven primary texts of these seven "world religions" owe a greater debt to Zoroastrianism than is usually realized, a fact reflected in Zoroastrian chapters in the two previous books and both expanded and particularized in *Seven Testaments of World Religion and the Zoroastrian Older Testament*.

Dr. Brown began his presentations with humor: "For years scholars have said that 'Zoroastrianism is the next big thing and always will be,' but Zoroastrians are getting the last laugh because right now Zoroastrianism is the big thing." He went on to assert how evidence is mounting that the Scriptures of the Avesta may be regarded as the reformed Vedic "Older Testament" of all seven testaments of the major world religions. Zoroastrianism has bequeathed to the major religions such concepts as creation and apocalypse, angels and demons, salvation and damnation, resurrection and final judgment, heaven and hell. Brown demonstrated to the conference how each of these religions has Zoroastrian roots in the Axial Age, found in various measure in the seven testaments that followed.

A review of Dr. Brown's presentations at the SSZ Conference in Chicago, October 19–21, 2018, submitted by Roshan Rivetna based on conversations with those in attendance.

The core of the Axial Age may be defined as the period between 550 BCE and 400 BCE in which Lao Tzu flourished at one end of the Silk Route and Socrates at the other. Foremost Greek philosophers, major Hebrew prophets, mystical Hindu avatars, the Buddha, and Cyrus the Great ranged along this narrow band of the globe, about the size and shape of Chile, laid horizontally through Asia. If one accepts the traditional Persian dates for Zoroaster (628–551 BCE), this places the development of these religions and their Scriptures in the immediate wake of Zoroaster's life and prophetic ministry. If one accepts the dates preferred by European scholars (eleventh or twelfth century BCE), the same eruption of Zoroastrian inspired religiosity on the Silk Route in the Axial Age would then be attributed to the Magi during the reign of Cyrus in the Persian Empire. This was the world's first superpower, and the ascension of Cyrus to the throne was followed by conversion of Vedic Magi from Turkey to China out of respect for, or to curry favor with, the king.

It was the ubiquitous Magi who carried the above concepts to every community on the Silk Route, as Vedic lore reformed and refined by Zoroaster. Polytheism was suddenly replaced by "The Oneness of God," accepted as monotheism in the West and as monism in the East. Monotheism is the belief that there is One God "out there" or "up there," separate from creation and worthy of worship. Monism is the belief that the whole universe is divine and humans are part of the divine order, though still praying to the Godhead or meditating on the divinity of the Universe. New religions East and West were inspired by Zoroastrianism, with monism being more typical of religions like Buddhism and the reformed Hinduism seen in the Bhagavad Gita. Monism appeared also in a Western version of Zoroastrianism called Zurvanism, which lasted only a few centuries in the Persian Empire side by side with the more normative monotheistic worship of God as Ahura Mazda. Confucianism remained with a simple monotheism, and monotheism became entrenched in the West (with small but notable exceptions in Judaism and Islam).

Zoroaster himself was born and grew up in a small town near the Caspian Sea. The young Vedic priest-in-training met Israelite exiles slowly migrating northward generation by generation toward Europe. At this time his Vedic Aryan people crisscrossed with the Israelites en route while themselves migrating south to Iran and India. Zoroaster's traditionalist dates make him a teenager sitting around the campfire with Israelite neighbors (and possibly in-laws?) during visits to exiles by the Jewish prophet Jeremiah. Hearing of the Oneness of God as a Divinity who places personal responsibility for goodness on each person, Zoroaster may have stored away such thoughts until ten years later during a social upheaval. At that time the young Vedic priest waded into river water to prepare a water sacrifice and was addressed by the Wise Lord, Ahura Mazda, who claimed to be the all-embracing Divinity, the One described by Jeremiah.

Zoroaster had entered the water as a Vedic priest but came out as the prophet of a new age, to begin a ministry that inspired and changed the world. Brown found the overlapping ages of Jeremiah and Zoroaster more than coincidental when possibly placing them in the same community at the same time. Brown maintains that cross-fertilization of Vedic and Semitic traditions could have happened in either this or other ways, but the communities did crisscross during Zoroaster's lifetime, and again when a group of exiled Jews surfaced in Babylon seventy years later as civil servants under Cyrus. Cyrus supported their dreams of returning to Jerusalem, where they rebuilt their temple and completed the final editing of the Torah Scriptures. By this time their original Semitic religion had been transformed by the above Zoroastrian concepts of the Magi priests of the court of Cyrus, with whom the Jewish priests and the prophets of Israel had been having daily contact for a generation.

This is just the most dramatic known example of how Magi of Zoroaster's now sophisticated religion interfaced with five of the seven major religions of the world during their formation in the Axial Age, followed later by Christianity and Islam, whose Zoroastrian influence came via Judaism. Two hundred years later, the actual texts of the Gatha poetic prayers of Zoroaster and subsequent portions of the Avesta were destroyed by the armies of Alexander the Great in 334 BCE. They were reconstituted from memory and surviving scraps, until destroyed again by the armies of Islam. The first such destruction was in Alexander's attempt to "civilize" Asia; the second was in Islam's eagerness to stamp out a dualistic variant of Zoroastrianism. Information about a third obliteration of the Zoroastrian community in China is only now becoming fully appreciated. After the second reconstitution of the Avesta, the Zoroastrian community retained only about 15 percent of the original Avesta writings, still in use today.

Copies of the lost portions possibly still exist, like the Dead Sea Scrolls of Hebrew Scripture, which had been hidden by Jews under similar circumstances in the Roman Empire. Dr. Brown has dubbed these missing chapters of the Avesta the *Dead Zee Scrolls*. He described the work of prominent archaeologists now engaged in the search, employing new techniques that scan for documents from outer space, yielding impressive results of late in other quests.

While the quest to find the Dead Zee Scrolls might seem like a stretch to some people, Dr. Brown presented the evidence for the recent identification of additional copies of the Cyrus Cylinder as an example of what is now being discovered. These include an apparently complete copy from China inscribed on large horse bones, now on display at the British Museum. He also took obvious delight in his "big reveal" of the tomb containing Zoroaster's bones, only to discover that two of the scholars present were already aware of that putative crypt beneath the famous Blue Mosque at Mazar-i-Sharif in Afghanistan. His additional evidence was welcomed.

Many of these matters are introduced in the Zoroastrian portions of the *Three Testaments* and *Four Testaments* books (available from Amazon.com and elsewhere). This aspect of work by Brian Arthur Brown has been of sufficient interest that the publishers have contracted with him for the third book in the series, *Seven Testaments of World Religion and the Zoroastrian Older Testament*. It will be primarily devoted to the Zoroastrian reforms of Vedic lore as found in the seven Scriptures, one of the places where they have been "buried." His three interfaith books in the *Seven Testaments Trilogy* are to be obtainable after being presented at a Niagara Falls launch conference in May 2020 attended by many of the world's top interfaith scholars.

Actor Morgan Freeman recently hosted *The Story of God*, an exploration of religions on the National Geographic TV network. The eighty-two-year-old actor asserted that Zoroastrianism has impacted him more than any other religion, despite his vast knowledge and faith acquired during his journey. Brown maintains that as a Christian, he himself now cherishes the New Testament of Christ, the Old Testament of Judaic prophecy, and the Vedic Older Testament that is the Zoroastrian foundation of it all. Of course, each component is to be respected as uniquely valid in its own right, as confirmed in the Quran and in the other Scriptures of the East. We can all learn from each other in the new Axial Age of our time.

Brown admits to "workshopping" some of the details of his next book in his appearances at the SSZ conference prior to submission for publication. Indeed, he got helpful assistance on several of his assertions from some of the Zoroastrian scholars in the crowd, including two senior scholars from Canada, Ervad Tehemton Mirza and Ervad Kobad Zarolia. Dastur Dr. Kersey H. Antia, senior scholar-priest at the Arbab Rustom Guiv Dar-e-Mehr in Chicago, expressed special gratitude to the speaker when Dr. Brown concluded his remarks to the scholars and the community by saying, "It's a great time to be a Zoroastrian."

zoroastrian creation story

> In the beginning, there was nothing in the world but Ahura Mazda, the Wise Lord, who lived in the Endless Light, and the Evil Spirit Ahriman, who lived in the Absolute Darkness. Between these realms was emptiness. One day, Ahura Mazda decided to make different creations. First, he shaped the sky made of metal, shining and bright. Second, he made pure water. Third, he created the earth, flat and round with no mountains or valleys. Fourth, he made the plants, moist with no thorns. Fifth, he created animals, big and small. Sixth, he created the First Man, called Gayomard, bright, tall, and handsome. And seventh, he created fire and distributed it within the creation.[1]

Ongoing difficulties in translation of Zoroastrian materials and continuing related controversies have led to a dependence on paraphrases in this volume, some derivative and others original, as was seen and appreciated earlier in part one. The above is a paraphrase based on close readings of material near the end of the Avesta canon.[2] It will be of particular interest when we do an examination of the Hebrew creation story developed in Babylon by the priestly source (P), who received this revelation from Zoroastrian sources and built on it out of the Jewish experience, with Christians, Muslims, and others following in this train.[3]

The ancient Vedic seven-phase creation story is attested and documented in detail in the *Three Testament* text of this trilogy. There are a number of Mesopotamian versions, but it is the Zoroastrianism rendition of the sixth century BCE that influenced the Jews in exile as work continued on the Torah, begun and completed in Israel/ Judah, but fleshed out by divine grace during the Babylonian Captivity. Counterintuitively, this realization may be difficult for the very scholars who hypothesize that the Avesta had long an oral tradition and was only written down in the Common Era. But the very fact that the text is late supports the possibility that much such matter did exist mainly in oral form for some centuries, perhaps from the beginning, or after the destruction of texts by Alexander's soldiers and Muhammad's followers, and that the material is ancient.

In the Rig Veda, the world's oldest Scripture in continuous use, the Sanskrit name of the first human is *Manu*, meaning "thinker," which is cognate with the English and German (Indo-European) man and Mann. Zoroaster revised this to *Gayomard* ("King of Mud"), which became *Gar-shāh* ("King of the Mountains") in Persian and *Adam* ("man from earth") in Hebrew, indicating the earlier provenance of the Gayomard story. In this and in general, the accepted techniques of form criticism illustrate persuasively that in comparing the creation story in Genesis chapter one with its Zoroastrian predecessor, it is clear that the refined biblical version follows the Zoroastrian model.

For those of us who hope and believe the Dead Zee Scrolls may be found, soon or eventually, the recovered portions of the Avesta will almost certainly provide additional testimony to the early provenance of this creation story. There is abundant ancient testimony referring to texts of the earliest Avestan scrolls, destroyed by Alexander. We know there were also oral traditions, eventually used to rewrite sections of the Avesta. Many of them were destroyed later by followers of Muhammad, the creation story surely among them, but it was so well known in oral presentation that it eventually got rewritten again, as cited above.

Even extant portions of the Avesta provide clues to the provenance we seek. The eighth book of *Denkard* makes reference to two of the missing portions of the Avesta, which refer to the more ancient versions of Zoroastrian creation stories. The *Chethrdat*, a portion identified earlier as having twenty-one chapters, and the *Varshtmansar*, of undetermined length, are quoted as making at least passing references to how the world and mankind were created, including the creation of "Gayōmart" by Ahura Mazda, as revealed to Zoroaster. From these references to still earlier material, we glean some scant information to the effect that[4] Gayōmart, the first human, was created by Ahura Mazda in the sixth phase of creation. He was created from mud at Eran-vedj (the middle of the earth) on the left side of the river Veh-Dāit, to be a companion to Ahura Mazda. He came not as a baby but fully developed as a young adult.

Through part two of this text, we will compare this Vedic-Zoroastrian creation story with similar stories in the other Scriptures under review, illustrating with archival pages and concluding with apocalyptic material, equally derivative or inspired by the Zoroastrian model.

zoroastrian apocalypse

The similar case that apocalyptic literature has its first appearance in the world in the Gatha prayer-poems of Zoroaster was made in both *Three Testaments* and *Four*

Testaments and appears here as the quintessential expression of the dualistic response to the creation story above. Due to helpful critical response to *Three Testaments* and *Four Testaments*, the subject deserves expansion in this *Seven Testaments of World Religion*. If there are skeptics regarding our exhibition of Zoroaster's creation story, presented as the model or inspiration for those that followed in the seven world religions, there is nobody who questions the fact that his Gathas contain several apocalyptic elements. They are recognized by all well-informed scholars as the first examples of this style of literary expression in the world, succeeded within two generations by several more in this series and then followed by others in train.

So a brief apocalypse will appear at the conclusion of each chapter in part two, none of them specifically Zoroastrian but all of them clearly derivative in style. Those that came after Zoroaster can hardly be imagined as being made up in this style independent of the Avesta and separate from each other, in most cases within the Axial Age in a suspiciously short period of time.

Presuming a similar ancient "Dead Zee Scroll" provenance, it may suit our purpose here to present the apocalyptic verses that appear in the *Bundahishn* immediately following that creation story above, identical in style to Avesta verses, extant and available to us. If our use of our own paraphrases makes the creation and apocalypse material seem almost childish, that is not more so than, say, the story of Adam and Eve in the Garden of Eden and other presentations we may consider. We remain confident in the ancient provenance, but again we express the expectation that additional ancient written texts of the following will be found within the Dead Zee Scrolls upon their discovery in a cave, a tomb, or a cache of documents somewhere. However, it is obvious that such materials are also buried within the sacred texts cherished by the seven world religions, as will become apparent.

The Evil Spirit peeked out of his dark world to see the Wise Lord's beautiful creations. The Wise Lord called him and said, "Evil Spirit! Aid my creatures and encourage them so that you will be immortal." The Evil Spirit snarled, "Why should I aid your creatures? Why should I encourage them? I am more powerful! I will destroy you and your creatures for ever and ever." Then he crawled back to his dark side to shape demons, witches, and monsters to attack the Endless Light.

The Wise Lord was all-knowing. He knew the Evil Spirit was making demons to destroy His good creations, and He also knew there would be a great battle in the Dark. So, the Wise Lord fashioned six Spirits—the Holy Immortals—to guard His creations against the Endless Dark. The Wise Lord shaped the Holy Immortals from His own soul, each sharing His own nature.

The first Holy Spirit was Khashathra, the Righteous Power, who became the guardian of the sky. Then the Wise Lord created Haurvatat, the Peace and Perfection. She became the protector of waters. Next was Spenta Armaiti, the Holy Devotion. She guarded the Earth. The other Holy Spirit, Ameretat, the Immortality, became the protector of plants. Vohu Manah, the Good Mind, was the fifth Holy Spirit, chosen to protect the animals. Asha Vihista, the Justice, became the protector of Humanity.

Ahriman saw the Wise Lord's Holy Immortals and was enraged. He cried, "Ahura Mazda! I will destroy you and all your creations. You will never be victorious." So, he and his demons attacked God's creations one by one. They tried to destroy the water but they could only bring bitterness to it. They tried to destroy the Earth but they could only get mountains and valleys into place. They tried to wither the plants but the plants only grew thorns.

The Evil Spirit and his demons brought sadness against happiness, pain against pleasure, pollution against purification, and death against life. They attacked Gayomard, the First Man, and gave him sickness and death. Ahriman thought he had destroyed humanity and that he had become victorious against the Light! But he was ignorant and foolish. When Gayomard, the First Man, died, from his bones grew a rhubarb plant. After forty years a man and a woman, Mashya and Mashyana, grew out of the rhubarb plant.

Mashya and Mashyana promised the Wise Lord that their children would help Him in His battle with Ahriman. Mashyana then gave birth to fifteen sets of twins and every pair scattered around the world and became a race. Then each person followed the good thoughts, good deeds and good words. Each became the follower of the Wise Lord in His battle with the Evil Spirit.

We can also summarize the various apocalyptic references in extant chapters of the Avesta, mostly from the Gatha sections,[5] composed by Zoroaster himself. They suggest that the end time will occur three thousand years after Zoroaster's own life. For scholars of Zoroastrianism who date his birth to around 1,000 BCE, that means the end could come very soon now. For Zoroastrian scholars who date his birth at 728 BCE, the world will struggle on for a couple hundred years more, though the signs of the coming end seem obvious to certain religious people in various related traditions, as we shall see.

The conclusion of the ancient battle between Ahura Mazda / Ormazd (or God) and his evil archenemy, Ahriman / Angra Mainyu (or Satan), will be joined when the sun and moon can no longer be seen in the sky and a long, dark winter commences. Modern Zoroastrians sometimes interpret this as the dust cloud from a nuclear winter blotting out all light and heat. In such circumstances religious devotion and family ties will temporarily decline—again a sign to some that the end is coming soon.

Much like imagery in the later Christian Book of Revelation, an evil creature with three heads appears to devour a third of the world's population. To counter these losses, a virgin comes forth to facilitate a savior, the third appearance of the Saoshyant (who previously appeared as an agent of creation and also near the time of Zoroaster . . . perhaps himself, perhaps Cyrus [as the Jews thought] or some other). The virgin bathes in a lake containing the ejaculated seed of the long-dead Zoroaster. She becomes impregnated by this seed and gives birth to the Saoshyant, the final of three appearances according to Zoroastrian beliefs. The Saoshyant raises all the dead and passes final judgment on their souls. Both the living and the dead are exposed to or submerged in a river of molten metal, which will burn and purge all their evils from them, with each soul suffering only to the degree that its "sins" warrant. By the time they reach the other side, they will all be purified to the point that the molten metal no longer hurts them at all.

Eventually Ormazd (as God is called in these later verses) leads this purified humanity and all the lesser deities in a final battle with Ahriman and the lesser demons, resulting in the permanent defeat of the forces of evil. They are finally seen to be illusions, and their forces are finally recognized as impotent. Ormazd and the Saoshyant accept the death of the animals that died in the service of humanity, and this sacrificial offering becomes the basis of a heavenly banquet as the earth and the universe are regenerated. The mountains are laid low and the valleys are filled up until earth is a perfectly smooth sphere, as it was before Ahriman ruined things so long ago. There is no sun since the light of God is everywhere, but the heavens swaddle the moon in beauty and the new earth rises up to blend into the heavens, where all souls will live forever with Ormazd in a state of perfection.

If it is reasonably assumed that the first creation story in the religions under consideration came through Zoroaster, the first apocalyptic eschatology is Zoroastrian without question. On this basis we may come to the profoundly significant conclusion that the first sense of time on a universal scale also originated through Zoroaster. This canopy over Western thought and the West's sense of meaningful advancement in a line of progress is reflected in the East as the beginnings and endings of circular eras, hinted at in Vedic lore. This idea is made explicit in the extant writings of Zoroaster, subsequently again in the Avesta, and in each of the Eastern traditions following in its train. The attribution of awareness of time, with a beginning and an end, might even be seen as the single most important contribution he made to world culture. Its significance is not dealt with adequately in this trilogy, but our heightened awareness leaves the development of the theme open to others.

an archive page from the dead zee scrolls

"Holiness is the best of all good: it is also happiness."

This is the copy of a fragment of a copy of the ancient Avesta referred to by Professor Freund in *Four Testaments*. It is a prayer that the Zoroastrian community happens to have already, though this is a copy at least a thousand years older than those cherished in recent centuries. It was found by Aurel Stein in Dunhuang, at the Chinese end of the Silk Route, in a trove of material, dating from the fifth to the ninth century CE. What we are looking for ultimately dates back even a thousand years before that, to the pristine classical Zoroastrian era in the same general area or even somewhat to the west of Dunhuang in the locale of old Sogdiana, in modern Uzbekistan and part of Tajikistan, one of the prime areas where the search continues on a daily basis at the present time "beneath the streets of Samarkand."

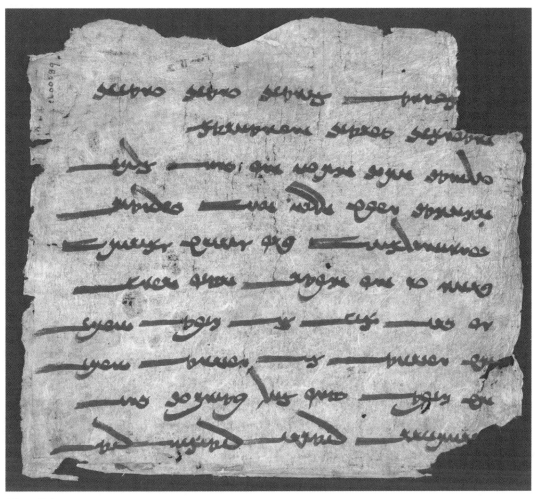

Ashem Vohu.
INTERNATIONAL DUNHUANG PROJECT BRITISH LIBRARY OR.8212/84.

notes

1. Adapted from *Book of Creation*, in the *Bundahishn* as paraphrased by Rebecca Cann in *Zoroastrian Kid's Corner*.

2. W. B. Henning, "An Astronomical Chapter of the *Bundahishn*," *JRAS* (1942), 229–48 (chap. II).

3. One-page note, interrupting the *textus receptus* of Professor Gildner's exordium.

4. Hamase-sarâ'i dar Iran, Tehran, 2000.

5. Textual references provided in the brief but more technical summary in the Exordium by Professor Geldner.

10
an essence of the torah

I N HER SPLENDID PREFACE TO THE TORAH IN VOLUME II, *THREE TESTAMENTS: TORAH, GOSPEL, AND Quran*, Ellen Frankel begins with a quotation from the Midrash Tehillim[1] to the effect that "in the beginning, two thousand years before the heaven and the earth, seven things were created: first came the Torah, written in black fire on white fire, and lying in the lap of God."

Far from challenging common sense with her choice of imagery, Frankel is here suggesting the importance of spiritual symbolism, a profound prelude to the critical analysis by her learnéd colleague, Marc Zvi Brettler, which followed.

It is perhaps by prescient intuition that in this quotation she anticipates the "seven" testaments of world religion that we are examining together, though Ellen has been part of this project since before her retirement after twenty years as senior editor and CEO of the Jewish Publication Society.

However, in her own excursion into the academic side of things, Frankel points to the fact that while the Gathas of Zoroaster's Avesta precede the Torah as we have it, there are ancient parts of the oral Torah that are older than any part of the Avesta (or any of the seven subsequent testaments), and that monotheism almost certainly came to Zoroaster from the Israelites of his neighborhood. She therefore happily claims Zoroastrianism, along with Christianity and Islam, as one of the "three daughter religions" of Judaism. There is no one-woman-upmanship in this, since she is very much aware of Judaism's debt to Zoroastrianism through their interface in Babylon—a happy acknowledgment of the interconnectedness of the subject we are pursuing.

Marc Zvi Brettler was coeditor of the earlier *Jewish Study Bible* for Oxford University Press, to which he offered an introduction to the Torah that was nearly as grand in sweep and scope as the introduction he presented in *Three Testaments: Torah, Gospel, and Quran* in 2012. Among other things in his *Three Testaments* contribution, the erudite Professor Brettler validates our use of the documentary hypothesis, "if not as 'documents,' then at least as an important starting point for understanding the prehistory of the Torah." While also acknowledging the importance of the Torah to other religions, in *Three Testaments* he points to the importance of respect for differing points of view, even when considering the same material: "The three great monotheistic religions all view the Hebrew Bible as significant, but we must remember that it is of different significance to each, and that each considers different parts of it to be especially significant, and that each interprets it differently."

This richness in shared resources, even across historic divisions, is currently expanding among seven world religions and others, as exemplified in Professor Brettler's more recent interface with Hinduism, to be addressed in the epilogue to this text. We do not have to agree on details to be stretched in our thinking and spiritual understanding and to be enriched in the traditions we hold dear.

hebrew creation story

The uniquely Hebrew creation story begins with Adam and Eve in the Garden of Eden, found as in the Yahweh source (J) at Genesis 2:4. But the Bible begins in chapter 1 with the account compiled from the Zoroastrian construction and polished by the priestly source (P) in Babylon under Zoroastrian influence. We should find that original in the Dead Zee Scrolls, but we have already seen the version that was preserved by oral tradition and finally written as a postscript to the Avesta.

GENESIS

When God Began to Create heaven and earth—²the earth being unformed and void, with darkness over the surface of the deep and a wind from God sweeping over the water—³God said, "Let there be light"; and there was light. ⁴God saw that the light was good, And God separated the light from the darkness. ⁵God called the light Day and called the darkness Night. And there was evening and there was morning, a first day.

⁶God said, "Let there be an expanse in the midst of the water, that it may separate water from water." ⁷God made the expanse, and it separated the water which was below the expanse from the water which was above the expanse. And it was so. ⁸God called the expanse Sky. And there was evening and there was morning, a second day.

⁹God said, "Let the water below the sky be gathered into one area, that the dry land may appear." And it was so. ¹⁰God called the dry land Earth and called the gathering of waters Seas. And God saw that this was good. ¹¹And God said, "Let the earth sprout vegetation: seed-bearing plants, fruit trees of every kind on earth that bear fruit with the seed in it." And it was so. ¹²The earth brought forth vegetation: seed-bearing plants of every kind, and trees of every kind bearing fruit with the seed in it. And God saw that this was good. ¹³And there was evening and there was morning, a third day.

¹⁴God said, "Let there be lights in the expanse of the sky to separate day from night; they shall serve as signs for the set times—the days and the years; ¹⁵and they shall

serve as lights in the expanse of the sky to shine upon the earth." And it was so. [16]God made the two great lights, the greater light to dominate the day and the lesser light to dominate the night, and the stars. [17]And God set them in the expanse of the sky to shine upon the earth, [18]to dominate the day and the night, and to separate light from darkness. And God saw that this was good. [19]And there was evening and there was morning, a fourth day.

[20]God said, "Let the waters bring forth swarms of living creatures, and birds that fly above the earth across the expanse of the sky." [21]God created great sea monsters, and all the living creatures of every kind that creep, which the waters brought forth in swarms, and all the winged birds of every kind. And God saw that this was good. [22]God blessed them, saying, "Be fertile and increase, fill the waters in the seas, and let the birds increase on the earth." [23]And there was evening and there was morning, a fifth day.

[24]God said, "Let the earth bring forth every living creature: cattle, creeping things, and wild beasts of every kind." And it was so. [25]God made wild beasts of every kind and cattle of every kind, and all kinds of creeping things of the earth. And God saw that this was good. [26]And God said, "Let us make humankind in our image, after our likeness. They shall rule the fish of the sea, the birds of the sky, the cattle, the whole earth, and all the creeping things that creep on earth." [27]And God created humankind in the divine image, creating it in the image of God—creating them male and female. [28]God blessed them and God said to them, "Be fertile and increase, fill the earth and master it: and rule the fish of the sea, the birds of the sky and all the living things that creep on earth."

[29]God said, "See, I give you every seed-bearing plant that is upon the earth, and every tree that has seed-bearing fruit; they shall be yours for food. [30]And to all the animals on land, to all the birds of the sky, and to everything that creeps on earth, in which there is the breath of life, [I give] all the green plants for food." And it was so. [31]And God saw all that had been made, and found it very good. And there was evening and there was morning, the sixth day.

2 The heavens and the earth were finished, and all their array. [2]On the seventh day God finished the work that had been undertaken: [God] ceased on the seventh day from doing any of the work. [3]And God blessed the seventh day and declared it holy—having ceased on it from all the work of creation that God had done. [4]Such is the story of heaven and earth when they were created.

hebrew apocalypse

There is no best illustration of Z derivative apocalyptic writing in the Hebrew text, but a rash of examples is provided by prophets preaching and writing during and immediately following the Babylonian Exile in which Jews participated in developments taking place in the wake of Zoroaster. We find these illustrations in Isaiah, Jeremiah, Daniel, Ezekiel, Amos, Micah, and Zechariah. The following from Zechariah presents the final battle motif as centred in and around Jerusalem, quoted often today by those who believe the end times are near.[2]

¹The word of the LORD concerning Israel: Thus says the LORD, who stretched out the heavens and founded the earth and formed the human spirit within: ²See, I am about to make Jerusalem a cup of reeling for all the surrounding peoples; it will be against Judah also in the siege against Jerusalem. ³On that day I will make Jerusalem a heavy stone for all the peoples; all who lift it shall grievously hurt themselves. And all the nations of the earth shall come together against it. ⁴On that day, says the LORD, I will strike every horse with panic, and its rider with madness. But on the house of Judah I will keep a watchful eye, when I strike every horse of the peoples with blindness. ⁵Then the clans of Judah shall say to themselves, "The inhabitants of Jerusalem have strength through the LORD of hosts, their God."

⁶On that day I will make the clans of Judah like a blazing pot on a pile of wood, like a flaming torch among sheaves; and they shall devour to the right and to the left all the surrounding peoples, while Jerusalem shall again be inhabited in its place, in Jerusalem.

⁷And the LORD will give victory to the tents of Judah first, that the glory of the house of David and the glory of the inhabitants of Jerusalem may not be exalted over that of Judah. ⁸On that day the LORD will shield the inhabitants of Jerusalem so that the feeblest among them on that day shall be like David, and the house of David shall be like God, like the angel of the LORD, at their head. ⁹And on that day I will seek to destroy all the nations that come against Jerusalem.

¹⁰And I will pour out a spirit of compassion and supplication on the house of David and the inhabitants of Jerusalem, so that, when they look on the one whom they have pierced, they shall mourn for him, as one mourns for an only child, and weep bitterly over him, as one weeps over a firstborn. ¹¹On that day the mourning in Jerusalem will be as great as the mourning for Hadad-rimmon in the plain of Megiddo. ¹²The land shall mourn, each family by itself; the family of the house of David by itself, and their wives by themselves; the family of the house of Nathan by itself, and their wives by themselves; ¹³the family of the house of Levi by itself, and their wives by themselves; the family of the Shimeites by itself, and their wives by themselves; ¹⁴and all the families that are left, each by itself, and their wives by themselves.

an archive page from a hebrew text

Ancient Hebrew Document Found at Dunhuang in China.
BRITISH LIBRARY OR.8212/166 (D.XIII).

notes

1. Midrash Tehillim 90:12.
2. Zechariah 12:1–14.

11

an essence of the tao

WHILE ALL OUR CONTRIBUTORS HAVE ILLUSTRIOUS CREDIBILITY, THE APPEARANCE OF Ellen Frankel and Marc Brettler immediately establishes a certain cachet of academic preeminence for *Three Testaments* in volume 2. The presence of Arvind Sharma, Richard Freund, Francis Clooney, and Victor Mair in *Four Testaments* does the same for volume 3. Considered by many to be the world's leading Sinologist across that vast field, Mair does at least hold preeminent standing in the area of Taoism and its Scripture, of particular interest to us.

In introducing the Tao Te Ching in *Four Testaments*, Mair writes, "In late 1973, when Chinese archaeologists working at Ma-wang-tui in central China, about a hundred miles south of the Yangtze River, unearthed two silk manuscripts of the *Tao Te Ching*, scholars of ancient China around the world were overjoyed." These manuscripts are at least half a millennium older than any commonly translated versions (a matter not unrelated to our quest to find certain other documents of that era). This translation of the Tao Te Ching is based wholly on these newfound manuscripts.

In his foreword to *Four Testaments*, Francis Clooney of the Harvard Divinity School asks, "What have the *Tao Te Ching* and the *Bhagavad Gita* to do with one another?" and answers, "This unexpected proximity also makes possible and perhaps inevitable another real benefit of the project: to read them *together*, paging through them, moving back and forth from text to text, allowing reading and the reader's imagination to bring them together." Mair takes this a step further in pointing to a more ancient connection.

Mair shows whole passages of the Tao Te Ching in which the words and images are identical to those of the Gita. For example, the obscuring of a mirror by dust as a metaphor for the clouding of the mind in the Gita[1] is also found in the Tao Te Ching.[2] Or take "closing all the doors of the body, shutting up the mind in the heart" of the Gita;[3] this compares with the practitioner of the Tao who "stopples the openings of his heart and closes its doors"[4]—the same thing in a different language. Mair says, "There are only three conceivable explanations for how this relationship could have developed:

1. China borrowed the yogic system and its attendant practices from India
2. India borrowed Taoism and its attendant practices from China
3. Both India and China were recipients of inspiration from a third source."

It appears that the Old Master of the Tao either taught the writer of the Gita or sat at his feet, unless they both really did have another source. In the absence of any evidence in support of the first two options to date, the answer may more properly be thought of as relating to the text of this study. The Avesta and Vedic-Zoroastrian influences become the model for "Scriptural Reasoning" and other examples of comfortable sharing in the twenty-first-century era of interfaith studies.

"If we use Christianity as a comparison, Baptist, Adventist, Lutheran, Catholic would be called schools. Different Taoist schools have different practices and different goals. Most modern Taoist schools are hybrids of Taoism and some other religion. Typical are Taoism and Buddhism, Taoism and Confucianism, and Taoism and Christianity."[5] Taoism may be a model for twenty-first-century religion, maintaining its ground but opening hearts and minds to insights from others.

taoist creation story

Creatio ex nihilo as the emergence of being from nothing is usually considered more typical of Western thought than Chinese discernment. However, Western mystical traditions have also articulated the view that God transcends "being" and is "nothing," which sounds more Chinese. In Taoist tradition, the nameless Tao gives rise to the Tao that can be named. At the border, leaving China and heading west in retirement, Lao Tzu penned these words:

> There was something featureless yet complete,
> Born before Heaven and Earth.
> Silent—amorphous—and formless,
> it stood alone and unchanging.
> We may regard it as the Mother of heaven and earth.
> Not knowing its name, I styled it the "Tao."
> If forced to give it a name I would call it "Tao."[6]
> The Tao that can be told
> is not the eternal Tao;
> The name that can be named
> is not the eternal name.
> The unnameable is the eternally real.
> Naming is the origin of all particular things.[7]

In the early centuries of the Common Era, we can identify Taoist creation stories in China, surrounding *Pan Gu* (meaning "from aboriginal abyss"), the first man. His name is thought by some to be a translation of the Babylonian *Tiamat*, "the Deep," a phrase employed in both Zoroastrian and Hebrew Scriptures at a time when such concepts reverberated at a pace only recently recognized. Said to have been born out of chaos within a giant egg where yin and yang competed, Pan Gu had two horns, two tusks, and a hairy body. He separated heaven and earth and set the sun, moon, stars, and planets in place. He divided the four seas of the earth and shaped the dry land by digging out valleys and piling up mountains, all achieved on the basis of yin and yang, used creatively by Pan Gu. Presented in Taoist art as a dwarf clothed in leaves, Pan Gu was plagued by parasites that evolved into true human beings.

taoist apocalypse

Apocalypse texts also exist in China, and the Taoist book *Divine Incantations* in particular is similar to the Zoroastrian model and the Western emulations. This Taoist text is believed to have been written in the fourth century CE and based on material coming into the religion from a source yet to be identified, but addressed in the next chapter. In a similar way, there were also those who later took the seventh-century ruler Li Hong to be the messianic figure, one who will return someday to elevate the faithful and destroy the rest of society and create a new society based upon Taoist teachings. Readers might keep these hints of another source related to Taoism in mind in reference to new identifications to be revealed in the next chapter.

The *Divine Incantations* offer ghostly soldiers to protect those who uphold Taoist teachings in the face of challenges by demon powers from a celestial realm. It persuades Taoists to work tirelessly in reaching out to those who are not yet enlightened so that they may join the winning side.

Even before the *Divine Incantations*, religious apocalyptic writings were being used to undermine the Han Dynasty during the Yellow Turban Rebellion from 184 to 205 CE. The vast peasant classes worked for a pittance and faced heavy taxation. This was seen by many Taoists as oppressive governance that would end in a period of destruction, from which new leadership would emerge. The Chinese saw the end of days as the end of a cycle in accord with the Chinese cyclical view of history.

an archive page from the tao te ching

Mawangdui Manuscript of Tao Te Ching Discovered in 1973.
WIKIMEDIA COMMONS.

notes

1. Book 3, stanza 38.
2. Chapter 54, lines 6 and 7.
3. Book 8, stanza 12.
4. Chapter 19, lines 4 and 5.
5. Open letter at www.the-taoism-for-modern-world.com.
6. Tao Te Ching 69 (traditional #25) based on the Mawangdui translation by Victor Mair in 1990 as used in *Four Testaments*.
7. *Tao Te Ching* chapter 1 in the Stephen Mitchell traditional translation of 1988.

12

an essence of the analects

I N ACKNOWLEDGING CURRENT DEVELOPMENTS IN THE SPIRITUAL REALM, CHINA'S CURRENT LEADER, Xi Jinping, has said, "Religions must be Chinese in orientation."[1] This is an almost eerie echo of the final suppression of Sogdian Zoroastrianism by Emperor Wuzong in 845 CE, along with other religions: "Syrian monks (Ta Ch'in) and Zoroastrian monks (Muh-hu-fo) to the number of more than three thousand are compelled to return to the world, lest they confuse the customs of China. With simplified and regulated government, we will achieve a unification of our manners, that in future all our youth may together return to the royal culture. We are now beginning this reformation; how long it will take we do not know."[2]

Jinping's pronouncement has been widely interpreted as a deliberate overture to Confucianism, but his comment is also being seized upon as collateral encouragement by Taoists and Buddhist. Christians in China had already begun to indigenize in the Three-Self Movement uniting historic Protestant mission denominations upon the expulsion of missionaries in 1950. A 2018 concordat between the Vatican and the Government of China brought unity between "underground" and state-recognized Catholics in an indigenized structure similar in certain respects to a long-standing concordat between the Vatican and France. These still-restricted but rapidly growing churches, together with American-style underground Protestant assemblies, are perhaps the greatest threat to the government. But it is the Muslim-scattered Hui Muslim population and the Uyghur Muslim majority in Xinjiang province who are the most severely harassed, with up to a million of the latter at any one time incarcerated for "vocational training." This is the whitewashing of minds called "re-education" for which China became famous during the Cultural Revolution under Mao Zedong, and which is still practiced for Buddhists in Tibet as well.

As for the religious spectrum in China today, Confucianism seems increasingly acceptable to the communist government, and the Muslim Hui and Uyghurs remain stubbornly entrenched, even as the situation of the Uyghurs has become dire. Buddhists are struggling to hold their own in Tibet, while Taoists keep a low but enduring profile. The church growth phenomenon may be for Christians the single most important story of the global church in the twenty-first century.

As with persecutions elsewhere in history, the old Chinese aphorism appears to say it all: "The Chinese people are like bamboo. When the wind blows, they bend over and touch the ground. When the wind drops, they come back to their full height." Westerners uncertain about the future of religion in North America and Western Europe might take note: There are more Christians in China than in the United Kingdom, more Muslims than in Saudi Arabia, more Taoists than in Korea, and more Buddhists than in the Indian subcontinent where the religion was born. The "Century of Religion" is young, and proponents are making common cause in many places, especially among the seven world religions, as will be described in the epilogue.

To the surprise of many, beginning in the 1990s the Chinese academic community developed a profound and vigorous interest in Zoroastrianism. This does not suggest a growing interest in religion in Chinese academia, but it does present a growing realization of how significantly the Zoroastrian phenomenon in China affected Chinese culture in the first millennium of the Common Era.[3] A flood of information too late to include in *Four Testaments*, but worth significant attention in this book, is introduced here and developed further on.

We know about incursions into China by Magi from Persia in the seventh century BCE, thanks to the work of Victor Mair, detailed in *Three Testaments* and alluded to shortly here. The manner in which they communicated Western ideas from their Iranian counterparts during the Persian Empire, including Zoroastrian influence, is helpfully reflected in the play *Older Testaments: Encounters on the Way* by William Thomas, presented in appendix D of this book. There had been previous "connections," and the Silk Route from China to the West was initially formulated during the reign of Emperor Wu (141–87 BCE) during the Han Dynasty, during which Zoroastrian and other ideas were beginning to be exchanged in a fashion more easily documented.

But it was during the Tang Dynasty (618–907, a high point in Chinese civilization) that Zoroastrians of the extended Sogdian community had more influence in Chinese history than realized until very recently. This influence was pervasive until one of their own rebelled against the Tang Dynasty and Zoroastrians faced a crackdown with a societal destruction equivalent to their near obliteration by Alexander and again under Islamic domination. The Sogdian Zoroastrians had become an integral part of Chinese society by the time An Lushan declared himself emperor. Though resembling Cyrus the Great in style, his insurgency was not an invasion but an integrated part of the culture, even though ill fated. The third historic denigration of Zoroastrianism in the aftermath of the An Lushan Rebellion (775–763) is only now coming to light in the modern era. Chinese experts, working together with Australian scholars of Zoroastrianism, point now to the significant influence of Zoroastrianism on Chinese culture before and during the An Lushan era, an influence that infiltrated Confucianism, at last making its mark within that distinctly Chinese singularity before it became a worldwide phenomenon.

Out of this influence came the Zoroastrian-style creation stories and apocalyptic visions counterintuitively referenced in the previous chapter on Taoism. Of equal significance, we can now begin to recognize that the Zoroastrianism of the Tang era may account for the dissonance between the Confucianism of the Analects by Confucius and his disciples and the practice of Confucianism as a public and spiritual phenomenon in the last thousand years. Confucius may have rejected the Zoroastrian ideas of the Magi at the Imperial Archives (however that actually happened in an enigmatic era), but Zoroastrian stimulus of a previous era may be found in Confucianism as practiced today. We can say with considerable confidence that it was when Zoroastrians became Confucianists following the An Lushan rebellion that Confucianism became a religion. The specifics of this significant development will be explicated in greater detail in appendix H for those readers wishing to master a growing and exciting field of Zoroastrian studies.

If Confucianism is indeed growing in Chinese government favor, or at least toleration, a continuing question remains among some scholars as to whether Confucianism qualifies as a religion. Some say it has never been a religion, while others aver that it was always a religion of wisdom or harmony, a "secular religion" with a focus on humanistic aspects of life in which humans can achieve ethical progress and live up to heavenly principles without the assistance of deities. None of this is sufficient to have Confucianism included in the *Norton Anthology of World Religions*, of which there are only six by that reckoning. We accept the affirmative thesis of Anna Sun's 2013 book, *Confucianism as a World Religion: Contested Histories and Contemporary Realities*.[4] In her 2018–2019 research project at Harvard Divinity School, she makes the case that Confucianism reads like something between Greek philosophy and Roman moral law but functions like a religion in the practice of people. We date this accurate description of Confucianism of the last thousand years or more from the revival of the Tang Dynasty in 763 CE and the subsequent integration of millions of Sogdian Zoroastrians into the mainstream of Chinese society, in which Confucian principles were enhanced by Zoroastrian spirituality.

Confucianism in practice does involve worship. It argues that humans are made up of two pieces: the *hun* (a spirit from heaven) and the *po* (soul from the earth). When a person is born, the two halves unite, and when that person dies, they separate and leave the earth. Sacrifice is made to the ancestors who once lived on earth by playing music (to recall their spirits from heaven) and drinking and spilling wine (to draw the soul from the earth). But one only needs to attend a Confucian tourist wedding in Niagara Falls (of which there are many, usually employing clergy of other traditions) or a funeral in Toronto's Chinatown (as local Chinese refer to it) to be certain that in popular culture, Confucianism is absolutely a religion, with prayers, Scripture readings, and all the trappings of spiritual expression. Such services have an almost Unitarian Universalist feeling about them, with readings from many sources and prayers addressed almost as if "To Whom It May Concern." Confucius himself promoted rituals, and in China today worshippers visit temples to show veneration of ancestors and of

Confucius. They ask for blessings, make offerings, and share ceremonial cups of tea in communion with each other and with the spirits. While there appears to be little or nothing of Zoroaster in the scriptural Analects of Confucius, there is enough in the practice of Confucianism to make modern Chinese secular scholars more than just a little suspicious that the spirit of Zoroastrianism lives on in China today.

traditional chinese creation stories

There are earlier Chinese myths of origin that seem unrelated, while those beginning in and after the Axial Age as cosmologies are more fruitfully compared to the Zoroastrian model. It appears that Confucius is to be distinguished by his resistance to and questioning of the new-think from the West, which the Magi brought to the realm before and during his lifetime. So the "Heavenly Questions" section of the *Songs of Chu*, a hundred years later in the Confucian tradition, begins by asking questions about creation myths that reflect issues still then in the air. The questions about darkness and light connect with Zoroastrian ideas, and the yin and yang reflect the drift to dualities in Zoroastrianism at exactly the same time. The questions are appropriate from the Confucian source; the connections are obvious.

> Who passed down the story of the far-off, ancient beginning of things? How can we be sure what it was like before the sky above and the earth below had taken shape? Since none could penetrate that murk when darkness and light were yet undivided, how do we know about the chaos of insubstantial forms? What manner of things are the darkness and light? How did Yin and Yang come together, and how did they originate and transform all things that are by their commingling? Whose compass measured out the heavens? Whose work was this, and how did he accomplish it? Where were the circling cords fastened, and where was the sky's pole fixed? Where did the Eight Pillars meet the sky, and why were they too short for it in the south-east? Where do the nine fields of heaven extend to and where do they join each other? The ins and outs of their edges must be very many; who knows their number? How does heaven coordinate its motions? Where are the Twelve Houses divided? How do the sun and the moon hold to their courses and the fixed stars keep their places?[5]

In 139 BCE, Han prince Liu An commissioned the compilation of *The Huainanzi*, a wide-ranging review of Chinese, and largely Confucian, material that contained two cosmogonic myths that develop the dualistic concept of yin and yang, probably from a time when dualistic Zoroastrian teachings were beginning to venture along the Silk Route.

> When Heaven and Earth were yet unformed, all was ascending and flying, diving and delving. It was called the Grand Inception. The Grand Inception produced the Nebulous Void. The Nebulous Void produced space-time, and space-time produced the original *qi* life force. A boundary divided the original *qi* energy. That which was pure and bright

spread out to form Heaven; that which was heavy and turbid congealed to form Earth. It is easy for that which is pure and subtle to converge but difficult for the heavy and turbid to congeal. Therefore, Hell was completed first; Earth was fixed afterward. The conjoined essences of Heaven and Earth produced yin and yang. The essences of yin and yang continually superseded each other causing the four seasons. The scattered essences of the four seasons created the myriad things. The hot *qi* life force of accumulated *yang* produced fire; an essence of fiery *qi* became the sun. The cold *qi* of accumulated yin produced water; An Essence of watery *qi* became the moon. The overflowing *qi* of the essences of the sun and the moon made the stars and planets. To Heaven belongs the sun, moon, stars, and planets; to Earth belong waters and floods, dust and soil.[6]

Of old, in the time before there was Heaven and Earth there were only images and no forms. All was obscure and dark, vague and unclear, shapeless and formless, and no one knows its gateway. There were two spirits, born in murkiness, one that established Heaven and the other that constructed Earth. So vast! No one knows where they ultimately end. So broad! No one knows where they finally stop. Thereupon they differentiated into the yin and the yang and separated into the eight cardinal directions. The firm and the yielding formed each other; the myriad things thereupon took shape. The turbid vital energy became creatures; the refined vital energy became humans.[7]

traditional chinese apocalypse

There was a certain amount of post-Zoroastrian Magian apocalypticism in China in the era following the Axial Age—in Taoism, as we have seen; vibrant in Buddhism, as we shall see; and based on revolution in Confucianism (so again almost compatible with the government in the present communist era). While rejecting the Vedic-Zoroastrian influence of the Magi, Confucius was drawn into apocalyptic thinking in refuting their arguments. In Confucianism, the cycle described in the apocalypse of Taoist universalist doctrine is dependent on the "Mandate of Heaven." This mandate was given by the heavens to emperors. It gave them the right to rule on the condition that they rule fairly. If the relationship between the masses and its emperor deteriorated to the point of mass unrest and dissatisfaction, the mandate would pass to those who overthrew the emperor and installed a fairer system of governance for the people.

This mandate of heaven has very ancient roots in Chinese history and has influenced the Chinese psyche to this day—an "apocalyptic" vision of revolution in this world as counter to the Zoroastrian image of a cataclysmic finale in a universal context. The Zhou Dynasty promoted the Mandate of Heaven concept well before the Axial Age, with the idea that there could be only one legitimate ruler of China at a time and that this ruler had the blessing of heaven. They used this mandate to justify their overthrow of the Shang Dynasty and their subsequent rule. It is a perfect example of what Confucius recognized and supported among the "noble traditions" of China, which, in his view, made the Magi-sponsored Western / Iranian concepts unnecessary and superfluous, as illustrated in the play *Older Testaments: Encounters on the Way*, in appendix D.

an archive page from the analects

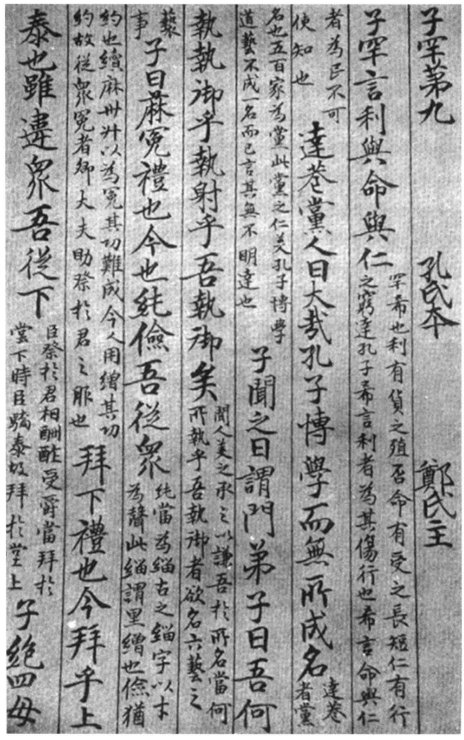

Title Page of Analects Book IX.

This title page illustration reproduces a leaf from a medieval hand copy of the Analects, dated 890 CE, recovered from an archaeological dig at Dunhuang, in the Western desert regions of China. The manuscript has been determined to be a schoolboy's hand copy, complete with errors, and it reproduces not only the text (which appears in large characters), but also an early commentary (small, double-column characters). The quality of schoolboy "handwriting"—actually brush and ink work—should probably make us all feel inadequate. . . . Recovery of this particular copy of the text was unusually valuable, because the second century CE commentary it includes is a famous one by a great early scholar that has otherwise been largely lost.[8]

notes

1. Speech by Xi Jinping, general secretary of the Nineteenth Communist Party Congress in Huaibei in China's eastern province of Anhui on October 18, 2017.
2. T. V. Philip, *East of the Euphrates: Early Christianity in Asia* (India: CSS & ISPCK, 1998).
3. See further Professor Dr. Zhang Xiaogui at zhshubenhua@163.com and as noted in the bibliography.
4. Princeton books, etc.
5. David Hawkes, ed., *The Songs of the South: An Anthology of Ancient Chinese Poems by Qu Yuan and Other Poets* (New York: Penguin, 1985), 127.
6. John S. Major et al., eds., *The Huainanzi: A Guide to the Theory and Practice of Government in Early Han China* (New York: Columbia University Press, 2010), 114–15.
7. Ibid., 240–41.
8. Robert Eno, University of Indiana, online teaching course.

13

an essence of the dhammapada

THERE IS A GROWING RECOGNITION OF THE ZOROASTRIAN CONTEXT OF THE BUDDHA'S CHILD-hood. He was born in the area of Lumbini in the Nepal-India border area in 563 BCE, when Zoroaster was an old man with headquarters at Balkh in nearby Bactria. Zoroaster was himself Scythian, and the Buddha was Saka, the Eastern Scythian tribe then inhabiting Nepal and northeastern India. Taxila University of the sixth century BCE was an early Vedic institution not far from there. Taxila was almost certainly in the thrall of the Zoroastrian phenomenon then sweeping the Silk Route and influencing the Shramana reform movement within northern Hinduism. During Buddha's childhood, Taxila itself was briefly the capital of the most easterly Persian province under the Achaemenids, an Iranian monarchy that was thoroughly Zoroastrian in religion. It may be presumed that in restricting Siddhartha Gautama to the palace as a boy, his father would have brought in tutors for his son, the most learned available being from Taxila. There is no suggestion that the Buddha's "awakening" under the bodhi tree was anything other than a unique phenomenon that led to the founding of Buddhism, as reflected in the Dhammapada, and the reform of Hinduism as seen in the Bhagavad Gita. But there is now little doubt that he expressed this experience of enlightenment in Zoroastrian terms.

In China, Buddhism built on Taoism, a monistic religion perhaps stimulated by the presence of Magi at the Imperial Archives and elsewhere in the time of Lao Tzu. In *Four Testaments*, Victor Mair makes a solid case that these Iranians were China's earliest Silk Route link to the west. The Magi were part of the mass conversion to Zoroastrianism in Iran under Cyrus the Great, presenting a stimulus in China similar to that experienced by the Buddha in India. The legendary confrontation between a conservative Confucius and a progressive Lao Tzu may be an apocryphal symbol of Chinese traditions reacting to monistic ideas from Iran. Confucianism defined itself by resisting change, while Taoism provided the environment in which Buddhism flourished with the same deep spiritual mindfulness and healing power available to us today.

If Victor Mair's stopple verse connects the Tao Te Ching and the Bhagavad Gita through a common Z source, the so-called parallel sayings of Jesus and the Buddha[1] are an even more impressive relational connection between two of our testaments in particular. *Three Testaments* addresses that matter in detail, proposing that while Jesus and the Buddha could never have met, both were in proximity to a common Z source, now lost to the world but seen in both the Christian Gospel and the Buddhist Dhammapada. The following essence of the Dhammapada was presented by Dr. Bhande Saranapala at a panel workshop on November 5, 2018, at the Parliament of the World's Religions in support of this text and to supplement a less than complete introduction to the Buddhist Dhammapada in *Four Testaments, Tao Te Ching, Analects, Dhammapada, Bhagavad Gita.*

ðhammapaða as the bible of buððhism

Just as Jesus was born a Jew and his transformational life gave the world Christianity, so too Siddhartha Gautama the Buddha was born into a Brahmanic/Hindu culture in the sixth century BCE, and his personal internal transformation gave the world Buddhism. Buddha's transformational life is depicted in the Tipitaka or Tripitaka, the Three Baskets. The Tipitaka contain Buddhist doctrine and ways to the transformational life of the Buddha. The Dhammapada, known as the Buddhist Bible and included in the *Four Testaments* compiled by Dr. Brian Arthur Brown, records fundamental doctrines of the Buddha. Buddhism in *Four Testaments* is limited to its Indian origins, as presented by Radhakrishnan's translation of the Dhammapada. I will critique this from the perspective of Buddhism both as it first appeared and as experienced today.

The story of Siddhartha Gautama's quest toward enlightenment is more than anything a story of the search for happiness and health (*Ariyapariyesana Sutta* of the *Majjhima Nikaya*). After 600 BCE, the Shramana movement progressed in the Hindu community as an offshoot of the Vedic religion, possibly an early response to what Brian Brown refers to as Zoroastrian stimulation. Shramanas, or "strivers or seekers," rejected the authority of the Brahmans as protectors of the Vedas and as agents of God, instead striving for an independent realization of the solution to the existential problem of suffering. These strivers renounced marital and domestic life, electing to adopt ascetic practices in hopes of purifying the soul or the mind. Where the Brahmans advocated external salvation through sacrifice and devotional practices, the Shramanas believed an internal realization of salvation to be possible.

We know that Siddhartha Gautama was greatly influenced by the practices of these Shramanas, spending several years of his life experimenting with extreme ascetic practices of self-mortification. When Siddhartha Gautama took this path to its limit, he still found no resolution to the problem of internal suffering. Contextualizing the Shramanic practices of extreme denial of the senses, against his former palace life of

---

Paper presented by Bhante Saranapala at the 2018 Parliament of World's Religions in Toronto.

complete sensual gratification, the Siddhartha Gautama found that neither of these two paths could ever lead to complete fulfillment, knowledge, wisdom, and utter liberation. It is here that the Siddhartha Gautama carved out a new way—namely, the noble eightfold path.

Siddhartha Gautama understood that all sentient beings experienced an inherent problem in life (*Mahasaccaka Sutta of the Majjhima Nikaya*); the problem of dissatisfaction he called *dukkha*. The theoretical framework provided by the teaching is the Four Noble Truths.[2] These truths center around the fact of suffering, understood not as merely experienced pain and sorrow but as the pervasive feeling of dissatisfaction that accompanies all conditional phenomena.[3] Siddhartha Gautama's profound wisdom was to recognize that the external world can never provide what we need to make us feel complete, but rather that the resolution to our feeling of disconnect lay internally. Siddhartha Gautama, the Buddha, stated in the Dhammapada:

> All experience is preceded by mind, led by mind, made by mind.
> Speak or act with a corrupted mind, and suffering follows
> as the wagon wheel follows the hoof of the ox.
>
> All experience is preceded by mind, led by mind, made by mind.
> Speak or act with a peaceful mind, and happiness follows
> like a never-departing shadow.[4]

The initial portion of the first stanza clearly delineates the mind as the forerunner to all experiences, imploring us to look internally, and prioritizing the mind as the path to freedom from dukkha. However, the second portion explains the benefits that will follow from setting the right intention. Act with a peaceful mind, free from agitation and corruption, and we can expect nothing less than mental health and well-being. To act with this peaceful mind, the mind must first be trained to go against the habitual external examination. Instead of keeping watch over the faults of others, the disciple is admonished to examine his own faults and to make a continual effort to remove internal impurities, just as a silversmith purifies silver.[5] Through training the mind to a deeper state of internal investigation, Siddhartha Gautama underwent a transcendental transformation, which resulted in him becoming the "Buddha"—the Awakened One.

The Buddha's plea to look internally defied the deeply rooted Vedic Brahmanic structures present throughout India before 600 BCE, challenging the rigid caste system and directly defying ritualistic sacrifice and salvation in external deities. Perhaps the most direct example of this shift was the establishment of Buddhist Sanghas, communities of spiritual wanderers ("Shramanas") made up of individuals formerly identifying as Brahmans (priests and academics), Kshatriya (warriors and rulers), Vaishya (merchants and landowners), Sudra (commoners, peasants, and servants), and Untouchables (outcastes). The Buddha's message to all these groups remained the same: true mental healing is attainable in this life, irrespective of caste, and through looking inward rather than outward. Where the Untouchables were irredeemable in the eyes of the spiritual tradition of the time, the Buddha stated that even if an individual has committed evil in the past, there is no need for dejection or despair: "A human's ways can be radically changed, and one who abandons the evil for the good illuminates this world like the moon freed from clouds."[6] It all looks very Zoroastrian.

Perhaps as a direct consequence of the defiance of old tradition, the Buddha's teachings could no longer survive in India after his death, as there was a fierce and direct opposition to Buddhist doctrine, even as a reform of Hindu practice. Subsequently, Buddhism moved to other locales that proved to be more hospitable hosts at the time. In China, the teachings of Confucius and Lao Tzu had already taken hold; therefore the population that was accustomed to notions of filial duty, on the one hand, and harmonious coexistence with nature, on the other, found Buddhist conceptualizations of karmic existence, personal rebirth, and internal investigation easy pills to swallow. Because the Buddha's teachings did not provide any direct major contradictions with the spiritual traditions present in China at the time, many individuals looked to Buddhism as offering a new hope for release from suffering.

While many factors can arguably be attributable to the spread of Buddhism to the west, they can all be encompassed in the Buddhist concept of dukkha. The problem of dukkha, which the Buddha talked about, was not simply a problem unique to the Axial Age in what is now northern India, but rather a problem of suffering and dissatisfaction that transcends time and place and is experienced universally.

The Buddha emphasized in the Dhammapada that health is attained through internal investigation. Richard Davidson, a renowned American neuroscientist at the University of Wisconsin, recently reminded us, "In the 2,500-year history of Buddhism, the religion has directed its energy inward in an attempt to train the mind to understand the mental state of happiness, to identify and defuse sources of negative emotion and to cultivate emotional states like compassion to improve personal and societal well-being." The adoption of Buddhism in the West has in many ways paralleled its transition in China. In the West, the prominent monotheistic ideologies resulted in a similar search for external salvation, with the belief being that devotional practices would result in eternal happiness and the end of suffering. With religion arguably being replaced by materialism in the nineteenth century, the search for true release shifted from *the* eternal creator to *an* eternal process of creation. In Apple, Google, and the like, however, the search still remains external rather than internal. Popular works such as Radhakrishnan's translation of Dhammapada, Dr. Walpola Rahula's *What the Buddha Taught*, Rick Hanson's *Buddha's Brain* and his *Hardwiring Happiness*, and Bhante Henepola Gunaratana's *Mindfulness in Plain English* provided helpful translations of the Buddha's teachings and excerpts designed to act as introductions to Buddhism for non-Buddhist Westerners.

With the Buddha's teachings now highly accessible, many neuroscientists have begun to express interest in applying the Western scientific model to study the effects the meditation practice of Buddhism had on the mind. Works such as Jon Kabat-Zinn's formulation of mindfulness-based stress reduction (MBSR) extracted the meditation practice of the religion, and applied it in a therapeutic context with great success to treat clinical depression. Since founding the Stress Reduction Clinic at the University of Massachusetts Medical School in 1979, Kabat-Zinn and his colleagues have treated over twenty thousand patients and taught more than two thousand health professionals the techniques of mindfulness meditation, which instructs a Buddhist-inspired nonjudgmental, total awareness of the present moment as a way of reducing stress. Objective data found that participants felt healthier, more positive, and less stressed.

The aforementioned works drew a great deal of attention and prompted a more secularized version of Buddhist meditation. This version appealed to the postmodern materialistic society where theistic religion was being shunned by many, leaving a gap in spiritual guidance, but perhaps remaining open to adopting a new religious mode of thought, well described in Dr. Brown's present forthcoming book relating monotheistic deism to monistic universal Divinity. With stress, anxiety, depression, and post-traumatic stress disorder affecting Westerners irrespective of religious upbringing, and despite, or perhaps in tandem with, technological advancement, the possibility of a secular method to attain mental health through the scientifically backed practice of meditation had a strong appeal, open to religious people and nonreligious alike. The Buddha's discovery at the bodhi tree 2,500 years ago transcended time and place and encouraged the same finding modern science now leans toward—namely, all suffering is happening within. New Western adherents of Buddhism have started to show great interest in original Buddhist doctrine, even at synagogue or church. Among the English translations of Buddhist texts, Dhammapada plays an important role to the people of all levels as it sheds light and offers hopes and solutions to human suffering.

Rather than imposing a blind acceptance of doctrine, the Buddha encouraged wise reflection. In the *Kalama Sutta* contained in the *Anguttara Nikaya*,[7] the Buddha encountered a group of ascetics called the Kalamas, who had doubt about which religious group expounded the true doctrine. The Buddha encouraged the Kalamas to refrain from following tradition simply because it is deeply rooted in society, following reports of others simply because the source seems credible, or following one's own inclinations toward practice because they resonate with personal preferences, but rather to test any view and belief through wise reflection of cause and effect. The Buddha praised this as the appropriate way to direct one's attention, even going as far as commending his disciples for not believing his own teachings with blind faith, but rather putting the principles into practice to develop experiential wisdom. As Matthieu Ricard, a French disciple of His Holiness, the Dalai Lama, once stated, "Buddhism is like science, based on experience and investigation, not dogma." This appeal to the investigative nature of human beings is perhaps one of the more compelling reasons why free-thinking elements in Western society are finding resonance in Buddhist meditation as a practice.

The Buddha found that all mental health–related problems are based on directing the clinging mind outward, toward projections of the past or future, rather than a mindful awareness of the present with dispassion and nonattachment. Much of this teaching is contained in the Dhammapada, a 424-verse compilation now contained in the *Khuddaka Nikaya* and encompassing various teachings through the Tipitaka. In the Dhammapada, the Buddha states, "Let go of the past, let go of the future, let go of the present. Gone beyond becoming, with the mind released in every way, you do not again undergo birth and old age."[8] The Dhammapada is intended to promote mental health and healing. While translations of his *nibbana* to the word *enlightenment* can sound quite esoteric, it is clear that the Buddha's compassionate teachings were pointing to the goal of true happiness, freed from all suffering and pain, rebirth, and death. The Buddha states, "Health is the foremost possession, contentment, the foremost wealth, trust, the foremost kinship, and nibbana, the foremost happiness," pointing once again to a mind free from agitation.[9]

Generally speaking, the Dhammapada contains practical ways of directing the mind internally and reflecting on the conditions of the mind to promote mental health and happiness in the present moment, the future, and eternally. The broadest counsel the Dhammapada gives is to avoid all evil, to cultivate good, and to cleanse one's mind.[10] More specifically, this is done by adhering to the five precepts, the fundamental moral code of Buddhism, which teaches abstinence from taking life, stealing, committing adultery, speaking lies, and consuming intoxicants.[11] No external hierarchical punishment is imposed for transgressing these precepts; however, one who violates these training rules "digs up his own root even in this very world"—in other words, uprooting the basis of their own mental health.[12] The observance of morality is justified by the fact that it is in harmony with universal law. Through the efficacy of karma, our willed actions become the chief determinant of our destiny, both in this life and in future states of becoming. Following ethical conduct leads upward to inner development, happiness, and joy, whereas, conversely, violating ethical conduct leads downward, to self-deprecation and unhappiness. This theme is announced by the pair of verses as quoted, which open the Dhammapada and are recurrent throughout.[13]

Much like exercising the body, these practices must be sustained consistently to strengthen the mind's ability to turn inward. Adhering to a set of moral precepts practiced in tandem with meditative investigation produces the wisdom necessary to release oneself from internal suffering. This is not only the Buddha's path to enlightenment, which he offers for us to partake if we so choose, but also synonymously the path to happiness in this lifetime. This can be clearly seen in the Dhammapada, produced in full in *Four Testaments: Tao Te Ching, Analects, Dhammapada, Bhagavad Gita*.

buddhist creation story

It is sometimes asserted that there could be no Buddhist creation story since there is no beginning of the endless cycles and no deity separate from the process, but it may be seen that the process itself recycles and that humans share in new beginnings in their awakenings to the reality of the universe. Indeed, the Buddha himself, with some humor, describes a creative process. The serious aspect of this particular teaching is its context, in which the Buddha is illustrating that despite the caste system of India, all people are equal and arise from the same process. Zoroaster and his sons endorsed social divisions of labor and function, but with flexibility of movement by individuals within society. Buddha was perhaps emulating that example of reform of the Rig Veda, which insisted on rigorous enforcement of caste divisions, when he personally broke immutable cast laws. The case of Upali, a low-caste barber who met the Buddha when he was called upon to cut the Buddha's hair, is often cited in this regard. Upali eventually approached the Buddha to ask to be ordained with a group of the Buddha's high-born kinsmen. The Buddha insisted on ordaining Upali first so that he would be their senior, and superior, in the order.[14]

The following story by the Buddha, retold here in a paraphrase of the Pali Canon version, should be seen in that context rather than as specifically "the Buddhist creation story," as is sometimes claimed. It presents a cosmology in which the universe expands and contracts over long periods of time, leading some to compare it with Zoroastrianism and modern models of the universe of the Big Bang at the beginning and the Big Crunch at the end.[15] The similarities are not great, but given the Axial Age timing and the relative certainty that other aspects of the Buddha's doctrine were triggered by the Zoroastrian stimulus, we may assume that the Buddha had at least heard Zoroaster's creation story. From his own perspective, and for his own purposes, the Buddha's version unfolded as he spoke to Vasettha, one of his monks who had been a Brahman. We mean no disrespect when we observe that it reads as if the Buddha was making it up as he went along, an aid to the point he was exemplifying.

Over the course of time, in very long periods, this world expands and contracts. In the last contraction-transition living beings were born into the *Abhasara Brahma* world.[16] The first humans there were neither male nor female at first, living in communities with cows and other domesticated animals. Their bodies were luminous but there was no sun, moon or stars in the beginning. The humans were able to move through the air and they gorged themselves on sweet natural fungus. There was no heavenly light or seasons or years. Their little earth area was surrounded by one vast ocean of water. As the world began to expand again the earth spread over the waters and colors appeared, and honey rice and other plants. Their bodies became physically stiff and erect, and sex organs developed. In lust many engaged in sexual activity, to the disgust of others who drove them out of the community, necessitating the establishment of new villages for the sexually active.

Agriculture developed in the new communities, based on private property which led to hoarding and greed. In the quest for justice, punishments were developed. The need for leadership and government led to the establishment of the Kshatriya caste of warrior leaders. Others chose to establish huts in the forest as chapel temples where they could meditate, while some wrote books about religion, establishing the Brahman caste. The economy required a merchant class, and the Vaishyas caste was born. They employed what became the caste of Sudras as herdsmen, hunters, laborers and house servants. Everyone became instructed in the Dharma laws of behaviour so each person could achieve Nirvana in this very life by responding to the call of personal destiny.[17]

buðdhist apocalypse: the buðdha's sermon of the seven suns

The Buddha's "Sermon of the Seven Suns" appears in the Pali Canon, where the Buddha pronounces the final fate of the universe in an apocalypse that engulfs the earth; its language clearly being in the tradition of the Vedic-Zoroastrian model. He presents an apocalypse that will be characterized by the sequential appearance of seven suns in the heavens, each sun wreaking havoc in its own way until the world is engulfed in utter collapse at the end of time, defined as the end of the cycle, a true *fin de siècle*, so to speak.

All things are impermanent, all aspects of existence are unstable and noneternal. Beings will become so weary and disgusted with constituent things that they will seek emancipation from them more quickly. There will come a season, O monks, when after hundreds of thousands of years, rains will cease. All seedlings, all vegetation, all plants, grasses, and trees will dry up and all things under the sun will cease to be. There comes another season after a great lapse of time when a second sun will appear. Now all brooks and ponds will dry up, vanish, cease to be.

A third sun will dry the mighty Ganges and other great rivers. A fourth sun will cause the great lakes to evaporate, and a fifth will dry the oceans. Again, after a vast period of time a sixth sun will appear, and it will bake the earth, even as a pot is baked by a potter. All the mountains will reek and send up clouds of smoke. After another great interval a seventh sun will appear and the earth will blaze with fire until it becomes one mass of flame. The mountains will be consumed, a spark will be carried on the wind and go to the world of God. Thus, monks, all things will burn, perish, and exist no more except those who have seen the path.

an archive page from the diamond sutra

Title Page of the Diamond Sutra. Intricate religious artwork on a copy produced in 868 CE, the oldest dated book in the world.
BRITISH LIBRARY OR.8210/P.2.

notes

1. A common phrase in the books on the subject by the Dalai Lama, Marcus Borg, and others in the bibliography.

2. Dhammapada 190–92.

3. Dhammapada 202–3.

4. Dhammapada 1–2.

5. Dhammapada 50, 239.

6. Dhammapada 173.

7. AN 3.65.

8. Dhammapada 348.

9. Dhammapada 204.

10. Dhammapada 183.

11. Dhammapada 246–47.

12. Ibid.

13. Dhammapada 15–18, 117–22, 127, 132–33.

14. Barbara O'Brien, "The Historical Buddha's Disciples," ThoughtCo, May 21, 2018, thoughtco.com/first-generation-of-buddhas-disciples-449657.

15. James J. Hughes, PhD, *Beginnings and Endings: The Buddhist Mythos of the Arising and Passing Away of the World*; Sulak Sivaraksa et al., *Buddhist Perceptions of Desirable Societies in the Future: Papers Prepared for the United Nations University* (Bangkok, Thailand: IRCD, 1993).

16. The current era of shape and change.

17. Digha Nikaya 27, the Aggañña Sutta.

14

an essence of the bhagavad gita

AVING ACCEPTED THE CONVENTIONAL WISDOM THAT THE ZOROASTRIANS WERE IN CONTROL of Babylon during the Jewish exile there, the evidence that the Magi were ubiquitous even in China (abundance of proof in volume 3, *Four Testaments*) and the all-too-obvious dating and teachings of Buddhism, it is also obvious that embryonic Vedic influence was preeminent in nascent Hinduism earlier on. The question of Zoroastrian influence in India is provided by the Bhagavad Gita during the Axial Age. The remaining pieces of the puzzle will then be connected in chapters 15 and 16 to the Z aspects of Christianity found in the New Testament and the identifiable Z-related sections "freshly revealed" to Muhammad in the Quran.

Much of what we now affirm was succinctly addressed at the September 11, 1893, Chicago meeting of the Parliament of the World's Religions by Swami Vivekananda, the head of the delegation from India at the first such Parliament of the modern era, three years before the Olympics were similarly revived. Vivekananda claimed the affinity of Hinduism with its Vedic roots, as reflected in the Bhagavad Gita, but also affirmed the overlapping sources in the validity of all religions. He sought neither to convert others nor to blend religions, but rather to support each other in affirming the contribution of each to a peaceable world. He addressed a fanaticism that is still too common in our world, perhaps even more so in our time, to which a correct appreciation of each other's testaments may be but part of the amelioration religion can bring to the world. Delegates to the Parliament of the World's Religions meeting in Toronto in 2018 worked on the arguments presented in the text of this volume 1 of our trilogy, no doubt feeling that it has taken too long for the influence of people like Swami Vivikananda to bear fruit and that works like this one may advance the cause Vivikananda addressed in the following words:

> Sisters and Brothers, it fills my heart with joy unspeakable to rise in response to the
> warm and cordial welcome which you have given us. I thank you in the name of the

most ancient order of monks in the world; I thank you in the name of the mother of religions, and I thank you in the name of millions and millions of Hindu people of all classes and sects.

My thanks, also, to some of the speakers on this platform who, referring to the delegates from the Orient, have told you that those from far-off nations may well claim the honor of bearing to different lands the idea of toleration. I am proud to belong to a religion which has taught the world both tolerance and universal acceptance. We believe not only in universal toleration, but we accept all religions as bearing truth. I am proud to belong to a nation which has sheltered the persecuted and the refugees of all religions and all nations of the earth. I am proud to tell you that we have gathered in our bosom the remnant of the Israelites, who came to southern India and took refuge with us in the very year in which their holy temple was shattered to pieces by Roman tyranny. I am proud to belong to the religion which has sheltered and is still fostering the remnant of the grand Zoroastrian nation. I will quote to you a few lines from a hymn which I remember to have repeated from my earliest boyhood, which is every day repeated by millions of human beings: "As the different streams having their sources in different paths which people take through different tendencies, various though they appear, crooked or straight, all lead to Thee."

The present convention, which is one of the most august assemblies ever held, is in itself a vindication, a declaration to the world of the wonderful doctrine preached in the Gita: "Whosoever comes to Me, through whatsoever form, I reach; all are struggling through paths which in the end lead to me." Sectarianism, bigotry, and its horrible descendant, fanaticism, have long possessed this beautiful earth. They have filled the earth with violence, drenched it often with human blood, destroyed civilization, and sent whole nations to despair. Had it not been for these horrible demons, human society would be far more advanced than it is now. But their time is come, and I fervently hope that the bell that tolled this morning in honor of this convention may be the death-knell of all fanaticism, of all persecutions with the sword or with the pen, and of all uncharitable feelings between persons wending their way to the same goal.

the hindu creation story

The earliest creation story in the world comes to us from the Rig Veda, just before the time of Zoroaster, whose own creation story is typical of his brilliant renovations of Vedic myths. This poem/hymn bears the Sanskrit title *Nasadiya Sukta*, which means *Not Non-Existence*.

In 2014, Swedish blogger Stefan Stenuud, with help from the Spokensanskrit.de dictionary, blended phrases lifted from seven of the most famous attempts to render into English the seven verses of this most ancient of all attempts to grasp the dawning of awareness of existential origins in the following synthesis, aided and abetted here by contributors to this volume. Readers may be forgiven for seeing connections to the *creatio ex nihilo* doctrine and the big bang theory popular in the West as well as obvious esoteric links to the Eastern creation concepts contemplated

नासदासीन्नोसदासीत्तदानीं नासीद्रजो नो व्योमापरो यत् ।
किमावरीवः कुहकस्यशर्मन्नभः किमासीद्गहनं गभीरम् ॥१॥

न मृत्युरासीदमृतं न तर्हि न राज्या।आन्ह।आसीत् प्रकेतः ।
आनीदवातं स्वधया तदेकं तस्माद्धान्यन्नपरः किंचनास ॥२॥

तम।आसीत्तमसा गूढमग्रे प्रकेतं सलिलं सर्वमा।इदम् ।
तुच्छेनाभ्वपिहितं यदासीत्तपसस्तन्महिना जायतैकम् ॥३॥

कामस्तदग्रे समवर्तताधि मनसो रेतः प्रथमं यदासीत् ।
सतोबन्धुमसति निरविन्दन्हृदि प्रतीष्या कवयो मनीषा ॥४॥

तिरश्चीनो विततो रश्मीरेषामधः स्विदासी ३ दुपरिस्विदासीत् ।
रेतोधा।आसन्महिमान ।आसन्त्स्वधा ।आवस्तात् प्रयतिः परस्तात्
॥५॥

को ।आद्धा वेद क।इह प्रवोचत् कुत ।आ।आजाता कुत ।इयं विसृष्टिः ।
अर्वाग्देवा ।आस्य विसर्जनेनाथाको वेद यत ।आबभूव ॥६॥

इयं विसृष्टिर्यत ।आबभूव यदि वा दधे यदि वा न ।
यो ।आस्याध्यक्षः परमे व्योमन्त्सो आंग वेद यदि वा न वेद ॥७॥

Nasadiya Sukta: The World's First Creation Story.

by Taoists, Confucianists, and Buddhists, with the Zoroastrian original carrying the most weight.

> There was neither existence nor non-existence then.
> There was neither sky nor heaven beyond it.
> Then all was covered and sheltered.
> And there was an abyss of water.
> There was then neither death nor immortality.
> There was nothing telling night from day.
> Until the One breathed autonomously
> There was nothing else.
> Darkness was then still concealed in darkness.
> All was chaos and water without shape.
> The One which had not been enclosed
> Emerged in a blinding flash.
> First to arise throughout the universe was desire.
> This was the primordial seed of conscious mind.
> Poets later searching their hearts found a bond
> between existence and non-existence.
> A cord stretched across, dividing the divinity from the chaos.
> What was in the heaven above and what in the earth below?
> Seeds were spread and mighty powers rose.
> Below was urge, above was will.
> Who knows these things and who can here tell
> Whence it came and whither this creation?
> Lesser divinities came later to this world.
> So who knows whence it came?
> So whence this creation came and whither it goes,
> Whether created or spontaneously making itself,
> The Godhead of it in the highest heaven,
> Only he knows, or doesn't "know."

From the Hindu perspective, there have been and will be more worlds and universes than there are creation stories. The above Rig Veda song, still employed in Hindu worship, is elaborated upon in many differing Indian traditions, much as Zoroaster himself obviously summarized and developed it in his own way before it came to the Hebrews in Babylon. In India, and in Hinduism around the world, we hear many other summaries, all from Vedic sources pre and post Zoroaster. We shall attempt our own synthesis here, easily relatable to the stories in the other world religions, but different enough from them that comparisons should be of great interest and foster mutual respect.

Universes are made by Lord Brahma the Creator, maintained by Lord Vishnu the Preserver, and destroyed by Lord Shiva. These three Divinities are all forms of the Supreme One and parts of the Supreme One. The Supreme One is threefold in Vedic lore and in Hinduism, not divided but one in cyclic rhythms of creation, life, and apocalypse, presided over by Brahma, Vishnu, and Shiva, though Vishnu has many consorts and divine companions who appear to humans as avatars, or personified representations of divinity.

According to Hindu interpretations of this agreed hypothesis, after each old universe is destroyed or collapses, nothing is left but an ocean of chaos. Floating on this ocean, resting on a great cobra snake associated with creation, is Lord Vishnu. Even in the chaos, everything around Vishnu is so peaceful and silent that he sleeps undisturbed by dreams or motion. From the depths a humming sound begins . . . a sound like Au-uummm but often pronounced as "OM" in discussion. (Hindus like to point out that this is the very sound picked up from space by modern probes.) The sound grows and expands, filling the emptiness and throbbing with energy. The night ends and Vishnu awakens. A first dawn flashes forth, and from Vishnu's navel grows a glorious lotus flower. From this comes Brahma, and it is from Brahma that the next creation comes.

Brahma creates grass, flowers, trees, and plants of all kinds, all sharing in a certain spirit. He then creates all other living things, birds to fly in the air and fish to swim in the sea, great animals and tiny insects, all of them emanating from parts of Lord Brahma's body. In many accounts he grows lonely and needs a mate, so he is split in two and becomes male and female, and in this way human beings are created. Every-thing comes from one Brahma, who identifies with the Supreme One—so everything is part of the Supreme One.

To Brahma one day is longer than four thousand million earth years. This universe, this world and its Brahma, like all those before and those to come, will be destroyed by Shiva. After such a day, when night falls, Brahma sleeps and the world is destroyed. Every morning when he awakes it is created again. Everything of the old universe has disappeared into the Supreme One. For an unimaginable period of time, chaos and water alone exist. Then, once again, Vishnu appears, floating with the snake on the vast ocean. From Vishnu comes forth the Brahma of the new universe, and the cycle continues for ever.

hindu apocalypse

The presentation of creation stories in the seven testaments and elsewhere appears to be derivative of, or at least strongly influenced by, the focus on this theme in the Avesta, extant, rewritten later, and almost certain to appear in the Dead Zee Scrolls, should they be found. This train of influence is even more pronounced in the case of apocalyptic derivations, the Zoroastrian example as given being but one of many in that tradition. As the very first examples of such writing in world literature, several apocalyptic episodes appear in the extant portions of the Avesta, still in everyday use in the Zoroastrian community. These are echoed in greater or lesser measure in the seven testaments that appear in the wake of Zoroaster's prophetic presentations, and with special poignancy in the reformation of Vedic tradition in Hinduism, dated to around 400 BCE in the Bhagavad Gita.

The Gita has been inserted into the middle of the ancient epic Mahabharata poem in a battle scene, an apocalyptic setting from its outset. This portrayal of life's struggle is presented as the conflict between the Pandava and Kaurava tribes, cousins, and other relatives in a vast extended family. This was a family feud of cosmic proportions, with huge armies arrayed on both sides. Thousands were about to fly at the throats of each other on the occasion for the giving of this testament, presented not in a temple or sanctuary, a school, college, or university, but on the field of battle. In *Four Testaments*, Gandhi makes it clear that in his judgment this "battle" has little or nothing to do with war and everything to do with the challenges of life. The Godhead appears as Lord Krishna, his "avatar" being in the form of the charioteer of Arjuna, a leading general of the campaign.

On one side of this battlefield were Arjuna's friends and family, and on the other his enemies, with whom he'd failed to negotiate peace. At Arjuna's own request, he and Krishna rode a chariot between the two armies on the battlefield before battle and parked there to survey the warriors he was going to command and those he would face in battle. Then Arjuna saw, in the midst of the armies of both parties, his grandfathers, uncles, brothers, sons, grandsons, friends, teachers, and more. He was overcome with emotion and lost the will to fight. He complained to Krishna and asked how he could possibly slay people he loved. Krishna responded to Arjuna's despairing attitude.[1]

> This attitude is not fit for a person of noble mind and knowledge. It is disgraceful, and it does not lead one to fame, Arjuna. Do not become a coward. Do not yield to this impotence. It does not befit you. Shake off this trivial weakness of your heart and get up for the battle. The worthy spirits among them are indestructible and it is only for their bodies that you grieve.

The Bhagavad Gita is a dialogue with important teachings from the mouth of God as an avatar in the human form of Krishna, addressed to this warrior Arjuna, on the battlefield of life in which the apocalypse, while engaging all, is intensely personal. There are battles we must face.

Krishna exhorts Arjuna to remember the higher duty of establishing dharma in the world over all else. *Dharma*, a difficult term to translate from Sanskrit, can mean righteousness, but also duty. Every human must follow his or her own duty or calling (dharma) in accordance with his or her nature and social responsibilities in order for society as a whole to be following the path of righteous order (dharma) and to be in sync with the cosmic order of things. Krishna puts it thus:

> Whenever and wherever there is a decline in dharma, and a predominant rise of irreligion, at that time I appear to save the righteous, to destroy the wicked, and to re-establish the truth of religion. It is for this that I appear in every age.[2]

The fact that the thoroughly apocalyptic Bhagavad Gita is also called *The Song of God* in popular Hindu culture is no irony. Its theme is peace in the midst of conflict and detachment from both desires for success and fears of defeat in life's battles. Indeed, though it mentions creation and re-creation, and while the entire context is apocalyptic, it is almost as if one of the great battle scenes in the active Christian apocalypse of the Book of Revelation is paused, or put on hold long enough for the Divinity to communicate the meaning of it all to the overawed humans. The scene is set to look at that next.

an archive page from the bhagavad gita

Bhagavad Gita: The Song of God.
BRITISH LIBRARY ADD. 26457—FOLIO # 17R.

notes

1. Bhagavad Gita 2:16–18.
2. Ibid., 4:7.

15
an essence of the gospel

I N INDIA PEOPLE OF PRACTICALLY ALL RELIGIONS BELIEVE JESUS WAS THERE DURING THE EIGHTEEN years he is missing from the biblical record. Perhaps he only reached Persia, or just Syria—trips for which the biblical record is univocal. The Bible suggests that his travels to Syria,[1] where Zoroastrianism was the state religion, were subsequent to previous trips, as researched in *Three Testaments*. At a minimum, the young man from Nazareth would have often crossed the Galilee, from which he could have reached Syria any day by midafternoon. He may well have gone farther, but our moderate projection takes this speculation out of the sphere of the bizarre and into the realm of the perfectly reasonable. If a young Muhammad was exposed to dualistic Zoroastrianism, for better and for worse, in caravan trips to Syria from even farther away, and if Jesus's family may have found refuge in Egypt to be within reach, we should conclude that Jesus traveled at least short distances as a single young man. If such travels did take place, we should expect they would be reflected in the stories of his life, his teaching, and his ministry; we now see that they are.

The river baptism that launched the vocation of Jesus, and the I AM motif used throughout his ministry, is related to the connections in which we now also see clear Zoroastrian imprints on both Christmas and Easter. In the New Testament, we have identified Zoroastrian elements with the appearance of the Magi in the Jesus birth narrative. The Roman December 25 holiday was previously dedicated to Mithra, the Vedic deva of light who had been reformed by Zoroaster as an "Immortal," or angel, and worshipped as "the Unconquered Sun" on the then winter solstice, when the light began its annual comeback into longer days. Was it mere coincidence that Christians took that as the appropriate date to celebrate the birth of Christ? It was Jesus himself who said, "I AM the *light* of the world,"[2] perhaps speaking as much as Saoshyant as Messiah.

The Zoroastrian connection continues in his teenage years when Jesus was growing up with an increase in "Wisdom" and "in favor with the people of the world."[3] The Zoroastrian motif occurs next in the baptism of Jesus with a river-scene revelation strongly reminiscent of Zoroaster's commissioning, followed again by the immediate appearance of "the tempter." We have indications of his exposure to Zoroastrianism in Sidon and Tyre, where a "Syro-Phoenician" woman challenges him to see the messiah as the Savior of all people rather than one who would merely restore the throne of the Jewish people.[4]

Throughout his ministry, Jesus makes use of the I AM phrase in a manner reminiscent of Zoroaster's use of that phrase, recorded in the *Little Avesta*, echoing God's words to Moses at the Burning Bush. Jesus also exhibits a stronger emphasis on the Last Judgment than any seen since Zoroaster. At the end or climax of his life, Jesus concluded his ministry profoundly in the Zoroastrian mode during the events leading up to and during the crucifixion and resurrection. At his preliminary trial, the high priest, Caiphas, asked him, "Are you the Messiah, the Son of the Blessed One?" The earliest Gospel has Jesus answer specifically, "I AM."[5] He then goes directly to Zoroastrian imagery, speaking again to Caiphas, "You will see the Son of Man . . . coming with the clouds of heaven,"[6] quoting a resurrection saying used also by the prophet Daniel in Babylon. (We might therefore speculate on the great likelihood that such words will be found in the Dead Zee Scrolls when found.) The gospel story ends in a penultimate closing scene with the repentant thief—"today you will be with me in *paradise*" (not "heaven"), in which Jesus appears to be operating in full Zoroastrian mode, leading to a three-day funereal event like the Zoroastrian model, and with no Jewish parallel. The influence of Zoroastrianism in Western monotheistic traditions can at last be recognized for what it is.

The church's understanding of the creation of the universe by the messiah, the perpetual light, hell, purgatory, and paradise, all imply direct connections with Zoroastrianism by the church beyond the personal experiences of Jesus, as does the church's understanding of salvation, the "ransom" theology of St. Paul, the apocalyptic material in Revelation, and liturgical remnants in church liturgy. At a minimum, we may assert that the usual Christian view of Jesus as both "Lord and Savior" points to his dual heritage as Davidic Messiah (Lord of the people in Israel) and Zoroastrian Saoshyant (Savior of the world), the second perhaps subsuming the first in the role of Redeemer, as understood by the Jewish Christians of early times.

the christian creation story

The Gospel According to John begins with the words "In the beginning"[7] from Genesis 1:1 in the first Hebrew creation story, as derived from the Zoroastrian prototype. It appears to some that chapter 1 of John's gospel is modeled on the first six days of creation, with day seven running on to chapter 2, again as in the Hebrew model in Genesis. The repeated expression *on the next day* serves as dividers indicating the eons of creation as presented in Genesis, where we find "and the evening and the morning were the first day," and so on. At first glance, it would seem that John has only five days, but that is because the versification of this Gospel is a later invention of the church.

Be that as it may, there is even more proof that John is aware of precedents. Even if there is no direct reference to the seven days of creation in the New Testament, it is accepted that there are sixty references to various aspects of creation. But John alone makes the direct connection with Zoroastrian precedents, perhaps by starting with the six days plus one in the lives of his own readers, but even more so in an almost startling dependence on the Zoroastrian conflict between light and darkness, and the presence of the Saoshyant at the beginning of creation.

Then, in the first verses of John, the Saoshyant Messiah is identified as the Word of God, the "Word" being the vehicle by which God created the world. "Let there be light" connects the creative act with the Word of God, identified by John as Jesus, "The Light of the World," and as the Saoshyant according to Zoroaster, with this dual identity confirmed subsequently in chapter 1:14–18. The Vedic–Hindu–Zoroastrian motif is obvious. The specifically Z connection continues in John: "All things came into being through him, and without him not one thing came into being. What has come into being in him was life, and the light was the life of all people. The light shines in the darkness and the darkness did not overcome it."[8]

That much establishes the Zoroastrian motif of the Saoshyant being present in creation. John next goes on to identify the second coming of such a Messiah in the Jewish Jesus of Nazareth, who people could behold in this life.[9] The bulk of John's Gospel is replete with such Zoroastrian references like the river baptism, the frequent refrains of I AM in a fashion so similar to the manner in which Zoroaster is thought to have quoted Moses after his encounter with the Israelites, and the clear emphasis on a physical resurrection of the body. Both angels and demons appear in John, and the emphasis on salvation ("God so loved the world"[10]) is largely in response to fourteen references to judgment in John's Gospel, which conclude with a promise to a dying thief that he will be resurrected in "paradise."

Those multiple references in the middle of life situations, while not as specific as St. Mathew's testimony to the presence of Zoroastrian Magi at the birth of Jesus, or St. Paul's "ransom" theology, when taken en masse, support the observation of Zoroastrian hallmarks in the darkness and light of the creation verses. All that is missing from John's testimony is a full-blown apocalypse.

the christian apocalypse

Tradition has identified the writer of the Book of Revelation (Αποκαλυψις, or Apocalypse in Greek) as John, the beloved disciple of Jesus who wrote the Gospel According to John. Modern scholarship suggests Revelation was written first in Hebrew by a Jewish elder named John in the church at Ephesus. The scroll would have been translated (badly in places) at some point into the Greek of the New Testament, but Ephesus has been described as a center of Zoroastrian tradition. It was the home of Heraclitus, the Greek philosopher traditionally credited as the first to have written about the Magi.

Revelation is classic Zoroastrianism in style, at once frightening in the rise of the evil one with a great tribulation at the end of the age, dramatic as it describes the final battle of good and evil, and victorious in the triumph of Jesus Christ over evil in his third coming at the dawn of a new creation.

It begins by presenting Jesus as the Saoshyant-Messiah who had appeared first in creation as "the world came into being through him."[11] He appeared again in the life of the world to call people to himself and bless them.[12] He will appear a third time, but first John addresses the seven churches of Asia Minor[13] in chapters where the word *repent* (μετανοέω or metanoew) is highlighted seven times. The rest of the scroll then describes the apocalyptic future in an almost modern split-screen effect, presenting terrifying scenes of both heaven and earth side by side. Believers who remain loyal to Christ will be protected from the trials and tribulations that will descend upon the rest of the earth to test its inhabitants.[14] The servants of God will be given seals upon their foreheads,[15] and spirits from the abyss are to torment only those who do not have the seal.[16]

The Revelation to John often reflects imagery found in the particular Hebrew Scriptures that are associated with the interface between Jews and Zoroastrians in Babylon, including the books of Isaiah, Job, Daniel, and Ezekiel.[17] Angels appear more than seventy times in Revelation and play an instrumental role in this prophetic text, which features warnings about the Day of Judgment. The number 7 resounds throughout Revelation, a Zoroastrian hallmark that often serves as a key to important events. There are the seven churches, seven angels, seven seals on seven scrolls, seven bowls of wrath, and seven trumpets of change.

> And the One who was seated on the throne said, "See, I am making all things new." Also, he said, "Write this, for these words are trustworthy and true." Then he said to me, "It is done! I am the Alpha and Omega, the beginning and the end. To the thirsty I will give water as a gift from the spring of the water of life. Those who conquer will inherit these things, and I will be their God and they will be my children. But as for the cowardly, the faithless, the polluted, the murderers, the fornicators, the sorcerers, the idolaters and all liars, their place will be in the lake that burns with fire and sulfur, which is the second death."[18]

It never gets more Zoroastrian than this. There are major or minor apocalyptic movements of some proportion today in all religions in the Zoroastrian train, most notably among Christians and Muslims, with sometimes disastrous consequences when this doctrine is presented in isolation from countervailing assurances of God's love, mercy, and power to redeem.

The first to highlight this emphasis among Christians of the modern era was Sir Isaac Newton, who predicted that the world would end in the year 2060, based on his deciphering of what he believed to be Bible codes. We still have some time left. Next came the followers of the teachings of William Miller, who, in 1833, proclaimed that the Second Coming of Jesus Christ would happen in the year 1844, recalled later by Millerites as the Year of Disappointment, but that movement has survived worldwide under the name Seventh-Day Adventists. Equally prominent are the Church of Jesus Christ of Latter-day Saints (until recently known as Mormons) and Jehovah's Witnesses, both of whom have survived "disappointments" but who now interpret present world turmoils as signs of the coming end that will arrive during the lifetime of some living members.

An end-times (or eschatological) system of apocalyptic theology devised in the mid-nineteenth century by John Darby is still influential in the twenty-first century and known as "premillennial dispensationalism." Darby was a founder of the Plymouth Brethren sect in Ireland and England, an Anglican offshoot, and his system was propagated in America and elsewhere through Cyrus Scofield's influential *Scofield Reference Bible*.[19] Darby's end-time scenario includes the imminent "rapture" of the saints, a period of "tribulation" dominated by the antichrist, the Battle of Armageddon when Christ and the raptured saints will defeat the antichrist and the earthly armies of unbelievers, a thousand-year millennial reign by Jesus, and the last judgment, which concludes the great human and universal drama that began with creation. This has become a classic form of Christian apocalypticism among fundamentalist, evangelical, and more conservative elements of Christianity—not to be taken lightly.

The *Left Behind* series of books by Tim LaHaye and Jerry Jenkins is a fictionalized treatment of Darby's system, which racked up sales of more than one hundred million copies late in the twentieth century. Hal Lindsey's *The Late Great Planet Earth* (1970) was the nonfiction best seller of the 1970s and has remained popular into the twenty-first century among the followers of Pat Robertson, Jerry Falwell, and James Hagee, the latter leading the American participation in ceremonies moving the US Israeli embassy to Jerusalem as a sign of the end times.

All of this leads us to recognize the ongoing importance of religion in world affairs, more significant in the twenty-first century than at any time since the Protestant Reformation in Europe, the Catholic Counter-Reformation, and the concomitant era of colonial missions. For example, the above adherents to Christian apocalyptic movements have obsessed over the end-time destiny of Jews in Israel. England's 1917 Balfour Declaration, supporting "a national home for the Jewish people," had important political support among "apocalyptic adventists," as did the founding of Israel in 1948, Israel's occupation of Jerusalem's Old City in 1967, and the planting of Jewish settlements in Gaza and the West Bank. They take these developments as the fulfillment of biblical prophecies and as a prelude to the occupation of all territory from the Euphrates to "the river of Egypt" by the Jews as described in Scripture,[20] with the rebuilding of the Jewish Temple in Jerusalem as preliminary to the millennial reign of Jesus. Significant numbers of Republican voters in the United States subscribe to these theories and affect American foreign policy to an appreciable extent, but the majority of Christians in America are not as panicked about the approaching end, and elsewhere in the world these notions are heard of among Christians but rarely adopted by mainstream branches of the church or sanctioned politically, except in Central and South America, where US-style evangelical Christianity is growing.

Zoroaster's vision of the apocalypse, reverberating in the Scriptures of Christianity, the other six world religions, and others as well, is also germane to the concept of the progress of time and a sense that all persons will participate in the end time, or possibly at the end of their own time, giving meaning and purpose to each life. Whether spiral or linear, the end of each era and the end of time as we know it will come as surely as the big crunch will someday follow the big bang, if not sooner, with each person's "death" (and resurrection) as a personal example of the universal principle.

While understood as revealed by God, the question of whether the Christian apocalyptic vision is modeled on Jewish or Zoroastrian precedents is appropriate, and we lean strongly toward noting the emerging importance of the latter. In the scriptural account of Jesus visiting the home of friends at Tyre in western Syria (Lebanon today), it is clear that he has been to this Zoroastrian territory previously,[21] perhaps often, maybe first in his travels during the so-called "lost years." The early church also had an affiliation with the same source through its interface with Mithraism, the Roman iteration of Zoroastrianism, adopted by Roman soldiers who eventually converted en masse to Christianity in certain units of the Roman Legion. This was about the same time that the church adopted the Roman public holiday of Mithra (god of light) as appropriate for the celebration of the birth of Jesus as the light of the world, just as the winter solstice passes and the light begins to be reborn in the lengthening of days. The apocalypse in Christian Scriptures also features good guys against bad guys exactly as found in the Zoroastrian precedents, which is not as prominent in Judaism's apocalypse or that of several others in this series.

The Zoroastrian apocalypse, both oral and written, was certainly in circulation when the Book of Revelation was being composed, as referenced in the Z version quoted[22] and others in the Gathas. Perhaps one person named John wrote the Gospel and another wrote the Revelation, but the two books or scrolls have always been connected through a succession of leaders named John in the Ephesus congregation, and we have already established that community's Zoroastrian context and the gospel's Zoroastrian-like struggle between light and darkness. The apocalypse in Revelation stands in the tradition of a Zoroastrian mode in the early church, only now coming to light in postcolonial studies reflecting the influence of Asia in the New Testament.

an archive page from the new testament

Chester Beatty Papyrus 46: II Cor 11:33–12:9. One of the oldest New Testament papyri.
USED BY PERMISSION OF THE UNIVERSITY OF MICHIGAN PAPYROLOGY COLLECTION.

notes

1. Mark 7: 24.
2. John 8:12 and 9:5.
3. A more accurate rendering of a familiar biblical verse at Luke 2:52.
4. Mark 7: 25–28.
5. Mark 14:62.
6. Daniel 7:13.
7. John 1:1.
8. John 1:3–5.
9. John 1:14–17.
10. John 3:16.
11. Revelation 1:10.
12. Revelation 1:11–14.
13. Revelation 2–3.
14. Revelation 3:10.
15. Revelation 7:3.
16. Revelation 9:4.
17. For example, the Son of Man in Daniel 7:13 is referenced in Revelation 1:13 and 14:14.
18. Revelation 21:5–8.
19. Oxford University Press, 1909.
20. Genesis 15:18.
21. Mark 7:24.
22. The *Bundahishn*, as referenced in chapter 9.

16

an essence of the quran

ASSALAMU 'ALAYKUM, PEACE BE WITH YOU—THANK YOU, MARK TOULOUSE, FOR YOUR INTRO-duction, thank you, Brian Brown, for putting this panel together; it is a pleasure to be here with all of you today.

Why are *Three Testaments* and *Four Testaments* important? Why is Scripture important, and why is bringing the world's greatest Scriptures together important in the new Axial Age? I am going to speak to this topic from an Islamic perspective, focusing on the Quran, the Scripture of my own religious tradition. I plan to highlight three features that I think are increasingly important in connection with Scripture: spirituality, women's interpretations, and interfaith relations.

Within this broad interreligious conversation between Western monotheism and Eastern monism, how does one conceptualize the Quran? The Quran is a spiritual method—indeed, an organized, superbly structured spiritual method that takes individuals and communities from the animal self (what we would call in Arabic the *nafs ammara bi'l-su'* [the self that commands us to do bad things]) to the completed self, the civilized, mature human being (*al-nafs al-kamila*), on a path of spiritual growth and closeness to God, or to what we would call *haqiqa*, Ultimate Reality.

Muslims who have trodden this path and have reached the higher stages speak of *fana'*, the annihilation of the ego, the experience of one's own nothingness, when everything one perceives is God and the bliss of God, and they also describe *baqa'*, subsistence in God, the transformation of the self that this knowledge of God and the love of God brings. From an Islamic perspective, the stages and states that are experienced on this inner journey resemble in some ways the Eastern religious traditions' illustrations of the realization of one's own nothingness, the path toward enlightenment and an experience of Ultimate Reality—except that in Islam the Light of the Heavens and the Earth is God.[1] It is one of the names of God, to whom belong the most beautiful of names,[2] so it is a path to the One who epitomizes everything that is beautiful and majestic on this planet. It is the path of love.

Paper presented by Navin Reda at the 2018 Parliament of the World's Religions in Toronto.

In terms of contents and emphasis, about 95 percent of the Quran deals with spirituality and belief and about 5 percent contains laws that regulate practice. You will find these three dimensions intertwined, communicated using various techniques that include prayers, stories, questions, and instructions—interspersed with meditations on the many beautiful names and attributes of God, always taking things back to God.

How is the Quran structured? It comes in the form of a prayer for guidance and a lengthy response. The prayer is the first sura or chapter in the Quran, and it is called the Opening (*al-Fatiha*). The rest of the Quran's 114 suras are God's response to that prayer. The second sura is *Surat al-Baqara*, which is the longest sura in the Quran, and it lays down the foundations for practice, belief, and spirituality in the Islamic tradition. Each sura after Sura 2 picks up one of its themes and elaborates it, organized by order of importance. For example, Sura 3, *Al 'Imran*, speaks of the importance of oneness in belief and community and of following God's messengers.

I have been asked to speak about a verse in Sura 4 and a verse in Sura 5, so I am now going to focus a little more on these two suras. Sura 4, called *al-Nisa'* or "Women," is about mindfulness of God (*taqwā*) and loving kindness in human relationships, particularly internal community relations, which is very important for spiritual growth. It begins with a section on the most vulnerable members of society—widows and orphans—followed by a section on the next most vulnerable members of society in the ancient world: women. As it teaches individuals and communities to curb the animal within them—their egos—it takes the broad foundations of the path as they are established in Suras 1–3 and narrows them down. This process of *taqwā*, narrowing down the path, is illustrated in three obnoxious practices that were current in many societies in ancient times: polygamy, seclusion of women, and wife beating.

This sura places constraints and conditions on these obnoxious practices and restricts them until they become practically impossible. However, because these unpleasant practices were widespread in the ancient world, some of the classical exegetes—who were mostly men—had problems accepting these limitations, so they used a variety of tools to get around them. Today, however, we are seeing an increasing number of women exegetes, and they are rereading these ancient interpretations of the sacred text and making them more accurate to the wording of the Quran and more intelligible to us today. One of these important women scholars is Dr. Laleh Bakhtiar, the author of the Sublime Quran translation in *Three Testaments*—Dr. Brian Brown's first book to be written in this set. She has a very interesting translation and interpretation of Verse 4:34, sometimes called the "beating" verse, which is the first of the two verses that I have been asked to speak about.

How does Verse 4:34 limit wife beating and make it practically impossible? The verse has four sentences, and I am going to go over each one and explain how it does this.

1. The first sentence is "Men provide for women with what God has privileged some over others [extra inheritance portion] and with what they spend of their wealth: (for) Good women are devoutly humble and guard the Unseen with what God has guarded." This sentence treats some of the underlying reasons for

domestic violence—the lack of generosity of spirit and inner stinginess that some men have toward women by making giving to women part of their practice. It also explains that men get something in return for their spending—that there is a spiritual benefit for them: women guard the Unseen, the inner dimension. How does this work toward spiritual growth? In order for men to experience the intimate connection of love of God, they need to learn to love someone else first, they need to develop an internal infrastructure for love, and, like charity, love begins at home.

2. The second sentence is "As for the women who you fear are going to walk out on you, advise them, desert them in bed and beat them," or—in Laleh Bakhtiar's new translation—"go away from them." This sentence provides the first of the conditions that narrow down wife beating, which is that the husband fears that his wife is going to walk out on him—the word *nushuz* in Arabic literally means to get up and walk away. The verse gives three options to such a man: to talk to his wife, embark on a trial period of separation in bed, and the third: wife beating (as traditionally translated). Of course, if a man is scared of his wife walking out on him and he beats her, it is just going to make her want to walk away all the faster. By juxtaposing two things that just don't go together—a man fearing his wife leaving him and beating her—this verse not only makes wife beating practically impossible but also gets men to think about consequences. Dr. Bakhtiar goes a step further and highlights the fact that the word for *beat* has twenty-seven different meanings in the Arabic language, and what makes the most sense here is "go away from"—an exegesis dealt with in careful detail in *Three Testaments* with considerable discussion in many quarters.

3. The third and fourth sentences in Verse 4:34 are "but if they voluntarily obey you, then do not oppress them in any way. God is High, Great." Here we get another restraint on wife beating or going away from a wife—which is that if the women stay and live together with the men, the men should not oppress them in any way, and, of course, desertion or beating is a form of oppression. This condition narrows down this obnoxious practice further no matter how you may wish to translate the word. The last verse is a reminder of God, and that loftiness and greatness belong to God, bringing the focus back to God and mindfulness of God.

So these are the different ways that this verse has narrowed down the ugly traditional practice of wife beating and made it impossible for someone who is mindful of God in human relations. It gets people to think ethically and compassionately as it nurtures spiritual growth from the animal self to the self-critical self.

The second verse that I have been asked to speak about is Q. 5:48, which is located in Sura 5, called *al-Ma'ida* or "The Table." While Sura 4, "Women," focuses on internal community relations, Sura 5, "The Table," is about external community relations between the Muslim community and other religious communities, which is also very important for spiritual growth. It teaches us to act with justice and fairness, even when faced with hate. The fact that faith relations and fairness in dealings with other religious communities is placed in Sura number 5 out of 114 suras demonstrates just how important this aspect is for spiritual growth, for as this sura explains, it is the closest thing to *taqwa*—God-consciousness or mindfulness of God. Verse 5:48 is addressed to the prophet Muhammad, and it is set in the context of non-Muslims coming to him for adjudication of their disputes with members of their own communities.

> We sent to you [Muhammad] the Scripture with the truth, confirming the Scriptures that came before it, and as a guardian over them: so judge between them according to what God has sent down. Do not follow their whims, which deviate from the truth that has come to you. We have assigned a law and a way to each of you. If God had so willed, He would have made you one community, but He wanted to test you through that which He has given you, so race to do good: you will all return to God and He will make clear to you the matters about which you differed.

As you can see, this verse speaks of truthfulness, justice, and integrity when dealing with members of other religious communities, and it also acknowledges the divine origins of their Scriptures and laws, or at least those of the major religious traditions that Dr. Brown is bringing together in *Seven Testaments*. The Quran tells us that God sent messengers to every single people on this planet[3] and that the core of these messages is the same. We call that core *Islam*. In the Arabic language, Islam literally means wholeness-making, making whole relations with God and God's creation, with everybody and everything on this planet, peace-making, wellbeing-making, and safety-making. This core ethos takes different forms and is expressed in different laws and rituals within the various Scriptures; however, they all preserve something of it, even if some of them have been edited, redacted, and otherwise modified across the ages. Some do not even center God anymore, maybe just a notion of oneness or even one's own nothingness and the need for enlightenment. Together, these Scriptures are a testament to God's gifts to humanity. Placing them side by side in a single work is in some ways an appreciation of this gift and of the Giver.

In conclusion, I highlight three things that are of increasing importance in the new Axial Age: the spiritual dimension of Scripture and how it builds spirituality as exemplified in the Quran, the increasing importance of women's interpretations that provide balance to male-centric inherited interpretations as demonstrated in Verse 4:34, and the importance of Scripture and its contribution to theologies of interfaith relations as indicated in Verse 5:48.

muslim creation story

In tracing the Quranic references to creation, it is helpful to recognize the Quran as the final testament in the Abrahamic family trilogy. To read the Quran, it is necessary to know the Hebrew Torah, or "Taurat," of the Old Testament and the Christian Gospel, or "Injil," of the New Testament. Muslims in the time of Muhammad knew both, either in the originals or in the summaries provided by the Prophet in his "sayings" known as the Hadith, written at his dictation. Muslims today know both Taurat and Injil better than either Jews or Christians know the Quran. While David and Goliath are mentioned in the Quran, as are Jesus and Mary and most other biblical stories, they are not repeated in complete form, on the assumption that the complete version is known. The same is true of the Zoroastrian/Hebrew/Christian story of creation. Parts of the story are mentioned as background to specific revelations and to make their meaning clear with reference to the purpose and meaning of existence.

In the Quran, God says that the earth and the sky were "joined as one unit" in the beginning,[4] after which they were "cloven asunder."[5] Next there were "lamps" (stars?) in the sky[6] as creation unfolded in six yawms,[7] or days similar to the Hebrew yoms, though the Quran is especially forthcoming in recognizing that these times represent vast eons or eras.[8] God made every living thing from water, including those that creep on their bellies, those that walk on two legs, and those that walk on four legs.[9] He made a human from the mud of the soft, wet earth,[10] using a quintessence of fluid.[11] He made him a spouse, that he might rest in her, and when he laid over her she accepted a light burden and moved about with it.[12] In the Quran, God told Adam to dwell in the garden with his wife and for them to enjoy everything except a certain tree, lest they run into harm and transgression. Then Satan (Shaitan) whispered suggestions of disobedience to them, bringing their nakedness into the open. And he said,

> God has only forbidden you this tree lest you become strong like angels and live forever. He swore to them both that he was a sincere advisor, and by this deceit he brought about their fall when they tasted the fruit of the tree. Their shame became obvious to them, and they sewed leaves together to hide their bodies. God called to them about their disobedience to Him and their obedience to Satan. They confessed their fault and begged forgiveness. But God ordered them to bow down, and put enmity between them. He decreed that they would need to work the earth in order to live, and that having come from the earth they would also return to it at the last.[13]

After finishing the created world, God "seated Himself upon His throne" to oversee His work.[14]

From Jews and Christians in his family and the community, Muhammad would have heard the common elements of this Middle Eastern creation story, but the above English paraphrase translation of Quranic verses obviously does not exactly follow the Genesis version of the Bible. Muslims believe nothing in the Quran was specifically copied from other sources, but rather was revealed afresh to Muhammad in a corrected or refined version God wished him to recite. Indeed, the raw material that God revealed afresh may well have been influenced by Zoroastrian sources since Muhammad even had one former Zoroastrian among his closest circle of companions. Any such Zoroastrian material in the Quran was refined by God there, much as the original Jewish Christians treated the Hebrew text and Zoroaster himself reformed the Vedic stories under Divine guidance.

muslim apocalypse

In its references to the apocalypse, the Quran exemplifies the sweeping aesthetic, literary, and spiritual grandeur of Islamic Scripture more than any other aspect of that text. A review of *The Quran, Epic and Apocalypse* by Todd Lawson, professor emeritus at the University of Toronto, suggests that the Quran may have been the inspiration for James Joyce insofar as "the Quran anticipates literary modernism as both epic and apocalypse. Its epic voice encompasses a vast temporal and spatial canvas—the cosmos, creation, humanity, time, history—while its chapters, singly and collectively, evoke an apocalyptic musicality. The apocalyptic vision of the Quran underscores its own true purpose: to herald and expedite a just community living in accordance with God's will, enjoying both peace and prosperity."[15] Some may simply attribute the style adopted by Joyce and other literary modernists to the apocalypticism of the whole Zoroastrian family tradition. But it is possible to regard literary modernism as nothing less than Quranic commentary on a grand scale, as the Western world in particular begins to recognize and appreciate the Quran's evocative beauty and power, especially as recited, even in the midst of life's mayhem and chaos as reflected in the apocalyptic portions.

References to the end of the world and the "Day of Resurrection" (*Yawm al-Qiyāmah*), which follows the "Day of Judgment" (*Yawm ad-Din*), are scattered artfully throughout the Quran, though elaborated upon more systematically in the Hadith, where several minor signs and twelve major signs are predicted to occur first. We happen to live in an era in which a sizable portion of this particular religious community (including ISIS, Al Qaeda, and the Wahhabis, so dominant in Saudi Arabia) believes the world is in the early stages of apocalypse, or actually joined in the final battle.

Moving beyond the apocalyptic revelation to Zoroaster as reflected in other apocalyptic expressions, in mainstream Islam the apocalypse of the Quran is defined more by majesty than by terror, and the majesty has a breathtaking *mysterium tremendum* about it. There is mention of smoke coming upon the earth during the Final Hour.[16] "And when the Word is Fulfilled against the unjust, We shall produce from the earth a beast to face them and warn them."[17] We find the awesome reversal of the sun rising in the West,[18] the ripping apart of the sky,[19] and the appearance of Yajuj and Majuj (Gog and Magog).[20]

Unlike the narrative we see in the Bible, unfolding from creation in Genesis to apocalypse in Revelation, the Quranic narrative of the end times is not reached at the end of a process, but rather suggests that the apocalypse can break out at any moment. The actual "battle" is joined with the appearance of Gog and Magog, identified earlier in the Hebrew Scripture as individuals and groups descended from a son of Noah named Japheth and as enemies of God's people prophesied by Ezekiel (called *Del Zel* in the Quran). Based on biblical references, they are sometimes thought of as "people of the East." Furthermore, Gog and Magog received special attention in Muslim apocalyptic literatures during the sack of Baghdad by Mongols in 1258 and the Soviet invasion of Afghanistan in 1979. The names Gog and Magog are applied to America and Europe by Al Qaeda and ISIS in more recent times, a phenomenon much like fears by certain American Christian apocalypticists about Muslim hordes from abroad or "caravans" of Hispanic "invaders" approaching from the south to "destroy the country."[21]

The Quranic apocalypse continues: "The earth then begins to move violently. It staggers, quakes, and is crushed and flattened. It brings forth what is inside of it and empties itself. Like a mirage the mountains assume variable forms. They collapse, are like teased wool and disintegrate into sand and dust. Heaven will be like molten metal and rent asunder, split open and full of gaping holes. The sun will be coiled up. The moon darkened . . . to foreshadow the terror that, at some time in the future, on the last day, will seize all of creation."[22]

In the Quran, there is no mention of fighting between Muslims, wars against Christians, or the killing of apostates, Jews, and nonbelievers, and yet all these became integral to the vision of Islamic extremists early in the twenty-first century, including Salafists, Wahhabists, and even the Muslim Brotherhood. This suggests that the governments of Iran and Saudi Arabia may not be as divergent as thought in this regard, as referenced in world affairs in the era of this book's publication, or in the similar Christian division among peoples of the Axis and Allied powers of the mid-twentieth century.

In the Muslim apocalypse, dreadful corruption and pandemonium will rule the earth, caused by an antichrist figure (Masih al Dajjal). At this point the Mahdi (Guided One) will appear as the central figure in the eschatological story. The Mahdi is a messiah-like figure, though the term *masih* in Islam is reserved for Jesus (Isa *al-Masih*), except in the few references to the Masih al Dajjal (antichrist). According to most, the Madhi will be a descendant of Muhammad through Muhammad's daughter Fatima and his cousin Ali. The Mahdi will confront and kill al Dajjal to end the disintegration of the Muslim community and to prepare for the reign of Jesus, who will rule for a time thereafter. The Mahdi will then fulfill his prophetic mission, a vision of justice and peace, before submitting to Jesus's eternal rule.

The high drama of the apocalypse in the Quran not only relates intimately to similar prophetic verses in the existing portions of the Avesta but also seems especially appropriate in a tradition that believes its Scripture to be the final testament. Like the other Abrahamic religions, Islam teaches that there will be a resurrection of the righteous dead after this *fitna*—known as *Armageddon* in some translations, or the Great Massacre (or *ghaybah* in Shī'a Islam, which emphasizes these cataclysms). The righteous are rewarded with the pleasures of Paradise (*Jannah* in Arabic), while wicked unbelievers are punished in Hell (*Jahannam*).

The Zoroastrian apocalyptic reality lives on today, not just in the immediate psychoses of Christians, Muslims, and other radical extremists but also in validation as a compelling concept in video games. Teenagers everywhere in the world seek to find meaning in the midst of chaos, to meet challenges and to survive beyond the pandemonium of their existence. Tellingly, the two bestselling launches are *Apocalyptic Game*, with popular series known as *Fallout*, *Doom*, and *War Frame*, followed by *Wasteland* with its multiple series games like *Dark Souls*, *Skyrim*, *Morowind*, and *Witches*, with post-death journeys through hell to a new world.[23] Being a hero and saving the world is the most common narrative in video games, whether it be through understanding of prophecy, discovery of power, solving a horrifying riddle, or being lucky enough to be the right person at the right time. The notion that teenagers are disinterested in religion is patently absurd, but this opening is rarely exploited by their elders.

Of course, free-standing apocalyptic visions are of little value in and of themselves, whether Zoroastrian, Islamic, or any of the others. The challenge is to find ways to share the whole gamut of spiritual resources so that people may deal with creativity, challenges of life, and mortality in the quest to find purpose in their existence. It may be that no generations before those coming to mature adulthood in the third, fourth, and fifth decades of the twenty-first century have been so primed and motivated to discover the essence of religious experience. Some may grasp and take advantage of rich, established traditions with deeper understanding. Others may venture into new contexts and formats introduced by academia, media, or popular culture, leading to self-fulfillment and personal expression in fields of service, self-giving, and positive action.

an islamic artifact

The Quranic text behind Mohamed Zakariya's *Ardently Anxious over You* is, "Certainly, a Prophet has come to you from among yourselves. He is grieved by how you have suffered. He is ardently anxious over you, sympathetic and merciful to the believers."[24] Zakariya singles out for special attention just two words of this verse, *harisun aleikum* (translated as "he is ardently anxious over you"), which create the structural axes of the composition, with the elongated letter *l* in *aleikum* driving upward to anchor the whole piece. The rest of the verse runs, in tiny letters, in a leftward-leaning style. The heraldic medallions provide stability to the composition, enhancing the rounded letter forms while softening the vertical thrust of the central letter.[25]

Both Easterners and Westerners have scarcely begun to appreciate the depth of sacred meaning in Islamic arts, a cultural deficit we hope to remedy, even slightly, in the *Three Testaments* text with outstanding calligraphy.

Ardently Anxious over You.
CALLIGRAPHY BY MOHAMED ZAKARIYA ACQUIRED BY AMIR HUSSAIN.

notes

1. Quran 24:25.
2. Quran 59:24.
3. Quran 16:36.
4. Quran 21:30 Yusuf Ali translation, "interwoven" in the *Sublime Quran* and "of one piece" in the Pickthall English version.
5. Ibid. Yusuf Ali, "unstitched" in the more feminine *Sublime Quran* and "parted" according to Pickthall.
6. Quran 41:11, "lamps" in Laleh Bakhtier's *Sublime Quran*, but "smoke" in Ali and Pickthall—a lantern image, perhaps.
7. Quran 11:7.
8. Quran 70:4 and 22:47.
9. Quran 24:45.
10. Quran 15:26.
11. Quran 32:7–8.
12. Quran 7:189.
13. Quran 7:19–25.
14. Quran 57:4.
15. Bruce B. Lawrence, Marcus Family Humanities Professor of Religion Emeritus, Duke University.
16. Quran 44:10–12.
17. Quran 27:82.
18. Quran 44:10.
19. Quran 84:1.
20. Quran 18:94.52.
21. Televised services addressed by Pastor John Hagee.
22. As summarized by Carl W. Ernst, *How to Read the Quran* (Chapel Hill: North Carolina Press, 2013).
23. Information supplied by Canadian teenagers James "Manu" Sinton and Olivier Lapierre.
24. Quran 9:128–29 (as from the Marmaduke Pickthall interpretation).
25. A critique from a *Christian Century* article on Zakariya's work, August 25, 2009, used with permission.

part three

APPENDICES

appendix a

Twelve Session Study Guides for Three Testaments *and* Four Testaments *by David Bruce*

My FIRST DEGREE, MANY DECADES AGO, WAS IN PHILOSOPHY AND RELIGIOUS STUDIES. I took courses in the phenomenology of religion, the anthropology of religion, the philosophy of religion, the sociology of religion, the psychology of religion, and comparative religion. I took all of these without any real dialogue with people of other faiths. In most cases, the textbooks and the professors were white, male Westerners seeking to embody a fictitious academic neutrality, and who spoke with unquestioned authority.

Times have changed! Sitting on an interfaith panel a few years ago, a question from the audience was fielded first by a rabbi, and then by an imam. When it was my turn, I leaned dramatically into the microphone and said in a deliberately rarified tone, "On behalf of two billion Christians . . ." My introduction had the intended effect, as the audience broke into laughter at the thought that there we were, three individuals on stage, each attempting to represent large swaths of humanity.

For all of our newfound humility, however, rising levels of education and use of the internet still leave us sorely tempted to satisfy ourselves with information *about* other traditions rather than hunger for authentic encounter *with* them.

The *Seven Testaments Trilogy* makes an excellent resource for people of all faiths and no faith at all to come together in dialogue to appreciate both the similarities and the differences of how and why people treasure their religious traditions. What follows is a pair of programs for twelve two-hour sessions using *Three Testaments* and twelve two-hour sessions using *Four Testaments*, with *Seven Testaments of World Religion* introducing both. These courses are suitable for academic settings, continuing education courses, and interfaith study groups either with mixed memberships or including visitors at host venues.

Leadership of these sessions should involve open-minded, inquisitive individuals rather than those seeking to elevate one point of view above all others. In colleges, universities, and seminaries, professors can expertly put the readings in historical or philosophical context. In a community setting, the leaders may rather take the avenue of "how my understanding of these traditions affects me." Whether you are an academic or a layperson, if you think that you don't have the necessary expertise to speak authoritatively on behalf of the world's major religious traditions, you're right—no one does. Almost anyone of good will, however, can invite others to genuinely listen to one another.

Guest participants can definitely make the experience richer, where someone personally invested in a particular tradition may be invited to express their appreciation of what it means to be a modern-day practitioner of their faith. Again, no Buddhist can represent all Buddhists, or Muslim all Muslims, or Christian all Christians. This can happen at particular sessions or be a feature of all of them, depending on the setting and the learning needs of the participants. Ideally in both academic and community settings, these days the class or group may itself be mixed. That ideal is more achievable now than at any other time in history and may be typical of classes and groups using these resources.

	The Three Testaments of Judaism, Christianity, and Islam (3T) + Three Testaments: Shalom, Peace, Salam and Seven Testaments of World Religion (7T)	
Week	First Half	Second Half
1	Video Presentation: *Three Testaments: Shalom, Peace, Salam* (via DVD or streamed via YouTube)	3T Preview/Review Foreword and Prologue (in remaining time)
2	a) 3T Play: dramatic reading of Prologue b) 3T: Torah: Preface, Introduction, and Translator's Notes	a) Torah reading: Genesis 1:1–3:24 b) Topic: the documentary hypothesis
3	a) 3T Play: dramatic reading of Act 1, scene 1 b) Torah reading: Exodus 20:1–18; Micah 6:1–8; Jeremiah 21:27–37 c) Topic: law, sin, and eschatological redemption	a) Torah reading: Deuteronomy 6:1–9; Psalm 95 b) Topic: polytheism, henotheism, monotheism
4	a) 3T Play: dramatic reading of Act I, scene 2 b) 3T: Gospel: Preface, Introduction, and Translator's Notes	a) Gospel reading: Matthew 5:1–10; Luke 6:17–26 b) Topic: the Synoptic problem
5	a) 3T Play: dramatic reading of Act I, scene 3 b) Gospel reading: Matthew 28:1–20; Colossians 1:12–20 c) Topic: Jesus the messenger and the Message	a) Gospel reading: John 20:19–31; Revelation 22:12–21 b) Topic: the risen and coming Christ
6	a) 3T Play: dramatic reading of Act II, scene 1 b) 3T: Quran: Preface, Introduction, and Translator's Notes	a) Quran reading: chapter 1, "The Opening"; chapter 48, "The Victory" b) Topic: Allah and his Prophet
7	a) 3T Play: dramatic reading of Act II, scene 2 b) Quran reading: chapter 2, "The Cow"; chapter 4, "The Women" c) Topic: religious duty in various religions	a) Quran reading: chapter 14, "Abraham"; chapter 50, "QAF" b) 7T reading: chapter 16, "An Essence of the Quran" c) Topic: creation and apocalypse in the Quran
8	a) 3T Play: dramatic reading of Act II, scene 3 b) Topic: revelation and/or religious development	a) 7T: chapter 9, "Zoroastrian Creation and Apocalypse" b) Topic: relative value of texts and traditions in the life of religious communities
9	a) 3T Play: dramatic reading of Act III, scene 1 b) 3T: chapter 1, "Also Sprach Zarathustra"; chapter 3, "Monotheism"	a) 3T: chapter 3, "From Zoroaster to Zorobabel"; chapter 4, "Israel's Redeemer" b) Topic: Torah creation and apocalypse

Week	First Half	Second Half
10	a) 3T Play: dramatic reading of Act III, scene 2 b) 3T: chapter 5, "Gospel and Torah"; chapter 6, "Gospel and Wisdom"	a) 3T: chapter 7, "Gospel and Avesta"; chapter 8, "Gospel and Quran" b) Topic: Gospel creation and apocalypse
11	a) 3T Play: Act III, scene 3 b) 3T: chapter 9, "Zoroastrians in the Quran"; chapter 10, "Torah in the Quran"	a) 3T: chapter 11, "Gospel in the Quran"; chapter 12: "Avesta in the Quran" b) Topic: unassigned
12	a) 3T Play: Act III, scene 4 b) Topic: options in interfaith relations: exclusivism, inclusivism, pluralism, etc.	a) 3T: "Epilogue" b) Choosing topics for final papers *or* c) Suggestions for next steps/future events

The Four Testaments of
Taoism, Confucianism, Buddhism & Hinduism (4T)
+ Older Testaments: Encounters on the Way
and *Seven Testaments of World Religion* (7T)

Week	First Half	Second Half
1	Video Presentation: *Older Testaments: Encounters on the Way* (via DVD or streamed via YouTube)	4T: Book One: Foreword and Prologue (in remaining time)
2	a) OT Play: dramatic reading of scene 1 b) 4T: Book One: "Introduction"; "Preface"	a) 4T: Book One: "Exordium"
3	a) OT Play: dramatic reading of scene 2 b) 4T: chapter 1, "From the Foundations of the Earth"	a) 4T: chapter 2, "A Priest Becomes a Prophet"
4	a) OT Play: dramatic reading of scene 3 b) 4T: chapter 3, "A Chance Meeting at the Edge of History," and chapter 4, "The Silk Route"	a) 4T: chapter 5, "The Extant Avesta"
5	a) OT Play: dramatic reading of scene 4 b) 4T: chapter 6, "The Fraternal Twins of World Religions"	a) 7T: "Visiting the Tombs of Saints and Prophets"
6	a) 4T: OT Play: dramatic reading of scene 5 b) 4T: chapter 7, "Tao Te Ching"	a) Topic: the Taoist creation and apocalypse
7	a) 4T: Book Three: "Introduction" and "Preface" b) 4T: chapter 8, "Analects"	a) Topic: the Confucian creation and apocalypse
8	a) 4T: Book Four: "Introduction" and "Preface" b) 4T: chapter 9, "Dhammapada"	a) Topic: the Buddhist creation and apocalypse
9	a) 4T: Book Five: "Introduction" and "Preface" b) 4T: chapter 10, "Bhagavad Gita"	a) Topic: the Hindu creation and apocalypse
10	a) 4T: Book Six: "Introduction" and "Preface" b) 4T: chapter 11, "Israel in Exile"	a) 7T: appendices F and G; briefly overview material about Sogdiana b) Review of creation story and apocalypse in Zoroastrian originals as found in *Seven Testaments* chapter 9
11	a) 4T: chapter 12, "Jesus as a Zoroastrian Saoshyant" b) 4T: chapter 13, "Chinvat Bridge"	a) 4T: Book Seven: "Preface: A Model for the Twenty-First Century" and "Appendix: Images of the Original Eastern Testaments"
12	a) 4T: Book Seven: "Introduction" b) 4T: chapter 14, "Among the Ruins"	a) 4T: chapter 15, "From Aurel Stein to Mary Boyce and Beyond" b) Choosing topics for final papers *or* c) Suggestions for next steps/future events

Materials should include:

- copies of *Seven Testaments* for all participants
- copies of *Three Testaments* or *Four Testaments* for all participants, depending on course
- the DVDs of the plays or access to YouTube presentations of *Three Testaments: Shalom, Peace, Salam* and *Older Testaments: Encounters on the Way*

Note that these session outlines presuppose that participants will have the opportunity, beginning with the second session, to pre-read each text to be discussed.

Session length can be adjusted to meet circumstances, but the outlines acknowledge that in both academic and community settings a two-hour schedule generally includes one hundred minutes of "run-time" and fifteen or twenty minutes of break time. Discussions of religion may be intense, even in the current interfaith milieu: leaders need to allow time for people to take a deep breath and reset.

Icebreakers can be used in each session to get participants "out of their heads" and into the fuller, lived reality of religious traditions. These can include sharing in pairs or groups responses to questions such as the following: "Can you name three people you know from different religious traditions?" "What was the first time you realized you were speaking with someone from a religious tradition different from yours?" "If there was one thing you would like people to understand about your religious tradition, what would it be?" Occasionally, the leader will recognize the need to open with a simple "So, how are we doing so far?"

The session format is adaptable, but many will open with icebreakers, followed by dramatic readings and discussion of one or more chapters of the text. In community there may be refreshments in the break between the first and second "half," with at least coffee or some libation in academic settings. Most experienced leaders will recognize that formal presentations should typically involve no more than one-third of the session, with two-thirds left for discussion. In some settings, such as fourth-year undergraduate or graduate classes, the presentations can be left to the students to do, with the professor acting principally as facilitator.

Closing comments are usually helpful when delivered by the participants, in response to an open-ended invitation such as "Name one thing from this session that you will probably want to think more about."

I have been fortunate enough to spend time in Jerusalem, a city important to my religious tradition. Once in the Old City I noticed a set of pillars standing alone where an ancient imperial structure had once stood. The building, like the empire, was long gone, but the pillars remained. It has probably occurred to you that religious texts cannot entirely capture the total richness of a religious tradition, and yet, because of their very nature *as* texts, they tend to stand the test of time, becoming pillars within each religious tradition, as interpretations, ceremonies, and local expressions that vary from time to time and place to place. Virtually anyone using the Dead Zee Scrolls in an academic or community setting will be pleasantly surprised at how much energy these discussions will produce. Both the ancient texts themselves and Brian Arthur Brown's commentaries are provocative and engaging all by themselves. If the experience of those who have used these materials to date is any evidence, leaders will struggle more with ending sessions on time than with getting them started. For all our sakes, let's keep the conversation going.

appendix b

Three Testaments: Shalom, Peace, Salam

THIS PLAY IS INTENDED FOR STUDY IN COLD READING OF SCENES IN SEMINAR ROOMS, FOR INSPIration at staged readings in congregations, and for the public in fully produced theatrical engagements. Ellen Frankel assumed responsibility for a final edit of the script before it was turned over to director Arthur Strimling, who made his own contribution to the staging of the work for the producer, James Flood, in premiere performances in upstate New York through June 2015.

There are certain things one cannot say or do in every society. In North America, for example, one may be arrested for shouting "Fire" without cause in a crowded theater, or for disseminating (or even possessing) pornographic pictures of minors. Just as offensive is the denial of the Holocaust, the wearing or display of a swastika, or uttering "the N word," for which a person may be fired from employment. More recently, the uttering of the word *faggot* has joined the N word on our list of tabooed utterances. While "the F bomb" still has some shock value, public sex talk and toilet talk are seen as more vulgar than profane. However, "free speech" notwithstanding, every culture puts limits on what can be said or depicted, and those who decry Islamic censorship would be first on the ramparts against child pornography.

When Russian officials employ the word *faggot* or when Islamist extremists deny the Holocaust, the North American community is outraged at the breaking of our taboos. In deference to similar sensitivities in the Islamic community, the artwork in *Three Testaments: Torah, Gospel, and Quran* is limited to calligraphy in Book III, avoiding human figures, especially of Prophet Muhammad, who is not to be adored like a sports or media icon or lampooned as any other kind of idol. This play employs a similar approach with respect to appearances on stage by historical figures, the Prophet Muhammad, his daughter Fatima, and Salman, a Zoroastrian companion.

Publisher's Note: *Three Testaments: Shalom, Peace, Salam* is Brian Arthur Brown's second play, following a local musical take-off on *Mamma Mia* called *Abba Daddy*. This play is based on dramatic episodes from *Three Testaments: Torah, Gospel, and Quran*, published by Rowman & Littlefield in 2012 and launched at Ground Zero in New York City and the Canadian Embassy in Washington in the aftermath of burning of the Quran by American Christian extremists. *Three Testaments* won the IPPY gold medal in Religion and the *Living Now* silver medal for "World Peace" in 2014.

In the early years of cinema, *The King of Kings* and *Jesus of Nazareth* were silent, black-and-white movies about Jesus. With the advent of sound in 1928, no "talkies" appeared with Jesus speaking for nearly forty years because in 1930 the Motion Picture Producers and Distributors of America adopted a Production Code ruling that "references to Deity, God, Lord, Jesus, and Christ shall not be trivial." This made it risky to invest in movies about Jesus, but he was glimpsed in non-speaking roles in Academy Award films like *The Robe* and *Ben Hur* in much the same way Muhammad appears in the recent film *The Message*, where we see only his footsteps and his staff. For Jesus, this modern "forty years in the wilderness" ended with a respectful remake of *The King of Kings* and *The Greatest Story Ever Told* in 1965. This play's staging of Muhammad's views required ingenuity, but in respecting such sensibilities we hope to earn respect for this work.

With nods to *The Birds* by Aristophanes and a Jewish medieval *Birds' Head Haggadah*, and with a debt to Farid al-Din al-Attar's great Sufi poem, *The Conference of the Birds*, in this play the hoopoe, the firebird, and the nightingale are not "appearances" of Muhammad, Salman, and Fatima on stage, as may be realized by their colorful plumage and birdlike (female) voices. In this device conceived by Dr. Nevin Reda, the birds employ historic and revered names in a quest for the meaning of the Scriptures, reporting what they heard Muhammad, Fatima, and Salman saying about religion, to the delight of theater critics and with the approval of respected Islamic scholars.

prologue

(Three actors on perches humming a simple Jewish niggun. Suddenly the TV screens, which provide scenery throughout the play, flash disturbing images of religious-based conflict, bombs and fleeing refugees drowning in the seas as the organ blares discordant music, the raucous opening portion of James Flood's "Overture to Peace." After a pause, a solo voice floats from the balcony with the first two portions of "I Know That My Redeemer Liveth" from Handel's Messiah.)

NIGHTINGALE

That's a song Christians love, but the words aren't necessarily Christian.

FIREBIRD

What do you mean?

NIGHTINGALE

The words are from the book of Job. They go back way before Christianity to Judaism, even back to Zoroastrianism before that. And Job is in the Quran too.

HOOPOE

Jews, Christians, Muslims: they are people of a common faith, the Abrahamic faith.

FIREBIRD

They don't act like people of a common faith. They're always fighting each other.

HOOPOE

Not . . . always. Sometimes they get along.

FIREBIRD

And then in the blink of an eye they're back at each other's throats.

NIGHTINGALE

In ancient Babylon, Jews and Zoroastrians lived in peace together.

FIREBIRD

Is that it? We have to go back 2,500 years to find a time when religions got along?

NIGHTINGALE

Well . . . I heard Muhammad talking to his daughter and a friend about that more recently, only about 1,500 years ago.

HOOPOE

Let's go check it out.

FIREBIRD

Can we do that?

HOOPOE

We can—that's the whole advantage of being celestial creatures in a play.

NIGHTINGALE (preening and warming up her "wings")

Oh, yes, I almost forgot.

HOOPOE

We can travel through time and space. We can go to times when religions lived together, and even nourished one another.

NIGHTINGALE

Oh, let's go! Maybe we could discover the common ground between them.

HOOPOE

The seeds of peace! Maybe we could bring the world what it needs to live in God's creation together.

FIREBIRD

What a waste of time! All we'll find is what we already know. It's natural for religions to be killing each other.

HOOPOE

But the yearning for peace . . . and the road to peace is also in the nature of religions. That is why we sing "I Know That My Redeemer Liveth" and other such songs of peace. Let's go! Let's find the road to redemption. Isn't it worth a try? Come with us, Firebird. We need you.

FIREBIRD

Well . . . you'll need protection, that's for sure.

HOOPOE

Good!

NIGHTINGALE (gesturing toward the audience)

Can we take them along?

HOOPOE

Yes, we can . . . All right! You out there—come with us on a quest through time in search of peace.

FIREBIRD

But we can't go back and visit Muhammad, because this is a play, and to represent the Prophet, "Peace be upon him," in a picture or on stage violates Islamic faith. Look at the riots that happened when cartoonists have published drawings, admittedly unflattering.

NIGHTINGALE

There could be a way to do this, to which even extremists could not take exception. A thousand years ago the Sufi Muslims recited a poem called *The Conversation of the Birds*, with feathered creatures representing the Prophet, his family, and friends. As birds, we could play the roles of those we saw and heard, and nobody could take offence.

(They take down their masks from nearby coatracks.)

HOOPOE

So tonight we will put on these bird masks to fly backward and forward in time, to get to the bottom of religious strife and find the way to peace in God's revelations to Muslims, Christians, Jews, and even Zoroastrians.

FIREBIRD (turns toward audience to speak directly to them)

Can peace come in your time, despite the terrors and horrors in today's news? Is there a role for religion that has not been tried in our time?

(They sing another niggun, and as they move with the masks they begin to embody birds, but they don't yet don the masks.)

HOOPOE (as she dons her mask)

Hoopoe is a bird in the Quran who told King Suleiman, "I have comprehended what you have not, and have come to you from Sheba with certain tidings." As Hoopoe, I heard

Muhammad's teachings from my perch on a bush near the family fire, and I will pass on his beliefs to you.

FIREBIRD (donning mask)

Firebird represents Salman, Muhammad's Zoroastrian companion and military advisor. (exits)

NIGHTINGALE (donning mask)

The Nightingale represents the Prophet's beloved daughter, Fatima. (moves to the fire pit)

HOOPOE

The atmosphere is electric here this evening. Some are worried lest the Prophet Muhammad (Peace Be upon Him) appear on stage. Others are nervous about his daughter and companion being filmed. We are not doing either. For example, I do not look like Muhammad, and I do not sound like Muhammad, so I cannot "depict" Muhammad, but I can stand in for him as a bird in this play in order to express his views as we heard them from a perch on a bush near the fire in his family compound. We want no riots here this evening, but if any of you intend to disrupt this play, we want you to know that there is security present. In the event of anything untoward happening, we ask everyone to please remain in your seats and to respect the peace that we are here to promote. (exits)

(Music shifts to the questing conclusion of "Overture to Peace")

act i

SCENE 1

(Evening. Fatima stokes campfire. Muhammad staggers in with Salman, wounded and hobbling.)

MUHAMMAD (HOOPOE)

Fatima . . . daughter . . . give us some help!

FATIMA (NIGHTINGALE)

Stretch him out by the fire; I'll get some water for him to drink, and to clean him up. He's bleeding; I'll need some bandages. I have some cloth. I knew something like this was going to happen. (dashing around to get a bucket of water and some cloth in white strips)

MUHAMMAD (HOOPOE)

I am glad I was around to break up that fight, my dear Salman. Those guards must be new. They mean well, but they took you for a spy because of your Persian clothes. Are you in much pain?

SALMAN (FIREBIRD) (bristling)

Never mind about my wounds, Muhammad. I was on my way to present you with a battle plan for the next incursion by your Arab enemies, but I now realize that the enemy within is just as significant, and I mean Muslims as well as Jews and Christians here who are giving you trouble. I'm bruised and bloodied, but I'll be ready for them next time and the results will be different. (Even while stretched out on his back by the fire he is punching the air like a prize fighter.)

MUHAMMAD (HOOPOE)

Please calm yourself; you're making things worse. I did announce that you are my house guest. Most of our people realize that you are the engineer whose moat saved our lives at the Battle of the Trench, and that you are discussing Persian life with me. As I say, those guards must be new.

FATIMA (NIGHTINGALE) (washing wounds from a bucket; bandaging an arm and a leg)

I hate to tell you, Father, but that's not exactly true. Your Muslims are not as virtuous as you think. They beat up Salman not because they thought he is a *spy*, but because he *is* Persian. They are jealous and don't want him around here. I share your dream of a new society where everyone has a place, but Arabs and Persians are always fighting, and maybe they always will be.

MUHAMMAD (HOOPOE) (after a bit of silence)

Salman, I'm so proud of this young girl! Ever since her mother, Khadija, died, she's been running the household. The two of them shared my devotion, and now she is educating the other women in our faith. Like her mother before her, she writes out the revelations God gives me. The true Quran is what we recite, but Fatima likes to get it all down in writing for future generations.

FATIMA (NIGHTINGALE)

I think Father is trying to distract you from your injuries, my friend! (She laughs.) But it's true that father feels honored that God would communicate with an illiterate person like himself — and he has agreed that Mother and I should write down the divine revelations. Like many Christians in her family, Mother was taught to read and write. She taught me, and I teach other women. Father's Jewish wives, Rayhana and Safiyya, also know how to read and write. My husband, Ali, is literate, but he's too busy defending us from our enemies to devote time to his pen. Most of the writing is done by those who Father calls "The People of the House," almost all women at the moment.

MUHAMMAD (HOOPOE)

I know that before joining us, you were briefly a Christian, Salman, but you were raised Zoroastrian. How was it that Zoroastrians came to believe in one God and a messiah, and other things that God is also now revealing to me, and commanding me to share with the Arab people?

SALMAN (FIREBIRD) (sitting up)

When Zoroaster was a young priest in Scythia, he received a vision from God. Since he had grown up among the Israelites exiled there by the Assyrians, it's likely that he had heard of similar divine revelations as reported by their visiting prophets. Some say Zoroaster may have had Israelite relatives, and that the great prophet Jeremiah possibly preached there.

MUHAMMAD (HOOPOE)

I've heard that many of the Israelites exiled to Persia eventually intermarried and adopted the religion and culture of the majority there. But this was not the case with the Jews who were exiled to Babylon a hundred years later. They stayed faithful to their traditions until they were allowed to return to Jerusalem to serve God there, as Jews were commanded to do in their Scriptures, which we also consider to be holy.

SALMAN (FIREBIRD)

I've been to Jerusalem. There are more Christians there than Jews these days, and lots of other people, too, from all over the world. But the Romans keep an eye on the Jews, and so should we.

MUHAMMAD (HOOPOE)

Jerusalem is especially sacred for Jews, but not for them alone. I myself was once transported by God's spirit to Al-Quds, as we call the city, riding on the back of my horse, *Al Buraq*. It was from there that I was elevated through the seven heavens and beheld all the prophets.

SALMAN (FIREBIRD)

And how did Jerusalem impress you? Did it live up to its name as the City of Peace?

MUHAMMAD (HOOPOE)

It was there that I began the practice of uttering "peace be upon him" at the mention of any of the prophets' names: Ibrahim, Musa, Yusuf, Yahya the Baptist, even Isa, Jesus, peace be upon them all. To me, Jerusalem, whose very name contains the word *shalom* or *salaam* has always been associated with peace. I often pray that there will *be* peace, some year, in Jerusalem.

SALMAN (FIREBIRD)

It is more pressing to bring peace to Medina here and now! The Jews are certainly your greatest challenge in doing so. They remain a people apart, among the most motivated, enterprising people in the city. It looks like they intend to keep their separate identity, even though you would like them to join our new faith. I predict that they will turn on you, and you better be prepared to fight them. Peace is a great idea, but you have to be ready to fight for it.

MUHAMMAD (HOOPOE)

You are constantly warning me to be on guard, Salman, and the revelations from God make it clear that we must be ready to defend ourselves, as you have already seen. But the revelations that take precedence speak of peace as the priority. Daughter, I am sure you can recite a verse.

FATIMA (NIGHTINGALE)

Of course, Father: "The worshippers of the All-Merciful are they who tread gently upon the earth, and when the violent address them, they reply, 'Peace!'"[1]

SALMAN (FIREBIRD)

That's fine, but when they approach in battle array, we'd better be ready to fight . . . sometimes even preemptively. If we know their intentions, Muhammad, we must strike the first blow.

MUHAMMAD (HOOPOE)

Perhaps, but we need to be just as ready for peace and seize that opportunity if it comes. It may not be human nature to extend your hand in peace to those who have been your enemies in the past, but there is another revelation that comes to mind that speaks directly to that. Fatima?

FATIMA (NIGHTINGALE)

"But if the enemy incline towards peace, do thou also incline towards peace, and trust in God: for He is One that heareth and knoweth all things."[2]

MUHAMMAD (HOOPOE)

You'd never know it by the empires of war in Rome and Greece, but even the Christians know this is true, at least those who read their book. According to the Christians in my first wife's family, the Bible says, "Whoever lives by the sword shall die by the sword."[3]

SALMAN (FIREBIRD)

I suppose the Jews know that too, since God spoke to them about their neighbors in their book. In one place it says, "These men are peaceable with us; therefore, let them dwell in the land, and trade therein; for the land, behold, it is large enough for them."[4] But what good did it do? The Jews tricked the neighbors into circumcision and then slaughtered them while they were sore. Perhaps this was for good reason, since the neighbors had earlier raped Jacob's daughter, and so it goes, round and round, and it will never stop.

MUHAMMAD (HOOPOE)

We can't say it will *never* stop, Salman, because peace is God's will. And for any group to be permanently secure and to really flourish, it must accept God's peace as revealed to them. They may appear to succeed for some time through warfare, but even the Jews have always known they cannot keep fighting forever. That is why their greeting is "Shalom" and they have tried peace, even when it did not work out for them. We, too, must accept what has been revealed to us. Ours is not a new religion, but a revival of truths revealed by God to all people, and we also say, "Salam."

FATIMA (NIGHTINGALE)

Arab pagans, Christians, Jews, Muslims—do such distinctions matter any longer, Father? Your new constitution for Medina takes us beyond tribe and race, even beyond religious differences. Everybody is offered a secure place where people can live in harmony and peace if they will.

MUHAMMAD (HOOPOE)

Our constitution has been adopted by all the tribes, by Jews, Christians, and Muslims, even by pagans, both slaves and free. This constitution was not revealed to us; it is just how I see the revelations are to be applied, and I have high hopes for peace among us all, despite the differences.

FATIMA (NIGHTINGALE)

(aside to Salman) At least we've written down the Medina Constitution, the first written constitution in the world, even if it is not revealed. I wonder if we can make it last. . . . When Father is gone, or even before, our constitution could fail. Somewhere, someday, Muslims will help make it happen, but I don't know if these people will achieve peace in this first attempt.

(Muhammad helps Salman to his feet. Salman dances around the fire, punching up into the air.)

SALMAN (FIREBIRD)

You may think your followers will understand that the society you're building is regulated by a constitution, which is aligned with the Quran, free of the prejudices of blood and kin. I say we have to be ready to fight. The peace we want in our community is worth fighting for.

(Martial music or *Ahdan* as two birds unmask and all three sit on stools on a wing of the stage.)

act í

SCENE 2

FIREBIRD (flitting across stage)

We are going back another thousand years to visit Israelite exiles by the Black Sea, gathering around an evening campfire. These exiles, expelled from Israel by the Assyrians a hundred years before the famous Babylonian Captivity, are often said to be among the "lost tribes" of Israel.

(Near fire, strumming guitar, actor leads the cast in a niggun, encouraging the audience to join in.)

CAMPFIRE HOST (addressing cast and audience)

Welcome to our weekly community campfire. Tonight we have a guest from Jerusalem, the City of David, with news of our cousins there. The young prophet Jeremiah has an impressive following in Jerusalem as he challenges the mores of the times, particularly in political circles. He confronts those who would forget the special destiny of our people to be a holy nation, different from other nations. Many believe we were exiled here by the Assyrians to punish us for a lapse in this understanding by Israelite leadership many years ago. Jeremiah, meet Israel in exile. Few here have ever returned to what was the

Northern Kingdom of Israel, from whence our ancestors came, or ever visited the Southern Kingdom of Judah. We remember the stories of our grandparents, and I even once had the privilege of traveling to Jerusalem, where I met your father.

ZOROASTER (leaping to his feet)

Cousin, don't forget to introduce those of us of Vedic faith to your guest. My tunic tells him I am in training for the priesthood, almost ready to be ordained. Many of our Eastern faith tradition have come this evening to hear how Israel's God fits into our pantheon, though I personally question that such a thing is possible. In fact, let me serve notice of my concern about the presence of this guest. We are living in peace together here; we don't need someone dividing us.

CAMPFIRE HOST

Yes indeed, Zoroaster. Jeremiah, your audience is mainly of Israelite descent, but we have those of other faiths among us, including Zoroaster, my brash young cousin here from a mixed marriage, who is sometimes a bit confrontational. Friends, this is Jeremiah, son of Hilkiah, high priest in the Jerusalem Temple. He comes bearing a special scroll, and to deliver a special message, a word from the God of Israel. Sit down, Zoroaster, you might learn something tonight.

JEREMIAH (large scroll in his arms)

Thank you, Eliphaz. You are perhaps the only person here who is known by my father. Thank you for welcoming me to your home when I arrived, and for the opportunity to address the campfire this evening. Some of the other communities I passed through also have Israelite residents, as this one does, but few have as many, and none live so far from home. It was to you that I was called to prophesy by my God and yours, responding to the prayers of my father.

(speaking in falsetto voice with arms raised in the air)

The word of the Lord came to me: "Before I created you in the womb, I selected you;
Before you were born, I consecrated you; I appointed you a prophet concerning the nations."
I replied, "Ah, Lord God! I don't know how to speak, for I am still a boy."
And the Lord said to me: "Do not say, 'I am still a boy,' But go wherever I send you
And speak whatever I command you. Have no fear, for I am with you to deliver you."[5]

Yes, I am young for a prophet, but the people of Jerusalem have become used to my preaching, and I hope to satisfy even young Zoroaster that the message I bring should enhance the faith of sincere people living together in peace. My father, Hilkiah, has been high priest for many years. About the time I was born he discovered an unknown scroll of the *Teachings of Moses* during a renovation of the Temple under the righteous young king, Josiah. I know you possess an old scroll of Israelite history, but in my hands is a copy of the *Second Scroll*, found by my father. It contains the speeches by the great lawgiver Moses, which were memorized by generations of Levites, most of whom came to Jerusalem from your own communities in Northern Israel. Since I was a child, it has been studied and copied and made available beyond the Temple precinct. My father believes it important for you to have your own copy of this *Scroll of Teachings* and felt compelled by God to have me deliver it to you. You may even know some of its words already:

Hear, O Israel. The Lord our God is one. Love the Lord your God
With all your heart, with all your soul and with all your strength.
Take to heart these instructions with which I charge you this day.
Impress them on your children and recite them when you stay at home,
When you are away, when you lie down and when you rise up.[6]

CAMPFIRE HOST

Let those of us who learned these words from our grandparents recite them together, slowly for the sake of young Israelites here, and for our neighbors who might like to know that our God is One, and that each person is to love and serve God. Please follow me line by line.

(gesturing to engage the theater audience also, line by line)

Hear, O Israel. (all repeat) / The Lord our God is one. (all repeat) . . .
Love the Lord your God / with all your heart, . . .
With all your soul, / and with all your strength. . . .
Take to heart these instructions . . . / With which I charge you this day . . .
Impress them on your children . . . /Recite them when you stay at home . . .
And when you are away . . . / When you lie down . . . / and when you rise up.[7]

JEREMIAH

I am called to prophesy to the nations, including Israel and Judah wherever our scattered people are found: in the Northern Kingdom and the Southern Kingdom, in Assyrian exile, in Babylon now, and in Egypt, even in Jerusalem, wherever our people are in danger of forgetting God. God calls us to serve Him in Jerusalem, but also in this foreign place. Each individual is responsible to God. The commandments of God are found in the ancient scroll in your possession, so you have no excuse. And the most precious commandments of all are eloquently summarized in this *Second Scroll* that I bring to you from the Holy City. The commandments are addressed to you as individuals. You cannot hide behind community failures or take refuge in only communal worship.

ZOROASTER (rising from his place near the fire)

We Vedic people have worshipped the divinities in many forms, from time immemorial, in our communities and at our open-air shrines. Spiritual forces, good and evil, are all around us, and we lift up our voices together in fear and supplication. We have begun to include Israelites in our rites, especially since so many of our families are intermarried now. But you have come to sow dissention and to have Israelites return to their old ways that never worked for them anyway. Is there truly but one God above all divinities? Does this God know each of us? Does your God expect things of mere individuals? I challenge your nonsense, and I resent what you are doing here. Let these people become part of our community and adopt our ways. People like you always bring strife, and the next thing you know we are fighting. Can't you leave us in peace?

JEREMIAH

Your protests go to the heart of the matter, Zoroaster! There are spiritual forces, but only one God. To bestow on other spiritual influences the status of gods is to put ourselves at the mercy of false gods. The God who made heaven and earth has a plan for the world and also a purpose for each person in it. As a people, we Jews are obligated to perform certain communal religious duties, which we have striven to maintain, not always successfully. But God also expects individuals to take personal responsibility in the fight against evil. Only then will peace prevail.

ZOROASTER

If I understand you, the Great God is the only God, whom other divinities must serve and individual people must obey. This is either nonsense or it changes everything. If you stay among us awhile to teach, don't engage just with Israelites like my cousin. Perhaps I need to think about this, so I'll be at your meetings, but we Vedic folk will keep our eyes on you before you drive a wedge between us and our neighbors. We are living at peace here; we don't want trouble! It's OK to let strangers into our country; we are a nation of immigrants, but when newcomers start up about their rights and wanting to supplant our culture, that is something else again. We can run you out of here, Jeremiah, and we will as soon as you begin to put our way of life at risk.

JEREMIAH

In the days and weeks ahead, I hope to meet with many of you, Israelites and Scythians alike, you especially, Zoroaster. Together we will study the *Second Scroll* and respectfully consider the needs of Vedic people as well as Israelites and Jews. We will consider what each person must do to serve God, and also what communities must do to be at peace among the nations, since that is what you are worried about. Bring your concerns to the table, but keep an open heart and mind.

(Campfire singer rises to lead the audience and cast in singing a niggun.)

act í

SCENE 3

FIREBIRD

So whatever happened to that Zoroaster? We catch up with him ten years later, still a young priest. Zoroaster wades into a river with his followers on the riverbank waiting for him to preach or lead a sacrifice, a scene similar to the baptism of Jesus many years later. He dips some water in a jug, holds it up gurgling, and wades out of the river in a reverie.

ZOROASTER

It's been awhile since I met that Jeremiah. I put up a strong argument against dividing the community, but his *Teachings* mean more to me all the time. I have been faithful to our Vedic religion in which we use the purity of water to cleanse the pollution of the land, and the heat of fire to sear away the dross of corruption and violence. Everybody loves my incantations, but times are tough. The people of our religious community are oppressed by nature and by crime. I am now thirty years old, as Jeremiah was when he opened my mind to the reality that there is but one God, and opened my heart to personal responsibility. I fetch this pure water from the middle of the river before I light our fire sacrifice, but I nearly despair. We need to hear a word from God.

(Quite unexpectedly an angel appears in the heavens as one who confronts and instructs.)

GABRIEL

Zarathustra, the name you were given in your native tongue means "camel-herder." But now you are called upon to guide people, not camels, and to share with everybody what you believe in your heart about God, to equip them spiritually as individuals, and to marshal them to join us in the fight against evil that is bedeviling the community. Only thus will you and they find peace.

ZOROASTER (falling to his knees)

Sacred Specter, are you a god?

GABRIEL

No, but I am immortal like the seven planets. I patrol an orbit assigned by God. I have been sent to invite and command you to turn to Ahura Mazda, Lord of Wisdom, the Great God described to you by Jeremiah. God is One, and God alone can redeem both communities and individuals. Worship by the community needs to be matched by each individual's personal commitment to God. You have been exposed to the God of the Israelites for a reason and a purpose. Are you at last ready to face God as an individual, to respond to God's invitation and command?

ZOROASTER

I am ready. I know that this personal responsibility to God is what is missing in the Vedic tradition. I bow in humility. I am ashamed that it has taken me so long.

GABRIEL

Then come into the presence of the Lord of Wisdom, Ahura Mazda, who is also the diva of universal justice, and who is attended by six Immortals.

VOICE OF GOD (off stage, as Zoroaster falls to his knees, the people seeming oblivious to this)

I am the transcendent Lord of Wisdom, and I am the immanent Spirit who is available to all people, though many hardly know Me except in the beauty and power of the communal assembly. Today I commission you, Zoroaster, to inspire people to oppose violence and to confront the terror of the time, each person as an individual. Even divine beings like the Immortal who unveiled My presence to you have all had to choose between order and disorder in support of either harmony or chaos. Some humans, like some of those Israelites you know, have already responded to my invitation. Now your people and the whole human race are being enlisted to join the benevolent forces of nature in a new era that will lead to victory of good over evil. You are a messenger to humanity. You came into the river as a good priest; you come out of the river to become a great prophet.[8]

ZOROASTER

It is clear that You are the Creator of the Universe, acknowledged in the sacred stories of Vedic lore, and also identified by Jeremiah. I acknowledge now that You are above all divinities, and that You are the uncreated Source of all life. Before You, all the forces of nature must become subservient, and in harmony with Your purpose all people must serve in the cause of justice. I have heard of You before, but now I have seen You, and heard Your voice. I am Your servant, and I know that You can redeem me and my people from the hell in which we now live.

VOICE OF GOD

Your people and all people! I send you to proclaim the way of peace to kings and queens, princes and priests, herders and peasants, to respect and bless each other beyond measure.

ZOROASTER (rising to his feet)

From my people and the Jews of our community, to the people of the road to the east and to the people of the road to the west, I will proclaim Your ways of truth and justice, that all people may live in peace together, Vedic in new understanding, Israelites leading the way, and others throughout the world as the light shines for them.

VOICE OF GOD

You will not be alone in this. My Redeemer was present in creation, to redeem the universe from chaos. My Redeemer will be present in the fullness of time to redeem all those who trust in Me from their distress. My Redeemer will be present at the end of time to redeem the Last Days in a Final Judgment, when all are required to account for themselves.

ZOROASTER

In the time I spent with your prophet, Jeremiah, I learned of the Messiah, a holy savior foretold by a prophet called Isaiah. Is that the Redeemer of whom you speak? And how will he redeem, and whom?

VOICE OF GOD

He will ransom My people Israel, and lead them as a shepherd leads the sheep to green pastures and still waters. He will give himself to redeem all people of every tribe and nation, each according to the light that has been given them, and according to their response to me in justice and peace.

ZOROASTER

What shall they do to obtain justice and peace?

VOICE OF GOD

Only their trusting response to Me can bring justice and peace.

ZOROASTER

And how will they know You to trust You?

VOICE OF GOD

Write these things down, so the power of religion can be passed on to all who can read and to those who will listen. Honor the holy Scriptures above all writings, whether by Jews, Vedic sources, or others. By honoring the Scriptures you honor Me, and you also secure my word for all time.

("I Know That My Redeemer Liveth"—female voice, first verse from offstage as light fades to black, curtain falls or music comes up.)

notes

1. Quran 25:63 (Yusuf Ali).
2. Quran 8:61 (Yusuf Ali).
3. Matthew 26:52.
4. Genesis 34:21.
5. Jeremiah 1:4–8, a prophetic utterance no doubt repeated many times, in the usual style of preachers, but actually fitting best here, when first uttered by the prophet as a young man.
6. Deuteronomy 6:4–7.
7. Ibid.
8. A story so important that it is repeated three times in the Avesta Scriptures. Yasna 31.8, 33.6–7, 43.5.

appendix c

Where the Bodies Are Buried

The Tomb of Absalom.
SHUTTERSTOCK IMAGES.

Called Absalom's Pillar, or *Yad Avshalom* in Hebrew, this structure, near the entrance to Jerusalem, is almost fifty feet high and eighteen feet square, surmounted by a round tower with a conical top, all built of smaller stones, resting on a massive solid stone cube some twenty feet in height and twenty feet square. The top is hollow, with a small door giving access to three burial chambers, of which one had once been occupied and sealed. The attribution to Absalom comes from the Hebrew Scripture: "Now Absalom, in his lifetime, had taken the pillar which is in the Valley of the King and set it up for himself; for he said, 'I have no son to keep my name alive.'"[1] He had named the pillar after himself, and it has been called Absalom's Tomb, Pillar, or Monument to this day.

Traditionally through the centuries, Jews, Christians, and Muslims living in Jerusalem would bring their children to this site to teach them the story of the rebellious child and to throw stones at the monument.[2] Doubts about its authenticity, at least as presently configured, come from the fact that the stone base is now chiseled with ionic columns in *bas relief* and a Doric frieze, styles introduced to Israel during the Seleucid Empire following Alexander the Great. Moreover, the Book of II Samuel says that at his death, Absalom's body was flung into a pit in the forest and covered with stones.[3] However, the tomb was apparently in existence in the time of Josephus in the first century CE, who referred to it as the Pillar of Absalom in his *Antiquities*.[4] It may have contained the bones of another king at some point, and been renovated in the Greek style, but its possible earlier association with Absalom is not without merit, at least in terms of it being a memorial.

Portico of Tomb of Confucius, His Family and Disciples.
SHUTTERSTOCK IMAGES.

The Cemetery of Confucius is in his hometown of Qufu in Shandong province. The tomb of Confucius is the largest and first constructed of the graves in this garden setting, entered by the portico above. It is a lengthy gray brick structure, four meters high and seven kilometers long with domed areas today. Inside the walls there are many ancient trees in the "Confucius Forest" flourishing inside, perpetually renewed from roots of the saplings collected by his disciples from the towns he visited. The other tombs in the cemetery each have many graves and stele statues, including those of his son, Kong Li; his grandson, Kong Ji; and disciples Kong Lingyi, Kong Yugou, Kong Wenshao, and Kong Shangren. Over time other graves and monuments were moved here during the Han Dynasty, as well as works by famous artists and calligraphers including Li Dongyang, Yan Song, Weng Fanggang, He Zhaoji, and Kang Youwei. The Tomb of Confucius itself is a veritable forest of steles and is visited by more than a million pilgrims per year at festivals that are so well organized that visiting tourists rarely feel swarmed or crowded. This, the tomb of Muhammad, and the Tombs of the Patriarchs and Matriarchs (family of Abraham and Sarah) in Hebron at Machpelah (the Al Ibrahim Mosque) would be the burial sites with the best attribution in this series, though several others are virtually beyond question in terms of verifiable provenance.

The Tomb of King David.
SHUTTERSTOCK IMAGES.

The Tomb of David might be the number one individual historical site for Jews in Jerusalem if its provenance were more secure, like that of Abraham in Hebron and Rachel in Bethlehem. The New Testament testimony regarding the existence of David's tomb in the first century CE is clear in the first sermon by Peter: "I can speak confidently to you about our ancestor, David. He died and was buried and his tomb is with us to this day."[5]

The sarcophagus purported to have held the bones of Israel's second monarch now reposes on the ground floor of what became an ancient Byzantine church. In 1173 CE, Benjamin of Tudela wrote that the tomb was discovered during repairs to that church. This building has also long been cherished as the site with an "upper room," where Jesus may have shared the Last Supper with his disciples. One holy site or memorial on top of another often tends to verify both or several.

After the crusades, the Roman Catholic Franciscans occupied the site for about two hundred years until, following a dispute with the Greek Orthodox patriarch of Jerusalem, their monastery was closed. The site was sold to a prominent Muslim family, who maintained it for some five hundred years, from whence in modern times it came into the possession of the *Diaspora Yeshiva*, a Jewish seminary. Until Israel obtained access to the Western Wall of the Temple, David's Tomb was the main focus of Jewish patriotic and religious fervor in Jerusalem.

The sarcophagus is covered by a blue cloth with white symbols and Hebrew inscriptions. There has been a determined effort to respect the tradition that this is David's tomb by resisting scientific analysis of anything inside. Questions about the tomb's authenticity revolve around interpretations of the evidence regarding the burial of David, much like the debates concerning the tomb of Absalom. However, again according to Josephus, such a tomb existed and was identified with King David in his time, when Herod the Great tried to loot it but found that by then it contained no valuables.[6]

Church of the Holy Sepulchre.
SHUTTERSTOCK IMAGES.

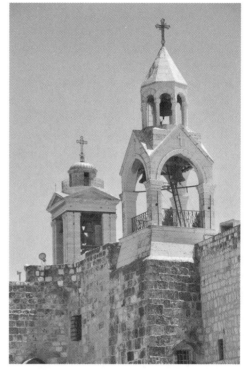

Church of the Nativity.
SHUTTERSTOCK IMAGES.

A more certain provenance surrounds the two foremost Christian sites in the Holy Land, though they too are complicated. The Church of the Holy Sepulchre, putative burial place of Jesus, and the Church of the Nativity, over the grotto cave in which he was born, were both built after 324 CE by funding and under the direction of St. Helena, the Christian mother of the Roman emperor Constantine. Despite advanced age, she undertook a journey to Palestine in the year 324 and "explored it with re-markable discernment" and "visited it with the care and solicitude of the emperor himself."[7] After she "had shown due veneration to the footsteps of the Saviour,"[8] she commissioned the erection of the two churches. One was in Bethlehem over the Grotto of the Nativity, then still memorialized in a community little changed in three hundred years, with one inn and a stable-cave out back. The other was in Jerusalem, where locals told her Jesus had been buried. However, Jesus had been buried near the crucifixion site that would have been outside the city walls, but by the time of St. Helena, this city had been destroyed and rebuilt. The site proposed to her by the "Chamber of Commerce" of the time now appears to be inside the city walls of Je-sus's time. The provenance of the Church of the Holy Sepulchre is not as secure as that of the Church of the Nativity, but no one dares mention that to the Catholic and Orthodox monks who jockey and jostle for control of every square inch of this site of sacred tradition. Many Protestants are content to visit and pray at the Garden Tomb, an Anglican shrine featuring a more typical Palestinian grave site of the first century, discovered "empty" in 1867, and outside the older city walls.[9]

Shrine of the Magi.
SHUTTERSTOCK IMAGES.

When St. Helena visited "the Holy Land," she collected various relics possibly associated with the life of Jesus, brought them home to Constantinople, and placed them in what would become the great Saint Sophia Church. The supposed bones of the "wise men" who attended the nativity of Christ were among her relics, the remains of three Magi who are described by Mathew in his gospel, having been brought from Persia to Bethlehem by the young church at an earlier time. When Constantine died during a dynastic upheaval, these relics were removed for safekeeping to a church in Milan. Around 1165 CE, Holy Roman Emperor Frederick I ("Barbarossa") sought aid to put down a revolt in Milan and received assistance in the form of an army on loan from the archbishop of Cologne. As part of the payment, he took (looted?) the bones of the three Magi from the Milan Cathedral and sent them to Cologne, where they might become an attraction for pilgrims to the great cathedral then under construction. These relics have been on display in the greatly expanded Cologne Cathedral to this day, their religious significance seemingly as attractively compelling in the twenty-first century as they were a thousand years ago.

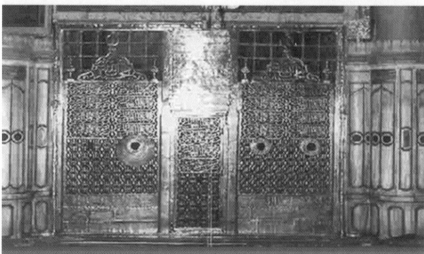

Tomb of Muhammad.
SHUTTERSTOCK IMAGES.

The tomb of the Prophet Muhammad in Medina has never been obscure or neglected. Lying beneath the dome of the Green Mosque, built up over what was once his compound, the complex also contains the tombs of the first two caliphs, Abu Bakr and Umar, to the right of his crypt. Muhammad's tomb was also intended for dual interment, with an unused tomb reserved, at the Prophet's expressed wish, for Jesus, the Messiah, after his second coming. Muhammad died on Monday, June 8, 632, in Medina, at the age of sixty-three. He was buried where he died, in the house of his youngest wife, Aisha, expanded and domed as shown. As the Messiah, in his second coming, according to Muslim tradition, Jesus will prepare humanity for Judgment. Jesus will then have a wife and children and eventually die as a mortal being. He will be buried beside Muhammad, to the left as pictured, as the Prophet himself directed, to await the final resurrection, according to Islamic doctrine.

Rachel's Tomb in 1880.
IMAGE FROM KLIGFIELD COLLECTION IN 3T COMPANION.

The Tomb of Rachel is one of the few that has periodically passed back into Jewish management, even when there was no Jewish state, as under the Ottoman Empire. The Tomb of Daniel, in Iran, is another example, where over the centuries perhaps 90 percent of visitors have been Jewish, and their contributions have generously supplemented maintenance grants from the Iranian government, though in this case the Jewish citizenry has never had outright control. In contrast, hundreds of other such sites, memorializing major and minor prophets, judges, and other patriarchal figures have received little notice by the Jewish Diaspora since 70 CE, under the circumstances of history. They were rescued from oblivion by the advent of Islam, in which they were cherished as tokens of God's gracious revelations and blessings to all peoples, a matter of some interest and considerable irony in present Middle Eastern circumstances.

Located in the Palestinian town of Bethlehem, where she died in childbirth, Rachel's tomb has an actual written historical provenance of at least 1,700 years in several records. This tomb of the wife of Jacob, the matriarch of Israel, has always been described as such in Muslim literature, though, in the recent political climate, it has also been referred to as the "Bilal ibn Rabah mosque." It has been under Jewish control and administration again since 1967, though, like other such sites, Rachel's Tomb is a spiritual and cultural treasure that the Palestinian people also wish to protect, asserting their intention to share it with the world, as has been the tradition. These tombs and the bones within them cry out for peace between Jews, Christians, and Muslims.

The Tomb of Caleb.
IMAGE FROM KLIGFIELD COLLECTION IN 3T COMPANION.

Caleb was the representative of the tribe of Judah among the twelve "spies" sent by Moses to reconnoiter the land of the Canaanites. His tomb is found in Kiphel-Haris, a Palestinian village. The Muslim provenance of the location is attested by the architectural dome, built over a site established in local tradition prior to the rise of Islam, and in decline or decay at that time. Many ancient tombs and related sites throughout the Middle East deserve consideration in this regard. Several purported tombs of Noah exist, but the one most venerated is at Nakhichevan in disputed territory between Armenia and Azerbaijan. Lot's tomb in Bani Na'im is only three kilometers away from that of his Uncle Abraham.

Other significant burial sites of biblical persons deserving of attention include the tombs of Asher, Gad, and Aaron in Jordan; Lamech in Afghanistan; Job, Aholiab, Shamgar, and Zephaniah in Lebanon; Ezra, Serah, Isaiah, Mordecai, and Esther in Iran; Ezekiel, Baruch, Jonah, and Nahum in Iraq; Jethro and Iddo in Syria; Joseph, Ephraim, Manasseh, Eliazar, Ithamar, Nun, Joshua, Samuel, Jesse, Ruth, Abner, and Amittai in Palestine; and Dan, Judah, Samson, Elkanah, Jehoshaphat, Huldah, Zedekiah, Zechariah, Hosea, Micah, Habakkuk, Deborah, Barak, and Yael, Haggai, and Malachi, all in Israel proper today.

Some 95 percent of such tombs are domed in the Muslim architectural style and have dated provenance of a thousand years or more. Of those listed and those yet to be pictured in Israel, several have had management pass from Islamic Trust organizations and Muslim boards of trustees into Israeli control in the last fifty years. A significant number of others in various Arab and other Muslim countries are managed by Muslim interests but are normally held open as much for local Jewish use as for Muslim pilgrimage sites, despite political tensions.

The Tomb of Othniel.
IMAGE FROM KLIGFIELD COLLECTION IN 3T COMPANION.

Othniel was one of the minor Judges of Israel soon after the conquest of the land of the Canaanites. His tomb is located not far from that of Caleb on the same hillside near Kiphel-Haris. For many Christian readers, the very existence of such sites is news. They have a historic and spiritual interest in the Holy Sepulchre site in Jerusalem, for example, with its complicated provenance, and the Nativity cave beneath the church in Bethlehem, which both go back to at least the time of St. Helena, the mother of Emperor Constantine. The Roza Bal shrine in India, which Sunni Muslims maintain as the Tomb of Christ, is a slightly different sort of "tomb," serving as a memorial, or a connection with some activity in the life of the person being so memorialized.

While some of these traditions may have archaeological bases or even DNA evidence, some appear close to the abuses associated with the collection of "relics" that helped trigger the Protestant Reformation by the time enough pieces of the cross had been collected to build an entire church. The importance of these tombs and other such traditions is that they ground this family's religious experience in bricks and mortar or flesh and bones of the believing community, rather than merely occupying the philosophical realm, speculation, or even "solid theology." This realization may be of particular value to Protestant Christians, whose popular understanding of the faith journey of this family extends back only five hundred years in popular conscious awareness, except for the brief New Testament era itself. Meanwhile, the rest of the family struggles with reconciling the moving testimony of Muslim dedication to preserving evocative remnants of the shared family history with the understandable Jewish interest in free access and a certain level of ownership and control of things intimately connected to Israel's existence and identity.

The Tomb of Benjamin.
IMAGE FROM KLIGFIELD COLLECTION IN 3T COMPANION.

Benjamin's tomb is an ancient domed building, located between the Palestinian village of Qalqilya and the Jewish city of Kfar Saba in central Israel. It was domed by the fourteenth-century Mamluk ruler, Tankiz, and the Muslim tradition is that it marks the burial site of "Nebi al-Yamin" or Ben-Yamin. The Muslims had venerated the youngest son of Jacob and Rachel by sculpting a goblet in relief above the doorway of the white-washed tomb, recalling the dramatic story of how Joseph, viceroy of Egypt, placed a goblet in Benjamin's pack, as a test of his brothers' intentions—conveyed in much the same detail in both the Quran and the Bible.

Since the establishment of the modern state of Israel, the tradition that this is indeed Benjamin's tomb was verified by the Jews, and the Israeli government has taken control of the site. Orthodox Jewish regulations mirror the Muslim practice of separate entrances for men and women. Inside, the domed ceiling is now painted with Moses's blessing to the Tribe of Benjamin: "Beloved of the Lord, he rests securely beside Him."[10] Jewish interest in this site is recent, but its provenance was established earlier and universal access was encouraged by Muslim authorities.

The first third of the twentieth century saw a measured growth in the Jewish presence in Palestine through immigration and property purchase. The Holocaust tragedy, perpetrated against Jews in Europe in the century's second trimester, dramatically accelerated a Jewish exodus from Europe. This happened in concurrence with an alliance between Arab nationalists and the Nazi and Fascist anti-Semitic regimes, whose support the Arabs cultivated against their British and French colonial rulers, drawing battle lines that remain today.

The Tomb of Simeon.
IMAGE FROM KLIGFIELD COLLECTION IN 3T COMPANION.

The Tomb of Simeon, son of Jacob and Leah, stands near the Arab town of Qalqilya, a community at present surrounded on all four sides by the Israli Security Barrier close to the Jewish city of Kfar Saba. The small, domed structure sits in a field not far from the Jewish Kibbutz Eyal, which has assumed administration of it. Until 1948 the site was holy only to Muslims, and Jews ascribed no holiness to it.

Today the dedicated inscriptions from the Mamluk period remain engraved on the stone walls of the tomb, but the cloths embroidered with verses from the Quran, with which the gravestones were draped, have been replaced by draperies bearing verses from the Hebrew Bible. Little or no sacred use is made of the site at present, and its appearance shows evidence of neglect, but it stands as testimony to both the history of Israel and the dedication to the legacy of the Patriarchs by the Muslims over the centuries.

The simplification of twentieth-century history presented above is offered to explain the status of the tombs and other sites traditionally administered by Muslim trust organizations. Jewish assertiveness in claiming their heritage is, of course, directly related to the perceived danger that what happened in Europe could happen again in the Middle East, with threats by Muslim extremists as a constant reminder of Jewish vulnerability. In a part of the world where most political entities are defined, at least in part, by religion, the Jewish majority state has a natural interest in historical sites that could secure its national identity and augment its historical, political, and spiritual ethos.

The Tomb of Obadiah.
IMAGE FROM KLIGFIELD COLLECTION IN 3T COMPANION.

Egeria (often also called Sylvia) was a Gallic noblewoman who made a pilgrimage to Palestine between 381 and 384. She wrote a Latin account of her journey in a long letter to a circle of women at home, which survives in fragmentary form. The part that survives includes information about her visit to Samaria, where she saw the tomb of John the Baptist, and also mentions visiting the tombs of the prophet Obadiah and Elisha, all at Sabaste, the present Arab village of Sebastia, seven kilometers northwest of Nablus.

Known in Hebrew as Shomron, Sabaste was the capital of the Northern Kingdom of Israel during the ninth and eighth centuries BCE, during the time of Obadiah and Elisha, prominent among the northern prophets of Israel. This capital was established by Omri, king of Israel, who bought it from a man named Shemer and called it Samaria.[11] The city was restored during the Roman period under Herod, who dedicated the city to the Roman emperor Augustus, whose Greek name was Sebastos.

The Crusader Kingdom was the next to reestablish the city as a pilgrim center because of the tomb of John the Baptist, despite reports that the Muslims had earlier transported his severed head to a shrine in either Damascus or Aleppo. Modern archaeological expeditions have uncovered magnificent buildings and Hellenistic cultural institutions from the various periods, including a theater, hippodrome, forum, and Roman temple, though the tombs, domed nearly twelve hundred years ago, have never been out of sight since accession to Muslim control, where they remain today.

The Tomb of Elisha.
IMAGE FROM KLIGFIELD COLLECTION IN 3T COMPANION.

Elisha is mentioned twice in the Quran as a prophet and is held in high esteem in Islam, as he is in Christianity and Judaism. He is mentioned only once in the Christian Scriptures, but in the Hebrew Scriptures, despite prophesying under the long shadow of Elijah, he lived longer, served God in confronting more kings, and performed more miracles than his mentor. The setting for his tomb in Sabastia is described in reference to Obadiah's tomb nearby.

In addition to the written record of Egeria in the fourth century, there are written references to Elisha's tomb by Italian pilgrims from Piacenza in 570 CE and the English saint Willibald in 724 CE. By that time Sabaste was the seat of a local Arab Christian bishop with twenty-five clergy serving congregations in the countryside, as well as three Orthodox churches dedicated to St. John the Baptist, St. Obadiah, and St. Elias in that city.

The Nabi Yahya (John the Baptist) main mosque of the city now stands within the precinct of the Cathedral of St. John, but of the tombs, Elisha's has always been the larger, an impressive structure, fully domed as befits a person of great honor, and still under Muslim administration.

The Tomb of Daniel.
IMAGE FROM KLIGFIELD COLLECTION
IN 3T COMPANION.

The Book of Daniel mentions that the prophet of that name lived in Babylon and visited Susa in Persia/Iran, where the tradition preserved among both Jews and Muslims has him buried. Today the Tomb of Daniel in Susa is a popular attraction among local Muslims and Iran's Jewish community, which remains vibrant in spite of the political situation. Jews continue to be welcome in activities at the tomb that overlooks the River U'lai, where Daniel had his vision of God as the Ancient of Days.

Syriac Christian writers reported the Jewish tradition in the fifth century, and the Persian historian, Al-Baladhuri, also recorded the belief that when the Muslim conqueror Abu Musa al-Ash'ari arrived in Susa in 638 CE, he found the coffin of Daniel. We may note that the tomb structure appears pre-Islamic. The first European description was by the Jewish traveler Benjamin of Tudela, who documented his visit in 1161 CE en route to western Asia, a hundred years before Marco Polo.

The current *Jewish Encyclopedia* refers to another tomb sacred to the memory of Daniel in the Kurdistan area of northern Iran. Another claimant site is within the citadel of the city of Kirkuk in a former Jewish synagogue, which became a church and in turn a mosque, and which also remains today. (It also claims to contain the graves of Hananiah, Mishael, and Azariah, the Hebrew names for Shadrach, Meshak, and Abednego.) The *Martyrologium Romanum* of 1583 CE ascribes the location of Daniel's tomb to a royal vault in Babylon, and there is another purported tomb of Daniel, located just outside of Samarkand, Uzbekistan, but Susa's tomb, pictured above, has always had the best providential claim.

Machpelah.
IMAGE FROM KLIGFIELD COLLECTION IN 3T COMPANION.

Also known as the Tombs of the Patriarchs and Matriarchs and the Al Ibrahim Mosque, this ancient shrine is the most spectacular of all these tomb sites. Located in Hebron, twenty miles south of Bethlehem, it would be little more than half an hour by car from Jerusalem were it not for roadblocks and security checkpoints. The name, Hebron, or *Chevron*, comes from the Hebrew word *chaver*, which, like the Arab name of the town, *Al Khalil*, means "friend," an abbreviation of the biblical phrase describing Abraham as the "friend of God." He bought the field and cave area from a local Hittite resident for four hundred silver shekels, the full market value, setting some precedent for land exchanges that may take place in our time. Abraham acquired this significant property four thousand years ago as a family burial site following the death of his wife, Sarah.[12] It became the place of his own burial,[13] at the decision of his sons Isaac and Ishmael, and grave space was reserved for two other of Israel's patriarchal-matriarchal couples, Isaac and Rebecca[14] and Jacob (Israel) and Leah.[15]

In the present political climate, few of these tombs, memorials, and cenotaphs convey anything like the harmony displayed by Isaac, Ishmael, and the extended family when they buried their father, Abraham, together,[16] in the gravesite known as Machpelah, of which the provenance has never been in question or dispute through all the ages. That site memorializes the burials of principal Patriarchs and Matriarchs of Israel: Abraham and Sarah, Isaac and Rebecca, Jacob and Leah.

Machpelah was a scene of intense Israelite activity some thirty centuries ago, as confirmed by twentieth-century analysis of artifact caches located deep within the cave. Two thousand years ago the whole site was surrounded by a massive structure built by Herod, king of Judea, to secure it as a place for Jewish prayers and gatherings at the graves of the Patriarchs. Herod built many such massive palaces and fortresses, but only this sacred shrine, with fifteen-meter-high walls and stones more massive than those of the pyramids, remains intact and fully functional for spiritual purposes today.

Between 290 and 320 CE, during the Byzantine Period, a massive Christian church measuring twenty thousand square feet was constructed inside those walls, over the original cave that contained the burial sites. In 614 CE, the site was taken over by Persian Zoroastrians, who leveled the church in preparation for making this high point into a mortuary shrine, according to their rites. They had not completed construction before Muslims took over in 637 and turned the place into a mosque on their way to conquering Jerusalem the next year.

Machpelah remained a mosque until 1100 CE, when it became a Christian church again under the Crusaders, whose new interior arches remain. It reverted to its status as a mosque in less than a hundred years. Saladin erected six main floor cenotaphs that resemble huge tombstones. As a mosque, Machpelah cycled through eras of generous public access and periods of severely restricted usage by Jews and Christians, depending on the political situation in various centuries. In 1967, this impressive shrine came under Jewish control again. For more than fifty years Machpelah has remained under Jewish control, but it is administered under Arab management through the Waqf, a typical Islamic Trust Society.

Despite ruthless episodes of violence at the site during the twentieth century, perpetrated first by one side and then another, some one million visitors visit Machpelah every year in ratios of almost equally one-third Jewish, one-third Christian, and one-third Muslim.

Machpelah is not the number one religious shrine in the area for Jews, Christians, or Muslims, perhaps fortunate as a potential sign of possible reconciliation between the children of Isaac and Ishmael, and including Christians adopted into the family and often referred to as the children of Abraham's third wife, Keturah. It may be providential that for Jews Machpelah is third in importance, after the Western Wall of the temple and the tomb of Rachel, mother of the nation. For Christians, Machpelah is number three, after the Church of the Holy Sepulchre and the Church of the Nativity. For Muslims, it is also third in importance in areas related to Palestinian claims, after the Al Aksa Mosque and the Dome of the Rock. No other tomb sites are of shared interest to the same extent. While none of them have been fought over as bitterly as the Tomb of Patriarchs and Matriarchs, none of them have Machpelah's potential to serve as the symbol of reconciliation *par excellence* in any future peace in the area.

The peace process is a never-ending quest, but as a sign and symbol of hope, this site is without equal. Jewish for two thousand years, Muslim for well over a thousand, Christian for several centuries, and even briefly Zoroastrian, Machpelah stands supreme as a beacon for those who believe the miracle of peace could be as transformative in the Middle East as it has been in East and West Germany, in South Africa or in Northern Ireland, all places where despair reigned for generations before peace arrived with a shock wave of unexpected harmony. Nothing less should be the goal in the Holy Land, despite the creative challenges to be faced in generously accommodating the passionate desires and understandable anxieties of the various parties in a peace that passes understanding.

notes

1. II Samuel 18: 18—"this day" being five hundred years later, around 550 BCE and the final recension of the Samuel–Kings corpus by the so-called deuteronomists.

2. *The Guide to Israel*, Zev Vilnay, Hamakor Press, Jerusalem, 1970, "Pillar of Absalom," 157–58.

3. II Samuel 18:17.

4. Josephus, *Antiquities of the Jews*, vii. 10, 3.

5. Acts 2:29.

6. Josephus, *Antiquities of the Jews*, 16:7:1.

7. Eusebius, xlii.

8. Ibid.

9. Also called "Gordon's Tomb," after the British general, Charles Gordon, who identified a prominent rocky crag in 1883 that looked like it could be the "place of the skull" mentioned in the Bible as the place where Jesus was crucified, similar in location and other details to the biblical record, as noted by German observers before him.

10. Deuteronomy 33:12.

11. Kings 16:24.

12. Genesis 23:1–20.

13. Ibid., 49:31.

14. Ibid., 35:29 and 49:31.

15. Ibid., 49:29–33 and 50:4–5, 12–13.

16. Genesis 25:9.

appendíx d

Older Testaments: Encounters on the Way, a one-act play by William Thomas

publisher's note: the play's the thing that says it all

AFTER SEEING *PEACE, SHALOM, SALAAM,* THE PLAY BASED ON *THREE TESTAMENTS,* AND KNOWING that *Four Testaments* was in development, William Thomas got hooked on the idea of writing a script based on *Four Testaments.*

Bill is an ordained minister in the United Church of Canada, presently serving the congregation of St. John's Stevensville United Church in Fort Erie, Canada. He additionally serves as the coordinator at the Embrace Centre, also in Fort Erie. Through their work and ministry, Bill and his wife, Cheryl, also a United Church minister, are associated with the Garrison Little Theatre.

Bill is a fellow of the Royal Society for the Arts. During his undergraduate and graduate studies in theology, he specialized in comparative religion. Initially conceived as a doctoral dissertation project, the play *Older Testaments: Encounters on the Way* has taken on a life of its own and is set to premiere at the Seven Testaments Trilogy Conference in Niagara Falls, New York, May 29–31, 2020, coinciding with the book launch for this volume, *Seven Testaments of World Religion.* The play's future is in seminary and university classroom readings and on stage in various settings, including congregational and other dinner theater events in an age of interfaith interest.

As playwright, Bill builds on the theatrical success of a Holy Week drama he wrote and had produced while serving as minister at Silver Spire United Church in St. Catharines, Ontario. That play is based on the painting *The Last Supper* by Bohdan Piasecki, where Jesus gathers in the upper room with a diverse gathering of people, including women and children. The author and contributing editor of this book was in the audience for this dramatization, so when Bill made his approach to write this script, the pitch for consent went to Rowman & Littlefield, the publisher of these books, and permission was granted.

Older Testaments: Encounters on the Way illustrates what the *Four Testaments* book needed five hundred pages to say. Just as the Three Testaments of Western monotheism may be related to each other through the Zoroastrian Older Testament, the Four Testaments of Eastern monism share a root system in Vedic lore. The syntheses are palpable while the differences stand out in contrast, which inform all Seven Testaments.

The poem "If" by Rudyard Kipling is in the public domain, used here to summarize the teachings of the Four Testaments and what they have in common with the Dead Zee Scrolls of the Avesta by Zoroaster. *Older Testaments: Encounters on the Way* is copyrighted 2019 in the name of William Thomas, and it is also available in script format from the United Kingdom at stageplays.com.

CAST OF CHARACTERS (IN ORDER OF APPEARANCE)

Qing Shan: A young female magi in her 20s
Ru Shi: A young male magi in his 20s
Yu Yan: A young woman in her early 20s
Lao Tzu: A man in his 40s or 50s
Confucius: A young man around 30
Yinxi: A man in his 50s
Saveeta: A woman in her 30s
Gautama: A man in his late 20s
Suddhodana: Gautama's father, a man in his 50s
Channa: A man in his 40s
Guard 1: A man
Guard 2: A man
An Ascetic: A man of nondescript age
Ananda: A man in his 20s
Arjuna: A man in his 20s
Krishna/Vishnu: A man in his 30s

In order to emphasize the continuity of thought and close relationship between traditions represented in these pages, it would be beneficial if the roles of Lao Tzu, Gautama, and Krishna/Vishnu were played by the same person. Alternatively, the connection between them might be made by costuming them in a blue shawl.

SCENE

Various locations

TIME

Various periods

Older Testaments: Encounters on the Way

PROLOGUE

AT RISE: Scenes of traditional markets are projected while the sounds of a market are heard. Accompanying these scenes is traditional Middle Eastern music and the voices of hawkers and street vendors. The sounds and voices become quieter and one voice rises out of the cacophony, proclaiming the words of Jeremiah:

"The Lord declares that the days are coming when I will make a new covenant with the people of Israel and the people of Judah. I will put my law in their minds and write it on their hearts. I will be their God, and they will be my people." (The words are projected as they are spoken.)

As the music becomes louder, it transitions to a more traditional oriental style and the images being projected transition to that of caravans moving through mountains and desert. Images of people and animals moving across the terrain.

(BLACKOUT)

(END OF PROLOGUE)

SCENE 1

SETTING: A courtyard outside the Imperial Archives.

AT RISE: A single female figure stands outside the door. Two figures, one male, one female, enter speaking to one another; one carries a large scroll.

QING SHAN

You see. I told you she would be here. And if Yu Yan is here, then the Master is inside.

RU SHI

Well, call out to her and let's see if we can speak to Lao Tzu. I think he will find our story and this scroll most interesting.

QING SHAN

(calling out)

Yu Yan, do you have a moment for an old friend?

YU YAN

Qing Shan? When did you return? I was told just last week that you had traveled to Tian-zhu with a group of traders.

QING SHAN

I returned just yesterday, but we traveled much further. We crossed the Indus River and continued to a grand city, filled with marvelous markets, called Nineveh.

RU SHI

The markets were overflowing with merchandise and livestock and produce. And we found some lovely spices and fragrances . . .

QING SHAN

(interrupting Ru Shi's recounting)

But, more importantly, we acquired this scroll from a faithful sister. It contains the words of one of the Hebrew prophets, Jeremiah. I thought the master might find some interest in it. Yu Yan, do you think we could speak with him, for just a moment?

YU YAN

Lao Tzu has been working on the archives for much of the day. Perhaps he could be convinced to take a short break. But you will have to be brief.

(turning to Ru Shi)

I didn't catch your name.

RU SHI

Ru Shi.

YU YAN

Ru Shi, my parents desired for me a soulmate, so they . . .

(turning toward the door)

I will see if the Master is available.

(Yu Yan disappears inside the doorway and emerges with Lao Tzu)

LAO TZU

Qing Shan and Ru Shi, is it?

(Ru Shi nods)

Yu Yan tells me you have returned from your journey with a scroll that you think might be of some interest to an old man.

QING SHAN

Yes, Lao Tzu, while in the city of Nineveh we acquired this scroll . . .

RU SHI

(interrupting Qing Shan)

There was a man standing on the street corner and he was addressing the crowds, speaking the words from this scroll and . . .

(Lao Tzu holds up his hand to stop Ru Shi and turns to Qing Shan, who looks at Ru Shi in frustration.)

QING SHAN

We were drawn by the words the man was speaking, and he told us they were the prophetic words of a Hebrew prophet, named Jeremiah. The man was accompanied by another, a sister Magi, Sheba. She, like us, is a Zoroastrian, living in Persia. Sheba gifted us with one of the scrolls and, knowing the work you are doing here at the Imperial Archives, we brought it to you.

LAO TZU

Thank you, Qing Shan, and you as well, Ru Shi. I will gladly accept this scroll from you, with gratitude and much anticipation. Of course, you have read it; what have you made note of?

QING SHAN

The prophet writes about the breakdown in the relationship between the people and their God. But close to the middle of the scroll he shares their God's promise that each person will understand fully for God's word will be written upon their hearts.

LAO TZU

That sounds very familiar, I have read that elsewhere. I will make note of that and study this scroll with great care.

(Lao Tzu bows towards Qing Shan and Ru Shi. They bow in return.
Lao Tzu and Yu Yan turn and enter the door to the Imperial Archives.
Qing Shan and Ru Shi exit in the opposite direction.)

(BLACKOUT)

(END OF SCENE)

SCENE 2

SETTING: Inside the Imperial Archives. The walls are lined with books and scrolls. There are scrolls that have fallen to the floor. There is a high table with two stools in front of it. There is also a sitting area with three chairs around a small table.

AT RISE: Lao Tzu and Yu Yan stand in front of a table with a number of scrolls unrolled before them.

YU YAN

Lao Tzu, Qing Shan brought you this scroll before the last new moon and you have not put it away since. I have watched as you have spent hours reading it, some days from dawn to dusk. What more do you hope to learn from it?

LAO TZU

Yu Yan, you are far too concerned with the passage of time. You will not remember this, but shortly after I began working here at the Imperial Archive we had a visitor. Her name was Scheherazade. She, like Qing Shan's friend Sheba, was from Persia, and she too brought a scroll from the west.

YU YAN

Is that one of these other scrolls you have opened on the table?

LAO TZU

Indeed it is. This one,

(picking a scroll up off of the table)

it is called the Avesta, and Scheherazade said at the time that it too contained the prophetic utterings of a man named Zarathustra. Over the years I have thought about the meaning and the importance of the Avesta. And from time to time new documents are brought to me that cause me to revisit it once again.

YU YAN

And this new scroll from Qing Shan is the newest of those documents? But why?

LAO TZU

Well, there are many words, phrases and sentiments found in this new scroll from the prophet Jeremiah that seem to echo the Avesta scroll. And I wonder if, like me, the Hebrew prophet might have read the words of Zarathustra. Or perhaps Zarathustra read the words of the prophet. It is not certain which came first.

YU YAN

Master, I have read these scrolls with you. What would make you think that there is any value in such things?

LAO TZU

Daughter, listen to these words from the new scroll that Qing Shan brought us: "I will put my law in their minds and write it on their hearts. I will be their God, and they will be my people." And then these words from the Avesta scroll: "Right teaching is available to the one who is able to understand the truth from you, O Lord of Wisdom, giver of all good. In your benevolence, you provide the most profound insights, those that are integral to your wise understandings."

(pauses)

Yu Yan, do you see that although the words may be different, they have similar meaning? The God of Jeremiah is related to the God of Zarathustra. Indeed, they may be speaking of the same God.

YU YAN

I think I understand.

LAO TZU

And then, in this earlier scroll, also from the Hebrew people, filled with wisdom sayings, "As a man thinketh in his heart, so shall he be." That sounds like something I said just the other day.

YU YAN

But master, why is that important? What difference does it make to you? To us? To the Emperor?

LAO TZU

My child, we must accept wisdom wherever we find it. There is much to be learned from our brothers and sisters in distant lands. Truth is not defined by time or geography, and so I am challenged to discern what can be learned from these scrolls before us.

(There is a knock at the door. Yu Yan looks at Lao Tzu. Lao Tzu nods. Yu Yan turns and opens the door.)

(A young man, Confucius, enters)

LAO TZU

Ah, Confucius, please come in. Yu Yan, can you please make us some tea?

(Yu Yan exits)

CONFUCIUS

Master, why do you continue to keep Yu Yan with you?

LAO TZU

Ah, Confucius, Yu Yan brings beauty into my life on many levels. She asks the questions that many think but dare not speak, and elicits answers I had not considered before. I have never heard her speak without kindness about anyone, even when my own mind was revelling in the thought. She has a most inquisitive mind. In fact, she may one day replace me as chief curator here at the Imperial Archive.

CONFUCIUS

Chief curator? But she is a woman—not even a woman, she is a girl.

LAO TZU

You must release yourself from such thoughts. The barriers you construct are untrue and not real. As we learn the Tao and travel the Way, such falsehoods are stripped away and our true selves are revealed. But finally, I am grateful to her parents, for they named her well. Her smile can brighten up the bleakest day. When my days are finished here, there is no one I will miss as dearly or whose friendship I will value as much as Yu Yan.

(pauses)

But enough of that. What shall we talk about today, my friend?

CONFUCIUS

I want to talk to you about these scrolls. But first, I have been thinking about our last conversation. And I am still left pondering how a society can ensure that the just and the upright advance ahead of the unjust and the crooked?

LAO TZU

Ah, in pursuing their affairs, people often fail when they are close to success. Therefore, if one is cautious at the end as at the beginning, there will be no failures.

CONFUCIUS

It is true that the cautious seldom err. But if one is always cautious and never taking risks, there may be no failure but also there will be no advancement.

LAO TZU

He who is brave in daring will be killed. He who is brave in not daring will survive. One of these two courses is beneficial, the other is harmful.

CONFUCIUS

But master, is it beneficial to survive with the unrighteous? Is it harmful to be killed in the name of what is right?

LAO TZU

If today I were to be courageous while forsaking compassion, be magnanimous while forsaking frugality, get ahead while forsaking the hindmost, THAT would be death.

CONFUCIUS

Then how do we know what is courageous? What is compassionate? What is magnanimous or frugal? What is the way forward as society advances? For by nature, men are nearly alike; it is by practice they get to be far apart.

LAO TZU

Confucius, my words are very easy to understand, very easy to practice. But no one is able to understand them. And no one is able to practice them.

CONFUCIUS

So, do I understand you Master? Are you saying that a person should let their words be sincere and truthful and their actions honorable and careful? For if their words be not sincere and truthful, and their actions be neither careful nor honorable, how could such a person be appreciated, even by their own neighbours and peers?

(Yu Yan enters carrying a tray with a tea pot and two cups.)

LAO TZU

Ah, here is Yu Yan with the tea. Confucius, words have authority and affairs have ancestry. It is simply because of ignorance that people cannot understand me. But those who do understand me are few; thus I am ennobled.

(turning to Yu Yan and realizing she has only brought two tea cups)

Yu Yan, please go get a third cup and join us for a cup of tea.

CONFUCIUS

No, none for me, thank you, I have to leave. But before I go, I would like to know what is contained in your collection of scrolls. I hear that you collect ideas from the West which you share with your followers as wisdom, equal to that of the Emperor.

LAO TZU

That is true. And with all of your concern about the world and its troubles, you might find the prophecies of Zarathustra of interest.

CONFUCIUS

I highly doubt it.

LAO TZU

He describes a heavenly Redeemer, called a Saoshyant, who was present when the world began. It goes on to say that this Saoshyant will come again in the fullness of time and will return finally when life on this earth is finished. What do you think of that?

CONFUCIUS

But Lao Tzu, we already have our Emperor, who is the Son of Heaven. And we are to obey him until he fails us. And then, if that happens, Heaven will bless the revolution which brings us our next Emperor, the next Son of Heaven.

LAO TZU

That is true, but . . .

CONFUCIUS

I think it would be wiser to stop our ears to this nonsense from the West. It only serves to confuse people. I came here today to protest your sharing of these foreign texts. They are profane. But now I must be going. Once again it has been a most challenging conversation, even if also quite troubling.

(Yu Yan accompanies Confucius to the door.)

YU YAN

So Confucius, your conversation with Lao Tzu became heated.

CONFUCIUS

Yu Yan, I understand the order of things, how fish swim, and birds fly, and animals run, but I have met with a Dragon and cannot grasp how he can levitate into the clouds and reflect on what can not be known.

(BLACKOUT)

(END OF SCENE)

SCENE 3

SETTING: A mountain pass with a guarded gate. A chair sits to the side of the gate. There is a wall with a doorway leading into a rustic room that is visible to the audience. In the room there is a table and three chairs.

AT RISE: Images of a lone figure, walking with oxen, are projected accompanied by music from northern India. Yinxi enters and sits in the chair beside the gate as the projection ends and Lao Tzu enters from off stage.

(the sound of a single ox is heard offstage)

YINXI

Greetings, traveler; I need to see your papers.

LAO TZU

My friend, I have just made the voyage from Kunming, traveling to Myitkyina. I need to get to the market there.

YINXI

That is a long trip, and you still have a way to go. But I still need to see some papers.

LAO TZU

It is long, but I am on the Way. Sadly, I have no documentation to see me past this gate.

YINXI

Master, it is true that you are on the Way, I recognized you as you approached. I, too, desire to know the Way.

LAO TZU

Friend, you have me mistaken for another. I am a simple farmer, trying to get to the market in Myitkyina.

YINXI

Master, my name is Yinxi; I am the son of Neng and Zhang. I know that you have come from a much greater distance than Kunming. In fact, you are Lao Tzu, a great and sage teacher, and until recently you were the chief curator at the Imperial Archives in Wangcheng.

LAO TZU

Of course, you are correct. But tell me, Yinxi, how do you know such things? Have we met each other before today?

YINXI

No, Master, but I am a student of the stars, and two moons ago I learned of your having left Wangchen and that you would be crossing into India at my checkpoint. I have been awaiting your arrival since.

LAO TZU

Well, then, friend, since you know me so well, I have little need of papers. Will you let me pass with my ox and simple possessions?

YINXI

Master, when I said I desired to know the Way, I was being sincere. I will let you pass if you will share with me the Way, the Tao.

LAO TZU

Yinxi, friend, there are many lessons, much to learn, and I do not have much time. Perhaps I can share with you the first lessons. For every journey begins with a single step.

YINXI

I am afraid I cannot let you pass if you don't, somehow, make it worth my while.

LAO TZU

Very well. You have obviously given this some thought, so what do you have in mind?

YINXI

My wife, Saveeta, is inside. She has prepared a stew for us to share. And although I am a simple man, Saveeta is able to read and write. Stay with us this night and share the wisdom of the Way. Saveeta will record your words and teachings, and tomorrow you can begin the trek to Myitkyina, if, of course, that is truly where you are headed.

(Yinxi leads Lao Tzu into the house and to a table set with three bowls, goblets and cutlery. They are joined by Saveeta, who arrives with paper and a writing utensil. The trio sits at the table and prepares to eat.)

YINXI

Ahum vaishva naro bhutva, praninaam deha maashritah.

Pranaapaana samaayukta,pachamyannam chaturvidham.[1]

LAO TZU

Thank you, Yinxi, for that blessing upon our meal and our time together. Saveeta, when you are ready, we can begin.

(The meal is shared.)

SAVEETA

Master, if you would like a cup of tea, Yinxi can prepare it and we can get started.

LAO TZU

That would be lovely.

(turning to Yinxi)

Thank you, my friend, a cup of tea will definitely help with my digestion.

(Yinxi departs)

LAO TZU

Perhaps I will begin thus:

The ways that can be walked are not the eternal Way;
The names that can be named are not the eternal name.
The nameless is the origin of the myriad;
The named is the mother of the myriad creatures.

(Yinxi enters with a tray, a teapot and three tea cups and sets them on the table. Yinxi pours three cups of tea as Saveeta continues to write. Yinxi sits down at the table.)

LAO TZU

While you cultivate the soul and embrace unity, can you keep them from separating? Focus your vital breath until it is supremely soft, can you be like a baby?

(The lights dim and come back up.)

YINXI

More tea, anybody?

(Yinxi pours more tea into the cups.)

LAO TZU

If it is bent, it will be preserved intact;
is crooked, it will be straightened;
is sunken, it will be filled;
is worn out, it will be renewed . . .

(The lights dim and come back up . . . Yinxi is sleeping in his chair, arms and head resting on the table.)

SAVEETA

Master, did you say, "The Way is eternally nameless"?

LAO TZU

Yes, Saveeta, I did.

As soon as one begins to divide things up, there are names;
once there are names, one should also know when to stop;
knowing when to stop, one avoids peril . . .

(The lights dim and come back up. Yinxi is gone.)

LAO TZU

And finally,

(pauses)

The way of heaven benefits but does not harm, the way of humanity acts but does not contend. And now I must be going. I trust Yinxi will now let me pass.

SAVEETA

Lao Tzu, thank you for sharing this wisdom. Yinxi and I will spend much time studying the Way as you have shared it. And once I have written these teachings out more legibly, we will share the Way with others as they pass through.

LAO TZU

Saveeta, the Way cannot be learned. If it could, it would not be the Way. The Way cannot be taught. If it could, it would be a falsehood.

SAVEETA

But we now have your words, your teachings. They should be shared with others seeking the Way.

LAO TZU

But Saveeta, the Way cannot be found in words and phrases or strokes upon a page. But it is also true that every musical composition begins with a single note, every great story begins with nothing more than a thought.

SAVEETA

Yinxi, Lao Tzu is preparing to leave, please make ready a traveling bag for him. The Way he is traveling will be long and arduous.

(Yinxi enters with a traveling bag and escorts Lao Tzu back out to the gate.)

YINXI

Safe travels, Master.

LAO TZU

And to you as well, Yinxi.

(Saveeta joins Yinxi, and he places his arm around her waist.)

LAO TZU

Thank you, Yinxi and Saveeta, for your hospitality and the many kindnesses you have shown to an old sojourner.

SAVEETA

Master, it is we who must thank you for the wisdom you have shared and the challenge you have put forth, to find the Way available to all.

(Lao Tzu bows slightly and Yinxi and Saveeta bow in return. Lao Tzu turns and exits as Yinxi and Saveeta wave farewell.)

(BLACKOUT)

(END OF SCENE)

SCENE 4

SETTING: The gateway to a courtyard of a palatial estate.

AT RISE: Gautama stands at the gate.

GAUTAMA

No, Father, I want to walk.

(Suddhodana, Gautama's father, enters)

SUDDHODANA

Gautama, be reasonable; we have carriages and chariots along with drivers and attendants. You can see the neighborhood just as well through a carriage window.

GAUTAMA

But I have seen the view from a carriage window many times. I want to feel my feet on the ground. I want to speak to the people who live outside of these gates.

SUDDHODANA

Gautama, the world is not always a kind place; you must concern yourself with your wife, Yasodhara.

GAUTAMA

Father, my wife will be fine here behind these gates. And I will fare just as well outside of them. If you must, have some of your attendants accompany me, or you can accompany me yourself.

SUDDHODANA

Very well. I can see that you won't be swayed. I will walk with you, but we will also ask Channa to join us. I know how much you enjoy your conversations with him.

(turning and calling out)

Channa!

(Channa enters)

CHANNA

Yes, Suddhodana? You called?

(seeing Gautama)

Gautama, are you preparing to go out? Shall I get your chariot?

SUDDHODANA

That won't be necessary, Channa. Gautama would like to take a walk outside of the gate. Something about feeling his feet on the ground and addressing the people.

GAUTAMA

I want to SPEAK to the people outside of the gates. Father, is that so wrong?

SUDDHODANA

Gautama, it is not that it is wrong, just unnecessary. But, as you desire, let us go for a walk.

(turning and smiling at Gautama)

Very well. I am ready to go.

(Gautama, Suddhodana and Channa depart, followed by two armed guards. While they are walking, images of aging are projected. The final image is that of a very elderly man's face.)

GAUTAMA

Channa, why does this man move so slowly and what is wrong with his body? It looks like he is losing his skin.

CHANNA

Gautama, this man has lived many years. All beings experience changes to their bodies as they age.

(Gautama appears troubled at Channa's words. They continue their walk. While they are walking, images of illness, disease, and poverty are projected. The final image is that of a young woman diseased by leprosy.)

GAUTAMA

Channa, here is a young woman, little older than a girl; yet she too is slow and unsteady and her body is misshapen. Why?

CHANNA

Gautama, this woman's body is being ravaged by disease and with the disease comes pain. All beings are subject to disease and pain.

(Once again, Gautama is troubled by Channa's words. They continue their walk. While they are walking images of death, mourning, funeral processions are projected. When the projection stops there is a body wrapped in a burial shroud lying at the side of the road.)

GAUTAMA

It appears that this person's journey has ended.

CHANNA

Yes, my young student. Today you have witnessed the inevitabilities of life. All beings get older. All beings are subject to illness, disease, and pain. And all beings will experience death.

GAUTAMA

But is this all there is? Is this the end? Is there no escape?

CHANNA

Gautama, you know that this man will be born again, and his station in the next life will be determined by how he lived this life. It is the karmic circle. That is samsara.

(Gautama appears dejected. The weight of this truth weighs heavily on him. Turning, he sees an ascetic, meditating with an alms bowl in front of him.)

CHANNA

Here is one who attempts to answer your questions. He meditates on the causes of human suffering and if it is possible to be released from samsara and the karmic cycle.

GAUTAMA

Why? What does he hope to gain from his meditations?

CHANNA

He hopes to find the answers that will be of benefit to all beings.

GAUTAMA

Why does the bowl sit on the ground before him?

CHANNA

He is reliant on the generosity of others. The bowl is for the collection of alms.

GAUTAMA

(turning to his father)

Father, do you have anything you can offer to this man? After all, he seeks answers that will be to my, and your, benefit.

SUDDHODANA

Son, we cannot be giving our hard-earned money to people who serve no function.

GAUTAMA

Very well, I will leave him some coins, and Channa, when we return to the house, gather some rice and bring me back here so I can offer it too to this man.

(Gautama drops some coins into the bowl and turns to walk home followed by the others.)

(The lights dim and come back up. Gautama and Channa are standing before the ascetic.)

GAUTAMA

Channa, please leave the rice here and return to my father's house.

CHANNA

I cannot leave you here on your own, Gautama.

GAUTAMA

Channa, you have been a trustworthy charioteer, a wise teacher, and a faithful friend. I have decided that this man's life is the life I want to lead. I too want to contemplate the questions of life in the service of all beings.

CHANNA

What shall I tell your parents? Your wife?

GAUTAMA

Tell them I have chosen the life of an ascetic and I will pray for them daily.

(Channa turns and leaves. Gautama begins his journey until he arrives at an old fig tree. Various images are projected, landscape, people, sky and mountains, etc., as Gautama walks.)

(Gautama sits beneath the tree in a meditative posture.)

(The lights dim and come back up. There are others sitting with Gautama, and they are in conversation.)

ANANDA

Buddha Gautama, can you show us the way to enlightenment?

GAUTAMA

Ananda, my cousin, I could show you the way, but then it would not be the way. I can teach you but, in the end, believe nothing, no matter where you read it, or who said it, no matter if I said it, unless it agrees with your own reason and your own common sense.

ANANDA

But then how will we know if something is true?

GAUTAMA

You will know. But doubt everything. Find your own light. And when you have found it you will know the truth.

ANANDA

Buddha Gautama, you are beyond wise and most compassionate. We desire the enlightenment you have attained. Please share the secret and save us from this world.

GAUTAMA

Ananda,

(looking around at the others)

my friends, no one saves us but ourselves. No one can and no one may. It is the self within which redeems the self without. We ourselves must walk the Way.

(BLACKOUT)

(END OF SCENE)

SCENE 5

SETTING: A battlefield at Kurukshetra (northern India)

AT RISE: Arjuna and Krishna stand together in an open chariot. Krishna's head is covered and his face obscured.

ARJUNA

O Krishna, look upon this battlefield; both sides have assembled and appear eager to fight.

KRISHNA

The lines appear to have been drawn and weapons are at the ready. Arjuna, the time for battle is quickly approaching.

(Arjuna lifts his bow and nocks his first arrow.)

(Looking out over both camps, Arjuna pauses and lowers his bow.)

ARJUNA

But Krishna, looking at the faces in both camps I see fathers and sons, grandfathers and grandsons, cousins and brothers, in-laws and other kin. I see teachers and sages, family and friends.

KRISHNA

Arjuna, you are, of course, correct. On one side are your brothers and other members of the Pandava family. But on the other side are your cousins and the rest of the Kaurava family.

ARJUNA

But this means at the end of the battle many of my friends and family, teachers and princes will be dead, some by my own hand.

KRISHNA

Again Arjuna, you are most certainly correct.

ARJUNA

(throwing down his bow and arrow and removing the sword from around his waist)

Then I cannot, I will not fight. I will not be responsible for the deaths of so many. I will remain here between the two camps. I will stop this battle.

KRISHNA

Arjuna, why do you distinguish between those you know and to whom you are related and others? This is not your first battle and these will not be the first deaths by your hand.

ARJUNA

But surely, if I strike my cousin with my sword, or if I pierce him with my arrow, he will die.

KRISHNA

Your mourning is misplaced and misspent. The wise mourn neither for the living nor the dead, for whether a king or a peasant none will cease to be hereafter.

ARJUNA

That is true. However, I must continue living knowing that I am responsible for the death of those I love.

KRISHNA

You are confusing the physical body, that can know both pleasure and pain and will surely know death, with the atman, the spiritual self, that cannot know death, for no one can destroy that immutable being.

ARJUNA

(with a look of dejection)

I believe you speak the truth. And I know my duty.

KRISHNA

Arjuna, you are a Kshatriya; to your caste is given the responsibility of governing during times of peace and fighting during times of war. There is no higher good for a Kshatriya than a righteous war.

ARJUNA

And therein lies the question, is this a righteous war?

KRISHNA

Arjuna, slain, you will gain heaven and, victorious, you will inherit the earth. Gather your weapons and arise. Determine to fight.

(Krishna reveals himself to be an avatar for Vishnu by uncovering his head and revealing his blue torso. Arjuna falls in a worshipful posture.)

VISHNU

Arjuna, the battle you are waging is an eternal battle and is waged by all people of every time and place. It is the battle between the finite and the infinite, the always changing and the immutable.

ARJUNA

Lord Vishnu, you would never ask me to act in a sinful manner, nor would you direct me to align myself with the unrighteous. Today, I will fight the doubts within me. Today, my bow will be drawn in your service and to your honor.

(The sounds of warfare are heard and images of battle scenes throughout the ages are projected. Arjuna engages in the battle with his bow and arrows, and then, drawing his sword, he runs off stage. Then there is silence, the screens go dark, and Arjuna emerges, bloodied but victorious.)

ARJUNA

Lord Vishnu, I have won the day. How could it have been otherwise with you by my side?

VISHNU

I am the source of all in the universe. Arjuna, now you must become my devotee; always think of me, act for me, worship me, and offer all homage unto me. Surrender to me alone and do not fear sinful reactions.

ARJUNA

Thanks to your grace, my delusion is destroyed, my understanding has returned. I stand secure, my doubts all dispelled; I will, from this day forward I will walk the Way of service to you.

(The lights dim, symbols from the seven traditions in *Seven Testaments* flash across the screen and a voice from offstage . . .)

VOICE #1

Then Zarathustra said, "Reveal unto me that name of thine, O Ahura Mazda! That is the greatest, the best, the fairest, the most effective, the most fiend-smiting, the best healing, that destroys best the malice of Daevas and men . . ."

Ahura Mazda replied unto him: "My name is the One of whom questions are asked, O holy Zarathustra!

. . . my fourth name is Perfect Holiness.
. . . my seventh name is the One with understanding.
. . . my eleventh name is He who produces weal.
. . . my twelfth name is Ahura, the Lord.
. . . my thirteenth name is the most Beneficent.
. . . my fourteenth name is He in whom there is no harm.
. . . my seventeenth name is the All-seeing One.
. . . my eighteenth name is the healing One.
. . . my nineteenth name is the Creator.
. . . my twentieth name is Mazda, the All-knowing One."

I AM the Keeper;

VOICE #2

I AM the God of your father Abraham

VOICE #3

I AM the Resurrection and the Life

VOICE #1

I AM the Creator and the Maintainer;

VOICE #2

I AM the Lord who made all things

VOICE #3

I AM the Light of the World

VOICE #1

I AM the Discerner;

VOICE #2

I AM El Shaddai

VOICE #3

I AM The Bread of Life

VOICE #1

I AM the most beneficent Spirit . . .

VOICE #2

I AM who I AM

VOICE #3

I AM the Way, the Truth and the Life

VOICE #1

I AM

VOICE #2

I AM

VOICE #3

I AM

(BLACKOUT)

(END OF SCENE)

(CURTAIN CALL)

EPILOGUE

(Gautama steps forward)

GAUTAMA

If you can keep your head when all about you
Are losing theirs and blaming it on you,
If you can trust yourself when all men doubt you,

But make allowance for their doubting too;
If you can wait and not be tired by waiting,
Or being lied about, don't deal in lies,
Or being hated, don't give way to hating,
And yet don't look too good, nor talk too wise:

If you can dream—and not make dreams your master;
If you can think—and not make thoughts your aim;
If you can meet with Triumph and Disaster
And treat those two impostors just the same;
If you can bear to hear the truth you've spoken
Twisted by knaves to make a trap for fools,
Or watch the things you gave your life to, broken,
And stoop and build 'em up with worn-out tools:

If you can make one heap of all your winnings
And risk it on one turn of pitch-and-toss,
And lose, and start again at your beginnings
And never breathe a word about your loss;
If you can force your heart and nerve and sinew
To serve your turn long after they are gone,
And so hold on when there is nothing in you
Except the Will which says to them: "Hold on!"

If you can talk with crowds and keep your virtue,
Or walk with Kings—nor lose the common touch,
If neither foes nor loving friends can hurt you,
If all men count with you, but none too much;
If you can fill the unforgiving minute
With sixty seconds' worth of distance run,
Yours is the Earth and everything that's in it,
And—which is more—you'll be a Man, my son.[2]

notes

1. I (God) become the fire of digestion (Vaishvanara) abide in all animals, and I am associated with the vital air of Life, going in and out of the body I digest all four kinds of food.
2. "If," Rudyard Kipling, 1895.

appendix e

Identifying the Tomb of Zoroaster

THE ORIGINAL CRYPT BENEATH THE BLUE MOSQUE IN AFGHANISTAN DATES TO MORE THAN A thousand years before Imam Ali, who locals believe to be also buried there. There is only one local candidate of sufficient celebrity from that earlier era to give the site its ancient name, *The Tomb of the Exalted* or "Mazar-i-Sharif." The name of the first occupant is revealed in the image of the "radiant camel" or "zarath-ustra," which, according to legend, carried thither the body of Imam Ali. The pronouncement on which this legend is based thus reestablished the splendid grandeur of Zoroaster's tomb, set now to become more important to all religions.

Crypt of Zoroaster under the Blue Mosque Tomb of Hazrat Ali.
SHUTTERSTOCK IMAGE.

Current scholarship is divided on the dates of the life of Zoroaster, but traditional Persian, ancient Hebrew, and early Christian sources agree that the Persian prophet died in 551 BCE during prayers in the chapel at Balkh, then the only city of importance in the Persian province of Bactria. If so, according to his teachings, his remains would not have been "exposed" to the elements inside the valley community of Balkh and buried there. The Greek historian Herodotus, writing in the fifth century BCE, described the use of "high places" by Zoroastrians from their earliest period: "It is not their custom to make and set up statues and temples and altars but they offer sacrifices on the high places of the mountains."[1] Over the course of time, these natural sacred sites were elaborated and simple shrines were built for the bones of those whose bodies had been exposed to nature. These mountain mausolea became the focus of the Zoroastrian pilgrimage tradition, as compared with the later fire temples of the cities and villages.

So Zoroaster's family and followers would have looked to the nearest "high point" of significance within walking distance, the place we call Mazar-i-Sharif, fifteen kilometers to the east, accessible on foot but high enough to honor the most important prophet of that age and location. Similar such ancient high points remain identifiable and unchanged near Yazd in Iran, near Petra in Jordan, and elsewhere. We call the one in question Mazar-i-Sharif, which translates as *Tomb of the Exalted*, a name it acquired only after the building of a mausoleum there. That site became identified by its current name only after mid-sixth century BCE as a memorial for the countless pilgrims then wishing to honor the life and ministry of the spiritual leader who had turned religious life upside down from one end of the Silk Route to the other. Otherwise, they might have named the tomb after the city (of whatever name), but that is how the community of Mazar-i-Sharif got its name, as a settlement grew around the site on the cusp of an era described by the *Economist* magazine. "Societies became recognizably 'modern' in the mid-first millennium BC, during the so-called 'Axial Age,' the period in which figures such as Plato, Buddha and Zoroaster appeared on the scene, promulgating their moralizing ideologies."[2] This observation, with sixth-century dates increasingly accepted for him in the twenty-first century, sets the search for Zoroaster's tomb right into the context of this book, which identifies him as the father of the Axial Age.

A tomb might be named after a person or after a place, but for a city to be named after a tomb, the person buried there must be exceptionally famous. Through all time there is simply no candidate in that region for such an honor other than Zoroaster. It was identified as Mazar-i-Sharif more than a thousand years before the next significant burial in that mausoleum, that of Hazrat Ali, when it was appropriately expanded again on the earlier Zoroastrian foundations. However, it was following the time of the first burial there that the settled area of Balkh began to stretch beyond the geographic Bactrian plain to a "capital" area that grew to become the more important center.[3] This fact is a key element in our contention that Zoroaster could not have died in the eleventh century BCE or earlier, since there was no such identifiable center as Mazar-i-Sharif for another five hundred years.

In his authoritative book on architecture in Afghanistan, the University of Edinburgh's distinguished archaeologist Warwick Ball comments on the Blue Mosque in Mazar-i-

Sharif, "There are many non-Islamic practices associated with this shrine, such as the raising of a pole at Nauruz on March 21 each year when Mazar-i-Sharif becomes the main centre of the annual Nauruz (New Year) festivities. It might be that the shrine represents an Islamization of a much older, pre-Islamic cult that was focussed on this site, perhaps even of Zoroaster himself, who is traditionally supposed to be buried in the Balkh region."[4]

Because the city is named after the tomb, it is only common sense that the tomb was there first. The community came into being and was settled in the sixth century BCE, coincident with the burial of obviously the most famous person who ever lived in that area, whose tomb became the name of the city that grew up around it. In fact, from that day until this there has never been any personage other than Zoroaster of such import functioning out of that region and buried there, with the possible exception of Ali, a thousand years later, and he was brought there from elsewhere.

We may, or may not, soon find missing pieces of the Zoroastrian Avesta (the "Dead Zee Scrolls"), a feature of this book, but increasing evidence identifying Zoroaster's tomb provides at least a measure of increased familiarity and some intimacy with this prophet, who, in certain respects, was the first to articulate a path to redemption for the world and its people. The earlier figures of Moses and Homer are profoundly significant, at least to Western culture, like a Zoroaster who might have lived and died back in the mists of time. However, a Zoroaster of the sixth century relates to us like well-known figures of the Axial Age: Hebrew prophets, Greek philosophers, Eastern mystics of popular religion. Identifying the *Tomb of the Exalted* as Zoroaster's resting place connects him directly with Parsees and other Zoroastrians today, and with devotees and practitioners of the seven religions whose testaments are the subject of this study.

This book identifies Zoroaster's tomb as being beneath the Blue Mosque in Mazar-i-Sharif, one of the most beautiful buildings in the world. Our identification of the tomb of Zoroaster fits the Islamic pattern of multiple burials in a single site, since he is regarded by Muslims as among the prophets of the People of the Book. Given the paucity of other possible candidates as occupant of a crypt beneath the tomb of Hazrat Ali, who could the original inhabitant of the mausoleum be except Zoroaster? It simply remains for experts with twenty-first-century high-tech equipment to prove that somebody was buried there at a lower level, somebody important enough to have the city named after his mausoleum. We will get to that, but first let us become more aware of the whole story of the Blue Mosque and its connections to Zoroaster.

Canadian journalist Terry Glavin (*National Post* and *Ottawa Citizen*) described this location in a column after a visit to the site in Afghanistan: "For centuries, Mazar's glorious Shrine of Hazrat Ali has been the journey's end for Shia pilgrims from afar, and an everyday refuge of gardens and esplanades for the local Sunni majority. The Blue Mosque, where everyone prays together, is also a fountainhead of Sufi cosmopolitanism. It is a marvel of classic Islamic architecture built in the grand Timurid style on deep Zoroastrian foundations."[5] The latter point is information he picked up on site as part of the local, but unofficial, lore.

Why does it matter where Zoroaster is buried? Discovery of the tomb of Zoroaster would be of great importance to Zoroastrians today as they assume a significant role in interfaith discussions based partly on facts at last, rather than legends about Zoroaster's dates and the importance of his teachings in the world of the Silk Route. Because of their interface in Babylon, this relationship is of interest to Jews, who may wish to know whether their connection with Zoroaster is direct or distant in relation to that era. Christians increasingly identify Jesus as the Savior of the World, the Saoshyant or "Redeemer" of Zoroastrianism, rather than merely the one who would restore the throne of David for the Jews of the early church. The location of the tomb in Afghanistan and its date also fits with self-identification of the four world religions farther east and others, as the Zoroastrian Avesta and the Dead Zee Scrolls begin to function as the Rosetta Stone of religion described in part two of this book. This may be a starting point in one of the most critical discussions in the shrinking world of the twenty-first century—namely, the place of religion as part of the problem or part of the solution to problems of divisions and relationships in our time.

Local Muslim residents of Mazar-i-Sharif appear to have no objections to identifying this site with Zoroaster. On the contrary, guides and tour books often refer to the legend that the Blue Mosque sits on an earlier Zoroastrian foundation. Our presentation of additional evidence in this regard at the 2018 Parliament of the World's Religions was greeted as big news, and it may be regarded by some as "the big reveal" of this book, though we are only presenting additional pieces of the puzzle, synthesizing them and making obvious inferences from them. It is our intention to move from legend and speculation to history and fact. In doing so, it may also be possible to finally settle the long-standing debate over the dates of Zoroaster's birth, life, and death.

This shrine is considered locally to be first and foremost the tomb of Hazrat Ali, the cousin, son-in-law, and eventual successor of Muhammad, even though most Muslims elsewhere in the world recognize Ali's tomb as being at the Imam Ali Mosque at Najaf in Iraq. Local Muslim devotees and tour guides in Mazar-i-Sharif have maintained the legend that says that the body of Ali was carried here on the back of a white (or "shining") camel, secretly, long years after his earlier burial in Najaf. Books, brochures, and tour guides recount the story of Ali being buried at Mazar-i-Sharif in a grave that had already been known for centuries as the *Tomb of the Exalted*, though the full antiquity of the name was not realized until quite recently.

In Sanskrit and related languages, the word *Zarah* is often rendered as golden, shining, or white in various traditions, though linguists are unanimous in lexicons that the very best translation is "radiant." In Sanskrit, as adopted in Arabic, Persian, old Avestan, and cognate languages, "camel" is *ustra* (or ushtra). The obvious, but only now articulated, meaning of the legend is that this memorial to Ali is mounted on Zarah-ustra, whose full name is usually translated as Golden Camel, though radiant or white camel works just as well in most languages.

The original crypt beneath the Blue Mosque in Afghanistan dates to over a thousand years before Imam Ali, who locals believe is buried there. The pronouncement on which this legend is based repurposed the apparent splendor of Zoroaster's more ancient mausoleum, the *Tomb of the Exalted*. Over time this phrase has been assumed to refer to Ali ibn Abu Talib, but the problem with assuming the title refers to Ali is confirmed by documentary evidence that the name of the tomb was there long before Ali arrived.

There is wide agreement with Dr. Ahmad Hasan Dani, a leading epigraphist and archaeologist of the Quaid-E-Azam University in Islamabad, that the city was named *Tomb of the Exalted* since 138 CE at the very least, half a millennium before Ali: "This more ancient date is witnessed by the *Mazar-I-Sharif Inscription*, clearly dated from the time of Veka, a local Shia ruler long centuries before Ali's death in 661 CE and his second burial in the year 701 CE."[6] The only prophet of note from that area was obviously buried sometime before 138 CE, but no earlier than the era soon after 550 BCE, when the capital of Bactria was moved from Balkh to the newly established community that became Mazar-i-Sharif, surrounding the tomb of "the exalted," a highly respected persona, one deserving of a mausoleum apparently like no other.[7]

The eventual attribution of the Mazar tomb to Imam Ali was perhaps understandable since it is known that Ali traveled in Afghanistan, where his "footprints" are preserved in stone memorials in two other cities. Mazar-i-Sharif was "revealed" or decreed to be the burial place of Ali by Harrun Al Rashid some forty years after Ali died in 661. Harrun was the fifth Abbasid caliph, who ruled in Baghdad from 786 CE to 809 CE. The fictional book *One Thousand and One Nights* is set in Harun's magnificent court, and some of its stories involve Harun himself, a figure of great imagination. He considered moving his court to the east, and eventually he did move it to Syria for safety, but he appears to have considered Afghanistan first.

Since there was already a mausoleum of a prophet in Afghanistan at the place called Mazar-i-Sharif, the *Tomb of the Exalted*, a tomb even then of interest to pilgrims, it suited his purpose for Harun to declare it to be also the tomb of Ali. He did so at the request of Ja'far as-Sadiq, who later became the sixth imam in the Shia tradition and was seeking to establish a Shia stronghold in Afghanistan. Ja'far was a descendant of Ali on the side of his father, Muhammad al-Baqir, and his story was eagerly accepted by the local population of Mazar-i-Sharif, largely Shia at the time, even if rejected by many other Muslims. It is as if these holy men were looking for a ready-made shrine, popular among pilgrims. There were no such Jewish, Christian, or Muslim sites that far east, but there was that mausoleum so impressive that the now substantial city was named for it, and the occupant was the prophet associated with the People of the Book named as Magian in the Holy Quran. Whether they brought the remains of Ali there physically or spiritually, the announcement had the desired effect of turning this shrine into a Muslim mosque.

It is possible that the remains of Ali were transferred there at a time when some could not remember who first was buried in the mausoleum. Others may have wished to deny that the prominent shrine tomb belonged to a non-Muslim persona, though, as we have seen, burial above any prophet from among the People of the Book was an established practice. The "Chamber of Commerce" would have encouraged the recognition of further enhancement of the site following the declaration also ascribing the tomb to Ali to this location.

The grave was then domed and greatly enhanced. Sultan Ahmed Sanjar of the Seljug Dynasty expanded the main structure to something even greater, resembling present proportions, some three hundred years after the reported reinterment of Ali. It was desecrated and then partially hidden under earthen embankment for protection during the invasion of Genghis Khan around 1220 CE. In the fifteenth century CE, Sultan Husayn Mirza Baygarah repaired and extended the superstructure in an outstanding example of the Timurid architectural style. It has been well maintained ever since as a priority budget item in the city, province, and nation. The latest addition is a monument to the national hero Ahmad Shah Massoud, a Mujahadin leader, who fought both the Soviets and the Taliban before his assassination in 2001.

The structure appears to be almost floating, a technique of this particular style of Islamic architecture, partially facilitated by intricately painted clay tiles, produced in a studio on site. Two square feet of tiling need to be replaced every day, having been damaged by the elements or stolen by pilgrims as religious mementos. A site plan of the foundations made by engineers early in the twentieth century showed that there had earlier been a crypt in the smaller walled precinct under the original mosque, razed later but with portals still remaining as gateways for the current shrine.

No carbon dating has yet been undertaken, though current techniques of archaeological investigation are equally effective. LiDAR scans from space, as described by Richard Freund in *Four Testaments*, can reveal much about the original site, and close-up electrical resistive tomography and ground-penetrating radar (ERT and GPR) scans might be able to flesh out the story of this mosque and its sacred precinct as to be presented by Freund and his team at the 2020 *Seven Testaments Trilogy* conference in Niagara Falls, New York. The team includes Harry Jol, an anthropologist at the University of Wisconsin–Eau Claire, who literally "wrote the book" on *Ground Penetrating Radar Theory and Applications*.[8]

Richard Freund is a leading field archaeologist who has worked around the world with Dr. Jol in non-invasive surveys of graves, tombs, and religious institutions. They find that this type of subsurface imaging often has surprising results, but their work reveals how this type of investigation needs to be done in a manner that protects the dignity of the site at the same time that new information can be gained.

Since Dr. Freund and I have had books published by Rowman & Littlefield, he was asked to vet the archaeological information embedded in this appendix. Though he had heard unsubstantiated rumors about the burial of Zoroaster, it was when he reviewed the collected source materials and oral reports listed below that he suggested a geoscience sub-surface mapping project to help further study of the tomb. Televised and written reports of the geoscientific expedition to investigate what lies beneath the Mazar-i-Sharif tomb will be available under the name *The Tomb of the Exalted*. Previous hints and clues about Zoroaster's tomb in a crypt beneath the Blue Mosque were earlier rejected by scholars as mere speculation because of the lack of any scientific information from the tomb. To provide a summary of the previously ignored evidence, we précis the support for our model in twelve categories, which move from speculation and conjecture to a more compelling concept when the new scientific information is included. Even before that, taking all the evidence together at last makes a good case for this site being confidently identified as the tomb of Zoroaster.

- History (only one candidate for this tomb within a thousand miles in any historical era)
- Geography (the appropriate high point is walking distance from Balkh, where he died)
- Demographics (population from the Bactrian plain slowly moving east to new capital at tomb in sixth century BCE)
- Nomenclature (regarding the name of the city and the tomb for which it was named)
- Common sense (regarding the significance of the tomb existing before the city)
- Local folklore (then and now)
- Burial practice (Muslims placing prophets' bones in sites already identified as holy)
- Linguistics (identifying Zoroaster as the "Zarah-ustra" in radiant camel legend)
- Politics (the theocratic mix of government and religion by early caliphs)
- Religion (facts about Ali in Afghanistan and other data regarding dates and personas)
- Architectural (reviews of structural engineering issues over the last century)
- Archaeological (expected verification by respected experts of the twenty-first century)

This much evidence and advance information from the site were enough for Freund to be confident that the proof is simply waiting to be announced at the launch conference for this book in Niagara Falls, New York, May 29–31, 2020. We know that the core of the shrine does contain a tomb chamber and an antechamber for prayer and worship, the starting point for high-tech investigations, untried heretofore. A question that remains concerns the possibility of any artifacts in the crypt. Could this be even a repository of the written materials for which Zoroaster was most famous? Missing portions of the Avesta found here may be the first cache of what we call *The Dead Zee Scrolls*, a mother lode of the missing chapters 6–27, thought by scholars like Mary Boyce to have been composed by Zoroaster himself. Such a tremendous possibility will be revealed in the future if the investigation by Professor Freund's 2020 team is able to indicate that there is more there than just the bones of Zoroaster.

At this point we get to the Indiana Jones–style speculation that some undergraduate students may enjoy, or the Dan Brown portion of the story for public library and congregational book clubs, except that some or all of it could well be proven true. The weeklong expedition is set to proceed under the local supervision of Dr. Julio Bendezu-Sarmiento, director of the French Archaeological Delegation in Afghanistan (DAFA), assisted by Blue Mosque guides. The earth-penetrating radar equipment is being set up at predetermined target locations identified by Dr. Harry Jol through preliminary scanning. Richard Freund's practiced eye looks down one visual shaft after another.

John Bedell of the NOW YouTube channel videotapes the sequential moments for the TV networks that frequently cover Freund's expeditions. Interviewer David Bruce keeps asking, "What do you see, Dr. Freund?" When the EPR cameras detect anything promising (bone, wood, even crypt-shape stones) at a depth of up to forty feet, Freund exclaims, "This could be it."

A discreet two-inch steel tube might then extract material from the level under consideration for identification and carbon dating. This all takes place under government permits issued through the American Institute of Afghanistan Studies in Kabul, in cooperation with the Archaeological Museum at nearby Termez, just over the Uzbekistan border.

It is my wife and research associate, Jenny Sutacriti Brown, who envisioned the aspirational moment in a made-for-television literary description. David Bruce again asks, "What do you see?" Jenny has Richard Freund replying, "I see a stone structure that appears to be a crypt, with a human skeleton, and some objects which could be scrolls on either side of the bones."

At this point in the actual expedition, Freund would interject. "Hold on, everybody. It is true that Brian Brown's evidence is enough for us to be sure that if there is anything that far down there, it is likely from 2,500 years ago, when Mazar-i-Sharif was founded around a mausoleum, rather than 1,500 years ago, when Ali was buried. In that case, we can presume that what we see is related to Zoroaster and that he was buried around 550 BCE rather than much earlier. But we are not going to find the Dead Zee Scrolls just like that. There may be something there, but much analysis remains to be done, and if its results are more specific, we still need Afghan government approval to actually excavate to the level which proves that in burying Ali here and others since that time, the custodians of this sacred precinct did indeed honor the memory and the earlier prophetic ministry of Zoroaster."

I and my colleagues in this quest are not particularly sanguine about the prospect of finding the Dead Zee Scrolls in the crypt beneath Hazrat Ali, but for many now the correlation of the above twelve factors pointing to Zoroaster's interment there (if there is indeed a crypt in that location) is enough to conclude that earlier uncoordinated speculations and scraps of evidence do combine to prove that "whatever is there" is indeed the remains of Zoroaster's bones. Buried in an identifiable site that did not exist prior to 550 BCE, any verification of the existence of a crypt there is sufficient to illustrate the veracity of the claim that the prophet who died nearby was buried there at a date coincident with the first human activity atop the "high place" identified as the *Tomb of the Exalted* ever since. In addition to the identification of Zoroaster's tomb, this discovery coincidently settles the dates of his life through the earlier part of the fifth century BCE and verifies the traditional Persian date of his birth as at 628 BCE.

Freund wrote to me on the eve of publication of this book, "If the double tomb is there, we will find it. If it is not conclusive because of depth, soil, obstacles, etc., we will write an appropriate and meaningful report on what we did, which itself will be very compelling." This will be the report to be presented at the Niagara conference following the expedition. Watch for it as a TV documentary or as a new book from Rowman & Littlefield. In a final note from Freund at this point, he writes:

The geoscience noninvasive nature of this study has the ability to add much to the discussion and preserve the dignity of the Blue Mosque. Subsurface imaging equipment will give us 3D models of a religious site that can be understood by the general public. This work in identifying the multi-layered tomb building is called "multi-cultural superimposition." The terms superposition or superimposition are borrowed from geology and archaeology. They are used by these disciplines to describe how the layers or strata of layers of historical materials are accumulated with the most ancient at the bottom and the younger layers on the top. It may seem counterintuitive but it seems that sometimes one holy site will be built over another holy site. In studies throughout the world we find that as people move around or come from other regions, they tend to gravitate toward known locations and they often build their own significant institutions on the same location that earlier peoples had sanctified. The idea of putting one tomb of a significant religious leader over the tomb of a more ancient religious leader is a form of what we call "multi-cultural or multi-religious superimposition," allowing the significance of the earlier religious leader's holiness to be, in a sense, absorbed by the tomb above. This is particularly important in the case of the Zoroaster and Ali, since the first was local and the second was transported from the place of death to a new location. In an archaeological sense, this is the equivalent of how Islam frequently absorbed the theological elements of Judaism and Christianity into its own theological constructs.

Tombs of varying dimensions were added to the Blue Mosque for a number of Afghan political and religious leaders over the years, which has led to the development of irregular dimensions that have done nothing except add character to the beautiful structure. It is already an attraction for pilgrims and visitors, and its putative recognition as also being the tomb of Zoroaster will increase the worldwide interest in this shrine. It already has national status similar to Westminster Abbey in the United Kingdom and Notre Dame in France, or Wat Arun in Thailand and the Taj Mahal in India. The Blue Mosque is one of the most beautiful edifices on the planet, but following verifications by the archaeological team under the leadership of Dr. Freund, this multilayered shrine may attain world status among both Muslims and Zoroastrians more like that attributed to the Vatican in Rome and the Kaaba in Mecca. This development will assist in the current quest to gain a better understanding of the story of Zoroaster, the dates of his life, where he was buried, and his impact on the world.

The House of One.
SHUTTERSTOCK IMAGE.

This spiritual center in Berlin contains a church, a mosque, and a synagogue with conjoining common space and areas for sharing with each other and with many others. Opened in 2019, it is the product of a grassroots group of the three religious communities who raised thirty-five million Euros in donations, plus ten million Euros each from the federal government and the city of Berlin. All parties recognized the importance of this modern cathedral-like structure in the establishment of a new community ethos among religious people in the country, which has possibly the world's most scurrilous record of religious conflict, Christian—Catholic and Protestant—and Jewish, countering trends verging on repetition of such tragedies with Muslim citizens in the early twenty-first century.

notes

1. *The Histories of Herodotus* 1:131.

2. *Economist*, March 21, 2019.

3. P. Leriche, "Bactria, Pre-Islamic Period," *Encyclopaedia Iranica*, Vol. 3 (1998).

4. Warwick Ball, *The Monuments of Afghanistan*, 248.

5. *Dissent*, April 5, 2011.

6. Ahmad Hasan Dani, *Proceedings of the Indian History Congress*, Vol. 61, Part One: Millennium Session (2000–2001), 132–35.

7. "Afghanistan: A Treasure Trove for Archaeologists," *Time*, February 26, 2009.

8. An Elsevier book, Amsterdam.

appendix f

The Sogdians: Prime Movers between Boundaries[1]

Jenny Rose

T HIS ARTICLE IS INTENDED TO PROVIDE A BRIEF BUT NUANCED OVERVIEW OF AN EASTERN IRA-nian people whose contribution to both the material and the ideological culture of the "Silk Road" has only recently become the focus of rigorous academic study. The evolution of Sogdian commercial activities in the region has been thoroughly explored—within the limits of currently available material—by Étienne de la Vaissière, in the updated, English edition of his history of Sogdian merchants.[2] My intention is not to replicate that research but to consider the impact of the Sogdians—particularly their adherence to ancient Zoroastrian beliefs and practices—on the language, culture, and religious expression of the trade routes between the fourth and eighth centuries CE.

historical background to sogdian trade and traffic

Traffic had existed between China and Central Asia since the mid-second millennium BCE, when nephrite jade from Khotan began to make its way to China, the Eurasian steppe, and Siberia.[3] But it was under the Ancient Persians (ca. 550–330 BCE) that more

---

Jenny Rose, at Claremont Graduate University, with Parsee ancestry herself, is a scholar of Zoroastrianism of the first rank. Here she describes activity related to ancient Sogdiana, known today as Uzbekistan plus part of Tajikistan, though she disagrees with the author on whether the Zoroastrian phenomenon in the sixth century BCE was soon after the life of Zoroaster or was triggered then by Magi activity. Presuming Zoroaster to have been born some centuries earlier, she presents insightful views of Zoroastrianism among Sogdians a thousand years after the height of its influence at the beginning of the Persian Empire. This article describes an era in an area in which portions of the Avesta may have been lost, hidden, or stored somewhere. While possible discovery sites for fragments of the Dead Zee Scrolls also exist in Western China and the Central Asian republics as well as in the Caucuses, Iran, and Turkey, Rose's description also gives readers an opportunity to see in Sogdiana the beating heart of Silk Route commerce and culture in later Zoroastrian times. Its influence within China proper will be seen in new and exciting research by Chinese, Australian, and other scholars presented in appendices G and H.

stable trade routes were established and that, as an Achaemenid satrapy, Sogdian involvement in commercial enterprise between "east" and "west" began in earnest.[4] An inscribed list of sources at Susa describes the origins of the materials used to build the Achaemenid king Darius I's palace complex there.[5] Although most of the craftsmen and some items came from the Near East—such as ebony and silver from Egypt and cedar from Lebanon—many of the raw materials were supplied by satrapies in the northeast of the empire: gold from Bactria; lapis lazuli and carnelian (or cinnabar) from Sogdiana; turquoise from Chorasmia; and ivory from Arachosia and India.[6]

In the late fourth century BCE, Alexander of Macedon pursued the last Achaemenid king, Darius III, to Bactria (the Zoroastrian stronghold) and then pushed his campaign farther into the eastern satrapies. Some of the ideas in this essay are further developed in a chapter on the Zoroastrians in Central Asia in my book *Zoroastrianism: An Introduction* (2011).

In about 327 BCE, Alexander besieged and captured a fortress in Sogdiana, known in his biographies as the "Sogdian Rock," where the local Bactrian chief, Oxyartes, had placed his wife and daughters for safekeeping.[7] One of those daughters was Rokhshana, whom Alexander later married. At about the time that the Parthians were rising to power against the Seleucids to the west, Sogdiana was briefly incorporated into the independent Greco-Bactrian kingdom but soon became an autonomous state, subject to successive incursions of nomadic groups from the steppes, including the Saka, the Hephthalites, and the Turkic Qaghans. In the late second century BCE, the Han imperial envoy Zhang Qian was sent to make an alliance with the peoples of Central Asia, particularly Sogdiana, in order to combat incursions into northern China from the Xiongnu steppe nomads.[8] The Han government used both diplomacy and force to counter the horse raids of the Xiongnu. On his second diplomatic mission between 119 and 115 BCE, Zhang Qian is said to have brought "tens of thousands" of cattle and sheep with him and to have offered gold and silk goods in great quantities to buy political influence on China's northwestern frontier.[9] Han gold was derived mostly from river deposits, as there were only a few gold mines in operation. The gold was cast primarily into round or "hoof" shapes or gold ingots for trading.[10]

The Han also used gold and silk to purchase the famous Fergana horses, which were larger and stronger than the steppe ponies and were used by the Chinese to breed battle steeds for cavalry counterattacks against the nomadic raids.[11] Han histories use epithets such as "blood sweating," "of dragon seed," and "heavenly" to refer to these prized horses.[12] The *Hou Han Shu*, a history of the Han compiled in the fifth century CE, records that a delegation of Sogdians and Xiongnu had brought Fergana horses to China as gifts, with the intention of furthering such trade relations as had been encouraged by Zhang Qian's reports and subsequent Chinese missions.[13] Records show that during the Tang period (618–907 CE), in one year the Chinese court exchanged more than a seventh of its revenue of silk for horses from Central Asia.[14] Tang period tombs include *mingqi*—terra cotta tomb figures—of horses and their Central Asian grooms and trainers, symbolic of the importance of the horse in the leisured lifestyle of the Chinese aristocracy.

In 117 CE, the Roman emperor Hadrian withdrew from Mesopotamia, and the Parthians took control of the sea route to Rome via Syria. At this time, Indian and Bactrian traders were more prominent on the eastern trade routes, but by the early fourth century CE, the Sogdians had established settlements throughout the Tarim Basin between Kashgar and Dunhuang, in the region now known as Xinjiang province. This migration may have been stimulated by the steady decline in urban life at the time, which was accompanied by a concurrent increase in the building of fortified castles across the fertile Zarafshan valley and by intensified agricultural development.[15] Such socioeconomic changes would have compelled some merchants to move to more promising locations to find customers.

From this period on, Sogdian manuscripts, inscriptions, and iconography are found along the northern trading routes, as well as in Ladakh, Kirghizia, Mongolia, and northern Pakistan.

evidence for widespread sogdian mercantile activity

In the Upper Indus Valley, at several sites along the Karakorum Highway, but primarily Shatial, more than six hundred Sogdian rock inscriptions in Aramaic script have been found.[16] This graffiti seems to date to about the mid-fifth century CE, and the information provided is mostly onomastic, signifying a predominance of Iranian personal names.[17] This material is located at sites on the southern trading route where Sogdian and Indian merchants bartered their wares. The many Buddhist-themed petroglyphs, alongside Kharoshthi and Brahmi inscriptions, attest that traders from India were predominantly Buddhist.[18] Recent analysis indicates that some of the Sogdians were en route for China, although it is not clear whether they passed over the Pamirs or through Bactria.[19]

Most merchants did not travel the entirety of the "Silk Road" but would trade goods through middlemen based in oasis towns such as Khotan or Dunhuang. The Sogdians, however, established a trading network across the fifteen hundred miles between Sogdiana and northern China that included staging posts with substantial communities. They settled at Gaochang, Toyok, and Hami in the north; Khotan in the south; Dunhuang, where the two routes converge on the eastern edge of the Taklimakan desert; and on into the Chinese cities of Changan, Luoyang, and Yangzhou.[20]

An indicator of the predominance of the Sogdians in the traffic and trade across this region is the fact that Sogdian became a lingua franca of commerce. The Sogdians had adopted the Imperial Aramaic script of Achaemenid official, commercial, and literary correspondence and continued to use it in various forms in successive centuries and locations.[21] A range of written and visual texts attests to both the ubiquity of the Sogdian language along the Central Asian trade routes and the extensive relocation of the Sogdians themselves. In fact, the Khotanese used the term *Sogdian* (Khotanese *suli*) as a generic reference to all merchants, regardless of their origins.[22]

Fourth-century CE Sogdian letters found near the trading post of Dunhuang tell us that local commodities included gold and silver, much of which had been worked into filigree ornaments, such as hair clasps and vessels in Persian style by artisans, whose metalwork then had a significant influence on Chinese forms.[23] Other goods mentioned in these "Ancient Letters" as being traded to the Chinese are woolen cloth (including Roman purple), hemp, linen, wheat, pepper, and camphor.[24] The last two items denote commercial relations with India and southeastern Asia. It was originally thought that silk was absent from the letters as a traded commodity, but recent research shows that the word used for silk is *pirchik*, a term derived from Khotanese.[25] Some of the items indicate that Sogdian reliance on trade was generally supported by agrarian production, which provided "famous horses, cattle, sheep, grapes, and all sorts of fruit. The water and soil of this country are excellent, which is why its grape wine is so famous."[26] Agriculture was sustained by artificial irrigation from the large rivers in the region. The grapevine and alfalfa were among plants imported from Sogdiana to be grown in China.[27] Presumably, the latter was used to feed the Fergana horses. Ancient Letter II, destined for Samarqand, refers to musk (which would have come from the borders of Tibet) being sent from Dunhuang, indicating that the postal service did not accompany the merchandise.[28] Musk was measured in vesicles.[29] Other quantities mentioned indicate that merchants concentrated on goods with a high yield of income per weight. The value of most of the goods was calculated in silver staters (Sogdian *styr*), the currency of the Sogdians based on the tetradrachms of Euthydemos.[30] The use of "coppers" (Sogdian *rwδk*) for small change is doubtless a reference to the cast copper currency of the Chinese.[31] The Ancient Letters[32] make no mention of the *drachm*, which is the exclusive unit of currency mentioned in the eighth-century Mount Mug documents.

The Ancient Letters were found in 1907 by the British archaeologist Aurel Stein in a postbag in the ruins of a watchtower near Dunhuang. They provide information not only about the goods exchanged and the early network of trade and commerce between Central Asia and China via the Tarim Basin but also about the Sogdian merchants and artisans who were involved. Later documents and murals reveal that traffic also involved people of faith, including monks and missionaries. Written in Old Sogdian Aramaic script on paper, with the name and location of the recipient on the outside, the Ancient Letters are mostly about trade, although one is from a Sogdian merchant's wife, named Miwnay, to her husband, Nanaidhat. The two had relocated from Samarqand to Dunhuang, where Nanaidhat seems to have got into financial trouble and left town. His wife, abandoned and destitute, had become a servant in a Chinese household to support herself and her young daughter, Shayn. The tone of the letter is along the lines of "I should have listened to my mother and never married you!"[33]

In another letter, to her mother, Chatis, in Samarqand, Miwnay bemoans her lot, complaining that she has asked several local Sogdians, including a relative, for a loan to return home, but no one has offered her any help, so she has been dependent on support from the priest. Miwnay writes that if she decided to leave the city, the priest would provide her with a camel and a man to accompany her.[34] The letters inform us that although Miwnay looked after her husband's business affairs, she did not have financial independence. Although Samarqand evidently continued to function as a home depot during this period, the allusion to a temple priest (*sgnpt*) in Dunhuang indicates that the Sogdian Zoroastrian population there was already numerous enough to support its own place of worship and a residential priest.[35]

sogðians in their homeland

By the mid-fifth century CE, the former urban districts of Sogdiana began to revive and new city walls were constructed.[36] Small city-states were established in the area of the Zarafshan Valley extending from the Amu Darya (Oxus) to the Syr Darya (Jaxartes), including Samarqand, Bukhara, Varakhsha, and Panjikent, and extending as far east as Chach (modern Tashkent). Sogdians were identified as belonging to one of three main groups: aristocrats, merchants, and workers, indicating that craftsmen and traders were significant members of this "Merchant Empire." It seems that, whereas in Sasanian Iran agriculture formed a constant basis for the economy, in Sogdiana it was less reliable as a result of frequent nomadic incursions[37] into its urban-centered society.[38] Local rulers came from the nobility, which was not as in Iran. As the cities developed, rich and poor alike decorated their houses—which were often two-storied structures—with murals and woodcarvings.[39] City streets and bazaar areas were lined with commercial stores and workshops, fronting residential buildings. Sogdiana was a midpoint on the trade routes: it functioned as a conduit between commercial centers in China, India, Sasanian Iran, and Byzantium. Initially, the Sasanians (ca. 224–651 CE) maintained a monopoly on the transport of goods, particularly silk, to Byzantium, denying access through Iran to foreign caravans. But in the late sixth century, as allies of the Turkic Qaghans, the Sogdians entered a trade agreement with Byzantium that gave them access across the Caucasus, circumventing Iran.

The Byzantine *History* of Menander Protector records that in 568 CE a Turco-Sogdian delegation headed by a Sogdian named Maniakh traveled to the Roman emperor in Constantinople to obtain permission to trade. This encounter, and subsequent negotiations, resulted in a flourishing traffic in silk between Sogdiana, the Western Turks, and Byzantium. Maniakh was able to briefly establish a western outlet for Sogdian commerce, an enterprise that was continued by his son but which Byzantine control seems quickly to have restricted to the northern coast of the Black Sea.[40]

sogðian religious expression

As evidenced by their literary relics, the Sogdians epitomize the religious plurality found along the trade routes traversing the region. From the late third century onward, both Christians and Manichaeans came to Central Asia, first as missionaries, and then as refugees from Sasanian Iran, and many learned Sogdian before continuing east to the oasis cities of Xinjiang and beyond.[41] Sogdian became, then, the principal language of dissemination of both Manichaeism and so-called Nestorian Christianity to the Chinese. That some Sogdians converted may be evidenced by Sogdian Christian texts from the Bulayïq monastery to the north of Turpan and the numerous Manichaean texts in Sogdian from nearby Qocho.[42] A wall painting of Manichaean *Electi* at Qocho identifies these adherents, in late Sogdian characters, as having Iranian names.[43]

Chinese Buddhist hagiographies record that from the second century CE onward, Sogdian Buddhist monks (with the surname "Kang") settled in the Xinjiang region and the main cities of inner China, such as Changan.[44] One Sogdian Buddhist monk, Kang Seng Hui, was a Sogdian merchant's son, whose family had lived in India for several generations and had then moved to Tonkin.[45] Brought up as an orphan in the early third century CE, Kang Seng Hui is said to have been the first to introduce Buddhism to the Nanking region of southern China.[46] Although the largest body of Sogdian texts is Buddhist, and Sogdians numbered among the main translators of Buddhist sutras into Chinese, Buddhism did not take root in Sogdiana itself.[47]

The predominant culture in Sogdiana remained Iranian and closely related to that of its Sasanian neighbors. Sogdians are mentioned in a Young Avestan text (*Videvdad* 1.4), preserved in writing by the Sasanians, as dwelling in one of the sixteen good lands fashioned for Iranians by Ahura Mazda, the "Wise Lord" of the Zoroastrian religion.

That the Sogdians' prime religious affiliation remained the Zoroastrian tradition is evidenced by the discoveries of murals depicting votaries making offerings before fire holders and a couple of actual fire holders. Clay ossuaries from Samarqand, Panjikent, and Er-Kurgan, dating to the fifth or sixth century, held the bones of the dead after exposure according to Zoroastrian ritual.[48] The ossuaries were then placed in vaulted family burial chambers. Some of these, and later ossuaries, incorporate Zoroastrian motifs.[49] A Chinese traveler, writing in about 605 CE, noted that there were many households outside the city walls of Samarqand specializing "in funerary matters," including looking after the dogs that would dispose of the corpses.[50] The practice of ossuary making disappeared in the second half of the eighth century, not long after the Islamic conquest, which suggests that the practice of exposure was largely abandoned and replaced by burial.[51] One of the last Sogdian kings, Devastich, was executed by the Umayyad Arab governor at the site of a Zoroastrian "bone depository" in 723 CE.[52]

The form of Zoroastrianism practiced by Sogdians included some elements not evidenced in Sasanian Iran, such as the veneration of indigenous Sogdian family or community divinities, who are depicted as personified beings in frescoes. One such divinity is Vesh-parkar, the Sogdian representation of Vayu, the *yazata* ("being worthy of worship") of the wind.[53] An illustration of Vesh-parkar in a building in Panjikent has an Indian appearance, with the three heads associated with his Buddhist equivalent, Shiva Mahadeva.[54] Elsewhere at Panjikent, one of the most commonly represented divinities, Nana, is portrayed centrally as a four-armed goddess on a lion. In Sogdian ideology and iconography, Nana seems to have been partly assimilated with the Iranian creative and chthonic *yazata*, Spenta Armaiti, but also to have retained elements associated with the Mesopotamian goddess Nanaia, such as holding the sun and moon in two of her hands.[55] The lion is also the vehicle of the multiarmed Indian goddess, Durga.[56]

One of the frescoes at Panjikent shows a scene of gods and humans lamenting the death of a young prince (or princess) who lies on a catafalque.[57] This may be a prototype of the cult of mourning centered on the Iranian hero Siyavush that is recorded by the tenth-century Islamic historian Narshakhi in his *History of Bukhara*.[58] Narshakhi relates that the people of Bukhara have lamentations on the slaying of Siyavush, "which is known in all regions, and the minstrels have made them into songs which they chant, and the singers call them 'the weepers.'"

These paintings are found on the walls of private houses and of a small shrine in Temple 2 Panjikent. A clay pilaster fire holder was found in Temple 1 Panjikent and a smaller, ceramic one at Er-Kurgan. In *Shahnama*, Siyavush was said to have founded the citadel at Bukhara.[59] Other illustrations at Panjikent have been identified as the Iranian themes of *razm o bazm*—"fighting and feasting"; the exploits of the legendary Iranian hero Rustam on his horse, Rakhsh; and animal fables similar to those of Aesop or the Indian *Panchatantra*.[60] A study of some of the earlier murals at Panjikent and Samarqand revealed the same distinctive treatment of drapery folds, and the appearance of a lotus-shaped motif, as appear on ninth-century Manichaean miniature paintings on manuscripts and walls at Qocho. It has been suggested that some of these stylistic approaches may have influenced—or at least stimulated—Islamic miniature painting in the Ilkhanid and later Timurid periods, the latter being centered in Sogdiana.[61]

sogðian merchant activity in china

A Chinese history of the Tang Dynasty, the *Xin Tang shu*, describes Sogdians in general as good at business: they enjoyed making a profit, and their young men at twenty would go out to neighboring countries to engage in commerce.[62] Evidence of such Sogdian expansionist trading venture has come to light in both Xinjiang and the Chinese interior in recent years.

During the fifth and sixth centuries CE, many Sogdians took up residence in the Hexi Corridor, then inner China, where they retained autonomy in terms of governance and had a designated official administrator named a *sabao*, derived from an earlier Sogdian title for a "caravan leader."[63] Textual sources from the Sui (581–618 CE) and Tang periods, as well as epitaphs on Sogdian funerary monuments, describe the arrival in China of ancestors from the homeland. For instance, a sarcophagus found at Xi'an in 2003 belonged to a Sogdian *sabao* named Wirkak (Chinese *Shi*), whose name denotes that his ancestors had come from Kish (modern Shahr-I Sabz).[64] The bilingual Sino-Sogdian epitaph informs us that Wirkak's grandfather had also been a *sabao* and that his wife, Lady Kang, was likewise of Sogdian origin.[65] Wirkak died in his eighty-sixth year, in 579 CE, and his wife a month later.[66]

Several intricately decorated stone funerary couches of wealthy Sogdian traders from northern China have also recently come to light. One such funerary bed was made for an anonymous merchant, who lived and died in sixth-century China. This artifact, now in the Miho Museum in Shigaraki, Japan, depicts a camel caravan, suggesting that the merchant may have died while on a trading journey, although such scenes of trade activity are echoed on Wirkak's sarcophagus and other Sogdian funerary monuments from China.[67]

By this time, Sogdians were becoming increasingly absorbed into the local Chinese population, but specifically Zoroastrian scenes on the mortuary couches and other memorials indicate that, although the surrounding culture of the deceased was Chinese, the predominant religious expression remained that of Sogdian Zoroastrianism.[68] The Zoroastrian faith of the anonymous merchant is indicated by one panel that portrays a priest wearing a *padan*—a mouth cover—to prevent him from polluting the sacred fire in its holder; a small table nearby contains round items which might be pomegranates or other ceremonial food.[69] The setting suggests the enactment of an *afrinagan* ceremony, such as is still performed by Zoroastrians on the fourth morning after death. Other aspects of the panel corroborate this identification of a Zoroastrian funerary ritual, alongside some elements of an eastern Iranian mourning cult.[70]

The stone funerary couch would have prevented the body of the deceased from coming into contact with the earth or water, in keeping with Zoroastrian custom. The eastern wall of Wirkak's sarcophagus seems to depict this moment. Zoroastrian priests with *padan* stand at the entrance to the Chinvat Bridge, where the soul is judged and its afterlife determined.[71] The bridge is guarded by two dogs. Wirkak and his wife are depicted leading a group of departed souls across the bridge. The souls have been judged favorably and cannot now be harmed by the two beasts in the raging waters below.[72] Such images appear to be pictorial representations of events relating to the fate of the soul as described in Zoroastrian texts. In those texts, however, the soul is not accompanied by others when it crosses the bridge.[73] Animals are also shown crossing the bridge, and the fact that one of them is a camel laden with wares reflects the particular concerns of the Sogdian merchant and his wife.

By the seventh century most of the larger northern Chinese towns with a Sogdian population of more than two hundred had a *sabao*, whose rank was respected and rewarded as the equivalent of a mandarin.[74] That local Chinese leaders were not granted the same rank shows the Sogdians' socioeconomic importance.[75] Although the *sabao* apparently acted as an administrator for the temple, it is not clear whether his role was also that of a priest.[76] Evidence of the construction of Zoroastrian temples (*xian*) in inner China include one that was restored in Changan in 631 CE.[77] These were, presumably, to serve the Sogdian community, although embassies from the Sasanians had also developed, so these temples could have been for trading relations with the Wei in the mid-fifth century.[78]

About 670 CE, the Sasanian crown prince, Peroz, and members of the court were granted refuge in China and the protection of the Tang court.[79] A Chinese document listing taxes paid on caravan trade in the Turpan region in the early decades of the seventh century discloses that twenty-nine out of thirty-five commercial transactions involved Sogdian merchants and that in thirteen of those operations both the buyer and the seller were Sogdian.[80]

Sogdian fire temples (*xian*) are mentioned at Turpan and Hami from the seventh century, and eighth-century Chinese sources mention a *xian* on the eastern edge of the town of Dunhuang, which had a courtyard and a main hall with religious paintings of "deities" and twenty niches.[81] According to later Chinese sources, the fire temple at Dunhuang lasted until the early second millennium.

Local government in these towns allocated material support to Zoroastrians for annual offerings (*saixian*).[82] This probably refers to *afrinagan* ceremonies or to seasonal festivals (*gahambars*) such as Fravardigan, which were also celebrated by the Chorasmians and Persians.[83]

After the Tang Dynasty had conquered the Turkic Qaghans in the mid-seventh century CE, the Sogdian city-states were accepted as nominal vassals of China. The king of Samarqand, Varkhuman (r. ca. 650–70 CE), acknowledged nominal Tang control, and Sogdian merchants were able to register as Chinese residents.[84] Gifts offered in diplomatic tribute each year by the Sogdians included the "golden peaches" of Samarqand, saffron, medicinal herbs, jewels, and gems, as well as living merchandise in the form of lions, leopards, horses, and dogs.[85] On a seventh-century CE mural in a palace at Samarqand, a king—possibly Varkhuman, who is named in an inscription on the western wall—is depicted enthroned, receiving delegates from many countries offering highly prized commodities.[86] The scene epitomizes the diplomacy of good trading relations. The so-called Ambassadors' Paintings could perhaps illustrate the Zoroastrian Nav Ruz ceremonies and may play a role similar to the representations of ritual gift-giving on the stairs to the *apadana* (the audience hall) at Persepolis.[87]

On the western wall of the hall at Samarqand, Turkish envoys are identified by their long plaits, and Chinese ambassadors are shown bringing gifts of silk in the triple form of cocoons, hanks, and rolls of cloth. By this time, the secret of silk making had been obtained in Central Asia, purportedly through a Chinese princess, who had smuggled silkworm cocoons in her headdress on her way to marry the king of Khotan. The legend maintains that this was to ensure that she had her own steady supply of silk for her clothing.[88] But high-quality silk textiles from China still demanded high prices and continued to dominate the market.

In the mural, three other envoys wear colorful robes with Iranian motifs—the boar, ducks with pearls, and the so-called *senmurv* (the "*Saena* bird" of Avestan myth), respectively—inside roundel designs. Although some of the murals at Samarqand imitate the Chinese style, such Iranian motifs are nonetheless found across the Xinjiang region, suggesting that it was the Sogdians who transported this iconography. The appeal of Iranian design to the Chinese is supported by a Sui-era report from 605 CE that a Sogdian named He Chou was placed, by imperial decree, in control of some of the Sichuan workshops producing silks woven with "western motifs."[89] A seventh- or eighth-century child's silk jacket and pants intended for a Tibetan prince exemplifies one such motif in its stylized pairs of ducks in roundels.[90]

By this time, silk made in Sogdiana was being exported along the trade routes to both east and west.[91] Decorating the tomb of St. Domitian in the Collegiate Church of Notre-Damein Huy, Belgium, was a piece of eighth-century Sogdian silk patterned with lions in medallions. This cloth has a Sogdian inscription identifying it as *zandaniji* (that is, from Zandan, near Bukhara), which may have been a general designation for specific motifs on a range of different textiles from Sogdiana.[92] The discovery of such fine goods outside Sogdiana may provide evidence of a trading model that reserved the most valuable goods for export.[93]

Although trading routes across Central Asia were closed during the Tibetan domination of the eastern Tarim Basin, they reopened when the Chinese assumed control of the region. The presence of Sogdians in the Tang courts is well documented in Chinese sources, where they are described as a people engaged in commerce, who are fond of music and wine.[94] Sogdian music was popular at court banquets, and another panel of the Miho couch shows the deceased merchant and his wife dining, while entertained by musicians and a Sogdian dancer.

Popular performers from Samarqand, Kish, and Chach at the Tang court in Changan were the "leaping" and "whirling" dancers, who presented the *hutengwu* and *huxuanwu* dances, respectively.[95] Tang poets describe the "western twirling girls" as wearing colorful shirts and flowing pantaloons, with boots of red deerskin.[96] Male dancers from Sogdiana were also popular and are represented on Tang-era *mingqi*. One such *mingqi* from Gansu province depicts a large-nosed male wearing an elongated Phrygian cap and a tight-sleeved tunic, such as ascribed to dancers from Chach by Tang court poets.[97] A contemporary account describes how a general of mixed Sogdian-Turkic descent named An-Lushan (Iranian *Rokhshan*) was taught the whirling dance by one of the Tang emperor's concubines.[98]

This apparently symbiotic relationship between Sogdians and Tang Chinese did not endure until the end of the dynasty. In fact, it was the military action of An Lushan in leading a revolt in northeastern China that brought an end to Sogdian mercantile dominance. This revolt, sometimes described as "the Sogdian rebellion," resulted in a war lasting from 755 to 763 CE. It was supported by many Sogdian traders in northern China, but the Uighur Qaghans' support for the Tang in the west resulted in those Sogdians being isolated from their bases in the Tarim Basin and Sogdiana.[99] Afterward, many Sogdians in China were brutally slain, and those who survived sought to change their names to hide their foreign identity.[100] From this point onward, not much is known about the Sogdian presence in northern China. It is clear, however, that Uighur Qaghans came into contact with resident Sogdian Manicheans in Luoyang and converted in about 762 CE, after which Manichaeism became the Uighur religion. With Uighur political backing, Manichean Sogdians in China received protection, and several new temples were constructed, including one in Changan and others in Luoyang and Yangzhou.[101] These Sogdians were free to engage in commerce and continued to flourish for the better part of a century, until the Uighur state was overrun by the Kirghiz in 840 CE, after which both the religion and its practitioners returned to a disadvantaged state, except in the area around Qocho, where most of the later Manichaean texts were found. Although the Chinese were still anxious to have good relations with the Central Asians on their borders, in between 843 and 845 recognition of all "foreign religions" including Buddhism was withdrawn by the Tang emperor, Wu-Tsung, in support of indigenous Taoism.

By this time Sogdians in the homeland were ruled by the Abbasid caliphate. Although there had been several uprisings in Samarqand and elsewhere in Sogdiana, Islam had become the dominant religion of the region. But the diversity of religious expression that had been one of the hallmarks of the Sogdian contribution to trade and culture lived on largely through the fine arts of the Islamic world. The Sogdians had learned the art of papermaking from the Chinese and were renowned for the quality of their paper.[102] This craft was put to use by the many Islamic savants in Samarqand and Bukhara during the rule of the Persian-speaking Samanids (819–999 CE) and quickly became a medium not only for the textual transmission of Islam but also for the articulation of Iranian mythology.

Remnants of the richness of the Sogdian culture may be preserved in the legends of Rustam and Siyavush in Ferdowsi's *Shahnama*; in the tales of the Indian *Panchatantra*, traditionally translated into Middle Persian by Khosrow I's physician, Burzoy, and later into Arabic as *Kalilah wa Dimnah*; in the songs, and acts, of mourning for fallen Iranian heroes; and, not least, in the intricate scenes of courtly life and poetic narrative expressed in Islamic miniatures.

A shrine entirely funded by the government of the Muslim majority state is shared by all seven world religions in Astana, Kazakhstan. In these and smaller interfaith facilities in universities, prisons, hospitals, and airports around the world, the publisher,

The Palace of Peace and Accord.
SHUTTERSTOCK IMAGE.

contributors, and readers have placed copies of *Three Testaments: Torah, Gospel, and Quran* and of *Four Testaments: Tao Te Ching, Analects, Dhammapada, Bhagavad Gita* on available sideboards for the use of those coming to pray or to meditate there. Anyone visiting is welcome to leave copies of these books in places yet to receive them or wherever they have "gone missing."

notes

1. Jenny Rose in Vol. 30, *Comparative Studies of South Asia, Africa and the Middle East* (2010).

2. Étienne de la Vaissière, *Sogdian Traders: A History*, trans. James Ward (Leiden: Brill, 2005).

3. Elena E. Kuz'mina and Victor H. Mair, *The Prehistory of the Silk Road* (Philadelphia: University of Pennsylvania Press, 2007), 3–4; Carol Michaelson, "Jade and the Silk Road: Trade and Tribute in the First Millennium," in *The Silk Road: Trade, Travel, War, Faith*, ed. Susan Whitfield and Ursula Sims-Williams (Chicago: Serindia, 2004), 44.

4. Old Persian cuneiform inscriptions mention Achaemenid hegemony over the satrapy of Sogdiana. See, for example, Darius's inscription at Bisitun, 1.16. Herodotus includes the Sogdians as one of the nations composing Xerxes's army. *Histories* 7.66.

5. Darius's inscription at Susa, f: see Roland G. Kent, *Old Persian Grammar, Texts, Lexicon* (1953; repr., New Haven, CT: American Oriental Society, 1983), 142–44. Citations are to the American Oriental Society edition.

6. For a discussion of the translation of Old Persian *Sinkabru* as cinnabar, rather than carnelian, see de la Vaissière, *Sogdian Traders*, 19.

7. Arrian, *Anabasis* 4.18.4–19.6; Strabo, *Geographia* 11.11.2–4.

8. de la Vaissière, *Sogdian Traders*, 29. The Chinese history *Shiji*, which incorporated information from Zhang Qian's reports, refers to the Sogdians (by the name *Kangju*) as a people who might be persuaded "by gifts and the prospect of gain" to ally with the Han (ibid.).

9. B. Watson, trans., *Records of the Grand Historian: Han Dynasty II*, rev. ed. (New York: Columbia University Press, 1993), 238.

10. Walter Scheidel, "The Monetary Systems of the Han and Roman Empires," Princeton/Stanford Working Papers in Classics, version 2.0 (Stanford, CA: Stanford University, 2008), 19, www.princeton.edu/~pswpc/ pdfs/scheidel/020803.pdf.

11. H. G. Creel, "The Role of the Horse in Chinese History," *American Historical Review* 70 (1965), 660.

12. For references to these epithets, see ibid., 661. Contemporary Chinese sources such as the *Shiji* call Fergana "Dayuan." See de la Vaissière, *Sogdian Traders*, 27.

13. Mariko Namba Walter, "Sogdians and Buddhism," *Sino-Platonic Papers*, no. 174 (2006), 15, www.sinoplatonic.org/complete/spp174_sogdian_buddhism.pdf.

14. X. Liu, "The Silk Road: Overland Trade and Cultural Interactions in Eurasia," in *Agricultural Pastoral Societies in Ancient and Classical History*, ed. M. Adas (Philadelphia: Temple University Press, 2001), 169.

15. G. V. Shishkina, "Ancient Samarkand: Capital of Sogd," *Bulletin of the Asia Institute* (*BAI*) 8 (1994 [1996]), 90.

16. Nicholas Sims-Williams, "The Sogdian Merchants in China and India," in *Cina e Iran: Da Alessandro Magno alla dinastia Tang* (*China and Iran: From Alexander the Great to the Tang*

Dynasty), ed. Alfred Cadonna and Lionello Lanciotti (Florence: Olschki, 1996), 52–53. Other sites of graffiti are Chilas, Thor North, and Dadam Das. Two Middle Persian, two Parthian, and about ten Bactrian inscriptions were also found. Nicholas Sims-Williams, *Sogdian and Other Iranian Inscriptions of the Upper Indus*, pt. 1, *Inscriptions of the Seleucid and Parthian Periods of Eastern Iran and Central Asia* (London: Corpus Inscriptionum Iranicarum and the School of Oriental and African Studies, 1989), 8.

17. Karl Jettmar considers whether the graffiti postdates the Hephthalite incorporation of Sogdiana in the late fifth century. Karl Jettmar, "Symbolic Systems in Collision: Rock Art in the Upper Indus Valley," in *Gandhara Art in Context: East-West Exchanges at the Crossroads of Asia*, ed. Raymond Allchin (New Delhi: Regency, 1997), 64. For further discussion of the significance of the site and the dating of the graffiti, see also Sims-Williams, "Sogdian Merchants," 52–54, and de la Vaissière, *Sogdian Traders*, 83. Some of the names are Middle Persian, one is Parthian, and others seem to allude to place names in Sogdiana. See Sims-Williams, "Sogdian Merchants," 54–55.

18. Jettmar, "Symbolic Systems in Collision," 56.

19. Sims-Williams ("Sogdian Merchants," 54–56) suggests that the prominence of names dedicated to the Oxus (*Wakhsh*) may indicate the latter route.

20. Judith A. Lerner, "The Merchant Empire of the Sogdians," in *Monks and Merchants: Silk Road Treasures from Northwest China; Gansu and Ningxia, Fourth through Seventh Century*, ed. Annette L. Juliano and Judith A. Lerner (New York: Abrams and Asia Society, 2001), 225.

21. The Sogdian language fell out of use after the tenth century CE but survives in the minority language of Yagnobi, still spoken in the Yagnob valley of northern Tajikistan.

22. Sims-Williams, "Sogdian Merchants," 46n6.

23. For a detailed analysis of the date of the letters, see Frantz Grenet and Nicolas Sims-Williams, "The Historical Context of the Sogdian Ancient Letters," in *Transition Periods in Iranian History, Studia Iranica* 5 (Paris: Association pour l'Avancement des Études Iraniennes, 1987), 101–22. The use of gold and silver is referred to in Nicholas Sims-Williams, "Sogdian Ancient Letter II," in Juliano and Lerner, *Monks and Merchants*, 47, and Susan Whitfield, *Life along the Silk Road* (Berkeley: University of California Press, 2001), 38.

24. On Roman purple, see Sims-Williams, "Sogdian Merchants," 60. On goods traded, see ibid., 48.

25. *Hou Han Shu*.

26. See John E. Hill, "The *Xiyu juan* 'Chapter on the Western Regions' from *Hou Hanshu*, 88, Second Edition," September 2003, depts.washington.edu/silk road/texts/hhshu/hou_ han_shu.html.

27. Sims-Williams, "Sogdian Merchants," 61.

28. de la Vaissière, *Sogdian Traders*, 48.

29. Sims-Williams, "Sogdian Ancient Letter II," 49.

30. Ibid.

31. Sims-Williams, "Sogdian Merchants," 50.

32. See Grenet and Sims-Williams, "Sogdian Ancient Letters," 113.

33. See Whitfield and Sims-Williams, *Silk Road*, 249.

34. Ibid.

35. On the reference to the temple priest, see Sims-Williams, "Sogdian Merchants," 48.

36. de la Vaissière, *Sogdian Traders*, 109.

37. Cf. Richard N. Frye, "Bukhara and Zanandaniji," in *Central Asian Textiles and Their Contexts in the Early Middle Ages*, ed. Regula Schorta (Riggisberg, Switzerland: Abegg-Stiftung, 2006), 76; de la Vaissière, *Sogdian Traders*, 100–101, 103–6.

38. Frye, "Bukhara and Zanandaniji," 76.

39. Lerner, "Merchant Empire," 223; de la Vaissière, *Sogdian Traders*, 234–37.

40. de la Vaissière, *Sogdian Traders*, 167, 248–49.

41. See Whitfield, *Life along the Silk Road*, 20, and Edward H. Schafer, *The Golden Peaches of Samarkand: A Study of T'ang Exotics* (1963; repr., Berkeley: University of California Press, 1985), 10.

42. These are mostly translations from Syriac biblical commentaries, homilies, and hagiographies. See S. Brock, *The Bible in the Syriac Tradition* (Piscataway, NJ: Gorgias, 2006), 146.

43. Hans-Joachim Klimkeit, *Manichaean Art and Calligraphy* (Leiden: Brill, 1982), 29. These eighth- or ninth-century paintings may, however, depict Persian Manichaeans.

44. See above, note 6, regarding the *Shiji* reference to the region as *Kangju*, whose inhabitants were known as "Kang." See also Walter, "Sogdians and Buddhism."

45. de la Vaissière, *Sogdian Traders*, 71–72.

46. Lerner, "Merchant Empire," 227, 228n1.

47. No Buddhist texts were found in Sogdiana proper. Most of the thirty Sogdian Buddhist texts found at Dunhuang are translations from Chinese, although the *Vessantara Jataka* appears to be a Sogdian retelling rather than a direct translation. It includes references to "Mithra, the Judge of Creation," along with other spirits that do not appear in the Pali version. See B. Stavisky, "Bactria and Gandhara: The Old Problem Reconsidered in the Light of Archaeological Data from Old Termez," in Allchin et al., *Gandhara Art in Context*, 29–34.

48. L. V. Pavchinskaia, "Sogdian Ossuaries," *BAI* 8 (1994 [1996]), 224. Before that, the earliest form was probably burial in jars. Vessels with food, golden coins, and bracteates were also often placed in the tombs.

49. See G. A. Pugachenkova, "The Form and Style of Sogdian Ossuaries," *BAI* 8 (1994 [1996]): 227–43, particularly 235–40.

50. Samuel N. C. Lieu, *Manichaeism in the Later Roman Empire and Medieval China* (Manchester: Manchester University Press, 1985), 182–83. According to Wei-Jie, the bones were collected and buried, but without a special coffin. The placement of bones in a decorated ceramic ossuary is evidenced as practiced throughout Sogdiana and Chorasmia and into Xinjiang, but not in inner China. Lerner, "Merchant Empire," 226.

51. Pavchinskaia, "Sogdian Ossuaries," 219.

52. Ilya Yakubovich determines that the Arabic term *nāwūs* refers in this instance to a Zoroastrian bone depository, not a place of interment: Ilya Yakubovich, "Mugh 1.1. Revisited," *Studia Iranica* 31 (2002), 249.

53. The name Vesh-parkar comes from an Avestan phrase *vaiiusˇ uparō.kairiiō*, "the wind whose activity is in the upper regions" (*Videvdad* 19.13, my translation, based on Sims-Williams's reading). See Nicholas Sims-Williams, "Some Reflections on Zoroastrianism in Sogdiana and Bactria," in *Realms of the Silk Roads: Ancient and Modern*, ed. David Christian and Craig Benjamin, *Silk Road Studies* 4 (Turnhout, Belgium: Brepols, 2000), 5.

54. Frantz Grenet, "Religious Diversity," 473.

55. See G. Azarpay, "Nana, the Sumero-Akkadian Goddess of Transoxiana," *Journal of the American Oriental Society* 96 (1976), 541. Azarpay compares Sogdian depictions of Nana with those of the Khotanese Saka *sˇs´andrāmatā*, whose name is the equivalent of Spenta Armaiti.

56. Nana is depicted on a lion on Kushan coins and was regarded as Ves-Shiva, the wife of Shiva—that is, Parvati/Durga. See G. Azarpay, *Sogdian Painting: The Pictorial Epic in Oriental Art* (Berkeley: University of California Press, 1981), 30.

57. Marshak later identified this scene, in Temple 2, as a cult mourning for a goddess. Marshak, "Panjikant,"16.

58. See Azarpay, *Sogdian Painting*, 129. Similar scenes are found on a vase from Merv and a chest from Tok-Kala.

59. Yarshater, "Ta'ziyeh and Pre-Islamic Mourning Rituals," 90.

60. Marshak, "Panjikant," 16–18.

61. Azarpay, *Sogdian Painting*, 170–80; Klimkeit, *Manichaean Art and Calligraphy*, 19–20.

62. de la Vaissière, *Sogdian Traders*, 160.

63. Whitfield and Sims-Williams, *Silk Road*, 21. The word *sabao* is found in the address of Ancient Letter V and seems to derive originally from an Indian *sarthavaha* (caravaneer), via Bactrian intermediary to Sogdians*'rtp'w*. Sims-Williams, "Sogdian Merchants," 51.

64. For an identification of the Chinese character Shi with Kish, see Grenet, "Religious Diversity," 465.

65. Lerner, "Shorter Notices," 151.

66. Grenet, "Religious Diversity," 465.

67. Another funerary couch from Anyang, in northern Xi'an, depicts a *sabao* named An Qie (d. 579 CE) in his garden receiving a delegation from the Sogdian community. Annette L. Juliano, "Chinese Pictorial Space at the Cultural Crossroads," *Ērān ud Anērān: Webfestschrift Marshak*, 2003, www.transoxiana.org/ Eran/Articles/juliano.html (2004).

68. Grenet, "Religious Diversity," 418.

69. See James R. Russell, "Zoroastrianism and the Northern Qi Panels," in *Armenian and Iranian Studies* (Cambridge, MA: Harvard University Press and Armenian Heritage Press, 2004), 1447; Judith A. Lerner, "Central Asians," 180.

70. For detailed analyses of these elements, see Lerner, "Central Asians," and Russell, "Zoroastrianism."

71. Grenet, "Religious Diversity," 469.

72. Ibid., 472.

73. Ibid., 475–76. Grenet maintains that the Zoroastrian elements of the scenes on Wirkak's sarcophagus are balanced by elements that belong to Manichaean eschatology.

74. de la Vaissière, *Sogdian Traders*, 152.

75. Ibid.

76. Ibid., 151.

77. Edward H. Schafer, "Iranian Merchants in T'ang Dynasty Tales," in *Semitic and Oriental Studies*, ed. W. J. Fischel (Berkeley: University of California Press, 1951), 408.

78. On Sasanian trade with the Wei, see ibid., 403.

79. On Sasanian trade with the Wei, see ibid., 403.

80. de la Vaissière, *Sogdian Traders*, 134.

81. On *xian* at Turpan and Hami, see ibid., 128, 129n23. On the Dunhuang *xian*, see Frantz Grenet and Zhang Guangda, "The Last Refuge of the Sogdian Religion: Dunhuang in the Ninth and Tenth Centuries," *BAI* 10 (1996 [1998]). See also Albert E. Dien, "A Note on Hsien 'Zoroastrorianism,'" *Oriens* 10 (1957): 284–88.

82. Grenet chooses the gloss *bao* for *sai* to translate the term as "thanksgiving" and considers this to allude to an *afrinagan* ceremony. The supplies at Dunhuang comprise thirty sheets

of paper "to paint the *xian* deities," but there is also reference to alcohol; at Turpan, cereals are mentioned for the "cult of the heavenly god," perhaps designating Ormazd. See Grenet and Guangda, "Last Refuge," 181–83.

83. On *afrinagan* ceremonies, see ibid., 182. On seasonal festivals, see Shkoda, "Sogdian Temple," 202, and also Nicholas Sims-Williams and François de Blois, "The Bactrian Calendar," *BAI* 10 (1996 [1998]), 152.

84. Marshak, "Sogdians in Their Homeland," 234. The Sogdians had to pay taxes and to perform military duties and corvée labor, like any Chinese citizen.

85. de la Vaissière, *Sogdian Traders*, 138; Schafer, *Golden Peaches of Samarkand*, 58–70, 76–77, 84–88, 117, 124–26, 188, 194, 222–49.

86. On the inscription, see Whitfield and Sims-Williams, *Silk Road*, 110.

87. Matteo Compareti, "Afrāsiāb: II. Wall Paintings," in *Encyclopaedia Iranica Online*, www.iranica.com/articles/afrasiab-ii-wall-Paintings-2 (2009).

88. S. H. Wriggins, *The Silk Road Journey with Xuanzang*, rev. ed. (Boulder, CO: Westview, 2004), 176.

89. From the *Sui shu*. See Matteo Compareti, "The Role of the Sogdian Colonies in the Diffusion of the Pearl Roundels Pattern," in *Ērān ud Anērān: Webfestschrift Marshak*, 2003, www.transoxiana.org/Eran/Articles/compareti.html (2004).

90. The outfit, in the Cleveland Museum of Art, dates from the period of Tibetan power in eastern Central Asia and the trade routes from Sogdiana to China (ca. 600–842 CE).

91. Whitfield, *Life along the Silk Road*, 30.

92. Frye, "Bukhara and Zanandaniji," 75, 79.

93. Ibid., 80.

94. Compareti, "Role of the Sogdian Colonies."

95. Lerner, "Shorter Notices," 153.

96. Schafer, *Golden Peaches of Samarkand*, 56.

97. Judith A. Lerner, "Dancing Central Asian," in Juliano and Lerner, *Monks and Merchants*, 254, 255, fig. 82.

98. Schafer, *Golden Peaches of Samarkand*, 56.

99. de la Vaissière, *Sogdian Traders*, 217–18.

100. Ibid., 221.

101. Sammuel L. C. Lieu, "Manicheism V. in China," in *Encyclopaedia Iranica Online*, www.iranica.com/articles/manicheism-v-in-china-1 (2002).

102. F. Wood, *The Silk Road: Two Thousand Years in the Heart of Asia* (London: The British Library, 2002), 67.

appendix g

Sogdians in China: A Short History and Some New Discoveries

Étienne de la Vaissière

THE SOGDIANS WERE THE INHABITANTS OF FERTILE VALLEYS SURROUNDED BY DESERTS, THE most important of which was the Zeravshan valley, in today's Uzbekistan and Tajikistan. This Iranian-speaking people had a fifteen-centuries-long historical identity between the sixth century BCE and the tenth century CE, when it vanished in the Muslim, Persian-speaking world. Although the Sogdians constructed such famous towns as Samarkand and Bukhara, they are now quite unknown. Only specialists on the Silk Road know that they were among the main go-betweens of the exchanges in the steppe, in Central Asia, and in China during the first millennium CE, and especially between the fifth and the eighth centuries CE. During this period, the "inland silk road" and the "Sogdian trading network" are almost synonymous. The contemporary Sogdian, Chinese, Arabic, Byzantine, and Armenian sources describe the Sogdians as the great traders of Inner Asia. They managed to sell their products—musk, slaves, horses, silverware, silk, and many other goods—to all the surrounding peoples. A Greek text describes their trading embassies to Byzantium; some caravaneers' graffiti prove that they were in India; Turkish jargon in their vocabulary is a testimony to their cultural and economic power in the Turkish steppe—but their main market was always China. The Chinese branch of their network is by far the best known, and in China the number of new discoveries on the Sogdians is quickly growing.

When did the first Sogdian arrive in China to trade? Various answers have been given to this quite simple question, but one of the most popular, which can still be found in many recent books or articles, makes Alexander the Great the villain of the story. Due to the disaster that befell Sogdiana during his campaigns there in 329–328 BCE, the Sogdians would have been forced to immigrate as far east as China. The creation of the Sogdian trading network between Samarkand and China thus was a by-product of the Greek conquest of the Achaemenid Empire. Needless to say, there is nothing in the available sources to support such an idea, which survived only because of its classical flavor and its familiar ring to the historians' ears. In fact, the Chinese, Yuezhi, Bactrians, Indians, and Sogdians who created the historical Silk Road did not need Greek help. Trade is yet another item that should be removed (after irrigation, town planning, and state formation) from the long list of supposed Greek influences in the history of Central Asia. The list of real influences is already full enough with coinage, iconography, and the alphabet (in Bactria)!

It has long been known that Chinese diplomacy toward the nomads in the second century BCE was instrumental in creating in Central Asia and farther west, in Parthia, a market for Han products, especially silk. Chinese embassies traveled with thousands of bolts of silk but at very irregular intervals. The merchants in northwestern India and eastern Iran were quick to appreciate the potential for this exchange and followed the steps of the Chinese ambassadors back to China. As Du Qin, a Chinese statesman, put it in 25 BCE, "There are no members of the royal family or noblemen among those who bring the gifts. The latter are all merchants and men of low origins. They wish to exchange their goods and conduct trade, under the pretext of presenting gifts" (from the Xiyu juan, "Chapter on the Western Regions" of the Hou Hanshu, from the translation by John E. Hill, September 2003). The Sogdians were doing exactly the same thing at the same time, and the first testimonies, in 29 and 11 BCE, on a Sogdian in China might also be found in the Han shu: "If in view of these considerations, we ask why [Kangju] sends his sons to attend [at the Han court], [we find] that, desiring to trade, they use a pretense couched in fine verbiage" (Han shu, Hulsewé 1979, 128). Kangju, a nomadic state, the center of which was in what is now the southern part of the Tashkent oasis, included Sogdiana during the first century BCE. This desire to trade was a Sogdian one.

It is difficult to understand the next step in the establishment of Sogdian communities in China. It seems that some of the ambassadors and their families settled in China, especially in Gansu. Some late genealogies of Sogdian families in China seem at least to imply such a reconstruction. We know on a firm textual basis that as early as 227 CE, in Liangzhou (Gansu), when a conquering army was approaching from the south, "The various kings in Liangzhou dispatched twenty men including Zhi Fu and Kang Zhi, the ennobled leaders of the Yuezhi and Kangju Hu, to receive the military commander, and when the large army advanced north they competed to be the first to receive us." (*The Records of the Three Kingdoms* is a Chinese historical text that covers the history of the late Eastern Han Dynasty and the Three Kingdoms period. The primary body of the text was written by Chen Shou in the third century and combines the smaller histories of Cao Wei, Shu Han, and Eastern Wu into a single text.) These Hu from Kangju are the Sogdians, while the Yuezhi are the traders from Bactria and Gandhara, the Kushan Empire created by the Yuezhi tribes. The leaders of the biggest trading communities in Gansu were sent to the invading army, and the Sogdians were already on a par with the greatest merchants of antiquity, the Kushan.

Sabo, a caravan boss.

The next step in the history of the Sogdians in China is provided by the "Sogdian Ancient Letters." These letters were left in the ruins of a Han watchtower, ninety kilometers west of Dunhuang in 313. Sir Aurel Stein discovered them there in 1907. They were sent by some Sogdian traders from Gansu to the West. One of them was sent from Gansu to Samarkand and described the political upheavals in northern China. The Xiongnu, who were then sacking the main towns there, were called for the first time in an Indo-European language by the name that would be theirs in Europe a century later: the Xwn, or "Huns." The letter described also the ruin of the Sogdian trading network in these towns: "The last emperor, so they say, fled from Luoyang because of the famine and fire was set to his palace and to the city, and the palace was burnt and the city [destroyed]. Luoyang is no more, Ye is no more! . . . And, sirs, if I were to write to you about how China has fared, it would be beyond grief: there is no profit for you to gain from it . . . [in] Luoyang . . . the Indians and the Sogdians there had all died of starvation."[2] But the same text describes a Sogdian network well established in Gansu, which was still there a century later. A Chinese text explains how "merchants of that country [Sogdiana] used to come in great number to the district Liang [the present Wuwei in Gansu] to trade. When Guzang [i.e., Wuwei] was conquered [by the Wei in 439] all of them were captured. In the beginning of the reign of Gaozong [452–465] the king [of Sogdiana] sent embassies to ask for their ransom."[3]

The fifth and sixth centuries were certainly the high days of Sogdian immigration to China. After the disruption of the inner China network in the fourth century, a new network of Sogdian communities was created. Many Sui and Tang texts or funerary epitaphs of Sogdian families describe how the great-grandfather came to China during the Wei as a *sabao*—that is, chief caravaneer. These families established themselves first in Gansu, the next generation moved into the main Chinese towns, and some Sogdians managed to reach the court. For instance, the biography of An Tugen in the Bei shi describes how An Tugen's great-grandfather came from Anxi (western Sogdiana) to the Wei and established himself in Jiuquan (the western end of Gansu). Later on, An Tugen rose from the position of merchant to grand minister of the Northern Qi in the middle of the sixth century.

New discoveries from Guyuan in the Chinese province of Ningxia (southern Ordos) provide a very good example of Sogdian families in China who did not achieve such high distinction. Six graves of one Sogdian family have been excavated there. (Luo Feng was the site of a Sogdian family completely excavated in 1996–2001 but poorly described until de la Vaissière and Trombert in 2004.) According to its name, the family should have originated from the Sogdian town of Kesh (Shahr-i Sabz, in Uzbekistan), and the texts of the funerary epitaphs indeed describe how the family migrated from the western countries. The archaeological content of these looted tombs confirms these western links, as some Byzantine and Sasanian coins, a seal stone inscribed in Pahlavi, and a Zoroastrian symbol were found there. The great-grandfather, Miaoni, and the grandfather, Boboni, "served their country in the capacity of Sabao." The father, Renchou, "idled away his life, accomplishing nothing in his official career." A member of the fourth generation, Shi Shewu (d. 610), was the great man of the family, and through him the family became integrated into Chinese society. He was a military officer of the Sui, and his grave and funerary epitaph are Chinese. His elder son, Shi Hedan (d. 669), was translator in the Imperial Secretariat of the Tang. Another son, Shi Daoluo (d. 658), was a soldier. A grandson, Shi Tiebang (d. 666), was in charge of an army horse-breeding farm near Guyuan. Shi Daode (d. 678), from another branch of the Shi clan, and his uncle, Shi Suoyan, who is buried in same graveyard, were also members of the military and officialdom.

We know also by name many other members of the family. Some of these names are simply transcriptions of Sogdian names: Shewu is the honorific personal name, but the public name was Pantuo. Shewu was pronounced Jia-mut, and Pantuo banda; together they provide Jimatvande, a well-known Sogdian name, "servant of Demeter," which was only divided in two halves for the need of the *interpretatio sinica*. The first names of the next generation sound Chinese, except in the elder branch: Shi Hedan and his son Shi Huluo have first names that seem to be transcriptions. After so many generations in China, some of the members of the families still married in the Sogdian milieu, among them Shi Hedan, great-great-grandson of Shi Miaoni, who married a Kang (the Chinese surname of the natives of Samarkand), and Shi Suoyan, who married an An (from Bukhara).

These data are fascinating, because with the Shi family we can follow the destiny of a specific Sogdian family in China and see how it became integrated first in the Sogdian milieu and then how it became sinicized in the Chinese administration. So far we lack other examples, due mainly to the novelty of the interest in the Sogdian families in Chinese archaeology. Some other Sogdian graveyards have been found but are badly published.[4]

The ancestors of Shi Shewu bore a title, *sabao*, which is very interesting for the history of the Sogdians in China. It proves that the Sogdian communities in China were deeply rooted in the caravan trade. This title is a transcription of the Sogdian word *sartapao*, itself a Sogdian transcription of the Indian *sârthavâha*, chief caravaneer, through a Bactrian intermediary. In India, the sârthavâha was not only the chief caravaneer but also the head of the traders' guild. In China, the title was imported first as early as the second century CE under the form *sabo* directly from India—for example, in Buddhist texts that described the Buddha as a chief caravaneer, and then a second time from the Sogdian form with the precise administrative meaning "head of the local Sogdian community." The "river of the sabao" in Chinese geography is the Zeravshan, which flows in Samarkand and Bukhara. So the heads of the Sogdian communities in China bore the titles of "chief caravaneer," and it is on this ambiguity that Shi Shewu played when he wrote that his ancestors "served their country in the capacity of Sabao." For a Chinese ear, they were officials, while for a Sogdian one, they were simply heads of caravans!

We can see in the textual and epigraphical sources many such sabaos installed in China. Most of the main towns of northern China had in the sixth and seventh centuries their Sogdian community headed by a sabao, who received a mandarinal rank in the official hierarchy, at least from the Northern Qi to the Tang. These nouveaux riches had some wealthy funerary beds carved for them, where they displayed both their Sogdian culture and their integration into Chinese society, in a way the iconographic counterpart of the epitaphs of the Shi family. These funerary beds were an old Chinese tradition well suited for Zoroastrian purposes because it isolated the body from earth and water. Some of them have been known for a long time—for example, the Anyang (Ye) one, which shows a sabao in his garden receiving the members of his community. Others have been found recently and have found their way into Chinese or foreign museums.

One of the most interesting was discovered two years ago near Taiyuan by a team of the Shanxi Archaeological Institute. The tomb of Yu Hong, who died in 593 at age fifty-eight, contained a funerary bed in the shape of a Chinese house, adorned by fifty-three carved panels of marble, originally painted and gilded. Yu Hong had traveled extensively, acting as an ambassador to the Ruanruan, in Persia and Bactria or Gandhara (Yuezhi), and to the Tuyuhun tribes near lake Qinghai. Then he served the Northern Qi and Zhou, and the Sui. He became sabao in 580 and then nominal governor of a town. We know this because the funerary epitaphs of Yu Hong and his wife were discovered in the tomb. And the iconography fits very well the geography of the texts: we see on the panels Yu Hong hunting with nomads on horses, but also hunting on an Indian elephant or banqueting with his wife. Zoroastrian symbols are clearly displayed: two priests, half-bird, half-human, wearing the traditional padam (a piece of cloth in front of the mouth), and Mithra and his sacrificial horse facing each other on each side of the entry.

The trade links with Central Asia provided the communities from the fifth to the eighth centuries with waves of new immigrants. One specific example of these links is from a discovery on the main stage of the route, Turfan, in Xinjiang. Many Chinese documents were used there to cut paper clothing for the dead who were buried in the Astana cemetery. Among them is a list of taxes paid on caravan trade in the Gaochang kingdom (Turfan) in the 620s. The text is not complete but gives a fairly good idea of the identity of the main traders in Turfan: out of thirty-five commercial operations in this text, twenty-nine involved a Sogdian trader. In thirteen instances, both the seller and the buyer were Sogdians.

In inner China, the seventh century saw an evolution in the official position of the Sogdian communities. It seems that the Tang transformed quite independent and autonomous Sogdian communities loosely integrated in the mandarin hierarchy into more controlled "submitted counties" without Sogdian hierarchy. The sabaos disappeared from the epigraphical and textual sources after the middle of the seventh century. But this period, up to the middle of the eighth century, was certainly the climax of Iranian influence on Chinese civilization. If the communities were suppressed, the families and individuals who were before inclined to stay within the Sogdian communities now were integrated more thoroughly into Chinese society.

We can see people with typical Sogdian surnames, such as Kang, getting involved in all the fields of Tang social life.

Obviously, many of them were merchants: around the main markets of the capitals, Chang'an and Luoyang, Sogdian temples, Sogdian taverns, and Sogdian shops flourished. They sold to the Tang elite the Western goods that were then à la mode (Schafer 1963). Many young nobles or drunken poets celebrated the charms of the Sogdian girls, and the most famous of them, Li Bo, wrote:

> The Western hour has features like a flower.
> She stands by the wine-warmer
> Laughs like with the breath of spring
> Dances in a dress of gauze, and asks
> "Will you be going somewhere, m'lord
> Now? Before you are drunk?"[5]

It was not just merchants but also soldiers, monks, and high or low officials who were of Sogdian descent. We have seen that the sons and grandsons of Shi Shewu served in the army. To quote another example, the New History of the Tang describes the family of An Chongzhang, minister of war from 767 to 777. His ancestors were sabao in Wuwei (Gansu) during three generations. In the fourth generation, a member of the family An Xinggui became "Wude-era meritous servant," and from then on the family belonged to the administration: the sixth-generation An Zhongjing was military vice-commissary-in-chief of Hexi, and An Chong-zhang was the leading member of the seventh generation.

Research on such materials is just beginning. Many funerary epitaphs of the Tang period should be used to understand the rapid pace of the sinicization of the Sogdians that took place under the Tang. It is already clear, though, that the rebellion of An Lushan was a major stage in this process. An Lushan was the main military governor of northeastern China on the frontier with Korea and the Kitans. His father was a Sogdian installed in the Turk Empire, and his mother was Turk; his first name is a straight transcription of the Sogdian Rokhshan, "luminous" (the same as Roxane, Alexander's wife). He established himself as a young boy in northeastern China, acted as a translator there in the markets, became a soldier, and climbed from the rank and file to the top of the army. His rebellion in 755 nearly destroyed the Tang Dynasty and put an end to one of China's Golden Ages. The rebellion was quelled only in 763 with the help of the Uighur nomads.

The rebellion has been described elsewhere as if it was only a military coup by autonomous and very powerful armies. The Sogdian identity of the rebels is only now being investigated as such. Yet many texts described it as a Sogdian rebellion and detailed how many Sogdian traders supported An Lushan. Furthermore, some new discoveries prove that this idea was not due to a xenophobic bias in the Chinese descriptions of the revolt but was something claimed by the rebels themselves: Shi

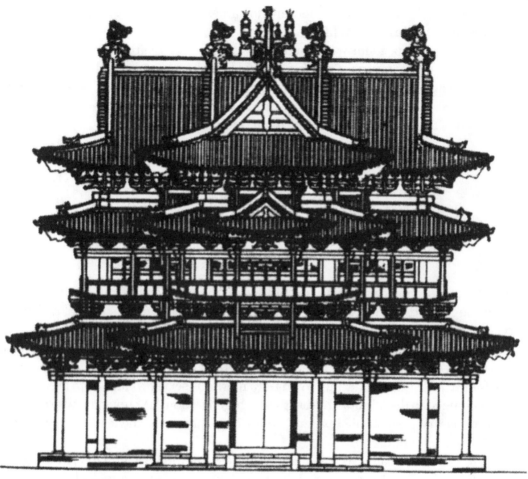

Zoroastrian temple.
IMAGE FROM *CHINA HERITAGE QUARTERLY*, BEIJING.

Seming, the second successor of An Lushan, himself a Sogdian, put the Sogdian royal title of *Jamuk* (Jewel, transcribed Zhaowu in Chinese) on par with Huangdi on his recently discovered ceremonial jades. The troops of the rebels bore the Sogdian name of Zhejie, a fair transcription of the Sogdian Châkar "professional soldier."

notes

1. *Silk Road Foundation Newsletter* 1, no. 2 (December 2003).
2. Sims-Williams, 1996, 49.
3. Enoki Wei shu, 1955, quoted in *française d'Extrême-Orient* (Paris, 2005). *Les Sogdiens en Chine*, edited by Étienne de la Vaissière and Eric Trombert.
4. See de la Vaissière and Trombert 2004 for other examples from textual sources.
5. Translation by Schafer in *The Golden Peaches of Samarkand*, 21.

appendix h

The Plot Summary for a Movie about a Zoroastrian Tragedy

I F SEX, VIOLENCE, AND POLITICAL INTRIGUE ARE THE STUFF OF BLOCKBUSTERS, THE AN LUSHAN Rebellion is worthy of consideration by the world's best film producers, whether in Hollywood or Bollywood. A century after Zoroastrians succumbed to Islamic power and influence in Persia, the dubious exploits of An Lushan led to the disappearance of huge Zoroastrian communities in China. The story is largely unknown, even by the Zoroastrian community of the twenty-first century, in which the role of China may again become paramount. We present here background information for the movie version of those events.

An Lushan was born in 703 CE in Yingzhou (now Chaoyang), China, to the well-placed Kang family within the burgeoning Sogdian immigrant community. Religion would play little or no role in the rise, rule, and demise of China's first Zoroastrian emperor, whose actions finally dragged the faith and its adherents into sudden oblivion. An exception to this rule would be the exemplary spiritual life of Shi Siming, Lushan's childhood friend and alter ego through his remarkable but checkered career. They all spoke Chinese, but Shi Siming knew the "Good Thoughts, Good Words, Good Actions" mantra by the Avestan words *Humata, Hukhta, Huvareshta,* and he taught them to his Chinese associates at every stage of the story, with little effect on his boyhood chum.

Twists and turns in the dramatic rise of An Lushan began an upward spiral in 741 when as a young general he became military governor in the area north of the Yellow River. He made the future Beijing his headquarters, but he traveled frequently to meet with Emperor Xuanzong, the Tang monarch reigning in the ancient capital, Luoyong. By this time Lushan had married twice, concurrently and advantageously, within the Sogdian minority, then a cultural and commercial elite. During one of his visits to the capital, he was adopted as a son by the slightly older Empress Consort Yang, with whom he was having a secret affair. How better to achieve access to the palace and to her? On this basis, on his next visit Lushan bowed to Consort Yang first before bowing to Emperor Xuanzong, stating, "Barbarians bow to mothers first before

275

fathers."[1] Xuanzong, now believing Lushan was submissive to him like a son to a father, showed him every imaginable favor. The late Canadian sinologist at the University of British Columbia, Edwin Pulleyblank, published an online article with flagrant but well-researched information suggesting that An Lushan was "an enormously fat man with a talent for buffoonery."[2] After receiving a gift of "Western twirling girls" (a skill preserved by Sufi Muslims today) from several Sogdian cities including Samarkand, Emperor Xuanzong was thrilled beyond expression. So despite his great weight, An Lushan and the Empress Consort, concubine Yang Guifei, determined to master "the Sogdian twirl" and did, now dominating life at court in every way.

At the beginning of 751, Lushan presented Emperor Xuanzong with eight thousand captives as slaves, and the emperor made him prince of Dongping, the only such appointment of a general outside the imperial Li family. The empress threw him a sumptuous birthday party on February 20 of that year to kick off a building project by the aging emperor, a magnificent mansion built for Lushan in the alternate capital of Chang'an (now known as Xi'an), sparing no expenses, and using jade, gold, and silver in special appointments.[3]

By this time, Lushan began to be worried what would happen once Emperor Xuanzong died. He had earlier refused to bow to Li Heng, the heir apparent, and there was bad blood between them, so he began to make preparations in case of retribution after the succession. He was already in a position to analyze the weak spots in the imperial defense system, and the first step he took was to organize a troop of eight thousand elite soldiers, ostensibly to defend the palace under his command. He sent them on ill-fated training expeditions until they were in supreme fighting condition, then placed them at the headquarters of his own armies, stationed just north of the Yellow River, until needed.

This elite guard was used for successful skirmishes in which he claimed to be defending the throne from rivals, presumptive heirs, pretenders, and future claimants. In the spring of 755, Lushan proposed replacing the thirty-two generals of traditional Han Chinese ethnicity with thirty-two "non-Han" generals (almost certainly Sogdian) under himself. We can surmise that the former generals were not as loyal to the emperor as the new generals would be to Lushan, "in defense of the throne." This plan was accepted by Emperor Xuanzong, himself also nervous about those who might wish to hasten the succession. Tensions with rivals continued until autumn, when the emperor finally became suspicious of Lushan as well and arranged for an alliance of adversaries as a check on, or balance of, Lushan's now obviously excessive power.

On December 16, 755, Lushan launched his own rebellion, claiming he had received a secret order from Emperor Xuanzong to advance on Chang'an to remove the most powerful of the emperor's potential challengers. His troops and generals chose to believe him, marched through Chang'an, occupied Luoyang, and the rebellion was over before it started. Emperor Xuanzong deserted his capital and fled to Sichuan, leaving Yang Guifie behind to negotiate on his behalf of his life. Li Heng fled in the opposite direction, to Lingwu, where he was declared emperor by the army. Li Heng's whole reign was then spent in attempting to reverse what became known in history as the

An Lushan Rebellion, though there were actually three Zoroastrian emperors before the rule of the Sogdian dynasty was over.

Meanwhile, in Luoyang on Lunar New Year's Day (February 5), 756, An Lushan had proclaimed himself emperor of China, launching the new Yan (or "peace") Dynasty, as he chose to call it. Tang officials of his new realm surrendered to him with few exceptions, and he made the leaders among them his chancellors, a move reminiscent of Cyrus the Great, still admired among Zoroastrians. He made his sons An Qingxu the prince of Jin and An Qing'en the prince of Zheng, two important provinces, though they all lived in the palace at Luoyang.

Despite this admirable beginning, Lushan was as ineffective a ruler as he had been an effective manipulator of events that brought him to power. His great girth, which made him look incredibly powerful upon his giant horse, made him look ridiculously obese on the throne. Years of hard living had caught up with him, and he suffered from ulcers and syphilis, the latter causing blindness. He became ill tempered, beating or even executing servants if they annoyed him. Once he achieved his goal of becoming emperor, he spent most of his time inside the Luoyang palace, where his officials and generals rarely saw him, except to receive gruff and excessive orders. The Sogdian Zoroastrian culture itself, outside the palace, was at its peak at this time.

Lushan had a bias for his son An Qing'en, a "weakling" born to his second and favorite wife, Empress Duan. He considered Qing'en the safe choice as the crown prince, instead of the stronger An Qingxu, who was slightly older and thought himself next in line. But even Qingxu feared that paranoia would cause Lushan to put him to death. He plotted an assassination with the help of his father's servant, Yan Zhuang, and Li Zhu'er, a favorite eunuch of the emperor, both of whom Lushan had beaten. On the night of January 29, 757, with Yan and Qingxu standing guard, Li Zhu'er smuggled a sword into the private quarters of the palace and attacked Lushan. The emperor, fat and blind, tried to fight back, but he could not find the sword he kept under his bed, and Li Zhu'er ran Lushan through with his rapier.

In the morning Yan Zhuang announced to the court that An Lushan was dying and was formally appointing An Qingxu crown prince. On that basis in a noon-hour ceremony, An Qingxu took the throne, even before announcing An Lushan's death, with nobody protesting or asking questions. His brief rule as the second Zoroastrian monarch was as chaotic as his father's.

In 759, Shi Siming, still quiet and unassuming, killed the erratic An Qingxu for the sake of the people and took the imperial title himself, the third Zoroastrian emperor. He recovered the body of An Lushan and performed Zoroastrian funeral rites for his friend. He then simply administered the affairs of state until overseeing an eventual surrender in 763 CE to Tang forces under a new emperor, Li Heng's son,[4] with new Uyghur allies, negotiating a just peace and amnesty for the Sogdian Zoroastrian population. Within a very short period of time there was an integration of millions of Sogdian Zoroastrians into the mainstream of Chinese society in which Confucian principles were enhanced by Zoroastrian spirituality. This was the "moment" in which Confucianism became a religion, as described in chapter 12 of this book.

A Mysterious Stranger in China.
IMAGE COURTESY OF THE MUSEO DI ARTE ORIENTALE (MAO), TURIN, ITALY.

Described as "A Mysterious Stranger in China" in a *Wall Street Journal* article by Lee Lawrence,[5] this burial figure from the eighth-century Yan Dynasty (shown in the photo) indicates a Zoroastrian spiritual vitality during the ill-fated An Lushan Rebellion of the Sogdian minority. It was seen as a mystery when first discovered in the ancient capital of Luoyang because art critics assumed it to be a person on a camel or on horseback riding side saddle. The population of the city was more than a million at the time, and at that moment about one-quarter were Sogdian. The Phrygian cap worn by Zoroastrians is an easy marker, but who wears the equally distinct *padam*, a facial veil of ritual sacrifice, while riding? The mystery was solved by identification of the yoga camel pose by Jenny Sutacriti in research for this text, showing the devotee here in a "half-camel" yoga position called "the Ustra-Sana." The persona thus memorialized is shown as probably leading a congregation in devotional exercises before the sacrificial flame; the hat may assist us in picturing this activity as being outdoors, as was customary.

This fits with the thinking of Marcello Pacini, who headed the Agnelli Foundation for twenty-five years and who acquired the statue at auction some twenty years ago for the MAO collection. "I have never seen a rider with such intensity in his eyes," he says. "His is the expression of a priest honoring a god, not that of a camel rider facing some banal complication."[6] The figure is solid and obviously sculpted by a master craftsperson, showing the sophistication of the vibrant Sogdian culture at its peak, and with obvious reference to the international context of Zoroastrian life in China, with yogic roots into India at that time.

With up to thirty-six million killed in its decade of rule, the final world-stage saga of the Zoroastrian tradition ended, until the current era in which the small surviving Zoroastrian community scattered around the world may play a role again in a New Axial Age. The An Lushan episode was even more ignominious than the collapse of Zoroastrianism under Alexander, and again following Muhammad, when they were merely the victims of calamity, rather than being directed to their demise by their leaders.

However, still well thought of by their neighbors for the most part, after the return to Tang rule following Shi Siming's amnesty, many Sogdians took Chinese names, and millions of Zoroastrians participated in Confucian religious ceremonies that accommodated their true spirituality across most of China. Was this one final example where furtive Zoroastrians might well have buried or accidently hidden one or more copies of their precious Scripture? The quest for the Dead Zee Scrolls expands now with the prime search area now extending from Sogdian Samarkand, eastward through all the areas of substantial Sogdian Zoroastrian activity along the Silk Route and well into China proper.

The restoration of lasting peace and prosperity by the Tang gave stimulus to an enriched Confucianism. A revised edition of five classic Chinese books known as the *Wujing* offered new commentaries on old traditions resulting in the rise of metaphysically significant Confucian texts, notably *Zhongyong* ("Doctrine of the Mean") and *Yizhuan* ("The Great Commentary of the Classic of Changes"). These appealed to some Buddhist and Taoist thinkers, but they were probably influenced by the influx of

Zoroastrian thought, recognized only of late. The most influential promoter of a Confucian revival was Han Yu, who spent part of his childhood in Chang'an and traveled throughout China, holding a number of distinguished government posts such as the rector of the Imperial University in Luoyang. He was a social associate and cultural companion of the respected Zoroastrians then prominent in the imperial court. Outliving both An Lushan and Shi Siming, Han Yu died after retiring back in Chang'an in 824 after a spectacular writing career. He is remembered for fending off Buddhist and Taoist influence with new ideas just as Zoroastrianism was being submerged into mainstream Chinese life, first in power and later in defeat.

Confucianists from that time forward have attributed the following verse to Confucius, without any textual proof. It appears in Confucian temples all over China to this day and in the West, where Taoists claim that it originated with Lao Tzu, again without evidence. The last lines may have been added by either, and after their encounters with a source our readers will easily recognize, the *Humata, Hukhta, Huvareshta*. These words demonstrate the give and take among religions that have roots in the Axial Age, and aspire to bless each other again in the New Axial Age, with again a certain inspiration rooted in the words of the Persian prophet of old:

> Watch your thoughts, they become words.
> Watch your words, they become actions.
> Watch your actions, they become habits.
> Watch your habits, they become character.
> Watch your character, it becomes destiny.

In the far east of China, a small group of Zoroastrian Sogdians continued with "business as usual," true to their identity for another century until they backed the wrong horse in a subsequent rebellion. In the far west, around Dunhuang and on down the Silk Route, it was Buddhism that became a default religion for many Zoroastrians. Several magnificent Zoroastrian temples became Buddhist in this area, where they are now being carefully reevaluated and restored as Zoroastrian historical monuments in the twenty-first century.

Twenty-first-century Chinese scholars are thoroughly investigating the Zoroastrian influence in Confucianism. They are also analyzing the influence of Taoism and Buddhism in relation to modern Chinese culture. They are even conducting examinations of minor crossover effects of Hinduism, Islam, Christianity, and Judaism in the secular state with its deep spiritual roots. This program is pursued with almost religious zeal in a communist idealism unlikely to reach proper conclusion without eventual acknowledgment of religious fundamentals. But we conclude by observing the irony that the religious quest in China today, with different goals and for different purposes, runs parallel to the project of the *Seven Testaments Trilogy* and employs many of the same methods and techniques.

Judging from sales of its two predecessors there, *Seven Testaments of World Religion* may be as welcome in China as in the radically secularized states of North America and Western Europe in a rapidly changing world. Western intellectuals on either side of the North Atlantic may be missing the boat for which Chinese intellectuals have already purchased tickets. It is sometimes suggested that the ideals and the programs of Christian missions triggered communist idealism, and now with religion again straining at the leash in China, at least some Chinese scholars will find themselves engaged by the spiritual dynamics they are investigating. China's "Great Leap Forward" under Mao Zedong was industrial. China's forward movement under Xi Jinping is the Road and Belt Initiative to recover control of the Silk Route. The future vitality of China, if present indications hold true, may well be in the spiritual realm.

notes

1. "An Lushan" article in *Zizhi Tongjian* by Bo Yang.
2. https://sogdians.si.edu/ from *The Sogdians: Influencers on the Silk Roads*, a series organized by the Freer Gallery of Art and Arthur M. Sackler Gallery, Smithsonian Institution with information and an outstanding exhibition of recent finds of Sogdian artwork from China.
3. Summary of information from the *Encyclopedia of China* (Chinese History Edition), 1st ed.
4. Ibid.
5. *Wall Street Journal*, September 3, 2011.
6. Ibid.

epilogue: an agenda for another twenty years

Finding and Identifying the Dead Zee Scrolls

IT TOOK TWENTY YEARS TO GET THIS MATERIAL SHAKEN DOWN INTO A MANAGEABLE TRILOGY. THE contributors join with me, as the author and contributing editor, in inviting the religious people of the world to shop at our bazaar over the next twenty years and to pass these products on to where they may be helpfully appreciated. Forty years is sometimes regarded as the gestation period for profound changes in the religious traditions under consideration, as also in politics and in "bell curve" social policy. I will be one hundred years old by then, but most of the contributors are younger than I am, and we are joined by adherents and promoters of our views daily, loyal to their own traditions, sharing what is precious to them and receiving treasures from others. A New Axial Age is a-birthing, and there is work to be done, including specific tasks we hope some of our readers will undertake.

Material that looks similar in the seven testaments themselves and elsewhere used to be explained by suggesting that it simply addresses the human condition in a manner consistent with life experiences and needs. A principal concept in *Seven Testaments of World Religion* is that this is not just coincidence—that such material is actually linked, in many cases connected to Vedic religious lore through Zoroastrian reforms and refinement, on to connections between the religions within Western and Eastern clusters. Apparently even in ancient China, Zoroastrians were open to adopting the spiritual treasures of others into the universal family of Zoroaster, illustrated in the appearance of yoga in the spiritual life of Zoroastrians there in the eighth century BCE and passed on the Confucians in due course, as illustrated in appendix H.

These connections may become more widely appreciated as we flesh out the details of links implicit in this book. The most obvious of these is the search for the Dead Zee Scrolls themselves, in whole, in part, or in more Z fragments buried in the texts of the Seven Testaments and elsewhere. Other identifiable projects will be proceeding from the international launch conference for the *Seven Testaments Trilogy* in May 2020 in Niagara Falls, New York.

The first of these is the absolute identification of the tomb of Zoroaster. This project will draw support from the chamber of commerce in Mazar-i-Sharif, two universities, and the departments of education, tourism, and religion of the government of Afghanistan. Western and Middle East Muslims may also be eager to demonstrate their role in maintaining the tombs of so many non-Muslim prophets among the People of the Book. These are, in addition to scholars of Zoroastrianism, Parsee philanthropists, universities, and other agencies from all over the world, represented at the conference, all under the leadership of Professor Richard Freund of Christopher Newport University. The opening pages of appendix B presented a rationale for this task.

The second such project to come out of that conference is the movie of the An Lushan Rebellion and its aftermath, in which Zoroastrianism was subsumed into Confucianism, giving it a religiosity not known in the more philosophical era of Confucius himself. Is it politically incorrect to note that Jewish interests are well represented in Hollywood, where such investigations have been undertaken successfully in reference to everything from *The Ten Commandments* to *Schindler's List*? Probably not more incorrect than to reference the fact that Bollywood productions are owned and controlled by Parsee Zoroastrians or that Muslims opened the trend in the twenty-first century with the Messenger of God telling the story of Muhammad. The list of specifically Christian movies runs from *The Robe* to *Jesus Christ Superstar*. Surely the blockbuster described in our appendix H is worthy of entrepreneurial attention or some cooperative effort in making this gripping Zoroastrian riff public in a day when Zoroastrianism is at last coming back into its own. The aforementioned ongoing conference has that agenda under control also in communications with Bollywood producers.

We now move to mutual enrichment among the seven religions of world culture in a New Axial Age. A simple example that comes easily to mind is the enjoyment of Christmas carols in honor of the Saoshyant in the homes and businesses of Zoroastrian friends and colleagues, or informally at their Deri Mer temples. Beyond the orthodoxies of the big seven, the next step will quite possibly benefit from Sufi and Ahmadi Muslims, Mormon and monist Christians, Jains, Kabbalists, and perhaps even nonproselytizing Jews for Jesus, a subject yet to be addressed. Get ready to meet and appreciate Sikhs, Baha'is, Unitarian Universalists, and adherents of other cherished traditions, each with their purpose and their place in the scheme of things. They all bring what they have experienced as fresh disclosures of Divinity to add to our shared appreciation of holy writ in the seven world religions and Zoroastrianism before them. Such enrichments may be challenging to the orthodoxy of some and rejected by others, but let us consider the more positive possibilities.

In her *Tastes of the Divine*, Michelle Voss Roberts describes possible reactions:

> We ecstatically step outside in the encounter with the divine and human others, but then we come back to ourselves once more. The journey affects us at many levels. When we read the texts of others, observe their religious practices, or simply attempt to understand

our neighbors, we are engaged as whole and complex persons. Intellectually, we may try to reconcile what we already believe with what we have encountered. Spiritually, we may consider how the encounter affects our commitment to our own religious tradition. But perhaps the most fundamental response occurs on an emotional or affective level. . . . By intensifying emotion within the reader, religious texts inspire the determination to live according to their reality.[1]

In his foreword to *Three Testaments*, Amir Hussain, then editor of the *Journal of the American Academy of Religion*, addressed this question: "The goal of interfaith dialogue as advanced by this book is not that we seek to convert each other (or even that we merely compare materials) but that we help each other to find what is most meaningful in our own traditions."

In his preface to *Without Buddha I Could Not Be a Christian*, Catholic theologian Paul Knitter takes it a step further:

I have come to realize that I have to look *beyond* the traditional borderlines of Christianity to find something that is vitally, maybe even essentially, important for the job of understanding and living the Christian faith: *other religions*. That is the scriptures, the traditions, the sacred texts, the past teachings, the living communities of other religious believers. It was only after I began to take seriously and to explore other religious scriptures and traditions that I was adequately able to understand my own.

Buddhism was at the center of one of the first such offerings of this sharing benefit. Nobody suggests that the awakening of the Buddha under the bodhi tree was anything but an authentic experience of the Divinity of the universe, unique in its origin with Siddhartha Gautama. But it was rooted in a reformed Vedic Zoroastrian impetus swirling around him since his early childhood and finally ripening in response to his struggle to reconcile the extremes of asceticism and indulgence witnessed in adult life. As he turned to the Hindu expressions of Vedicism so dominant in his culture, he found a ready audience for the refinements recently stimulated by Zoroaster and spread to his homeland by Magi and others in contiguous parts of the Silk Route. His own nascent reform movement was so welcomed and successful that "Buddhism," as it would later be called, was soon eclipsed by the resurgent Hinduism it triggered in India. Buddhists did not become Zoroastrians, but if Vedic lore is the Older Testament of Zoroastrianism, the Z context becomes the Older Testament within Buddhism, which itself gives birth or provides the context for the New Hinduism expressed so beautifully in the Bhagavad Gita. The Hindus did not become Buddhists, but many of them say they all became better Hindus at that juncture.

After the death of the Buddha, the movement passed on to other venues such as China, where sharing in the opposite direction took place as Buddhism itself built on the Taoist base fostered two generations earlier by Lao Tzu. This second exchange was profitable to both sides at various times in their histories. In like fashion, Buddhists sometimes taught that Lao Tzu was actually Siddhartha Gautama visiting China, and Taoists have believed that upon leaving China, it was to India that Lao

Tzu journeyed, where he eventually sat under the bodhi tree until he was ready to teach the shared message within the context of Hindu culture. The truth behind these legends is complex—not literal, but something of a model for sharing profound and precious insights in our time.

Taking the Eastern experience of sharing a step further in *Older Testaments: Encounters on the Way*, playwright William Thomas imaginatively sets the appearance of Zoroastrian Magi in the heart of Chinese culture. He recognizes the confrontation between Confucius and Lao Tzu as a conflict illustrating a universal pattern seen in the initial influence of Zoroastrianism on the thinking of Lao Tzu and the initial reaction of Confucius in defense of Chinese traditions. In the play, the emptying of everything into the at-One-ment that comes from awakening to the positive nature of Universal Reality was subsequently described and written down by a border guard as Lao Tzu left China. It was repeated by Buddha in his own awakening in the Hindu context and made universal by Krishna in the Bhagavad Gita—Krishna being presented as the avatar of the Lao Tzu/Siddhartha Gautama divine personas in this play.

A similar history occurred over many centuries in the West between Judaism, Christianity, and Islam, though with only rare instances of goodwill and mutual appreciation. Judaism provided the foundation, perhaps modeling, molding, or facilitating Zoroaster's refinement of Vedic lore in important respects. The first generation of Christians were all Jewish, and a Jewish majority prevailed for a century after that, followed by a separation from Rabbinic Judaism that had developed from the same roots in becoming a "new" Judaism after the 70 CE destruction of the temple in Jerusalem. Both were descended from the Hebrew Scriptures, often described by Christians as their Old Testament, the teachings and prophecies of which permeated the Middle East until the time of Muhammad in the seventh century CE and onward. These same Scriptures are indeed also the Old Testament of the new Rabbinic Judaism, complete in themselves but also related to the Older Testament of which we speak.

Even as we begin to recognize both Zoroastrian influence and portions of Christian Scripture in the Quran, the Hebrew Scriptures appear as the dominant context of the Quran, though in all these cases we acknowledge the Muslim proclivity to see the whole of the Quran as the "words" of God presented afresh. To Muslims, these words were revealed to Muhammad as the manner in which all previous expressions of "The Book" should then be presented in corrected or supplemented format for the Arab world and all who would receive this revelation. Jews and Christians need to ask themselves what is revealed in that book that they might appreciate, just as Muslims, Christians, and Rabbinic Jews all need to acknowledge the earlier Hebrew Scriptures as the "Old Testament" of all three, even while now also recognizing the Vedic Older Testament of the whole world.

In the opinion of many, God's words in the Quran have profound literary meaning in addition to sometimes less weighty "literal" meanings, but only of late might a leading scholar like Amir Hussain dare apply his familiarity with Christian or Jewish manners of interpretation in becoming a better Muslim.

Muslim readers will thus benefit from understanding the Quran in its historical and cultural contexts—asking when and why and how the verses were revealed to Muhammad. They can also learn about the truth of metaphor in discussion of literary analysis in the work of profound believing critics like Northrop Frye.[2] . . . What might have been understood as literally true is now also seen as metaphorically true at a deeper level of meaning. The Quran itself seems to give allowance for such understanding: "It is God who revealed the Book to you. In it are clear revelations which are the foundations of the book, while others are metaphorical."[3, 4]

In 2004, when the text of *Noah's Other Son* was still in preparation for publication, a lecture by Rabbi Reuven Firestone, who was visiting in Buffalo, New York, provided me with an opportunity to interview six local rabbis about the question of including mention of Messianic Jews (or "Jews for Jesus"). All six of them and Firestone himself expressed dismay bordering on revulsion at the prospect, with Reuven and my future friend and contributor to *Four Testaments*, Rabbi Jacqueline Mates-Muchin, declaring it a "toxic topic" for Jews, akin to touching a fatal "third rail" on an electric train track. "Don't do it if you wish to sell any books at all to your important Jewish market."

The separation of the church from the synagogue in the second century CE was followed by a rash of adverse behaviors toward Jews, whose continued presence in the "Holy Land" and the diaspora elsewhere led to their dreadful persecution in Europe and beyond to many parts of the world. This is consistent with the twentieth-century Holocaust and atrocities continuing to the present day in parts of North America, Europe, and elsewhere. All this is despite the remarkable contributions of Jewish people to every culture they joined, and it justifies their desire to establish a secure refuge in their ancient homeland. It was the Romans who killed Christ, and Jesus was himself Jewish, so the epithet "the Jews killed Christ" is patently absurd, despite the fact that he had Jewish enemies—similar to the experience of many religious leaders in history. So reasons for this shameful behavior by Christians must be found elsewhere: possibly in the resistance of Jews to full integration with their surrounding societies, or perhaps jealousy over their remarkable success in professional endeavors within areas permitted to them when they were forbidden to possess land, the true repository of wealth in traditional societies. Or this blight may be a scapegoat for the failures of others, or simply but tragically irrational, or all of the above.

This brief inquiry into the history of persecution of Jews by Christians is an attempt to explicate the standoff that prevents many of the adherents of Western religions from entering into the type of interchanges Eastern religions have enjoyed over the centuries and to illustrate the challenges faced by coreligionists. Even Muslims, after centuries of relative harmony with Jews in many places, got sucked into a hateful vortex by finding themselves allied with the Jew-hating "Axis Powers" during World War II. As the twenty-first century unfolds, similar challenges exist, such as for Muslims and Christians to avoid becoming entrenched in acrimony; for Buddhists to overcome rancor symbolized by the ethnic cleansing of Rohingya Muslims in Myanmar and Tamil Hindus in Sri Lanka; and the counterintuitive rise of Hindu nationalism in India and the Christian Right in America. There is much work to be done, and the onus is on religious people, as seemingly intractable divisions remain in the hearts of those fearful of losing privileged positions.

The Jewish community itself, consisting of both religious and secular Jews, is open to accommodating atheist, Buddhist, Taoist, and even Jewish people who are Muslim by birth and conviction, but not Christian Jews. Christians have earned this disapprobation by attempting to co-opt Judaism in certain respects and by behaviors that have been anything but Christlike over the millennia. It should be possible for Jews to allow for messianic consideration of Jesus, but they can hardly be expected to do so in the face of adventist theology described in our piece about the Christian apocalypse whereby the end will come only when all Jews are converted or killed. Congregations of Messianic Jews are scrupulous about traditional Jewish observances and could be a growing presence to strengthen Jewish populations of Israel and elsewhere, but not when attitudes of radical Christian minorities continue to be "hellbent" on the destruction of the Jewish community in one way or another regardless of "politically correct" rhetoric on the matter.

Messianism itself is not off the table in the case of other claimants. For example, claims by certain Jewish groups that Menachem Mendel Schneerson (April 18, 1902–June 12, 1994) is the Messiah, soon to return, are not widely entertained, but adherents of his movement are certainly regarded as Jewish in a manner opposite to that extended to messianic Christian Jews. According to Conservative Judaism, Jews who believe Jesus is the Messiah have "crossed the line out of the Jewish community."[5] Reform Judaism, the modern progressive movement, agrees: "For us in the Jewish community anyone who claims that Jesus is their savior is no longer a Jew and is an apostate."[6]

However, the tragic history of this relationship notwithstanding, a profoundly sophisticated Jewish academia remains able to enter into sharing conversations and even offer leadership appropriate to the times. Two prominent Jewish academics, Amy-Jill Levine of Vanderbilt University and Marc Zvi Brettler of Duke, have generously produced *The Jewish Annotated New Testament* to provide information for Christians about the Jewish context of their Scriptures and a perhaps more correct appreciation of the Jewishness of Jesus.

Brettler, a prominent contributor to the *Three Testaments* text, has also joined with Professor Leela Prasad to present a program of Jewish and Hindu studies in which the Duke University calendar description summarizes what is going on as well as any explanation of similar programs at places like Claremont, Harvard, Hartford, and McGill in North America, and the School of Oriental and African Studies in the United Kingdom and Singapore, to mention but a few:

> Using interdisciplinary comparative frameworks, this course will study how two major world religions, Hinduism and Judaism, create a dynamic cosmos that brings abiding meaning to the daily lives of millions of believers. It explores concepts such as ritual and myth by examining Jewish and Hindu materials from early to modern times. The broader aims of the course are to understand how each tradition imagines time, space, and matter, and

to explore how claims about the sacred are transformed in modernity. Ultimately, it aims to inspire reflection on how religion, identity and culture function in the modern world.[7]

Professors at Duke reach out to mixed student bodies of Hindus, Jews, Christians, and others, as do contributors to this trilogy in a trend of expanding significance. At Duke and elsewhere, a major aspect of the conversation will be the interplay between monotheistic and monistic understandings of Divinity and the Universe as the Eastern and Western clusters of world religions increasingly interact. Spinoza may be right to be silent before the awesomeness of a whole Divine Universe, but others may have news for Spinoza with respect to a Godhead who cares for and responds to each individual toenail within the one universal body. There are both monotheists in this world and monists detached from it who experience divine energy and a universal transpersonal engagement with each element of what may also be described as a multiverse.

So we are into a New Axial Age of stimulation and sharing in which the "evangelism" of the time is aimed at ourselves first, for Christians to become better Christians, Taoists to become wiser Taoists, and Confucianists in particular taking from other religions everything they need these days while reminding the rest of us how these advances can be fitted into traditional practices. As recounted earlier by an attendee at presentations I personally offered to the North American Zoroastrian community meeting in Chicago in 2018, I can adhere to my Christian New Testament, find a profound foundation for my faith in the Hebrew Old Testament, and also acknowledge my debt to the Older Testament of Zoroastrian Scriptures, extant among Zoroastrian friends and colleagues, buried within the *Seven Testaments of World Religion* (and perhaps still to be found among the Dead Zee Scrolls).

Indigenous religious traditions in Canada are now referred to as the Canadian Older Testament,[8] rescuing the broader society from environmental degradation and providing sacred models for "sustainable development" of resources needed by the world. As religious people in the twenty-first century incline increasingly toward appreciation of the various Older Testaments of the world, there will be less judgment of others as "wrong" and going to hell unless they become "like us." Nobody is required to give up their religious traditions, but those who remain blind and deaf to the riches offered to them by others are poorer for missing out on the Divinity everywhere.

"Getting the word out" may remain an imperative of proselytizing religions that are eager to share their own precious treasure. They may find more receptive audiences when they approach others with the attitude of St. Paul when he prefaced his presentation of the Gospel to the intellectual elite in Athens with respect for the religious quest that preceded him there. "Athenians, I see how extremely religious you are in every way"[9] is how he begins in reference to the insights of their own poets. Indeed, Greek philosophy and "mysteries" may be listed with Hebrew, Zoroastrian, and other influences in the Christian New Testament in much the same way that Eastern monism affects Western monotheism today, whether in Kabbalism and across Judaism, in Sufi Islam and beyond, or as illustrated by a Catholic who can hardly maintain his Christianity without Buddha. Fellow Christians and others will find that such a one has much to offer of growing value out of his expanding faith experience, increasingly so in the New Axial Age of the twenty-first century.

When I served a church in Toronto at the turn of the century, Russians fleeing the collapse of the Soviet Union often joined my church, and many sang in the choir. Some would have a nonattending spouse, excused as being an atheist. On visiting such homes, I would sometimes ask, "Would you like to tell me about the God you don't believe in?" Invariably the willing answer was some variation on the Angry Bearded Grandfather in the sky, reminiscent of an out-of-touch old Germanic "Gott" figure (from the Proto-Indo-European *gutos*), capricious enough to intervene in human affairs only on a whim. My usual reply, "Hey, that's the same God I don't believe in," was often greeted with a laugh, followed by a good conversation on the quest for meaning in existence. But there are even Christian clergy who have difficulty believing in an occasionally "interventionist" God, given the state of the world and the undeserved pain experienced by many people.

We could illustrate how in the New Axial Age of the twenty-first century, something of a monist position can facilitate Christians in engaging the deeper meanings of orthodox doctrine both in belief and in vibrancy of prayer and meditation. As one empties oneself of desires and personal ambitions, into the fullness of the complete divinity of the universe, one experiences the interconnectedness of All, centered on the Godhead, which, for Christians, has the face of Jesus. As the Godhead sacrificially gives of God's Divinity to all, the earthly incarnation of the story makes sense of the Godhead's initiative (the virgin birth), the eternal life (resurrection), and everything in between in both the scriptural story and human experience. But perhaps we have heard enough from Christians already, who may now need a season of listening before offering again their particular treasures in Christ. We have noted one particular Christian professor whose spiritual vitality is enriched by his engagement with Buddhism, and we have seen examples of monists from the East who just as comfortably slip into monotheistic expressions when addressing the Godhead. We have recognized the appreciation of a professor of Islamic theology in strengthening Muslim awareness of new depths of his own tradition, not through assimilation but in a broadening perspective.

Congregational ministries may display the richness of cross-pollination from different traditions. Jacqueline Mates-Muchin is the Chinese senior rabbi at Oakland's Temple Sinai, a contributor and a great friend of this project. Her arrival from Buffalo as assistant rabbi in 2005 prompted questions from a congregant, in the normal course of things. That interview by Oakland writer Ilana DeBare found its way onto the internet, where it reveals how certain aspects of monism and monotheism blend naturally in our era of sharing among those who are wise to the times.

Q: Let me jump right into the middle of things. Do you believe in God, and what is your conception of God?

A: I believe that there is a oneness to the universe and a connection to every aspect of the universe. The things that make up our bodies are the same things floating out in space. It's the same stuff that was there at the big bang and the same stuff that will be there when our sun explodes, however many billions of years from now.

And ultimately what we do has an effect around the universe. By virtue of that connection, I believe we are commanded to behave in certain ways—in particular with other human beings, but with the world around us as well.

That's why within a Jewish context, the notion of "command" makes so much sense. It's that idea that there is no other choice. When we understand what our actions mean, how can there be any other choice than for us but to behave in a certain way?

Q: With that idea of God as the oneness of the universe, how do you then make sense of the Torah's portrayal of God as an actual consciousness that communicates with people?

A: I think the Torah is a great story. It's mythology like any other myth. What we learn from it is that there is a separateness that we have to be responsible to. It is, on the one hand, everything, but, on the other hand, it is so separate that we cannot mistake it for ourselves. That is ultimately what the Torah teaches by offering the picture of God that it does—to create that analogy so we understand what the separateness is, and how we have to be responsible to that.

Visualizing God working in the same way, we see people working was a way to help people with the notion of "it's not all me." The problem with talking about everything being connected is that we can mistake the things we want with Godness. But that's not what it (Godness) is. It has to be something more elevated and loftier than any one piece of our reality.

Q: So when you're reading a part where God is speaking through a prophet—Moses, Jeremiah—what do you make of that? Is it the person's conscience speaking, which they call God? Or is there something that was actually channeled through them?

A: It is a person. We all use God-talk to motivate people in different ways. You can use it responsibly. You can use it irresponsibly too. I imagine the prophets believed things about how we have to respond to the world, and told the story in such a way that people could hear it.

Q: So do you read the words of a Jeremiah as the words of a human making something up, or a human channeling oneness?

A: I would say it's an inner struggle with . . . how to encourage people to create a society that is going to be positive and productive. Each of those prophets is having an inner struggle that is very painful, and is also attempting to call up aspects of tradition and text to determine what is the best course of action.

You can say it is a human being responding to God's command, in that it is a human being recognizing that ultimate connectedness of everything and attempting to get other people to recognize it and respond in a responsible and positive way.

I have known Rabbi Mates-Muchin since her years in Buffalo. As noted, she has helped shape some of my views, and her early studies contained a significant component on the Analects of Confucius. When I first read this interview, I wondered, despite this being California, how her new congregation might feel about having a monist rabbi. She answered me clearly, with a reply I should have expected:

> I don't think it is accurate to say that I have a reputation as a monist or that my congregant picked up on that and that is why she decided to interview me. I would say that my perspective is wholly Jewish and so would my congregants. I don't think that is a stretch, as we could look at many Jewish thinkers and philosophers through time whose teachings I have merely echoed. However, I know I am a product of my time, society and experience, so I understand if, from an academic perspective, you view my theology as a blend.

So Jacqueline Mates-Muchin is obviously conducting her ministry within normative rabbinical canons. Indeed, she has been so popular and respected in her ministry that ten years after her arrival in Oakland, she was elevated to the position of senior rabbi of that prestigious congregation (in the news in 2017 after the temple was desecrated by racist anti-Semitic graffiti, countered by congregants and neighbors wrapping the ugly slogans in white paper banners displaying words of peace and love). The senior rabbi's theology is offered appropriately in a monotheistic context, despite aspects that may appear monistic in reference to the spirit of the times and in the context of this study.

Not all clergy are as able to articulate such a blend of tradition and current context. Some of those who lately describe themselves as "non-theistic" ministers might run into fewer congregational objections and denominational hurdles if they would stop saying that there is no divinity anywhere when they really mean that Divinity is not somewhere separate from everything. They might be more helpful to those they serve if they would simply affirm that Divinity is everywhere. In doing so, they may find new depth, great richness, and vibrant truth in the traditions in which they stand, as surely as the sunsets and sunrises continue to move us all in a post-Copernican age. When we ascribe Divinity to the whole Universe, we are then called to respond to the "commands" or requirements of such Divinity in the way described by Mates-Muchin, herself an earlier contributor to *Four Testaments*.

And religion is not dead on campus either, but its main locus has shifted from the seminaries to departments of religious studies. Dalhousie University, where I enrolled in 1959 when it had only one half-course in religion, now has sixty-four such courses (not all in every year) and nine professors for more than a thousand students, many taking religious electives while studying for other degrees. Many North American Christian seminaries have departments of study in Judaism, Islam, Hinduism, and

Buddhism in which non-Christian professors and students join in programs of *Scriptural Reasoning* in a New Axial Age.

It is a high privilege for seminarians and others to focus on Divinity as still "the queen of the sciences," but in the majority of North American universities that were founded by Christian denominations, many seminaries are becoming part of the department of religious studies (or vice versa). They currently offer complete and recognized training for Christian clergy under the interfaith umbrella alongside students of other faiths seeking accreditation not only in relation to their traditions but also with respect to requirements for government-funded chaplaincies in prisons, hospitals, universities, and the armed forces. This type of training context may be adopted in the United Kingdom and certain parts of Europe by the second quarter of the twenty-first century, and we hope to see similar developments in Africa, Israel, and elsewhere in the Middle East, and perhaps in South America and Asia later in the century as the new Axial Age unfolds.

As stated several times previously, "Faith relations have become as important as race relations in the twenty-first century." For example, in the launch conference brochure for this book, Dr. Michelle Voss Roberts, principal of Emmanuel Theological College in the University of Toronto, is described as a specialist in Hindu-Christian comparative theology, but she describes the context of her work as "exploring how multifaith theological education enables participants to become deeply rooted in their own traditions while studying alongside people of other faiths."

Chaplaincies themselves are another area where interfaith sharing takes place in many countries. This is a natural outcome of government parsimony in funding multiple religious personnel in response to demand in the military, universities, hospitals, and prisons. In those situations, it is common for chaplains and those to whom they minister to move instinctively past barriers in order to study together, worship together, and pray together much in the manner described by David Bruce in the introduction to this volume. In Japan, this sharing is usually Buddhist, Shinto, and Christian, the latter especially in universities, but the combinations vary from country to country. In Europe and America, Muslims have begun to find their way into mutuality, beginning with prisons. In Canada, chaplains take their government-approved training for the most part in Christian seminaries, where there are Muslim, Hindu, Jewish, and Buddhist departments, though this may shift to departments of religious studies if the latter can ever get over their suspicion of the actual practice of religion, as opposed to merely examining and studying it. Various interfaith chaplaincy models are springing up in Africa, with a few in India; no such thing exists as yet in the Middle East, ironically the original home of several faith traditions.

Increasingly, congregations of various religions are also able to embrace a New Axial Age reality, occasionally building beside each other to share parking lots for services on different days (Netherlands, Canada), doing joint programs of care for the wider community (Michigan and other states, Ontario and other provinces except Quebec), praying together on special occasions or in the midst of tragedy, and studying together in varying circumstances. Community study programs like those described in our study guide are sometimes held on neutral ground such as in a public library. This is less necessary for religious folk than for those who consider themselves atheist or agnostic, whereas programs shared mainly by congregational members are enhanced by hosting each other at the various temples.

While remaining to practice their faith in the tradition in which they grew up, we may soon find Messianic Muslims at the mosque experiencing growing appreciation of Jesus (Isa Ibn Maryam) as respected by Muhammad[10] and as the Masih mentioned more than a hundred times in the Quran by that and other titles. We may find "Jewish Buddhists" who appreciate the Divinity of the Universe in every synagogue. One can attend yoga classes in many Christian churches these days, and transcendental meditation is popular among Unitarian Universalists and in temples across the religious spectrum. Like the Zoroastrians mentioned above, Taoists make a practice of singing Christmas carols and plumbing their meaning. The Chinese government contemplates endorsing Confucianism as a philosophy, while the *guojiao* movement, under the respected religious leader Jiang Qing, seeks to have Confucianism recognized as the state religion, in which practitioners would be applying religious rites and prayers openly borrowed from the other world religions, especially Christianity.[11]

When I visit the relatives of my wife in Trinidad, most of whom are Hindu, I find portraits of Jesus in almost every home, where he is seen as an avatar of God by people who attended Canadian Christian mission schools in earlier days. Can they be followers of Jesus as their avatar without formally joining a church? Sincere Christians are learning from others, but these are also issues for Buddhists and Hindus, Muslims and Jews, as well as Confucianists and Taoists. The conversation about the new evangelism is full of promise, but is just at its humble beginning.

There are multicultural challenges in my country, but Canada has become something of a world model for life in the New Axial Age. My own faith experience and expression is that of traditional Christianity, and I am always eager to share the things of Christ, which others may accept within their own context or mine, but I am also blessed in my reception of spiritual gifts from others. In particular, I am increasingly blessed by the realization of how my rather orthodox Christian beliefs can be expressed within a monist framework. When I experienced a challenging life situation some years ago in Toronto, my close friend, Santoch Singh, a Sikh, presented me with a commanding statuette of Ganesh for my desk. This Hindu representation of Divinity, with a human body, an elephant head, and bulging muscles, was to remind me that the Godhead is "the remover of obstacles." Two of this friend's four Sikh children have married United Church spouses, remaining active in their Christian congregations after typically Sikh marriage ceremonies, where the grooms arrived on horseback to meet the brides arriving on elephants on a back street of a Toronto suburb. This is not syncretism, but rather mutual enrichment and blessing.

On such occasions nobody is being unfaithful to their faith; everybody is being enriched within their own context and offering what they cherish to others. Muslims and Christians appear to have the greatest anxiety and the most to learn in this connection. Any of the latter who are alarmed at the prospect are referred for further reading to the American Baptist publication, *Side by Side: Being Christian in a Multifaith World*, included in our bibliography. Muslims are directed to *The Three Abrahamic Testaments: How the Torah, Gospels and Qur'an Hold the Keys for Healing Our Fears*, by California physician and eloquent lay theologian Ejaz Naqvi, past president of his mosque in Oakland.

The Court of Akbar.
PHOTO FROM THE *THE BIBLE AND ASIA* BY R. S. SUGIRTHARAJAH, LICENSED BY BRIDGEMAN IMAGES.

Some hallmarks of the New Axial Age might be Christians offering Christ to the world, but more humbly; Muslims reciting the Quran at a mixed wedding where "a cord is touched" connecting everyone to the Divine; Jews stressing Divinity in community; Hindus celebrating the Divinity of the Universe; Buddhists engaged in mindful meditation; Taoists living gracefully within the Flow; Confucianists finding stability in noble traditions; and followers of Zoroaster sharing his reforms that provide a veritable "source code" for the Axial Age in his time and ours. To each their own, without rancor to others and in appreciation of what treasures they may receive. The world will breathe a sigh of relief when such a day comes, and harbingers of that day's approach may be actually closer than even the most ecumenical among us realize.

Christian Jesuits arrived in India in 1541 to find a literate community of religious scholars at the court of Emperor Akbar, most appearing to be Parsee. Mughal court historian Badayuni has stated, "Fire worshipers from Navsari came to the Mughal capital at that time and proclaimed the religion of Zardusht as the true one."[12] In J. J. Modi's "The Parsis in the Court of Akbar and Dastur Meherji," Rana says, "The influence of the Parsis on the enlightened Emperor was such that Akbar incorporated Zoroastrian motifs, including the veneration of the fire and sun,"[13] along with the visible symbols viz the sacred shirt and thread. Akbar ordered his vizier, Abul Fazl, to ensure that the sacred fire be kept burning day and night at the palace and is said to have stated, "To light a candle is to commemorate the rising of the sun."[14] The conversation continues.

notes

1. *Tastes of the Divine*, 185.
2. Northrop Frye (July 14, 1912–January 23, 1991) was a Canadian literary critic and literary theorist, considered one of the most influential of the twentieth century in the realm of the deeper profundities of myth.
3. Quran 3:7 Yusef Ali, Pickthall, and other translations render this word as "allegorical."
4. *Three Testaments*, foreword, x.
5. Jonathan Waxman, "Messianic Jews Are Not Jews," United Synagogue of Conservative Judaism. Judaism has held that the Mashiach will come and usher in a new era, not that he will proclaim his arrival, die, and wait centuries to finish his task. To continue to assert that Jesus was the Mashiach goes against the belief that the Mashiach will transform the world when he does come, not merely hint at a future transformation at some undefined time to come. Judaism rejects the claim that a new covenant was created with Jesus and asserts instead that the chain of tradition reaching back to Moshe continues to make valid claims on our lives, and serve as more than mere window dressing.
6. Contemporary American Reform Responses, #68, "Question 18.3.4: Reform's Position On . . . What is unacceptable practice?" faqs.org.
7. Duke University Catalogue: Religion 216S Hinduism and Judaism.

8. As, for example, in *True North, Strong and Free*, 78 and 81.

9. Acts 17:22.

10. *Sahih al-Bukhari*, Volume 4, Book 55, Number 657, and many additional Sunnah entries of the second Islamic century.

11. Anne Sun, *Confucianism as a World Religion*, xv.

12. Ashleshaa Khurana, *Emperor Akbar's Parsi Counsel*, TNN, March 31, 2015, at https://timesofindia.indiatimes.com/city/surat/Emperor-Akbars-Parsi-counsel/articleshow/46753047.cms.

13. Ibid.

14. Ibid.

afterword

Continuing the Magi Journey, including an article by Mark Rose

S O WE KNOW NOW THAT THE MAGI WERE ACTIVE IN CHINA IN EARLY TIMES AND INFLUENCED both Confucianism and Taoism directly and indirectly. Without question they were in northern India around the time of Buddha's birth, setting the context for his teachings, reflected in the sacred writings of both Hinduism and Buddhism. The Zoroastrian priests in conversation with Hebrew prophets in Babylon were undoubtedly Magi. The adolescent Muhammad met the Jewish rabbi Tayma and the Christian monk Bahira in Syria, and it would be passing strange if the adult caravanner met no Magi in a place where Zoroastrianism was the state religion, where he learned the Avesta verses he presented in the Quran in the manner dictated afresh by the Divine in his experience.

Christians are entranced by the famous gospel story of the Magi visiting the holy family after the birth of Christ.[1] Catholics believe a star hovering a few hundred feet above the stable was a unique phenomenon. Evangelicals believe that since God can do anything, he chose to do this. Progressives probably believe that if there were Magi in the neighborhood, they were attracted by the shepherd visitors and others surrounding the hullabaloo of a baby in a barn and rightly discerned that they had been "guided" there, or that the story points to a greater truth that Jesus came as fulfillment of the Saoshyant prophecies of Zoroaster, as recounted by St. Matthew, who wrote his gospel during his apostolic mission to Persia.

The following article is presented by permission as a response to the opening foreword by Karen Hamilton, which featured the movement of Magi around the ancient world. We reserve our own final comment on the significance of the Magi connection to follow this material from Mark Rose, who served as managing editor, senior editor, and online editor for the respected *Archaeology* magazine from 1985 to 2015.

It may be noted that the Cologne Cathedral attracts more than seven million pilgrims per year, a daily average of twenty thousand visitors to the Shrine of the Magi, Germany's most important "tourist site," surpassing the Brandenburg Gate, remnants of the Berlin Wall, and even Munich's Oktoberfest. This may be hard for religious skeptics to understand, but the truth is that people of the twenty-first century are as hungry for something pointing to spiritual meaning as in any other age. The thirst for religious authenticity may be met by less debunking and more by pointing to the meaning beyond the symbols.

"the three kings and the star"[2]

One of the most evocative tales in the Bible is that of the journey made by the wise men to Bethlehem. Today, the three kings and the star are celebrated in Christmas carols, on greeting cards, and with front-yard light displays. But the popularity of the story is not new. From just a few lines in the book of Matthew, the story and veneration of the three grew over the centuries. And in Cologne, Germany, there is a gilded shrine that, if you choose to believe, has held the remains of the wise men since the Middle Ages.

Matthew calls the three travelers "magi" and says that they came from the east, having seen a star. After their interview with Herod, "The star which they had seen in the east went before them till it came to rest over the place where the child was." Having located the infant Jesus and presented their gifts of gold, frankincense, and myrrh, they departed, returning home by another route so as to evade Herod. Beyond that, there is nothing. In Matthew, we aren't told their names, how many there were, or even if they were all men. They were not even kings.

The elaborate story that we know today can be found in the *Historia Trium Regum*, the *History of the Three Kings*, which is attributed to the fourteenth-century cleric John of Hildesheim. In this compilation of the legend, we are told much more about the star: "When the day of the nativity was passed the Star ascended up into the firmament, and it had right many long streaks and beams, more burning and brighter than a brand of fire; and as an eagle flying and beating the air with his wings, right so the streaks and beams of the Star stirred about." And we are told that the three wise men, named Melchior, Balthazar, and Gaspar, are the kings of "Ind, Chaldea, and Persia." They only meet on the outskirts of Jerusalem, having traveled from their own lands "in great haste" and without stopping. And so they reach Bethlehem and present their gifts. When the kings depart, they continue together until they reach the Hill of Vaws, or Hill of Victory, on the border of Ind, where a watchtower was maintained (it was here that the star was first sighted). There, before departing to their own countries, the three made "a fair chapel in worship of the Child they had sought. Also they agreed to meet together at the same place once in the year, and they ordained that the Hill of Vaws should be the place of their burial."

John of Hildesheim continues the story of the wise men: "after many years" a star appeared above the cities in which the kings dwell just before Christmas, indicating to them that their lives were nearing an end. "Then with one consent they built, at the Hill of Vaws, a fair and large tomb, and there the three Holy Kings . . . died and were buried in the same tomb by their sorrowing people." If we were to assume that this actually happened, that all three died at the same place at the same time, it might have been in the mid-first century (since the kings were adults already in Bethlehem). If so, the kings had little more than two centuries of rest in their tomb before beginning another journey.

Their tour director would be Helena, the mother of Constantine and now St. Helena. After 323–324, when he defeated his last rival, Constantine began rebuilding the city of Byzantium. He rededicated it as Constantinople in the year 330. One of the new buildings was the church Saint Sophia (Holy Wisdom), the first of three that would have that name. In the same period, Helena went to the Holy Land and collected various relics, including the true cross, and brought them home to Constantinople (see Cynewulf for an unusual retelling of this). The relics of the wise men were among her trophies: "Queen Helen . . . began to think greatly of the bodies of these three kings, and she arrayed herself, and accompanied by many attendants, went into the Land of Ind . . . after she had found the bodies of Melchior, Balthazar, and Casper, Queen Helen put them into one chest and ornamented it with great riches, and she brought them into Constantinople . . . and laid them in a church that is called Saint Sophia."

John of Hildesheim is rather brief about the wise men's later career. On Constantine's death, he says a persecution of Christians led to the relics being moved by the emperor Mauricius, who had them placed in a church in Milan. This may refer to the attempted pagan restoration under Julian (361–363), but Mauricius is a bit later (582–602). Much later, Frederick I, the holy Roman emperor, was at war in Italy and requested aid against Milan, which the archbishop of Cologne, Rainald von Dassel, provided in the form of an army. The grateful Frederick rewarded him with the relics of the wise men in 1164. And to Cologne the relics were taken, and there—whoever the bones belong to—they remain today.

THE MUMMY DETECTIVE AND THE MAGI

The Learning Channel's *Mummy Detective* series takes on the biblical wise men in an episode titled "The Three Kings" to be broadcast on December 23. It starts with some engaging hook lines from the show's host, Egyptologist Bob Brier, a contributing editor to *Archaeology*, who presents the wise men as the "most mysterious characters in the Bible" and promises to track down what may be the "only relics of people who actually knew Jesus." At the end of an hour, will we agree that these "could just be the real deal"?

The program has the hallmarks of Bob Brier in pursuit of something—animated and sometimes quirky language ("Herod was not a happy camper") and a fast pace. The Three Kings subject provides opportunities to look for evidence in unusual places. A card store and Christmas light displays in front of houses provide examples of the traditions about the kings we know today. These scenes are instructive in showing what comes from the few biblical references to the wise men (or is appropriate for the time) and what was added later: camels on the cards okay; crowns not. Footage takes us from Bronx neighborhoods to the Persian capital of Persepolis to Bethlehem (where a local shepherd is asked what time of year he watches his flocks by night), to Cologne, Germany.

From Ravenna, Italy, we see the famous mid-sixth-century mosaic of the wise men from the Basilica of St. Apollinarius (they are also in a mosaic of the Byzantine empress Theodora, appearing as embroidered figures on the hem of her mantle, at Ravenna's San Vitale). The mosaic is used to establish the Eastern origins of the wise men based on their clothing. Their hats and trousers are compared to reliefs from Persepolis showing what are identified as Parthians in pointy hats and trousers. Brier says this Parthian connection and the Greek word used to name them, *magoi*, identifies the wise men as members of the Zoroastrian religion from Persia (the footage showing a Zoroastrian temple in Iran today is very interesting). One could argue that the caps worn in the Ravenna mosaic are the same old, floppy Phrygian caps long known in classical art or that the trousers are known from many steppe peoples, such as the Scythians. At any rate, we have the wise men coming from the East, as the Bible says, and as their costume (depicted centuries later) indicates.

So, what were they following? Brier quickly runs through the errors of the monk Dionysius, who was assigned the job of revising the calendar but left out five years by accident. The traditional date of Christmas, he says, is nothing more or less than the birth date of the Roman sun god Sol Invictus. This leaves us with a birth of Jesus in 6–5 BC, at some unknown time of year. This is where the program digs into the astronomy, using an expert from Rutgers University. Their candidate for the Star of Bethlehem? The conjunction of the planets Venus, Saturn, and Jupiter rising among the constellation Aries the ram in April of 6 BC. It's an interesting proposal and uses the biblical text, an ancient coin stamped with a sheep and star, and computer simulations of the movements of the planets millennia ago. But viewers of "The Three Kings" should be aware that there are other explanations of the star that seem to fit the evidence—for example, the conjunction of Saturn and Jupiter in the constellation Pisces that occurred three times in the year 7 BC (see astronomer Anthony Aveni's November/December 1998 *Archaeology* article on this topic). Both possibilities have pros and cons.

Meanwhile, Brier and "The Three Kings" move on to Cologne and its magnificent cathedral and the shrine that supposedly contains the remains of the magi. We are shown a fourteenth-century fresco of St. Helena, but is this evidence that the relics are from Constantinople, or merely evidence that the painters were illustrating the well-known story of her finding the relics? And, after all, there's no guarantee Helena got the right men since Matthew doesn't say that there were three (or that they were all men) to begin with. Fragments of textiles from within the shrine are dyed purple and consistent with Syrian weaving of the second through third centuries, so the cloth in which the relics are laid does not suggest this is just another example of the medieval faking of holy relics.

And what about the bones? Well, access was limited, to say the least, but using a photograph of the shrine in which the backs of three gold-crowned skulls can be seen, Brier comes up with a neat bit of evidence. In the Ravenna mosaic, the three kings are shown as an older, middle-aged, and young man, respectively. At the C. W. Post Campus of Long Island University, Brier's home base, they zoom in on the skulls and print out the image at poster size. Sure enough, the sutures (which knit together the bones of the cranium) indicate that the three are younger (sutures open), middle (partly fused), and older (fused and smoothed over). So the skulls in Cologne do match the sixth-century Ravenna mosaic. And the cloth in the shrine looks even older. But does this mean that the wise men—said in John of Hildesheim's account to have lived for "many years"—somehow kept their cranial sutures unchanged from the time they went to Bethlehem to the time they passed away? Hmm . . .

Frederick I (Barbarosa) and Beatrice of Burgundy at the Shrine of the Magi.
MEDIEVAL DRAWING BY KOBLENZ STAATSARCHIV FROM WIKIMEDIA COMMONS.

There is just enough evidence here to weave an engaging story, and Brier has done that (and added new evidence), but for many reasons I was not convinced at the end that the bones in Cologne are "the real deal." Ultimately, the basic facts, from the few lines in Matthew, give too little to go on. Relying on the later tale raises questions of circular arguments. Could the Cologne relics simply reflect the later story rather than being the originals? Perhaps they are three gentleman from Constantinople or somewhere in Palestine who were available for the role when Helena went on her search. Regardless of the answer, "The Three Kings" is entertaining and covers a lot of ground. It's worth having a look at.

Well, we have looked at it and the program is still played on English-speaking TV networks around the world every December. People, Christian and other, and some with no religion, are not necessarily convinced that the relics in Cologne are the actual bones of the Magi to which the Bible refers, but there must be something to the story. At the very minimum, this "evidence" reminds us that St. Matthew, writing from a Persian culture where Magi were still the dominant religious establishment, wished to place some Zoroastrians in the nativity scenes to make the point that Jesus can be seen as the fulfilment of prophecies regarding the Saoshyant as the Savior of the world. At maximum, the story is also associated with the newer realization that Magi were ubiquitous in the ancient world and that they carried a message that resonates still within the pages of seven testaments of world religion and elsewhere. The details differ, and the differences produce the treasures that we are able to share in the New Axial Age, giving and receiving that which is precious, like the gold, frankincense, and myrrh that are used to this day in Zoroastrian worship.

In a similar way, we may or may not soon find the physical Dead Zee Scrolls, some or all of them, but the "evidence" remains that such material either exists or can be gleaned from the extant Avesta, and as buried between the lines of the Seven Testaments and elsewhere. The religions of the world are connected; each has cherished gems to share, and all have needs to which others may contribute. Until we learn and accept this truth, religions will be as much part of the problem as the solution to the rancorous divisions that beset the world of the twenty-first century. It is the hope of the contributors to this book and to the trilogy of which it is a part that these compendia may be an appropriate starting point for many in this quest.

notes

1. The Gospel According to St. Matthew, 1:1–12.
2. *Archaeology*, December 21, 2004.

bibliography

*Indicating items of special interest to those eager to pursue the "breaking news" out of China.

Abdul al Rauf, Imam Feisal. *What's Right with Islam, A New Vision for Muslims and the West.* New York: HarperCollins, 2004.

Ali, Abdullah Yusuf. *The Meaning of the Holy Qur'ān.* Brentwood, MD: Amana, 1991.

Anthony, David W. *The Horse, the Wheel and Language: How Bronze-Age Riders from the Eurasian Steppes Shaped the Modern World.* Oxford: Princeton University Press, 2007.

Armstrong, Karen. *The Great Transformation.* New York: Anchor, 2007.

Ayoub, Mahmoud. *A Muslim View of Christianity.* New York: Orbis, 2007.

Bakhtiar, Laleh, translator. *The Sublime Quran, Revised Edition.* Chicago: Kazi, 2011.

Bakhtiar, Laleh, and Shaykh Muhammad Hisham Kabbani, eds. *Encyclopedia of Muhammad's Women Companions.* Chicago: ABC International Group, 1998.

Ball, Warwick. *The Monuments of Afghanistan.* London: I. B. Tauris, 2008.

Barazangi, Nimat Hafez. *Woman's Identity and the Qur'an: A New Reading.* Gainsville: University Press of Florida, 2004.

Barlas, Asma. *"Believing Women" in Islam: Unreading Patriarchal Interpretations of the Qur'an.* Austin: University of Texas Press, 2002.

*Beckwith, Christopher I. *Empires of the Silk Road.* Princeton, NJ: Princeton University Press, 2009.

Bhote, Keki R. *Zoroastrianism: Mother of All World Religions.* Glencoe, IL: Bhote Press, 2015.

Bleeck, Arthur H. *Avesta: The Religious Books of the Parsees. Volumes 1–3.* Lexington: Elibron Classics, 2005.

*Boqin, Jiang. *The Zoroastrian Art of the Sogdians in China.* Sizihwan, Kaohsiung, Taiwan: Zhongshan University Press, 1996.

Boyce, Mary. *A Persian Stonghold of Zoroastrianism.* Oxford: Clarendon Press, 1977.

———. *Textual Sources for the Study of Zoroastrianism.* Chicago: University of Chicago Press, 1990.

———. *Zoroastrians: Their Religious Beliefs and Practices.* London: Routledge, 1979.

———. *Zoroastrianism.* Chicago: University of Chicago Press, 1990.

Brettler, Marc Z., ed. *The Jewish Study Bible.* London: Oxford, 2004.

Brettler, Marc Z., and Levine, Amy-Jill, eds. *The Jewish Annotated New Testament.* New York: Oxford University Press, 2017.

Brown, Brian. *Forensic Scriptures*. Eugene, OR: Cascade, 2009.

———. *Noah's Other Son*. New York: Continuum, 2007.

———. *Three Testaments: Torah, Gospel, and Quran*. Lanham, MD: Rowman & Littlefield, 2012.

———. *True North, Strong and Free*. Niagara Falls: 3T Publishing, 2017.

Bruce, David. *Guide to the Bible*. Toronto: United Church Publishing House, 2010.

———. *The Resurrection of History*. Eugene, OR: Wipf and Stock, 2014.

Burton, John. "Abrogation." In *Encyclopaedia of the Qur'an (EQ)*, edited by Jane McAuliffe. Leiden: Brill, 2001–2006.

Cramer, Samuel. "Mennoniten." In *Realencyclopedie für Protestantische Theologie and Kirche*. 24 vols., edited by J. J. Herzog and Albert Hauck, 3rd ed. Leipzig: J. H. Hinrichs, 1896–1913.

Darmesteter, James. *The Zend-Avesta*. 3 volumes. Oxford: Oxford University Press, 1880.

*de la Vaissière, Étienne. *Sogdian Traders: A History*. Translated by James Ward. Leiden: Brill, 2005.

*de la Vaissière, Étienne, and Eric Trombert. *Les Sogdiens en Chine*. Paris: Ecole Francaise Extreme Orient, 2004.

*Dillon, Michael, ed. *Encyclopedia of Chinese History*. London: Routledge, 2018.

Easwaran, Eknath. *The Dhammapada*. Tomales, CA: Nilgiri Press, 2007.

*Encyclopaedia Iranica. "Chinese–Iranian Relations in Pre-Islamic Times." Accessed on February 1, 2019, at http://www.iranicaonline.org/articles/chinese-iranian-i.

Finkel, Irving, ed. *The Cyrus Cylinder*. London: I. B. Tauris, 2013.

Foltz, Richard. *Religions of the Silk Road*. New York: Palgrave MacMillan, 2010.

Freund, Richard. *Digging through History*. Lanham, MD: Rowman & Littlefield, 2012.

———. *Digging through the Bible*. Lanham, MD: Rowman & Littlefield, 2009.

Friedman, Richard Elliott. *The Bible with Sources Revealed*. New York: HarperOne, 2005.

———. *Who Wrote the Bible?* New York: HarperCollins, 1997.

Fronsdal, Gil. *The Dhammapada*. Boston: Shamballa, 2006.

Gershevitch, Ilya. *The Avestan Hymn to Mithra*. London: Cambridge University Press, 1967.

Ghandi, Mahatma. *The Bhagavad Gita*. New Delhi: Young India, 1931.

Gilliot, Claud. "Creation of a Fixed Text." In *The Cambridge Companion to the Qur'ān*, edited by Jane Dammen McAuliffe. Cambridge: Cambridge University Press, 2006.

Glassé, Cyril. *The New Encyclopedia of Islam*, 4th edition. Lanham, MD: Rowman & Littlefield, 2013.

———. *The Second Coming of the Judeo-Zoroastrian Jesus of the Dead Sea Scrolls*. New York: Revelation, 2014.

*Graff, David A. *Medieval Chinese Warfare 300–900*. London: Routledge, 2001.

*Gulacsi, Zsuzsanna, and Jason Beduhn. "The Religion of Wirkak and Wayusi: Zoroastrian Iconographic Program on a Sogdian Sacrophagus from 6th Century X'ian." Bloomfield Hills, MI: *Bulletin of the Asia Institute*, New Series, Vol. 26, 2012.

Hansen, Valerie. *The Silk Road: A New History*. New York: Oxford University Press, 2012.

*Hawkes, David, ed. *The Songs of the South: An Anthology of Ancient Chinese Poems by Qu Yuan and Other Poets*. New York: Penguin, 1985.

Henning, W. B. *Zoroaster: Politician or Witch-Doctor?* Oxford: Oxford University Press, 1951.

Herzfeld, E. E. *Zoroaster and His World*. Princeton, NJ: Princeton University Press, 1947.

Holy Bible, New Revised Standard Version. Iowa Falls: World Bible Publishers, 1989.

Hussain, Amir. *Oil and Water: Two Faiths, One God*. Kelowna: CopperHouse, 2006.

Hussain, Amir, and Willard G. Oxtoby, eds. *World Religions*, 3rd edition. New York: Oxford University Press, 2010.

Jol, Harry M. *Ground Penetrating Radar Theory and Applications*. Amsterdam: Elsevier, 2009.

Khan, Daisy. *Born with Wings*. New York: Spiegel & Grau, 2018.

Knitter, Paul. *Without Buddha I Could Not Be a Christian*. Oxford: Oneworld, 2009.

Krotz, Douglas Roper. *The Man Who Sent the Magi*. Peoria, AZ: Intermedia, 2011.

Landau, Brent. *Revelation of the Magi*. New York: HarperOne, 2010.

Lings, Martin. *Muhammad: His Life Based on the Earliest Sources*, 2nd US edition. Rochester, VT: Inner Traditions, 2006.

*Liu, Xinru. *The Silk Road in World History*. New York: Oxford University Press, 2010.

Madigan, Daniel. "Themes and Topics." In *The Cambridge Companion to the Qur'an*, edited by Jane Dammen McAuliffe. Cambridge: Cambridge University Press, 2006.

Mair, Victor H. *Tao Te Ching, The Classic Book of Integrity and the Way*. New York: Bantam, 1990.

———. *Wandering on the Way*. Honolulu: University of Hawaii Press, 1998.

*Mair, Victor H., and J. P. Mallory. *The Tarim Mummies*. London: Thames and Hudson, 2000.

*Major, John S., et al., eds. *The Huainanzi: A Guide to the Theory and Practice of Government in Early Han China*. New York: Columbia University Press, 2010.

Malandra, William W. *An Introduction to Ancient Iranian Religion*. Minneapolis: University of Minnesota Press, 1983.

Malandra, William W., and Pallan Ichaporia. *The Pahlavi Yasna of the Gathas and Yasna Haptanhaiti*. Wiesbaden: Reichert, 2013.

Mallory, J. P. *In Search of the Indo-Europeans*. New York: Thames and Hudson, 1989.

McAuliffe, Jane Dammen, et al. *Encyclopaedia of Qur'an*, 1st edition. 5 vols. Leiden: Brill, 2001–2006.

McLaren, Brian D. *A Generous Orthodoxy*. Grand Rapids, MI: Zondervan, 2004.

Michie, David. *The Dalai Lama's Cat*. New York: Visions, 2012.

Motzki, Harald. "Alternative Accounts of the Qur'an's Formation." In *The Cambridge Companion to the Qur'an*, edited by Jane Dammen McAuliffe. Cambridge: Cambridge University Press, 2006.

Nanavutty, Piloo. *The Gathas of Zarathushtra*. Ahmedabad: Mapin Publishing, 1999.

Naqvi, Ejaz. *The Three Abrahamic Testaments: How the Torah, Gospels and Qur'an Hold the Keys for Healing Our Fears*. Ashland, OR: White Cloud Press, 2017.

Nigosian, S. A. *The Zoroastrian Faith*. Montreal: McGill-Queens, 2007.

Olson, Richard P. *Side by Side: Being Christian in a Multifaith World*. Valley Forge: Judson Press, 2018.

Philip, T. V. *East of the Euphrates: Early Christianity in Asia*. India: CSS & ISPCK, 1998.

Prabhupada, A. C. *Bhagavad-Gita as It Is*. Los Angeles: International Society for Krishna Consciousness, 1979.

Radhakrishnan, S. *The Dhammapada*. New Delhi: Oxford University Press, 1950.

Reda, Nevin. "Holistic Approaches to the Quran: A Historical Background." *Religion Compass* 4, no. 8 (2010): 495–506.

Reddish, Mitchell G., ed. *Apocalyptic Literature*. Nashville: Abingdon Press, 1990.

*Rose, Jenny. "The Sogdians: Prime Movers between Boundaries." *Comparative Studies of South Asia, Africa and the Middle East* 30 (2010).

———. *Zoroastrianism: An Introduction*. London: I. B. Tauris, 2011.

Schafer, Edward H. *The Golden Peaches of Sanarkand: A Study of T'ang Exotics*. Berkeley: University of California Press, 1963.

Scheidel, Walter, ed. *State Power in Ancient China and Rome*. Oxford: Oxford University Press, 2015.

Sharma, Arvind. *Our Religions*. New York: HarperOne, 1993.

Sims-Williams, Nicholas. *The Sogdian Merchants in China and India*. Firenze: Olschki, 1996.

Stein, David E. S., et al., eds. *The Contemporary Torah*. Philadelphia: Jewish Publication Society, 2006.

Sugirtharajah, R. S. *The Bible and Asia*. Cambridge, MA: Harvard University Press, 2013.

Sugirtharajah, Sharada. *Imagining Hindusim*. London: Rutledge, 2003.

Sun, Anna. *Confucianism as a World Religion*. Princeton, NJ: Princeton University Press, 2013.

Tanakh: The Holy Scriptures. Philadelphia: Jewish Publication Society, 1985.

Taraporewalla, I. J. S. *The Divine Songs of Zarathustra*. Whitefish, MT: Kissinger Publishing, 2010.

Ten Elshof, Gregg A. *Confucius for Christians*. Grand Rapids, MI: Wm. B. Eerdmans, 2015.

Thich, Nhat Hanh, and Elaine Pagels. *Living Buddha; Living Christ*. New York: Riverhead, 1995.

Voss Roberts, Michelle. *Tastes of the Divine*. New York: Fordham University Press, 2014.

Wadud, Amina. *Qur'an and Woman: Rereading the Sacred Text from a Woman's Perspective*. New York: Oxford University Press, 1999.

West, E. W. *Pahlavi Texts of Zoroastrianism*. Oxford: Oxford University Press, 1860.

West, M. L. *Hymns of Zoroaster: A New Translation of the Most Ancient Sacred Texts of Iran*. New York: I. B. Tauris, 2010.

Whitfield, Susan. *Life Along the Silk Road*. Los Angeles: University of California Press, 1999.

Wolf, Laibl. *Practical Kabbalah*. New York: Three River Press, 1999.

*Wushu, Lin. *Zhong gu san yi jiao bian zheng / Lin Wushu zhu* (Debate and Research on the Three Persian Religions: Manichaeism, Nestorianism, and Zoroastrianism in Mediaeval Times). Beijing Shi: Zhonghua shu ju, 2005.

Xiaogui, Zhang. *Zonggu huahua xianjiao kaoshu* (A Study of Sinicized Zoroastrianism in Medieval China). Beijing: Cultural Relics Press, 2010.

*Yang, Bo. *Zizhi Tongjian* (Comprehensive Mirror in Aid of Governance). Modern Chinese Edition (English). Taipei: Yuan-Liou Publishing, 2006.

Yogananda, Paramahansa. *The Yoga of Jesus: Understanding the Hidden Teachings of the Gospels*. Los Angeles: Self Realization, 2007.

index

about the contributors
(in order of appearance)

Rev. Dr. Karen Hamilton was general secretary of the Canadian Council of Churches from 2002 to 2017. Dr. Hamilton is a long-time member and chair of the World Federalists of Canada and a member of the council for the World Federalist Movement, which was nominated for the 2002 Nobel Peace Prize. Published author and popular speaker, she was co-chair of the Trustees of the Parliament of the World's Religions through its Toronto meetings in 2018.

Dr. David Bruce is the author of *The Resurrection of History* from Wipf and Stock and of the four-volume adult curriculum, *Jesus 24/7*, from the United Church Publishing House. He has been a leading contributor to *Three Testaments*, *The Three Testaments Companion*, and *Four Testaments* preceding this introductory volume while serving in administrative capacities for the Roman Catholic Archdiocese of Toronto.

Rev. Dr. Bhante Saranapala is the Buddhist chaplain at the University of Toronto. Born in Chittagong, Bangladesh, after monastic education in Sri Lanka, he undertook studies at the University of Toronto and McMaster University. He teaches his own tested approach to mindfulness and insight meditation.

Roshan Rivetna and her husband, Rohinton Rivetna, have been key players in the promotion of academic advances in the worldwide Zoroastrian diaspora. She was editor of *FEZANA Journal*, the publication of the Federation of Zoroastrian Associations of North America, from 1991 through 2005.

Dr. Nevin Reda is assistant professor of Muslim studies at Emmanuel College of Victoria University in the University of Toronto. Her primary area of research is the poetics and hermeneutics of Quranic narrative structure, often utilizing insights from biblical studies and literary theory. Her secondary area of research is Islamic legal theory (*uṣūl al-fiqh*), occasionally from a feminist perspective.

Rev. William Thomas is the playwright of an interfaith drama for this volume based on his studies in comparative religion at Concordia University in Montreal. He is a senior United Church minister in Canada's exhilarating Niagara region, a fellow of the Royal Society for the Arts in the United Kingdom, a doctoral candidate in his studies in the United States, and a theologian associated with the World Alliance of Reformed Churches.

Contributors associated with the other volumes in the trilogy are introduced there, including:

Volume 2: Amir Hussain, Ellen Frankel, Marc Brettler, Henry Carrigan, David Bruce, Laleh Bakhtiar, Nevin Reda, and

Volume 3: Francis X. Clooney, Victor H. Mair, Jacqueline Mates-Muchin, Arvind Sharma, Cyril Glassé, Richard Freund, Ed Eduljee, and the ubiquitous David Bruce, ever helpful and always appreciated.

about the author/ contributing editor

Prior to completing this trilogy, **Brian Arthur Brown** authored twenty books on the quest for peace and harmony between First Nations and other Canadians, French and English in Canada, Canadians and Americans at war and in peace, and Jews, Christians, and Muslims worldwide. His bestselling two-volume compendium *Three Testaments: Torah, Gospel, and Quran* (2012) and *Four Testaments: Tao Te Ching, Analects, Dhammapada, Bhagavad Gita* (2016) was described by reviewers as his magnum opus prior to the present volume. *Seven Testaments of World Religion* addresses the new reality that "faith relations" have joined "race relations" as the hot-button issues of the twenty-first century. This trilogy reestablishes the study of religion as what used to be referred to as "the queen of the sciences."

Brown holds a bachelor's degree in classics from Dalhousie University in Halifax, a master's degree in theology from McGill University in Montréal, and a doctorate in organizational behavior from the University of California, and he has done postdoctoral studies in executive leadership at Harvard University. He is currently a member of the Oxford Round Table at Oxford University, and in 2015 he was elected as a fellow of the Royal Society for the Arts.

Brown is currently scholar-in-residence at First Baptist Church in Niagara Falls, New York, where he writes for Rowman & Littlefield internationally. He is also minister emeritus at St. John's Stevensville United Church in Niagara Falls, Canada, writing for Wood Lake Books on Canadian themes. He is research associate at St. James United Church in Montreal, formulating visions for the future of Christianity in a multifaith Canada. Brian and Jenny Sutacriti love their hundred-year-old rambling brick house in the "American Foursquare" architectural style, within earshot of the thunderous Niagara Falls, awaiting the weekend visits of their children and grandchildren and making sure they all get to church.